Blackstone's Police Manual

Evidence and Procedure

Blackstone's Police Manual

Volume 2

Evidence and Procedure

2024

David Johnston

LLB, LLM, Barrister

and

Glenn Hutton

BA, MPhil, FCIPD

Consultant Editor: Paul Connor

OXFORD
UNIVERSITY PRESS

OXFORD
UNIVERSITY PRESS

Great Clarendon Street, Oxford, OX2 6DP,
United Kingdom

Oxford University Press is a department of the University of Oxford.
It furthers the University's objective of excellence in research, scholarship, and education by publishing worldwide. Oxford is a registered trade mark of Oxford University Press in the UK and in certain other countries

First Edition published in 1998
Twenty-sixth Edition published in 2023

Published in the United States of America by Oxford University Press
198 Madison Avenue, New York, NY 10016, United States of America

British Library Cataloguing in Publication Data
Data available

ISBN 978–0–19–889064–5

DOI: 10.1093/law/9780198890645.001.0001

Printed in the UK by
Bell & Bain Ltd., Glasgow

Foreword for 2024 Blackstone's Police Manuals

As the Chief Executive of the College of Policing, the professional body for policing, I am pleased to provide the foreword for *Blackstone's Police Manuals 2024*.

The role of the College is to set standards, provide training and share good practice for policing nationally. Practitioner knowledge is at the heart of everything we do, and we use evidence of *what works*, to make a difference in fighting crime and protecting the public.

Attention has intensified on the challenges of policing because of shocking tragedies, violence and abuse committed by police officers and, as a result, public trust in policing is declining. It has never been more important than now, that knowledge and standards are the cornerstones of the policing profession. Blackstone's Manuals are the definitive reference source for all who are involved in police law and procedure and those seeking to progress or specialise in a role. They are widely used in the professional development of police officers and staff in a variety of roles.

Whilst Oxford University Press produce these titles independently, the College develops, maintains and tests standards to ensure suitability for promotion by producing a comprehensive and relevant syllabus. The Blackstone's Manuals are the official study guide for the College's National Police Promotion Framework that underpins the national legal examination, which candidates must pass, to be promoted to the ranks of sergeant and inspector.

If you are using these Manuals as a reference guide for continuous professional development, thank you for your commitment. If you are using the Manuals as a professional reference to ensure your work is of the highest possible standards, thank you for your dedication and, finally, if you are referencing these books to study for promotion or progression into a specialist role, I wish you every success.

Chief Constable Andy Marsh QPM
Chief Executive, College of Policing

Preface

The *Blackstone's Police Manuals* are the only official study guides for Police Promotion Examinations—if the law is not in the Manuals, it will not be in the exams.

All the Manuals include explanatory keynotes and case law examples, providing clear and incisive analysis of important areas. As well as covering basic law and procedure, they take full account of the PACE Codes of Practice and human rights implications. They can also be used as a training resource for police probationers, special constables and police community support officers, or as an invaluable reference tool for police staff of all ranks and positions. In relation to being used as a reference tool, this is particularly relevant to officers and others involved in the procedures connected with the custody, identification and interviews of offenders, all of which are detailed in chapters 2.6 to 2.8 of the Manual.

The *Evidence and Procedure* Manual contains a wide range of activities to cover the complex and demanding legislative framework governing the increasing depth and breadth of policing delivery. In an attempt to present this shifting and growing body of national and European law, the Manual has been structured in three distinct parts: chapters 2.1 to 2.3 cover the criminal justice system; chapters 2.4 and 2.5 cover the law of evidence; and chapters 2.6 to 2.8 cover police station procedure.

The 2024 edition of the Manual includes updated case law across the chapters. As with previous editions, the findings of the College of Policing review of the most recent police promotion examinations, together with editorial and customer feedback, have been taken into account in the revisions to the Manual.

Although every care is taken to ensure the accuracy of the contents of the Manual, neither the authors nor the publisher can accept any responsibility for any actions taken, or not taken, on the basis of the information contained within it.

Oxford University Press are always happy to receive any useful written feedback from any reader on the content and style of the Manual, especially from those involved in or with the criminal justice system. Please email this address with any comments or queries: police@oup.com.

The law is stated as at 1 June 2023.

Acknowledgements

The *Evidence and Procedure* Manual, as with each edition, has been greatly influenced by the support it receives from across the police service and other parts of the criminal justice system. In particular, we would like to express our thanks to the staff of the Legal Services Department of the College of Policing and Examinations and Assessment. The monthly Digest produced by the Legal Services Department is an invaluable reference and the informative review conducted by Examinations and Assessment helps to shape the content and style of the Manual.

Thanks to George Cooper (Northamptonshire Police), Stuart K. Fairclough (Metropolitan Police), Paul Murphy (Greater Manchester Police) and Kevin Whitehouse (West Midlands Police).

Our thanks, as always, to all the staff involved in the production of the Manual in the Academic and Professional Law Department at Oxford University Press. Special thanks also to Rosalie for her continued support and forbearance and thanks to Bertie and Hilda.

David Johnston and Glenn Hutton

Contents

Table of Cases

Table of Statutes

Table of Statutory Instruments

Table of Codes of Practice

PACE

Table of European Legislation

Table of Home Office Circulars

Table of International Treaties and Conventions

How to use this Manual

Volume numbers for the Manuals

The 2024 *Blackstone's Police Manuals* each have a volume number as follows:

Volume 1: *Crime*
Volume 2: *Evidence and Procedure*
Volume 3: *General Police Duties*

The first digit of each paragraph number in the text of the Manuals denotes the Manual number. For example, chapter 2.3 is chapter 3 of the *Evidence and Procedure* Manual and chapter 3.3 is chapter 3 of the *General Police Duties* Manual.

All index entries and references in the Tables of Legislation and the Table of Cases, etc. refer to paragraph numbers instead of page numbers, making information easier to find.

Material outside the scope of the police promotion examinations syllabus—blacklining

These Manuals contain some information which is outside the scope of the police promotion examinations. A full black line down the margin indicates that the text beside it is excluded from Inspectors' examinations.

PACE Code Chapters

The PACE Codes of Practice have been taken out of the appendices and are now incorporated within chapters in the main body of the *Blackstone's Police Manuals*. A thick grey line down the margin is used to denote text that is an extract of the PACE Code itself (i.e. the actual wording of the legislation) and does not form part of the general commentary of the chapter.

The PACE Codes of Practice form an important part of the police promotion examinations syllabus and are examinable for both Sergeants and Inspectors. They are not to be confused with 'blacklined' content that is excluded from the syllabus for Inspectors' examinations (see 'Material outside the scope of the police promotion examinations syllabus—blacklining' section).

Length of sentence for an offence

Where a length of sentence for an offence is stated in this Manual, please note that the number of months or years stated is the maximum number and will not be exceeded.

Any feedback regarding content or other editorial matters in the Manuals can be emailed to police@oup.com.

Police Promotion Examinations Rules and Syllabus Information

The rules and syllabus for the police promotion examinations system are defined within the Rules & Syllabus document published by College of Policing Selection and Assessment on behalf of the Police Promotion Examinations Board (PPEB). The Rules & Syllabus document is published annually each September, and applies to all police promotion assessments scheduled for the calendar year following its publication. For example, the September 2023 Rules & Syllabus document would apply to all police promotion assessments held during 2024.

The document provides details of the law and procedure to be tested within the National Police Promotion Framework Step 2 Legal Examination, and also outlines the rules underpinning the police promotion examination system.

All candidates who are taking a police promotion examination are strongly encouraged to familiarise themselves with the Rules & Syllabus document during their preparation. The police promotion examination rules apply to candidates undertaking the National Police Promotion Framework.

The document can be downloaded from the Development Section of the College of Policing website, which can be found at <https://www.college.police.uk>. Electronic versions are also supplied to all force examination officers.

If you have any problems obtaining the Rules & Syllabus document from the above source, please contact the Candidate Administration Team via the 'Contact us' section of the College of Policing website (see above).

Usually, no further updates to the Rules & Syllabus document will be issued during its year-long lifespan. However, in exceptional circumstances, the College of Policing (on behalf of the PPEB) reserves the right to issue an amended syllabus prior to the next scheduled annual publication date.

For example, a major change to a key area of legislation or procedure (e.g. the Codes of Practice) during the lifespan of the current Rules & Syllabus document would render a significant part of the current syllabus content obsolete. In such circumstances, it may be necessary for an update to the syllabus to be issued, which would provide guidance to candidates on any additional material which would be examinable within their police promotion examinations.

In such circumstances, an update to the Rules & Syllabus document would be made available through the College of Policing website, and would be distributed to all force examination contacts. The College of Policing will ensure that any syllabus update is distributed well in advance of the examination date, to ensure that candidates have sufficient time to familiarise themselves with any additional examinable material. Where possible, any additional study materials would be provided to candidates free of charge.Please note that syllabus updates will only be made in exceptional circumstances; an update will not be made for every change to legislation included within the syllabus. For further guidance on this issue, candidates are advised to check regularly the College of Policing website, or consult their force examination officer, during their preparation period.

2.1 Instituting Criminal Proceedings

2.1.1 Introduction

There are many ways in which the appearance of a defendant before a magistrates' court can be secured:

- by the accused being arrested and, following CPS advice, charged by the police and brought before a court; or
- by the accused being arrested and then granted police bail to give the CPS time to decide whether to prosecute; the CPS may then start a prosecution by using the 'written charge and requisition procedure'; or
- by the accused being arrested and then granted bail subject to a requirement to return to the police station on a specified date; where the CPS decide there is sufficient evidence to charge the police will charge the accused when they answer their bail; or
- by the accused being served with a 'written charge and requisition' without first having been arrested; or
- in the case of a private prosecution, by the laying of an information by the prosecutor before a magistrate resulting in the issue of a summons requiring the accused to attend at court on a specified day to answer the allegation in the information; or
- by the laying of an information by a prosecutor before a magistrate resulting in the issue of a warrant for the defendant to be arrested and brought before the court. Alternatively, the warrant may be backed for bail where the defendant is arrested and then released on bail to attend court on a specified day.

2.1.2 Written Charge and Requisition

The procedure in relation to instituting criminal proceedings is provided by the Criminal Justice Act 2003, s. 29, which states:

(1) A relevant prosecutor may institute criminal proceedings against a person by issuing a document (a 'written charge') which charges the person with an offence.

(2) Where a relevant prosecutor issues a written charge, it must at the same time issue—
  (a) a requisition, or
  (b) a single justice procedure notice.

(2A) A requisition is a document which requires the person on whom it is served to appear before a magistrates' court to answer the written charge.

(2B) A single justice procedure notice is a document which requires the person on whom it is served to serve on the designated officer for a magistrates' court specified in the notice a written notification stating—
  (a) whether the person desires to plead guilty or not guilty, and
  (b) if the person desires to plead guilty, whether or not the person desires to be tried in accordance with section 16A of the Magistrates' Courts Act 1980.

(3) Where a relevant prosecutor issues a written charge and a requisition, the written charge and requisition must be served on the person concerned, and a copy of both must be served on the court named in the requisition.

(3A) Where a relevant prosecutor issues a written charge and a single justice procedure notice, the written charge and notice must be served on the person concerned, and a copy of both must be served on the designated officer specified in the notice.

(3B) If a single justice procedure notice is served on a person, the relevant prosecutor must—

(a) at the same time serve on the person such documents as may be prescribed by Criminal Procedure Rules, and

(b) serve copies of those documents on the designated officer specified in the notice.

(3C) The written notification required by a single justice procedure notice may be served by the legal representative of the person charged on the person's behalf.

KEYNOTE

Criminal proceedings are instituted by the issue of a written charge. A failure to issue a requisition and/or serve the documents is a procedural error and does not render the institution of proceedings a nullity (*DPP* v *McFarlane* [2019] EWHC 1895 (Admin)).

In relation to s. 29(2B), a single justice procedure notice is where the case is heard by a single justice. The accused must have attained the age of 18, be charged with a summary offence that does not carry imprisonment, intend to plead guilty and agree to the case being dealt with by a single justice without a hearing and in the absence of the parties and, if a party appears, must proceed as if the party were absent (s. 16A of the Magistrates' Courts Act 1980).

A 'relevant prosecutor' for the purposes of s. 29(5) includes a police force, the DPP (and therefore the CPS), the Director of the SFO, the Director General of the NCA and those persons specified by the Secretary of State, for example the Secretary of State for Work and Pensions.

2.1.3 Service of the Summons or Requisition

The Magistrates' Courts Rules 1981, r. 99, as amended by the Magistrates' Courts (Amendment) Rules 2019 (SI 2019/1367), states:

(1) Subject to paragraph (7), a summons requiring a person to appear before a magistrates' court may be served by—

(a) handing it to the person in person or, where the person is a corporation, to a person holding a senior position in that corporation;

(b) posting it to the person at an address where it is reasonably believed that the person will receive it or, where the person is a corporation, the address for service in accordance with paragraph (2);

(c) addressing it to the person and leaving it for the person at an address where it is reasonably believed that the person will receive it;

(d) where the person has given an electronic address and has not refused to accept service at that address, sending it by electronic means to the address which the person has given;

(e) where the person to be served is given access to an electronic address at which a document may be deposited and has not refused to accept service by the deposit of a document at that address, by depositing it at that address and making it possible for the recipient to read the document, or view or listen to its content, as the case may be, and notifying the recipient of the deposit of the document (which notice may be given by electronic means);

(f) where the person is in custody, sending it to his or her custodian, addressed to the person;

(g) where the person has given a document exchange (DX) box number, and has not refused to accept service by DX, addressing it to the person at that DX box number and leaving it at that document exchange;

(h) where the person is legally represented, serving it on the person's legal representative in the same manner as it could be served on the person under subparagraphs (a), (b), (c) and (g);

(i) where the person is legally represented and the person's legal representative has given an electronic address, sending it to that address;

(j) where the person to be served is legally represented and the legal representative is given access to an electronic address at which a document may be deposited by depositing it at that address and making it possible for the recipient to read the document, or view or listen to its content, as the case may be, and notifying the recipient of the deposit of the document (which notice may be given by electronic means); or

(k) any other method specified by the court.

KEYNOTE

Where the person is a corporation, the address for service under this rule is the person's principal office, and if there is no readily identifiable principal office, then any place where it carries on its activities or business (para. (2)).

A witness summons may only be served in accordance with para. (1)(a), (d) or (f) (para. (6)).

Paragraph (7) provides that this rule does not apply in relation to a judgment summons (for which r. 58 requires service on the judgment debtor personally).

Where a summons or requisition is served on a defendant under 18, a copy must also be served on a parent or guardian of the defendant, and if the court requires the parent or guardian to attend, the copy may impose that requirement or a separate summons or requisition may be issued for that purpose (r. 7.4 of the Criminal Procedure (Amendment) Rules 2022 (SI 2022/45)). The court must require the parent or guardian to attend where the defendant is under 16 (s. 34A of the Children and Young Persons Act 1933).

2.1.4 Service Outside England and Wales

The following legislation deals with the service of documents outside England and Wales:

- Section 39 of the Criminal Law Act 1977 (service in Scotland and Northern Ireland) provides that (a) a summons, (b) a written charge, (c) a requisition and (ca) a single justice procedure notice, requiring a person charged with an offence to appear before a court in England or Wales, and any other document which, by virtue of any enactment, may or must be served on a person with, or at the same time as, a document mentioned in para. (a), (b), (c) or (ca) above, may, in such manner as may be prescribed by rules of court, be served on him in Scotland or Northern Ireland (s. 1). This also applies to a summons directed to a person that is issued after the person's trial has begun (s. 1A).
- Section 1139(4) of the Companies Act 2006 (service of copy summons etc. on company's registered office in Scotland and Northern Ireland).
- Sections 3 and 4 of the Crime (International Co-operation) Act 2003, and rr. 49.1 and 49.2 of the Criminal Procedure Rules 2020 (service of summons etc. outside the United Kingdom).
- Section 1139(2) of the Companies Act 2006 (service on overseas companies).

2.1.5 Issue of Warrants

Section 125 of the Magistrates' Courts Act 1980 deals with the execution of warrants and provides:

(1) A warrant of arrest issued by a justice of the peace shall remain in force until it is executed or withdrawn or it ceases to have effect in accordance with rules of court.
(2) A warrant of arrest, warrant of commitment, warrant of detention, warrant of control or search warrant issued by a justice of the peace may be executed anywhere in England and Wales by any person to whom it is directed or by any constable acting within his police area.

2.1.5.1 Warrant of Arrest

An arrest warrant can be issued for a suspect by a justice of the peace if an information in writing is laid before them that a person has committed or is suspected of having committed an offence (s. 1(1)(b) and (3) of the 1980 Act). Such warrants can only be issued for persons aged 18 or over if the offence the warrant relates to is an indictable offence or is punishable with imprisonment or the person's address is not sufficiently established for a summons or written charge and requisition to be served on him/her (s. 1(4)).

In relation to witnesses, an arrest warrant may be issued by a justice of the peace where they are satisfied that it is in the interests of justice to secure the attendance of a person who could give material evidence or produce any document or thing likely to be material evidence. However, a warrant may only be issued where evidence is given on oath that a summons would not procure the attendance of the person (s. 97(2)), or that the person, with no just excuse, has failed to attend court in response to a summons (s. 97(3)).

2.1.6 Execution of Warrants

The Criminal Procedure Rules 2020, r. 13.5 states:

(1) A warrant may be executed—
  (a) by any person to whom it is directed; or
  (b) if the warrant was issued by a magistrates' court, by anyone authorised to do so by section 125 (warrants), 125A (civilian enforcement officers) or 125B (execution by approved enforcement agency) of the Magistrates' Courts Act 1980.
(2) The person who executes a warrant must—
  (a) explain, in terms the defendant can understand, what the warrant requires, and why;
  (b) show the defendant the warrant, if that person has it; and
  (c) if the defendant asks—
    (i) arrange for the defendant to see the warrant, if that person does not have it, and
    (ii) show the defendant any written statement of that person's authority required by section 125A or 125B of the 1980 Act.

KEYNOTE

Certain warrants issued by a magistrates' court (arrest, commitment, detention, distress or in connection with the enforcement of a fine or other order) may be executed anywhere in England and Wales by a civilian enforcement officer (s. 125A) or by an approved enforcement agency (s. 125B). In either case, the person executing the warrant must, if the defendant asks, show a written statement indicating: that person's name; the authority or agency by which that person is employed or in which that person is a director or partner;

that that person is authorised to execute warrants; and, where s. 125B applies, that the agency is registered as one approved by the Lord Chancellor. A warrant to which s. 125A applies may be executed by any person entitled to execute it even though it is not in that person's possession at the time (s. 125D).

In order to execute a warrant of arrest issued in connection with, or arising out of, criminal proceedings, or a warrant of commitment issued under s. 76 of the 1980 Act, a constable may enter and search any premises where he/she has reasonable grounds for believing the person sought is on the premises. The search may only be to the extent required and is restricted to the parts of the premises where the constable reasonably believes the person may be. Reasonable force may be used when necessary. These powers are derived from ss. 17(1)(a) and 117 of the Police and Criminal Evidence Act 1984. Civilian enforcement officers and approved enforcement agencies may be authorised to enter and search premises for the purposes of executing a warrant (for or in connection with any criminal offence), only to the extent reasonably required, and where they have reasonable grounds for believing the person is on the premises (sch. 4A to the 1980 Act).

The Criminal Procedure Rules 2020, r. 13.5(3) states that a person who executes a warrant of arrest requiring the defendant to be released on bail must make a record of:

- the defendant's name;
- the reason for the arrest;
- the defendant's release on bail; and
- when and where the warrant requires the defendant to attend court; and
- serve the record on the defendant and the court officer.

Other types of warrants that may be executed by a constable are listed in s. 125D(3) of the 1980 Act as a warrant under the: Armed Forces Act 2006; Tribunals, Courts and Enforcement Act 2007 (control of goods); Family Law Act 1996 (failure to comply with occupation order or non-molestation order); Crime and Disorder Act 1998 (unwilling witnesses); and Powers of Criminal Courts (Sentencing) Act 2000 (offenders referred to court by youth offender panel).

Where a person is arrested by a constable under warrant, they must be informed of the reason for their arrest and the fact that the constable is acting under warrant (Police and Criminal Evidence Act 1984, s. 28).

Rule 13.4(3) provides that a warrant for detention or imprisonment must include such an indication of the defendant's physical and mental health as may be needed to alert those to whom the warrant is directed: (a) to any vulnerability of the defendant; and (b) to any risk to others that may be posed by the defendant.

2.1.6.1 Disclosure of Information for Enforcing Warrants

The Magistrates' Courts Act 1980, s. 125CA states:

> (1) A magistrates' court may make a disclosure order if satisfied that it is necessary to do so for the purpose of executing a warrant to which this section applies.
> (2) This section applies to a warrant of arrest, commitment, detention or control issued by a justice of the peace in connection with the enforcement of a fine or other order imposed or made on conviction.
> (3) A disclosure order is an order requiring the person to whom it is directed to supply the designated officer for the court with any of the following information about the person to whom the warrant relates—
> (a) his name, date of birth or national insurance number;
> (b) his address (or any of his addresses).
> (4) A disclosure order may be made only on the application of a person entitled to execute the warrant.

KEYNOTE

The disclosure order may require that basic personal information (name, date of birth, national insurance number and address or addresses) held by a relevant public authority be supplied by that authority to the court for the purpose of facilitating the enforcement of a s. 125A(1) warrant which is so specified (s. 125C(1)).

A 'relevant public authority' means a Minister of the Crown, government department, local authority or chief officer of police specified in an order made by the Lord Chancellor (s. 125C(2)).

The information supplied for the purpose of facilitating the enforcement of a s. 125A(1) warrant may be supplied to any person entitled to execute the warrant; any employee of a body or person who, for the purposes of s. 125B, is an approved enforcement agency in relation to the warrant; or any justices' clerk or other person appointed under s. 2(1) of the Courts Act 2003 (s. 125C(3)).

Under s. 125C(4) it is an offence for a person to intentionally or recklessly disclose information supplied to him/her under this section otherwise than as permitted by subs. (3), or use information so supplied otherwise than for the purpose of facilitating the enforcement of the s. 125A(1) warrant concerned. However, it is not an offence to disclose any information in accordance with any enactment or order of a court or for the purposes of any proceedings before a court, or to disclose any information which has previously been lawfully disclosed to the public (s. 125C(5)).

2.1.6.2 Execution of Warrants throughout the United Kingdom

Section 136 of the Criminal Justice and Public Order Act 1994 states:

(1) A warrant issued in England, Wales or Northern Ireland for the arrest of a person charged with an offence may (without any endorsement) be executed in Scotland by any constable of any police force of the country of issue or of the country of execution, or by a constable appointed under section 24 of the Railways and Transport Safety Act 2003, as well as by any other persons within the directions of the warrant.

(2) A warrant issued in—

(a) Scotland; or

(b) Northern Ireland,

for the arrest of a person charged with an offence may (without any endorsement) be executed in England and Wales by any constable of any police force of the country of issue or of the country of execution, or by a constable appointed under section 24 of the Railways and Transport Safety Act 2003, as well as by any other persons within the directions of the warrant.

(3) A warrant issued in—

(a) England or Wales; or

(b) Scotland,

for the arrest of a person charged with an offence may (without any endorsement) be executed in Northern Ireland by any constable of any police force of the country of issue or of the country of execution as well as by any other persons within the directions in the warrant.

(4) A person arrested in pursuance of a warrant shall be taken, as soon as reasonably practicable, to any place to which he is committed by, or may be conveyed under, the warrant.

KEYNOTE

In addition to a warrant for the arrest of a person charged with an offence, this section also relates to: (a) a warrant of commitment and a warrant to arrest a witness issued in England, Wales or Northern Ireland; and (b) a warrant for committal, a warrant to imprison (or apprehend and imprison) and a warrant to arrest a witness issued in Scotland. In addition, the section also applies to a warrant for the arrest of an offender referred back to court by a youth offender panel (sch. 1, para. 3(2) to the Powers of Criminal Courts (Sentencing) Act 2000), issued in England and Wales.

Section 38A of the Criminal Law Act 1977 provides for the cross-border execution of Scottish commitment warrants for non-payment of fines, and s. 38B contains similar provisions for such warrants being executed between England, Wales and Northern Ireland.

The Indictable Offences Act 1848, s. 13 provides that warrants from the Isle of Man and the Channel Islands may be executed in England and Wales where they have been endorsed by a justice of the peace.

2.2 Release of Person Arrested

2.2.1 Introduction

The release of persons arrested is regulated by the Bail Act 1976, the Police and Criminal Evidence Act 1984 and the Criminal Justice and Public Order Act 1994.

Significant changes to the existing legislation have been made by the Police, Crime, Sentencing and Courts Act 2022. The 2022 Act establishes a neutral position within the legislation, by removing the presumption against pre-charge bail. It creates a set of risk factors to be taken into account when considering whether to grant pre-charge bail. This makes particular reference to the safeguarding of the victim, witness and/or suspect, particularly where they are vulnerable.

2.2.2 Person Arrested Elsewhere than at a Police Station

Where a person is arrested at any place other than a police station, or taken into custody by a constable following an arrest made by a civilian, the constable is normally obliged to take that person to a designated police station (Police and Criminal Evidence Act 1984, s. 30(1), (1A), (1B) and (2)), or in certain circumstances to a non-designated police station ((s. 30(3)–(6)).

An arrested person may, instead of being taken to a police station, be released with bail (known as 'street bail') or without bail to attend at a police station at a later date. The provisions of the 1984 Act in relation to this are detailed below.

2.2.2.1 Release of Arrested Person Elsewhere than at a Police Station

The Police and Criminal Evidence Act 1984, s. 30A provides for persons arrested elsewhere than at a police station to be released with or without bail without being required to attend a police station.

The Police and Criminal Evidence Act 1984, s. 30A states:

> (1) If subsection (1A) applies, a constable may release a person who is arrested or taken into custody in the circumstances mentioned in section 30(1).
>
> (1A) This subsection applies if—
>
> (a) the constable is satisfied that releasing the person on bail is necessary and proportionate in all the circumstances (having regard, in particular, to any conditions of bail which would be imposed), and
>
> (b) a custody officer authorises the release on bail having considered any representations made by the person.
>
> (1B) In determining whether releasing the person on bail is necessary and proportionate in all the circumstances, the constable must have regard in particular to—
>
> (a) the need to secure that the person surrenders to custody,
>
> (b) the need to prevent offending by the person,
>
> (c) the need to safeguard victims of crime and witnesses, taking into account any vulnerabilities of any alleged victim of, or alleged witness to, the offence for which the person was arrested where these vulnerabilities have been identified by the constable, and
>
> (e) the need to manage risks to the public.
>
> (1C) If subsection (1A) does not apply, a constable may release without bail a person who is arrested or taken into custody in the circumstances mentioned in section 30(1).

(2) A person may be released under subsection (1) or (1C) at any time before he arrives at a police station.
(3) A person released on bail under subsubsection (1) must be required to attend a police station.
(3A) Where a constable releases a person on bail under subsection (1)—
 (a) no recognizance for the person's surrender to custody shall be taken from the person,
 (b) no security for the person's surrender to custody shall be taken from the person or from anyone else on the person's behalf,
 (c) the person shall not be required to provide a surety or sureties for his surrender to custody, and
 (d) no requirement to reside in a bail hostel may be imposed as a condition of bail.
(3B) Subject to subsection (3A), where a constable releases a person on bail under subsection (1) the constable may impose, as conditions of the bail, such requirements as appear to the constable to be necessary—
 (a) to secure that the person surrenders to custody,
 (b) to secure that the person does not commit an offence while on bail,
 (c) to secure that the person does not interfere with witnesses or otherwise obstruct the course of justice, whether in relation to him or any other person, or
 (d) for the person's own protection or, if the person is under the age of 18, for the person's own welfare or in the person's own interests.
(4) Where a person is released on bail under subsection (1), a requirement may be imposed on the person as a condition of bail only under the preceding provisions of this section.
(5) The police station which the person is required to attend may be any police station.

KEYNOTE

Section 30A(3B) enables the officer granting bail to consider attaching conditions relevant and proportionate to the suspect and the offence. The conditions that may be considered are the same as those available to a custody officer as contained in s. 3A(5) of the 1976 Act, except for those specified in s. 30A(3A).

A constable who is satisfied that there are no grounds for keeping the arrested person under arrest or releasing him or her on bail under s. 30A must release that person (s. 30(7) and (7A)).

The reference to a custody officer in s. 30A(1A)(b) includes a reference to an officer other than a custody officer who is performing the functions of a custody officer where a custody officer is not readily available (s. 36(7C)).

2.2.2.2 Notice in Writing

The Police and Criminal Evidence Act 1983, s. 30B states:

(1) Where a constable releases a person under section 30A, he must give that person a notice in writing before he is released.
(2) The notice must state—
 (a) the offence for which he was arrested,
 (b) the grounds on which he was arrested, and
 (c) whether the person is being released without bail or on bail.
(3) A notice given to a person released on bail must inform him that he is required to attend a police station.
(4) The notice must also specify—
 (a) the police station which the person is required to attend, and
 (b) the time on the bail end date when the person is required to attend the police station.
(4A) If the person is granted bail subject to conditions under section 30A(3B), the notice also—
 (a) must specify the requirements imposed by those conditions,
 (b) must explain the opportunities under sections 30CA(1) and 30CB(1) for variation of those conditions.
(5) ...
(6) The person may be required to attend a different police station from that specified in the notice under subsection (1) or to attend at a different time or an additional time.
(6A) A person may not be required under subsection (6) to attend at a police station at a time which is after the bail end date in relation to the person.

(7) He must be given notice in writing of any such change as is mentioned in subsection (6) but more than one such notice may be given to him.

(8) In this section 'bail end date', in relation to a person, means the last day of the period of 3 months beginning with the day after the day on which the person was arrested for the offence in relation to which bail is granted under section 30A.

KEYNOTE

The section requires that the bail notice must, in addition to the existing requirements, set out the date, time and place at which bail must be answered. The date is required to be three months beginning with the day after the day on which the person was arrested. There is no provision to extend bail granted under s. 30A, nor can the bail return date be altered where its use extends street bail beyond the three-month limit.

The only exception for bail to be extended beyond three months is if, at any time on the day on which the applicable bail period in relation to a person would end, the person is in hospital as an in-patient. The running of the applicable bail period in relation to the person is to be treated as having been suspended for any day on which the patient was in hospital as an in-patient (s. 47ZM).

2.2.2.3 Release, Attendance and Re-arrest

The Police and Criminal Evidence Act 1984 states:

(1) A person who has been required to attend a police station is not required to do so if he is given notice in writing that his attendance is no longer required.

(2) If a person is required to attend a police station which is not a designated police station he must be—
   (a) released, or
   (b) taken to a designated police station, not more than six hours after his arrival.

(3) Nothing in the Bail Act 1976 applies in relation to bail under section 30A.

(4) Nothing in section 30A or 30B or in this section prevents the re-arrest without warrant of a person released under section 30A if, since the person's release, new evidence has come to light or an examination or analysis of existing evidence has been made which could not reasonably have been made before the person's release.

2.2.2.4 Variation of Bail Conditions: Police

The Police and Criminal Evidence Act 1984, s. 30CA states:

(1) Where a person released on bail under section 30A(1) is on bail subject to conditions—
   (a) a relevant officer at the police station at which the person is required to attend,
   (b) ... may, at the request of the person but subject to subsection (2), vary the conditions.

(2) On any subsequent request made in respect of the same grant of bail, subsection (1) confers power to vary the conditions of the bail only if the request is based on information that, in the case of the previous request or each previous request, was not available to the relevant officer considering that previous request when he was considering it.

(3) Where conditions of bail granted to a person under section 30A(1) are varied under subsection (1)—
   (a) paragraphs (a) to (d) of section 30A(3A) apply,
   (b) requirements imposed by the conditions as so varied must be requirements that appear to the relevant officer varying the conditions to be necessary for any of the purposes mentioned in paragraphs (a) to (d) of section 30A(3B), and
   (c) the relevant officer who varies the conditions must give the person notice in writing of the variation.

(4) Power under subsection (1) to vary conditions is, subject to subsection (3)(a) and (b), power—
   (a) to vary or rescind any of the conditions, and
   (b) to impose further conditions.

(4A) If it is reasonably practicable to do so, the investigating officer must seek the views of the alleged victim (if any) of the relevant offence on—

(a) whether any of the conditions that are relevant conditions should be varied under subsection (1), and
(b) if so, what variations should be made to those conditions.

(4B) The investigating officer must inform the relevant officer of any views obtained under subsection (4A).

(4C) If any of the conditions which are relevant conditions are varied under subsection (1), the investigating officer must, if it is reasonably practicable to do so, notify the alleged victim of the variations.

(4D) If the alleged victim of the relevant offence appears to the investigating officer to be vulnerable, subsection (4A and (4C) apply as if references to the alleged victim of the offence were to a person appearing to the officer to represent the alleged victim.

KEYNOTE

Section 30CA introduces a number of terms that require further explanation.

Investigating Officer

The 'investigating officer', in relation to the relevant offence, means the constable or other person in charge of the investigation of the offence.

Relevant Offence

The 'relevant offence' means the offence for which the person making the request under subs. (1) was under arrest when granted bail under s. 30A(1).

Relevant Condition

The 'relevant condition', in relation to the relevant offence and an alleged victim of that offence, means a condition that relates to the safeguarding of the alleged victim.

Relevant Officer

The 'relevant officer', in relation to a designated police station, means a custody officer but, in relation to any other police station (s. 30CA(5)):

(a) means a constable who is not involved in the investigation of the relevant offence, if such a constable is readily available, and
(b) if no such constable is readily available:
  (i) means a constable other than the one who granted bail to the person, if such a constable is readily available, and
  (ii) if no such constable is readily available, means the constable who granted bail.

Alleged Victim

For the purposes of s. 30CA, a person ('P') is an alleged victim of an offence if (s. 30CA(6)):

(a) an allegation has been made to a constable or other person involved in the investigation of the offence that P has suffered physical, mental or emotional harm, or economic loss, which was directly caused by the offence, and
(b) P is an individual.

Vulnerable

For the purposes of s. 30CA, an alleged victim of an offence is vulnerable if the alleged victim (s. 30CA(7)):

(a) was aged under 18 at the time of the offence, or
(b) may have difficulty understanding a communication from an investigating officer under this section, or communicating effectively in response to it, by reason of:
  (i) a physical disability or disorder,
  (ii) a mental disorder within the meaning of the Mental Health Act 1983, or
  (iii) a significant impairment of intelligence and social functioning.

2.2.2.5 Variation of Bail Conditions: Court

The Police and Criminal Evidence Act 1984, s. 30CB states:

(1) Where a person released on bail under section 30A(1) is on bail subject to conditions, a magistrates' court may, on an application by or on behalf of the person, vary the conditions if—
  (a) the conditions have been varied under section 30CA(1) since being imposed under section 30A(3B),
  (b) a request for variation under section 30CA(1) of the conditions has been made and refused, or
  (c) a request for variation under section 30CA(1) of the conditions has been made and the period of 48 hours beginning with the day when the request was made has expired without the request having been withdrawn or the conditions having been varied in response to the request.

KEYNOTE

Where the court varies the conditions they must be seen as necessary for any of the purposes mentioned in s. 30A(3B)(a)–(d), and bail continues subject to the varied conditions (s. 30CB(3)(b) and (c)). It was held in *R (On the Application of Ajaib)* v *Birmingham Magistrates' Court* [2009] EWHC 2127 (Admin) that in deciding to vary bail conditions, the court was entitled to rely on a police officer's evidence whilst allowing him to withhold specific information. In this case the police asserted that they held material disclosure of which would prejudice their inquiries, suggesting that the suspect was liquidating his assets to travel abroad.

2.2.2.6 Power of Arrest for Non-attendance and Breach of Bail Conditions

The Police and Criminal Evidence Act 1984, s. 30D states:

(1) A constable may arrest without warrant a person who—
  (a) has been released on bail under section 30A subject to a requirement to attend a specified police station, but
  (b) fails to attend the police station at the specified time.

(2) A person arrested under subsection (1) must be taken to a police station (which may be the specified police station or any other police station) as soon as practicable after the arrest.

(2A) A person who has been released on bail under section 30A may be arrested without a warrant by a constable if the constable has reasonable grounds for suspecting that the person has broken any of the conditions of bail.

(2B) A person arrested under subsection (2A) must be taken to a police station (which may be the specified police station mentioned in subsection (1) or any other police station) as soon as practicable after the arrest.

(3) In subsection (1), 'specified' means specified in a notice under subsection (1) of section 30B or, if notice of change has been given under subsection (7) of that section, in that notice.

KEYNOTE

Section 30D(1) and (2) relate to a person's failure to answer his/her bail at the specified time and place. Section 30D(2A) and (2B) provide a power of arrest where a constable has reasonable grounds to suspect that a person has broken any of the conditions of bail.

An immigration officer or a constable may arrest without warrant a person on immigration bail if there are reasonable grounds for believing that the person is likely to fail to comply with a bail condition, or that the person is failing, or has failed, to comply with a bail condition (sch. 10, Immigration Bail, para. 10(1) of the Immigration Act 2016).

2.2.3 Pre-charge Release of Person Arrested and Bail

The Police and Criminal Evidence Act 1984 provides for the following pre-charge scenarios:

- the custody officer determines that there is sufficient evidence to charge that person with the offence for which they were arrested and may detain them at the police station for such period as is necessary to enable them to do so (s. 37(1));
- the custody officer determines that there is insufficient evidence to charge that person with the offence for which they have been arrested, the person shall be released pending the obtaining of further evidence with bail where the pre-conditions for bail are satisfied or without bail (release under investigation) where the pre-conditions for bail are not met (s. 37(2));
- if the custody officer determines that he/she does not have sufficient evidence to charge a person with the offence for which they were arrested and the pre-conditions for bail are not satisfied, then the person arrested must be released without bail (subject to subs. (3)) (s. 37(2A));
- the custody officer has reasonable grounds for believing that the person's detention without being charged is necessary to secure or preserve evidence, then the person may be kept in police detention (s. 37(3));
- subject to s. 41(7) (below), if there is sufficient evidence to charge the person the custody officer shall release the person without charge and on bail or keep the person in police detention, for the purpose of enabling the DPP to make a decision under s. 37B (s. 37(7)(a));
- there is sufficient evidence to charge and the custody officer releases the person without charge and without bail unless the pre-conditions for bail are satisfied (s. 37(7)(b));
- there is sufficient evidence to charge and the custody officer releases the person without charge and on bail if those pre-conditions are satisfied but not for the purpose under s. 37B (s. 37(7)(c));
- there is sufficient evidence and the person is charged (s. 37(7)(d));
- a review officer concludes that the detention of a person without charge can no longer be justified and the custody officer releases the person without bail unless the pre-conditions for bail are satisfied (s. 40(8));
- a person, who at the expiry of 24 hours after the relevant time is in police detention and has not been charged, shall be released at that time without bail unless the preconditions for bail are satisfied, or on bail if those pre-conditions are satisfied (s. 41(7)). This subsection does not apply to a person whose detention for more than 24 hours has been authorised or otherwise permitted (s. 41(8)).

KEYNOTE

The decision as to how a person is to be dealt with under s. 37(7)(a)–(d) above shall be that of the custody officer (s. 37(7A)).

A person released on bail under ss. 37(7)(a) and 37(7)(b) who breaches that bail and is arrested under s. 46A (**see para. 2.2.3.3**) shall be charged or released without bail unless the pre-conditions for bail are satisfied, or on bail if those pre-conditions are satisfied (ss. 37C and 37CA).

Where a person is released under s. 41(7) (expiry of 24 hours' detention), s. 42(10) (expiry of authority of continued detention) or s. 43(18) (expiry of warrant of further detention), they shall not be re-arrested without a warrant for the offence for which they were previously arrested unless, since the person's release, new evidence has come to light or an examination or analysis of existing evidence has been made which could not reasonably have been made before their release.

2.2.3.1 **Pre-conditions for Bail**

The Police and Criminal Evidence Act 1984, s. 50A states:

(1) For the purposes of this Part the following are the pre-conditions for bail in relation to the release of a person by a custody officer—
 (a) that the custody officer is satisfied that releasing the person on bail is necessary and proportionate in all the circumstances (having regard, in particular, to any conditions of bail which would be imposed), and
 (b) that the custody officer has considered any representations made by the person or the person's legal representative.
(2) In determining whether releasing the person on bail is necessary and proportionate in all the circumstances, the custody officer must have regard in particular to—
 (a) the need to secure that the person surrenders to custody,
 (b) the need to prevent offending by the person,
 (c) the need to safeguard victims of crime and witnesses, taking into account any vulnerabilities of any alleged victim of, or alleged witness to, the offence for which the person was arrested where these vulnerabilities have been identified by the custody officer,
 (d) the need to safeguard the person, taking into account any vulnerabilities of the person where these vulnerabilities have been identified by the custody officer, and
 (e) the need to manage risks to the public.

2.2.3.2 **Period of Bail and Extensions**

The Police and Criminal Evidence Act 1984 provides a regime of time limits and extensions introduced in respect of pre-charge bail. The following is an overview of these changes.

Applicable Bail Period: Initial Limit (s. 47ZB)

When the custody officer is releasing a person on bail to attend at a police station under s. 47(3)(c), he/she must appoint a time on the day on which the 'applicable bail period' in relation to the person ends (s. 47ZA(1) and (2)).

Section 47ZB(1) states that the 'applicable bail period', in relation to a person, means:

(a) in a Financial Conduct Authority (FCA), His Majesty's Revenue and Customs (HMRC), National Crime Agency (NCA) case or Serious Fraud Office (SFO) case, the period of six months beginning with the person's bail start date, or
(b) in any other case, the period of three months beginning with the person's bail start date.

A person's bail start date is the day after the day on which the person was arrested for the relevant offence (s. 47ZB).

The applicable bail period may be changed by the custody officer where the person is on bail in relation to one or more offences other than the relevant offence and it is appropriate to align the person's attendance in relation to the relevant offence with the person's attendance in relation to one or more other offences (s. 47ZA(3)). This subsection applies where the custody officer believes that a decision as to whether to charge the person with the relevant offence would be made before the end of the applicable bail period in relation to the person (s. 47ZA(4)). Where subs. (3) or (4) applies, the power may be exercised so as to appoint a time on a day falling before the end of the applicable bail period in relation to the person (s. 47ZA(5)).

Applicable Bail Period: Extension of Initial Limit in Standard Cases (s. 47ZD)

Section 47ZD allows a relevant officer (an officer of inspector rank or above (s. 47ZD(6)) to extend bail from three months to six months where the conditions A to D set out in s. 47ZC are met. The relevant officer must arrange for the suspect or their legal representative to be invited to make representations, and must consider any that are made before making a decision. The suspect (or their representative) must be informed of the outcome. The four conditions outlined in s. 47ZC are:

Condition A—the decision-maker has reasonable grounds for suspecting the person in question to be guilty of the relevant offence.

Condition B—the decision-maker has reasonable grounds for believing:

(a) in a case where the person in question is or is to be released on bail under s. 37(7)(b) or 37CA(2)(b), that further time is needed for making a decision as to whether to charge the person with the relevant offence, or

(b) otherwise, that further investigation is needed of any matter in connection with the relevant offence.

Condition C—the decision-maker has reasonable grounds for believing:

(a) in a case where the person in question is or is to be released on bail under s. 37(7)(b) or 37CA(2)(b), that the decision as to whether to charge the person with the relevant offence is being made diligently and expeditiously, or

(b) otherwise, that the investigation is being conducted diligently and expeditiously.

Condition D—the decision-maker has reasonable grounds for believing that the release on bail of the person in question is necessary and proportionate in all the circumstances (having regard, in particular, to any conditions of bail which are, or are to be, imposed).

KEYNOTE

Conditions A to D: 'Decision-Maker'

In relation to a condition which falls to be considered by virtue of s. 47ZD, the 'decision-maker' will be the relevant officer in question (i.e. an officer of the rank of inspector or above).

Applicable Bail Period: Further Extension of Limit in Standard Cases (s. 47ZDA)

If a relevant officer (an officer of inspector rank or above) has authorised an extension of the applicable bail period in relation to the person under s. 47ZD, that period has not ended and a senior officer is satisfied that conditions A to D are met in relation to the person, the senior officer (an officer of the rank of superintendent or above (s. 47ZDA(6)) may authorise the applicable bail period in relation to the person to be extended so that it ends at the end of a period of nine months beginning with the person's bail start date.

Before deciding on an authorisation, the senior officer must arrange for the person or the person's legal representative to be informed that a determination is to be made and must consider any representations made by the person or the person's legal representative.

The senior officer must arrange for the person or the person's legal representative to be informed whether an authorisation has been given in relation to the person.

KEYNOTE

Conditions A to D: 'Decision-Maker'

In relation to conditions A to D which fall to be considered by virtue of s. 47ZDA, the 'decision-maker' will be the senior officer in question (i.e. an officer of the rank of superintendent or above).

Applicable Bail Period: Extension of Limit in Non-standard Cases (s. 47ZDB)

If the applicable bail period in relation to a person is the period mentioned in s. 47ZDB(1)(a), that period has not ended and an appropriate decision-maker is satisfied that conditions A to D are met in relation to the person, they may authorise the applicable bail period in relation to the person to be extended so that it ends at the end of the period of 12 months beginning with the person's bail start date.

The person or the person's legal representative must be informed that a determination is to be made, any representation must be considered and they must be informed whether an authorisation has been given in relation to the person.

KEYNOTE

An extension under s. 47ZDB relates to cases involving the FCA, HMRC, NCA or SFO (s. 47ZB(1)(a)) and an initial 'applicable bail period' of six months.

Conditions A to D: 'Decision-Maker'

In relation to conditions A to D which fall to be considered by virtue of s. 47ZDB, the 'decision-maker' will be the 'appropriate decision-maker'.

'Appropriate Decision-Maker'

Section 47ZDB(6) states that the 'appropriate decision-maker' means:

(a) in an FCA case, a member of staff of the Financial Conduct Authority who is of the description designated for the purposes of this section by the Chief Executive of that Authority,
(b) in an HMRC case, an officer of Revenue and Customs of a grade that is equivalent to the rank of superintendent or above,
(c) in an NCA case, a National Crime Agency officer of a grade that is equivalent to the rank of superintendent or above, and
(d) in an SFO case, a member of the Serious Fraud Office who is of the Senior Civil Service.

Applicable Bail Period: Extension of Limit in Designated Cases (s. 47ZE)

This section provides that if a senior officer has authorised an extension of the applicable bail period in relation to a person under s. 47ZDA, the DPP may designate the person's case as being exceptionally complex (a 'designated case'). If a qualifying police officer (an officer of the rank of commander or assistant chief constable or above) is satisfied that conditions A to D are met in relation to the person in a designated case, the officer may authorise the applicable bail period in relation to the person to be extended so that it ends at the end of the period of 12 months beginning with the person's bail start date.

The qualifying officer must consult the DPP and arrange for the person or the person's legal representative to be informed that a determination is to be made, any representation must be considered and they must be informed whether an authorisation has been given in relation to the person.

Any authorisation for extending the bail period must be given before the applicable bail period in relation to the person has ended.

KEYNOTE

Conditions A to D: 'Decision-Maker'

In relation to conditions A to D which fall to be considered by virtue of s. 47ZDA, the 'decision-maker' will be the qualifying police officer in question (i.e. an officer of the rank of commander or assistant chief constable or above).

Applicable Bail Period: First Extension of Limit by Court (s. 47ZF)

If a senior officer has authorised an extension to the applicable bail period in relation to the person under s. 47ZDA, the appropriate decision-maker has authorised an extension of the applicable bail period in relation to the person under s. 47ZDB or a qualifying police officer has authorised an extension of the applicable bail period in relation to the person under s. 47ZE, a qualifying applicant (a constable, a Crown Prosecutor or a designated member of the FCS, HMRC, NCA or SFO) may apply to the magistrates' court for it to authorise an extension of the applicable bail period in relation to the person. This must be before the applicable bail period in relation to the person ends under this section.

Where a court is satisfied that conditions B to D as set out in s. 47ZC are met, it may authorise an extension of bail. Dependent on the nature of the application, the court may authorise an extension of 12, 18 or 24 months beginning with the person's bail start date.

Section 47ZG provides that further extensions of the bail period for up to six months may be authorised by the court where conditions B to D as set out in s. 47ZC are satisfied.

Withholding Sensitive Information

Section 47ZH provides that the police or prosecutors may apply to the court to withhold certain information relevant to the application to extend bail from the person on bail and their legal representatives. The court may only allow information to be withheld for the four grounds set out in subs. (4)—essentially: that there are reasonable grounds to believe that disclosing that information would lead to evidence being interfered with; a person coming to harm; another suspect escaping arrest for an indictable offence; the recovery of property obtained as a result of an indictable offence being hindered.

Applicable Bail Period: Cases Referred to the DPP

Bail time limits do not apply in cases where an individual is bailed under s. 37(7)(a) or 37C(2)(b) while waiting for a charging decision to be made by the DPP. However, where a charging decision has been requested from the DPP, but the DPP requests further information from the police before reaching that decision, bail time limits will re-apply during the period that the police are gathering that information and, accordingly, the police must set a new bail return date that is not after the end of the person's applicable bail period. If, at the point that the DPP makes the request for further information, the person's applicable bail period would end within seven days of the DPP's request, the person's applicable bail period is extended to seven days from that request in order to give the police time to gather the information, seek a bail extension or release the suspect from bail. Where the information requested by the DPP is provided, the bail time limit is again suspended (s. 47ZL).

Applicable Bail Period: Special Cases of Release on Bail under Section 30A and Periods in Hospital (s. 47ZM)

Where a person is granted bail under s. 30A (**see para 2.2.2.1**) or s. 47ZB (**see para 2.2.3.2**), their bail end date means the last day of the period of three months beginning with the day after the day when they were initially bailed. However, the running of the applicable bail period is to be treated as having been suspended for any day on which the person is in hospital as an in-patient.

Duty to Seek Views of Alleged Victims on Conditions and Pre-charge Bail

Section 47ZZA imposes a duty to, where reasonably practicable, seek views from alleged victims on whether relevant conditions should be imposed on the release of a person on pre-charge bail.

The Police and Criminal Evidence Act 1984, s. 47ZZA states:

(1) Subsections (2) to (5) apply if—
   (a) a person has been arrested for an offence, and
   (b) a custody officer proposes to release the person on bail under this Part (except section 37C(2)(b) or 37CA(2)(b)).

(2) If it is reasonably practicable to do so, the investigating officer must seek the views of the alleged victim (if any) of the offence on—
   (a) whether relevant conditions should be imposed on the person's bail, and
   (b) if so, what relevant conditions should be imposed.

(3) In this section 'relevant condition', in relation to an offence and an alleged victim of that offence, means a condition that relates to the safeguarding of the alleged victim.

(4) The investigating officer must inform the custody officer of any views obtained under subsection (2).

(5) If the person is granted bail subject to relevant conditions, the investigating officer must, if it is reasonably practicable to do so, notify the alleged victim of the offence of those conditions.
(6) If the alleged victim of the offence appears to the investigating officer to be vulnerable, subsections (2) and (5) apply as if references to the alleged victim of the offence were to a person appearing to the officer to represent the alleged victim.
(7) Subsections (8) to (11) apply if—
 (a) a person has been arrested for an offence,
 (b) the person has been released on bail under this Part subject to conditions, and
 (c) the person requests a custody officer to vary the conditions under section 3A(8) of the Bail Act 1976.
(8) If it is reasonably practicable to do so, the investigating officer must seek the views of the alleged victim (if any) of the offence on—
 (a) whether any of the conditions that are relevant conditions should be varied, and
 (b) if so, what variations should be made to those conditions.
(9) The investigating officer must inform the custody officer of any views obtained under subsection (8).
(10) If any of the conditions which are relevant conditions are varied, the investigating officer must, if it is reasonably practicable to do so, notify the alleged victim of the variations.
(11) If the alleged victim of the offence appears to the investigating officer to be vulnerable, subsections (8) and (10) apply as if references to the alleged victim of the offence were to a person appearing to the officer to represent the alleged victim.

KEYNOTE

'Investigating Officer'

In this section, 'investigating officer', in relation to an offence, means the constable or other person in charge of the investigation of the offence (s. 47ZZA(12)).

'Alleged Victim'

Section 47ZZA(13) states that for the purposes of this section a person ('P') is an alleged victim of an offence if:

(a) an allegation has been made to a constable or other person involved in the investigation of the offence that P has suffered physical, mental or emotional harm, or economic loss, which was directly caused by the offence, and
(b) P is an individual.

'Vulnerable'

Section 47ZZA(14) states that for the purposes of this section an alleged victim of an offence is vulnerable if the alleged victim:

(a) was aged under 18 at the time of the offence, or
(b) may have difficulty understanding a communication from an investigating officer under this section, or communicating effectively in response to it, by reason of:
 (i) a physical disability or disorder,
 (ii) a mental disorder within the meaning of the Mental Health Act 1983, or
 (iii) a significant impairment of intelligence and social functioning.

2.2.3.3 Power of Arrest for Failure to Answer to Police Bail

The Police and Criminal Evidence Act 1984, s. 46A states:

(1) A constable may arrest without a warrant any person who, having been released on bail under this Part of this Act subject to a duty to attend at a police station, fails to attend at that police station at the time appointed for him to do so.

(1ZA) The reference in subsection (1) to a person who fails to attend at a police station at the time appointed for him to do so includes a reference to a person who—

(a) attends at a police station to answer to bail granted subject to the duty mentioned in section 47(3)(b), but

(b) leaves the police station at any time before the beginning of the proceedings referred to in sub-paragraph (i) of that provision.

(1ZB) The reference in subsection (1) to a person who fails to attend at a police station at the time appointed for the person to do so includes a reference to a person who—

(a) attends at a police station to answer to bail granted subject to the duty mentioned in section 47(3)(b), but

(b) refuses to be searched under section 54B.

(1A) A person who has been released on bail under this Part may be arrested without warrant by a constable if the constable has reasonable grounds for suspecting that the person has broken any of the conditions of bail.

(2) A person who is arrested under this section shall be taken to the police station appointed as the place at which he is to surrender to custody as soon as practicable after the arrest.

(3) For the purposes of—

(a) section 30 above (subject to the obligation in subsection (2) above), and

(b) section 31 above, an arrest under this section shall be treated as an arrest for an offence.

KEYNOTE

In subs. (1ZA)(b), sub-para. (i) of s. 47(3)(b) relates to proceedings held for the purposes of s. 51 of the Criminal Justice Act 2003 (directions for live links in criminal proceedings) so far as that section applies to preliminary hearings.

In subs. (1ZB)(a) the reference to s. 47(3)(b) relates to 'live link bail'.

The offence for which a person is arrested under subs. (1) is the offence for which he/she was granted bail (s. 34(7)).

Section 46A(1) provides a power of arrest only where a person fails to attend at that police station at the time appointed. This should be contrasted with s. 46A(1A) where a person released on bail under s. 47 may be arrested if there are reasonable grounds for suspecting that the person has broken any of the conditions of bail.

2.2.3.4 Breach of Pre-charge Bail Conditions Relating to Travel

OFFENCE: **Breach of Pre-charge Bail Conditions Relating to Travel—*Policing and Crime Act 2017, s. 68***

• 12 months' imprisonment and/or a fine on indictment • Six months' imprisonment and/or a fine summarily

The Policing and Crime Act 2017, s. 68 states:

(3) The person commits an offence if—

(a) the person's release on bail is subject to the travel restriction condition mentioned in subsection (2)(a) and he or she fails to comply with the condition, or

(b) the person's release on bail is subject to a travel restriction condition mentioned in subsection (2)(b) to (f) and he or she fails, without reasonable excuse, to comply with the condition.

KEYNOTE

This offence relates to a person who breaches certain travel-related conditions of pre-charge bail for those arrested on suspicion of committing a terrorist offence.

Each of the following is a travel restriction condition contained in s. 68(2):

(a) the person must not leave the United Kingdom,

(b) the person must not enter any port, or one or more particular ports, in the United Kingdom,

(c) the person must not go to a place in Northern Ireland that is within one mile of the border between Northern Ireland and the Republic of Ireland,
(d) the person must surrender all of his or her travel documents or all of his or her travel documents that are of a particular kind,
(e) the person must not have any travel documents, or travel documents of a particular kind, in his or her possession (whether the documents relate to that person or to another person),
(f) the person must not obtain, or seek to obtain, any travel documents (whether relating to that person or to another person) or travel documents of a particular kind.

The offence would apply where a person has been arrested under s. 24 of PACE or art. 26 of the Police and Criminal Evidence (Northern Ireland) Order 1989 on suspicion of committing a terrorist offence, as listed in s. 41 of the Counter-Terrorism Act 2008, has been released on pre-charge bail subject to a travel restriction condition and subsequently breaches, without reasonable excuse, any of those conditions. The offences listed in s. 41 of the Counter-Terrorism Act 2008 cover a range of offences including membership of a proscribed organisation, fundraising in support of terrorism and encouraging terrorist acts.

This section provides another tool for the police to tackle terrorism by deterring those arrested on suspicion of a terrorist offence from breaching a travel restriction condition imposed under the terms of their pre-charge bail, and by adding to the range of offences which might be prosecuted in cases where such a person has returned to the United Kingdom.

A 'travel document' means anything that is or appears to be a passport, or a ticket or other document that permits a person to make a journey by any means from a place in the United Kingdom to a place outside the United Kingdom (s. 69(2)). 'Passport' means a UK passport, a passport issued by or on behalf of the authorities of a country or territory outside the United Kingdom (or by or on behalf of an international organisation) or a document that can be used (in some or all circumstances) instead of a passport (s. 69(3)).

The offence can be tried on indictment in the Crown Court, which means that the Criminal Attempts Act 1981 applies so as to make it an offence to attempt to breach a travel restriction condition.

2.2.3.5 Notification of Decision not to Prosecute

The custody officer is under a duty to notify a person released under s. 34, 37 or 37CA of the Police and Criminal Evidence Act 1984, if a decision is made not to prosecute that person, either due to there being insufficient evidence, or where there is sufficient evidence but a decision is made that the person should not be charged or cautioned (s. 34(5B)). A notice in writing that the person is not to be prosecuted must be given to the person (s. 34(5C)). However, this does not prevent the prosecution of the person for an offence if new evidence comes to light after the notice was given (s. 34(5D)). These provisions also apply to a person released after the expiry of 24 hours' detention under s. 41(7) (s. 41(10)–(12)).

2.2.4 Police Bail After Charge

Where a person is charged at the police station (otherwise than a warrant backed for bail) the custody officer must make a decision to keep the person in custody until they can be brought before a magistrates' court, or to release the person either on bail or without bail, unless one or more conditions in the Police and Criminal Evidence Act 1984, s. 38, are satisfied (s. 38(1)).

Where the custody officer decides to bail a person who has been charged, s. 47(3) of the 1984 Act provides they may do so:

(a) to appear before a magistrates' court at such time and such place as the custody officer may appoint;

(b) to attend at such police station as the custody officer may appoint at such time as he may appoint for the purposes of—
   (i) proceedings held for the purposes of section 51 of the Criminal Justice Act 2003 (directions for live links in criminal proceedings) so far as that section applies to preliminary hearings (within the meaning of that section), and
   (ii) any such hearing in relation to which a direction under that section is given requiring or permitting the person on bail to take part through a live audio link or a live video link (within the meaning of that section); or

(c) to attend at such police station as the custody officer may appoint at such time as he may appoint for purposes other than those mentioned in paragraph (b) (subject to section 47ZA).

KEYNOTE

If bail conditions have been imposed by the custody officer, these may be varied by a magistrates' court on the application of the suspect (s. 47(1E)). The magistrates may confirm or remove the existing conditions or impose other conditions (Criminal Procedure Rules 2020, r. 14.6). Irrespective of the outcome, it continues to be police bail.

Nothing prevents the re-arrest without warrant of a person released on bail subject to a duty to attend at a police station if new evidence justifying a further arrest has come to light since his/her release (s. 47(2)).

Where a custody officer grants bail to a person to appear before a magistrates' court, he must appoint for the appearance a date which is not later than the first sitting of the court after the person is charged with the offence. If informed by the court that the appearance cannot be accommodated until a later date, that later date.

Where a custody officer has granted bail to a person subject to a duty to appear at a police station, the custody officer may give notice in writing to that person that his/her attendance at the police station is not required (s. 47(4)).

Where a person has been granted bail to attend at a police station (s. 47(3)(b)), a custody officer may subsequently appoint a different time, or an additional time, for attendance to answer bail and must give the person notice in writing of any changes (s. 47(4A) and (4B)). A custody officer may not appoint a time for a person's attendance under subs. (4A) which is after the end of the applicable bail period in relation to the person (s. 47(4D)). The reference to s. 47ZA in s. 47(3)(c) relates to 'applicable bail periods' (**see para. 2.2.3.2**).

In *Williamson* v *Chief Constable of West Midlands* [2003] EWCA Civ 337, it was clarified that the Bail Act 1976 does not apply to 'breach of the peace' as it is not a criminal offence.

2.2.4.1 Searches of Persons Answering to Live Link Bail

The Police and Criminal Evidence Act 1984, s. 54B states:

(1) A constable may search at any time—
   (a) any person who is at a police station to answer to live link bail; and
   (b) any article in the possession of such a person.

(2) If the constable reasonably believes a thing in the possession of the person ought to be seized on any of the grounds mentioned in subsection (3), the constable may seize and retain it or cause it to be seized and retained.

(3) The grounds are that the thing—
   (a) may jeopardise the maintenance of order in the police station;
   (b) may put the safety of any person in the police station at risk; or
   (c) may be evidence of, or in relation to, an offence.

(4) The constable may record or cause to be recorded all or any of the things seized and retained pursuant to subsection (2).

(5) An intimate search may not be carried out under this section.

(6) The constable carrying out a search under subsection (1) must be of the same sex as the person being searched.

KEYNOTE

A constable may retain a thing seized under s. 54B in order to establish its lawful owner where there are reasonable grounds for believing that it has been obtained in consequence of the commission of an offence (s. 54C(2)).

If a thing seized under s. 54B may be evidence of, or in relation to, an offence, a constable may retain it for use as evidence at a trial for an offence, or for forensic examination or for investigation in connection with an offence (s. 54C(3)).

Nothing may be retained for either of the purposes mentioned in subs. (3) if a photograph or copy would be sufficient for that purpose (s. 54C(4)).

Designated detention officers, as well as constables, can use the powers in ss. 54B and 54C to search and seize. Anything seized by a designated detention officer must be delivered to a constable as soon as practicable and in any case before the person from whom the thing was seized leaves the police station (Police Reform Act 2002, sch. 4, part 3, para. 27A).

Section 46A(1ZB) (**see para. 2.2.3.3**) provides a constable with a power of arrest for defendants who attend the police station to answer live link bail but refuse to be searched under s. 54B.

2.2.5 Police Bail Restrictions

The Criminal Justice and Public Order Act 1994 provides for those occasions when bail may only be granted in *exceptional circumstances* where a person is charged with certain specified offences. Section 25 of the 1994 Act states:

(1) A person who in any proceedings has been charged with or convicted of an offence to which this section applies in circumstances to which it applies shall be granted bail in those proceedings only if the court or, as the case may be, the constable considering the grant of bail is of the opinion that there are exceptional circumstances which justify it.

(2) This section applies, subject to subsection (3A) below, to the following offences, that is to say—

(a) murder;
(b) attempted murder;
(c) manslaughter;
(d) rape under the law of Scotland;
(e) an offence under section 1 of the Sexual Offences Act 1956 (rape);
(f) an offence under section 1 of the Sexual Offences Act 2003 (rape);
(g) an offence under section 2 of that Act (assault by penetration);
(h) an offence under section 4 of that Act (causing a person to engage in sexual activity without consent) where the activity caused involved penetration within subsection (4)(a) to (d) of that section;
(i) an offence under section 5 of that Act (rape of a child under 13);
(j) an offence under section 6 of that Act (assault of a child under 13 by penetration);
(k) an offence under section 8 of that Act (causing or inciting a child under 13 to engage in sexual activity), where an activity involving penetration within subsection (3)(a) to (d) of that section was caused;
(l) an offence under section 30 of that Act (sexual activity with a person with a mental disorder impeding choice), where the touching involved penetration within subsection (3)(a) to (d) of that section;
(m) an offence under section 31 of that Act (causing or inciting a person, with a mental disorder impeding choice, to engage in sexual activity), where an activity involving penetration within subsection (3)(a) to (d) of that section was caused;
(ma) to (mh) [equivalent offences under the law of Northern Ireland]
(n) an attempt to commit an offence within any of paragraphs (d) to (mh).

(3) …

(3A) This section applies where—

(a) the person has been previously convicted by or before a court in any part of the United Kingdom of any offence within subsection (2) or of culpable homicide, and

(b) if that previous conviction is one of manslaughter or culpable homicide—

(i) the person was then a child or young person, and was sentenced to long-term detention under any of the relevant enactments, or

(ii) the person was not then a child or young person, and was sentenced to imprisonment or detention.

(4) This section applies whether or not an appeal is pending against conviction or sentence.

(5) In this section—

'conviction' includes—

(a) a finding that a person is not guilty by reason of insanity;

(b) a finding under section 4A(3) of the Criminal Procedure (Insanity) Act 1964 (cases of unfitness to plead) that a person did the act or made the omission charged against him; and

(c) a conviction of an offence for which an order is made discharging the offender absolutely or conditionally;

and 'convicted' shall be construed accordingly;

'the relevant enactments' means—

(a) as respects England and Wales, section 91 of the Powers of Criminal Courts (Sentencing) Act 2000 or section 250 or 250A of the Sentencing Code;

(b) as respects Scotland, sections 205(1) to (3) and 208 of the Criminal Procedure (Scotland) Act 1995;

(c) as respects Northern Ireland, section 73(2) of the Children and Young Persons Act (Northern Ireland) 1968.

KEYNOTE

Section 25 provides that bail may not be granted where a person is charged with murder, attempted murder, manslaughter, rape or attempted rape if he/she has been previously convicted of any of these offences unless there are exceptional circumstances. A person charged with murder may not be granted bail except by order of a Crown Court judge (s. 115 of the Coroners and Justice Act 2009). This does not apply to attempted murder or conspiracy to murder.

Even where a person's custody time limit had expired, s. 25 could still be applied and the evidential burden was on the defence to demonstrate that exceptional circumstances existed. Also, in the case of *Hurnam* v *State of Mauritius* [2005] UKPC 49, the Privy Council stated that the seriousness of the offence is not a conclusive reason for refusing bail and the court must consider whether or not the accused is likely to abscond if released on bail.

In all other cases the custody officer must consider the issue of bail and s. 38(1) of the 1984 Act sets out the occasions where bail can be refused.

2.2.6 Grounds for Refusing Police Bail

The Police and Criminal Evidence Act 1984, s. 38(1) provides that where an arrested person is charged with an offence, the custody officer, subject to s. 25 of the Criminal Justice and Public Order Act 1994, need not grant bail if the person arrested *is not an arrested juvenile* and one or more of the following grounds apply:

- the person's name or address cannot be ascertained or the custody officer has reasonable grounds for doubting whether a name or address furnished is his/her real name or address;
- the custody officer has reasonable grounds for believing that the person arrested will fail to appear in court to answer to bail;

- in the case of a person arrested for an imprisonable offence, the custody officer has reasonable grounds for believing that the detention of the person arrested is necessary to prevent him/her from committing an offence;
- in a case of a person aged 18 or over, where a sample may be taken from the person under s. 63B (where there is a provision for drug testing in force for that police area and station), the custody officer has reasonable grounds for believing that the detention of the person is necessary to enable the sample to be taken;
- in the case of a person arrested for an offence which is not an imprisonable offence, the custody officer has reasonable grounds for believing that the detention of the person arrested is necessary to prevent him/her from causing physical injury to any other person or from causing loss of or damage to property;
- the custody officer has reasonable grounds for believing that the detention of the person arrested is necessary to prevent him/her from interfering with the administration of justice or with the investigation of offences or of a particular offence;
- the custody officer has reasonable grounds for believing that the detention of the person arrested is necessary for his/her own protection; or
- the person is charged with murder.

If the person arrested is *an arrested juvenile* and one or more of the following grounds apply:

- any of the requirements of paras (a) to (h) above, but in the case of para. (d) only if the arrested juvenile has attained the minimum age;
- the custody officer has reasonable grounds for believing that the arrested juvenile ought to be detained in his/her own interests.

KEYNOTE

Juveniles being detained 'in their own interests' means for their own welfare. The expression 'welfare' has a wider meaning than just 'protection' and might apply to juveniles who, if released, might be homeless or become involved in prostitution or vagrancy (Bail Act 1976, sch. 1, part I, para. (3)). Section 38 of PACE and s. 21 of the Children Act 1989 make clear that there are very limited circumstances to justify the detention of children at police stations. However, in *Archer* v *Commissioner of Police of the Metropolis* [2021] EWCA Civ 1662, it was held to be lawful where a juvenile was detained for a short period overnight until he could be brought to court. There was no secure accommodation in the local area for juveniles and therefore no reasonable alternative and there was also a real risk that the juvenile might be attacked if released.

In taking the decisions required by s. 38(1), except where a defendant's name and address cannot be ascertained, detention is necessary for the person's own protection, or a juvenile is detained in his/her own interests, the custody officer is required to have regard to the same considerations as those which a court is required to have regard to in taking corresponding decisions under the Bail Act 1976, sch. 1, part I, para. 2(1) (s. 38(2A)).

Schedule 1, part I, para. 2(1) provides that the defendant need not be granted bail if the court (custody officer) is satisfied that there are substantial grounds for believing that the defendant, if released on bail (whether subject to conditions or not) would:

- fail to surrender to custody; or
- commit an offence while on bail; or
- interfere with witnesses or otherwise obstruct the course of justice, whether in relation to him/herself or any other person.

In *R (On the Application of Ajaib)* v *Birmingham Magistrates' Court* [2009] EWHC 2127 (Admin), it was held that a police officer's opinion that the accused is a 'flight risk' was sufficient even though the source of information giving rise to the officer's opinion was not disclosed.

Schedule 1, part I, para. 9 provides that in taking the decisions required by para. 2(1), the court (custody officer) will have regard to such of the following considerations as appear to be relevant:

(a) the nature and seriousness of the offence or default (and the probable method of dealing with the defendant for it);
(b) the character, antecedents, associations and community ties of the defendant;
(c) the defendant's record as respects the fulfilment of his/her obligations under previous grants of bail in criminal proceedings;
(d) except in the case of a defendant whose case is adjourned for inquiries or a report, the strength of the evidence of his/her having committed the offence or having defaulted;
(e) if the court is satisfied that there are substantial grounds for believing that the defendant, if released on bail (whether subject to conditions or not), would commit an offence while on bail, the risk that the defendant may do so by engaging in conduct that would, or would be likely to, cause physical or mental injury to any person other than the defendant, as well as to any others which appear to be relevant. This includes domestic violence where a person is associated with the accused within the meaning of the Family Law Act 1996, s. 62.

Where bail is refused, the custody officer must inform the detained person of the reasons why and make an entry as to these reasons in the custody record (s. 38(3) and (4)). This must be done as soon as the decision to refuse bail is made unless the conditions set out in PACE, Code C, para. 1.8. apply, i.e. the person is incapable of understanding, is violent or is in urgent need of medical attention. In such cases, the person must be informed as soon as practicable.

The decision regarding bail is part of the process of investigation of crime with a view to prosecution and so the police enjoy immunity in respect of decisions to refuse bail (*Gizzonio* v *Chief Constable of Derbyshire* (1998) *The Times*, 29 April).

In relation to the detention of juveniles where bail has been refused, **see para. 2.6.19, Charging Detained Persons.**

2.2.7 Custody Officer—Granting Bail

The granting of bail in criminal proceedings is provided by s. 3 of the Bail Act 1976 and this section examines the general provisions in relation to bail granted by a custody officer, the conditions that may be attached and applications to vary or remove those conditions.

2.2.7.1 General Provisions

Section 3 states:

(1) A person granted bail in criminal proceedings shall be under a duty to surrender to custody, and that duty is enforceable in accordance with section 6 of this Act.
(2) No recognizance for his surrender to custody shall be taken from him.
(3) Except as provided by this section—
  (a) no security for his surrender to custody shall be taken from him,
  (b) he shall not be required to provide a surety or sureties for his surrender to custody, and
  (c) no other requirement shall be imposed on him as a condition of bail.
(4) He may be required, before release on bail, to provide a surety or sureties to secure his surrender to custody.
(5) He may be required, before release on bail, to give security for his surrender to custody. The security may be given by him or on his behalf.
(6) He may be required to comply, before release on bail or later, with such requirements as appear to the court to be necessary—
  (a) to secure that he surrenders to custody,
  (b) to secure that he does not commit an offence while on bail,

(c) to secure that he does not interfere with witnesses or otherwise obstruct the course of justice whether in relation to himself or any other person,

(ca) for his own protection or, if he is a child or young person, for his own welfare or in his own interests.

KEYNOTE

Subsection 3(7) relates to a parent/guardian standing surety for a person under the age of 17 (see para. 2.2.7.4).

Guidance to courts, applicable also to a custody officer, when approaching the decision to grant bail was given in *R* v *Mansfield Justices, ex parte Sharkey* [1985] QB 613, where it was held that any relevant risk, for example, absconding, must be a 'real' risk, not just a fanciful one.

Where a custody officer grants bail there is a requirement for a record to be made of the decision in the prescribed manner and containing the prescribed particulars. If requested, a copy of the record of the decision must, as soon as practicable, be given to the person in relation to whom the decision was taken (s. 5(1)).

2.2.7.2 Custody Officer: Conditions of Bail

The power of a custody officer to impose bail conditions is provided by s. 3A of the 1976 Act, which states:

(5) Where a constable grants bail to a person no conditions shall be imposed under subsections (4), (5), (6) or (7) of section 3 of this Act unless it appears to the constable that it is necessary to do so—

(a) for the purpose of preventing that person from failing to surrender to custody, or

(b) for the purpose of preventing that person from committing an offence while on bail, or

(c) for the purpose of preventing that person from interfering with witnesses or otherwise obstructing the course of justice, whether in relation to himself or any other person, or

(d) for that person's own protection, or if he is a child or young person, for his own welfare or in his own interests.

KEYNOTE

Where a custody officer decides to grant bail and considers one or more of the requirements in s. 3A(5)(a)–(d) apply, one or more of the following conditions can be imposed:

- the accused is to live and sleep at a specified address;
- the accused is to notify any changes of address;
- the accused is to report periodically (daily, weekly or at other intervals) to his/her local police station;
- the accused is restricted from entering a certain area or building or to go within a specified distance of a specified address;
- the accused is not to contact (whether directly or indirectly) the victim of the alleged offence and/or any other probable prosecution witness;
- the accused is to surrender his/her passport;
- the accused's movements are restricted by an imposed curfew between set times (i.e. when it is thought the accused might commit offences or come into contact with witnesses);
- the accused is required to provide a surety or security.

In *McDonald* v *Dickson* [2003] SLT 476, it was held that a condition for an accused to remain in his dwelling at all times except between 10 am and 12 noon did not amount to detention or deprivation of his liberty and did not constitute an infringement of his right to liberty under the European Convention on Human Rights, Article 5.

A bail condition prohibiting a person from residing at their home address was held to be disproportionate even where the police were investigating a serious offence of racially aggravated harassment against neighbours (*R (On the Application of Carson)* v *Ealing Magistrates' Court* [2012] EWHC 1456 (Admin)).

In relation to non-imprisonable offences it has been held that a hunt protester who was arrested for an offence under s. 5 of the Public Order Act 1986 was rightly required as a condition of his bail not to attend another hunt meeting before his next court appearance (*R* v *Bournemouth Magistrates' Court, ex parte Cross* [1989] Crim LR 207).

2.2.7.3 Applications to Vary or Remove Bail Conditions

The power to vary or remove conditions is provided by s. 3A(4) of the Bail Act 1976 which states:

> Where a custody officer has granted bail in criminal proceedings he or another custody officer serving at the same police station may, at the request of the person to whom it was granted, vary the conditions of bail and in doing so he may impose conditions or more onerous conditions.

KEYNOTE

Section 3A(5) (see para. 2.2.7.2) also applies on any request to a custody officer to vary or remove conditions of bail.

There is a requirement that a custody officer either imposing or varying the conditions of bail must include a note of the reasons in the custody record and give a copy of that note to the person in relation to whom the decision was taken (s. 5A(3) and (4)).

An accused may also apply to the magistrates' court under s. 43B(1) of the Magistrates' Courts Act 1980, to vary conditions of police bail. The prosecution may apply to the magistrates' court to reconsider bail and vary the conditions of bail, impose conditions in respect of bail that has been granted unconditionally, or withhold bail (s. 5B(1)). This only applies to bail granted by the magistrates' court or a constable and only in relation to offences triable on indictment or either way (s. 5B(2)). The application can only be on the basis of information that was not available to the court or constable when the original decision was taken (s. 5B(3)).

2.2.7.4 Police Bail: Surety

The Bail Act 1976, s. 8 states:

> (1) This section applies where a person is granted bail in criminal proceedings on condition that he provides one or more surety or sureties for the purpose of securing that he surrenders to custody.
> (2) In considering the suitability for that purpose of a proposed surety, regard may be had (amongst other things) to—
> (a) the surety's financial resources;
> (b) his character and any previous convictions of his; and
> (c) his proximity (whether in point of kinship, place of residence or otherwise) to the person for whom he is to be surety.

KEYNOTE

The question as to whether or not sureties are necessary is at the discretion of the custody officer (or court).

A person cannot stand as his/her own surety (s. 3(2)).

There is no power to grant conditional bail with a surety to ensure no further offending; a surety can be sought only for the purpose of securing surrender to custody and not for any other purpose (*R (On the Application of Shea)* v *Winchester Crown Court* [2013] EWHC 1050 (Admin)).

The decision as to the suitability of individual sureties is a matter for the custody officer. Where no surety, or suitable surety, is available, the custody officer can fix the amount of cash or security in which the surety is to be bound for the purpose of enabling the recognizance of the surety to be entered into subsequently (s. 8(3)).

Where a court grants bail but is unable to release the person where no surety or no suitable surety is available, the court may fix the amount in which the surety is to be bound, and the recognizance of the surety may later be entered into before a police officer who is either of the rank of inspector or above or who is in charge of a police station, or other person as specified in s. 8(4) in conjunction with the Criminal Procedure Rules 2020, r. 14.14.

The normal consequence for a surety, where an accused fails to answer bail, is that he/she is required to forfeit the entire cash or security in which he/she stood surety. The power to forfeit recognizances is a matter for a court (Magistrates' Courts Act 1980, s. 120).

It is not necessary to prove that the surety had any involvement in the accused's non-appearance (*R* v *Warwick Crown Court, ex parte Smalley* [1987] 1 WLR 237). However, in *R* v *York Crown Court, ex parte Coleman* (1988) 86 Cr App R 151, it was held that where a surety had taken all reasonable steps to ensure the accused's appearance the recognizance ought not to be forfeited.

The Bail Act 1976 provides that a surety may notify a constable in writing that the accused is unlikely to surrender to custody and for that reason he/she wishes to be relieved of his/her obligations as surety. This written notification provides a constable with the power to arrest the accused without warrant (s. 7(3)).

Where a parent or guardian of a person under the age of 17 consents to be surety, they may be required to secure that the person complies with any requirement imposed by virtue of s. 3(6) (**see para. 2.2.7.1**). No requirement shall be imposed on the parent or guardian where it appears that the person will attain the age of 17 before the time to be appointed for their surrender to custody (s. 3(7)).

2.2.7.5 Security

A person granted bail may be required to give security for his/her surrender to custody (Bail Act 1976, s. 3(5)). The security can be money or some other valuable item which will be liable to forfeiture in the event of non-attendance in answer to bail.

A security may be required as a condition of bail but only if it is considered necessary to prevent the person absconding.

A third party may make an asset available to an accused to enable him/her to provide it as security for his/her release on bail (*R (On the Application of Stevens)* v *Truro Magistrates' Court* [2001] EWHC Admin 558).

2.2.7.6 Acknowledging Bail

OFFENCE: **Acknowledging Bail in the Name of Another—*Forgery Act 1861, s. 34***

• Triable on indictment • Seven years' imprisonment

The Forgery Act 1861, s. 34 states:

> Whosoever, without lawful authority or excuse (the proof whereof shall lie on the party accused), shall in the name of any other person acknowledge any recognizance or bail, ... or judgment or any deed or other instrument, before any court, judge, or other person lawfully authorised in that behalf, shall be guilty of felony ...

KEYNOTE

This offence occurs where a person impersonates another person for the purpose of acting as a surety.

Provided the bail or recognizance is valid, this offence would appear to apply equally to bail granted by a court or the police.

2.2.8 Liability to Arrest for Absconding or Breaking Bail Conditions

The Bail Act 1976, s. 7 states:

(1) If a person who has been released on bail in criminal proceedings and is under a duty to surrender into the custody of a court fails to surrender to custody at the time appointed for him to do so the court may issue a warrant for his arrest.

(1A) Subsection (1B) applies if—

(a) a person has been released on bail in connection with extradition proceedings;

(b) the person is under a duty to surrender into the custody of a constable; and

(c) the person fails to surrender to custody at the time appointed for him to do so.

(1B) A magistrates' court may issue a warrant for the person's arrest.

(2) If a person who has been released on bail in criminal proceedings absents himself from the court at any time after he has surrendered into the custody of the court and before the court is ready to begin or to resume the hearing of the proceedings, the court may issue a warrant for his arrest but no warrant shall be issued under this subsection where that person is absent in accordance with leave given to him by or on behalf of the court.

(3) A person who has been released on bail in criminal proceedings and is under a duty to surrender into the custody of a court may be arrested without warrant by a constable—

(a) if the constable has reasonable grounds for believing that person is not likely to surrender to custody;

(b) if the constable has reasonable grounds for believing that that person is likely to break any of the conditions of his bail or has reasonable grounds for suspecting that that person has broken any of those conditions; or

(c) in a case where that person was released on bail with one or more surety or sureties, if a surety notifies a constable in writing that that person is unlikely to surrender to custody and that for that reason the surety wishes to be relieved of his obligations as a surety.

KEYNOTE

Breach of conditions of bail is not a Bail Act offence, nor is it a contempt of court unless there is some additional feature (*R* v *Ashley* [2003] EWCA Crim 2571).

Where a person is arrested under s. 7 he/she shall be brought before a magistrate as soon as practicable and in any event within 24 hours (s. 7(4)(a)). However, in the case of a person charged with murder, or with murder and one or more other offences, he/she must be brought before a judge of the Crown Court (s. 7(8)).

This section requires that a detainee not merely be brought to the court precincts or cells but actually be dealt with by a justice within 24 hours of being arrested (*R (On the Application of Culley)* v *Dorchester Crown Court* [2007] EWHC 109 (Admin)).

In *R* v *Evans* [2011] EWCA Crim 2842, the Court of Appeal stated:

> The general practice of accepting surrender by way of entry into the dock accords not only with common experience and general practice but also with principle ... Crown Court surrender may also be accomplished by the commencement of any hearing before the judge where the defendant is formally identified and whether he enters the dock or not.

The word 'court' includes a judge of the court or a justice of the peace. Also a bail notice stating a particular time of attendance is a notice that may happen at any time from 9.30 am onwards. Mere arrival at the Crown Court building does not constitute surrender, neither does reporting to an advocate. Surrender has to be accomplished personally by the defendant.

Section 7 does not create an offence, it merely confers a power of arrest (*R* v *Gangar* [2008] EWCA Crim 2987).

2.2.9 Offence of Absconding by Person Released on Bail

The Bail Act 1976 s. 6 creates two offences in relation to absconding and states:

(1) If a person who has been released on bail in criminal proceedings fails without reasonable cause to surrender to custody he shall be guilty of an offence.

(2) If a person who—

(a) has been released on bail in criminal proceedings, and

(b) having reasonable cause therefor, has failed to surrender to custody, fails to surrender to custody at the appointed place as soon after the appointed time as is reasonably practicable he shall be guilty of an offence.

KEYNOTE

Section 6 applies where:

- the police grant bail to a suspect to appear at the police station;
- the police grant bail to a defendant to appear at court on the first appearance;
- the court grants bail to the defendant to return to court at a later date.

The burden of proof in relation to showing 'reasonable cause' (s. 6(1)) is a matter for the accused (s. 6(3)).

A person who has 'reasonable cause' still commits the offence if he/she fails to surrender 'as soon after the appointed time as is reasonably practicable'. Where an accused was half an hour late in appearing at court it was held that he/she had absconded (*R* v *Scott* [2007] EWCA Crim 2757). In *Laidlaw* v *Atkinson* (1986) *The Times*, 2 August, it was held that being mistaken about the day on which one should have appeared was not a reasonable excuse. Also, there is no requirement on the court to inquire as to whether a person arrested for failing to comply with bail conditions had any reasonable excuse for breaching bail (*R (On the Application of Vickers)* v *West London Magistrates' Court* [2003] EWHC 1809 (Admin)).

Failure to give to a person granted bail in criminal proceedings a copy of the record of the decision does not constitute reasonable cause for that person's failure to surrender to custody (s. 6(4)).

Failing to answer bail granted by a police officer is a summary offence and the decision to initiate proceedings is for the police/prosecutor using the written charge and requisition procedure. Such an offence may not be tried unless proceedings are commenced either within six months of the commission of the offence, or within three months: (a) after the person surrenders to custody at the appointed place; (b) is arrested, or attends at a police station, in connection with the bail offence or the offence for which he/she was granted bail; or (c) the person appears or is brought before a court in connection with the bail offence or the offence for which he/she was granted bail (s. 6(12)–(14)).

2.2.10 Remands in Police Custody

Where a person is remanded in custody it normally means detention in prison. However, s. 128 of the Magistrates' Courts Act 1980 provides that a magistrates' court may remand a person to police custody:

- for a period not exceeding three clear days (24 hours for persons under 18 (s. 91(5) of the Legal Aid, Sentencing and Punishment of Offenders Act 2012) (s. 128(7));
- for the purpose of inquiries into offences (other than the offence for which he/she appears before the court) (s. 128(8)(a));
- as soon as the need ceases he/she must be brought back before the magistrates (s. 128(8)(b));
- the conditions of detention and periodic review apply as if the person was arrested without warrant on suspicion of having committed an offence (s. 128(8)(c) and (d)).

2.3 Court Procedure and Witnesses

2.3.1 Introduction

This chapter deals with the conditions where an accused can plead guilty by post for certain summary offences, the procedure in dealing with offenders for summary, either-way and indictable offences, and the law in relation to witnesses.

2.3.2 Plea of Guilty by Post

The procedure for a defendant to plead guilty by post is provided by the Magistrates' Courts Act 1980 and applies to proceedings for summary offences started by way of summons (or requisition) in the magistrates' court (s. 12(1)), or in the youth court for persons aged 16 or 17 (s. 12(2)). The summons (or requisition) is served on the defendant together with a 'statement of facts' and a prescribed form of explanation. This allows the defendant an opportunity to plead guilty and put forward any mitigation in his/her absence. The magistrates' designated officer informs the prosecution of any written guilty plea.

KEYNOTE

This section is most commonly used for driving offences, and provision is made for a printout from the DVLA to be admissible as evidence of previous convictions for traffic offences without the need to give an accused notice of intention to refer to these previous convictions (Road Traffic Offenders Act 1988, s. 13).

2.3.3 Mode of Trial

The classification of the offence determines in which court the trial takes place; generally, summary offences in the magistrates' court and indictable offences in the Crown Court.

In the case of an either-way offence the magistrates must determine whether a person who has attained the age of 18 should be tried summarily in the magistrates' court or be sent to the Crown Court to be tried (ss. 17A to 21 of the Magistrates' Courts Act 1980).

2.3.3.1 Pre-trial Hearings

In the magistrates' court there is a system of pre-trial hearings. These are known as an 'Early First Hearing' where a guilty plea is anticipated or an 'Early Administrative Hearing' where a not guilty plea is expected. Section 8A of the Magistrates' Courts Act 1980 provides that at a pre-trial hearing, once a not guilty plea has been entered, the court may make rulings on any question as to the admissibility of evidence and any other question of law relating to criminal cases to be tried in the magistrates' court.

These rulings are binding and will continue to be so until the case is disposed of by the accused being acquitted, the prosecutor deciding not to proceed with the case, or the information is dismissed (s. 8B).

2.3.4 Summary Trial

Summary trials take place in the magistrates' court before at least two lay justices or a single District or Deputy District Judge (Magistrates' Courts). The prosecution and defence may conduct their own case in person or be represented by counsel or solicitor (s. 122(1) of the Magistrates' Courts Act 1980).

Where there is a 'guilty' plea in the magistrates' court, the hearing starts with the prosecution stating the facts of the case and introducing the offender's relevant previous convictions. The defence then put any mitigation to the court before sentence is passed.

Where there is a 'not guilty' plea the prosecutor may summarise the prosecution case, concisely identifying the relevant law, outlining the facts and indicating the matters likely to be in dispute. To help the members of the court to understand the case and resolve any issue in it, the court may then invite the defence concisely to identify what is in issue (Criminal Procedure Rules 2020, r. 24.3). The prosecution will then present their case to the court. Following this the defence may then call their evidence and finally address the court in a closing speech.

2.3.5 Trial on Indictment

Trials on indictment take place in the Crown Court before a judge of the High Court, circuit judge, a recorder or a qualifying judge advocate.

The prosecution must appear by legal representative, but the accused may still conduct his/her own case and may be allowed a friend to accompany him/her as an adviser, though such an adviser may not question witnesses or address the court (*McKenzie* v *McKenzie* [1971] P 33).

Where there is a 'guilty plea', which must be entered personally by the accused (*R* v *Ellis* (1973) 57 Cr App R 571), the only evidence which the prosecution needs to call is details of the accused's antecedents and criminal record. Occasionally, where there is disagreement about the precise facts of the offence, the prosecution may be required to call evidence to support their version of the facts; known as *Newton* hearings (*R* v *Newton* (1983) 77 Cr App R 13).

Where there is a 'not guilty' plea, the prosecution are required to satisfy the jury beyond reasonable doubt that the accused committed the offence. Where the prosecution fail to provide sufficient evidence as to *any* element of the offence, the accused is entitled to be acquitted. This acquittal would take place on the direction of the judge, at the end of the prosecution case, following a defence submission of 'no case to answer'. The prosecutor has the right to make representations if a submission of no case to answer is made (*DPP* v *Berry* [2019] EWHC 825 (Admin)).

2.3.6 Defendant's Non-appearance

Where an accused fails to appear in the magistrates' court in answer to bail the court may:

- issue a warrant for the accused's arrest under s. 7 of the Bail Act 1976 (**see para. 2.2.9**);
- appoint a later time when the accused has to appear in accordance with s. 129(3) of the Magistrates' Courts Act 1980;
- proceed in the accused's absence under s. 11(1) of the Magistrates' Courts Act 1980.

Where the accused's appearance was by way of summons, the court must be satisfied that the summons was served in the prescribed manner before commencing in the accused's absence (s. 11(2)).

Where an accused is under 18 years of age the court *may* proceed in his/her absence (s. 11(1)(a)), and if the accused has attained the age of 18 the court *shall* proceed in his/her absence unless it appears to the court to be contrary to the interests of justice do so (s. 11(1)(b)). The court is not required to inquire into the reasons for the accused's failure to appear (s. 11(6)). On occasions where a person is deliberately absent, and indifferent to the consequences of their absence, the court may proceed without the accused being present (*R* v *Allad* [2014] EWCA Crim 421).

2.3.7 Witnesses

A witness is a person called by a party in court proceedings with a view to proving a particular matter material to the case. This section examines the key issues in relation to witnesses.

2.3.7.1 Attendance of Witnesses at Court

The prosecution or defence can apply for a summons, warrant or order requiring a witness to attend a magistrates' court (s. 97 or 97A of the Magistrates' Courts Act 1980, or para. 4 of sch. 3 to the Crime and Disorder Act 1998) or the Crown Court (s. 2 of the Criminal Procedure (Attendance of Witnesses) Act 1965). Where appropriate, such an application can be used as a pre-emptive measure to secure the attendance of witnesses.

The procedure for the service of a witness summons is contained in the Magistrates' Courts (Amendment) Rules 2019 (SI 2019/1367), r. 99(1)(a), (d) or (f) (**see para. 2.1.3**).

In *R* v *Popat* [2008] EWCA Crim 1921 it was held that a witness summons did not have to be served in accordance with the Rules if the date of the court hearing was actually brought to the attention of the witness.

2.3.7.2 Competence and Compellability

In looking at witnesses, it is crucial to consider two related questions:

- whether there are any restrictions to a witness being called to provide testimony. This question is frequently one of whether a witness is *competent*;
- whether a witness may be compelled or made to provide testimony. This is a question of whether a witness is *compellable*.

Competence in its simplest interpretation is whether in law a witness is allowed to be a witness. For a witness to be compellable two aspects must be considered:

- the witness must be competent; *and*
- the law requires the witness to give evidence even if the witness would rather not do so.

2.3.7.3 General Rule of Competence and Compellability

At every stage in criminal proceedings all persons are (whatever their age) competent to give evidence (Youth Justice and Criminal Evidence Act 1999, s. 53).

2.3.7.4 The Accused

Evidence on Behalf of the Prosecution

The competence of the accused to give evidence on behalf of the prosecution is dealt with under s. 53 of the Youth Justice and Criminal Evidence Act 1999, which states:

> (4) A person charged in criminal proceedings is not competent to give evidence in the proceedings for the prosecution (whether he is the only person, or is one of two or more persons, charged in the proceedings).

(5) In subsection (4) the reference to a person charged in criminal proceedings does not include a person who is not, or is no longer, liable to be convicted of any offence in the proceedings (whether as a result of pleading guilty or for any other reason).

The 1999 Act provides that should the prosecution wish to use the testimony of an accused against a co-accused, they must first make that person competent to be able to give that evidence. In *R* v *McEwan* [2011] EWCA Crim 1026, it was held that where the accused pleads guilty, they are competent for the prosecution even if they suggest in their evidence that they were not a participant in the offence, unless the plea is set aside.

Evidence on Behalf of the Defence

The Criminal Evidence Act 1898 sets out the position of whether an accused person is competent and compellable for the defence. Section 1 of the 1898 Act states:

(1) A person charged in criminal proceedings shall not be called as a witness in the proceedings except upon his own application.

...

(4) Every person charged in criminal proceedings who is called as a witness in the proceedings shall, unless otherwise ordered by the court, give his evidence from the witness-box or other place from which the other witnesses give their evidence.

2.3.7.5 Accused's Spouse or Civil Partner

The Police and Criminal Evidence Act 1984, s. 80 states:

(1) In any proceedings the wife or husband of the accused shall be competent to give evidence—
  (a) subject to subsection (4) below, for the prosecution; and
  (b) on behalf of the accused or any person jointly charged with the accused.

(2) In any proceedings the spouse or civil partner of a person charged in the proceedings shall, subject to subsection (4) below, be compellable to give evidence on behalf of that person.

(2A) In any proceedings the spouse or civil partner of a person charged in the proceedings shall, subject to subsection (4) below, be compellable—
  (a) to give evidence on behalf of any other person charged in the proceedings but only in respect of any specified offence with which that other person is charged; or
  (b) to give evidence for the prosecution but only in respect of any specified offence with which any person is charged in the proceedings.

(3) In relation to the spouse or civil partner of a person charged in any proceedings, an offence is a specified offence for the purposes of subsection (2A) above if—
  (a) it involves an assault on, or injury or a threat of injury to, the spouse or civil partner or a person who was at the material time under the age of 16;
  (b) it is a sexual offence alleged to have been committed in respect of a person who was at the material time under that age; or
  (c) it consists of attempting or conspiring to commit, or of aiding, abetting, counselling, procuring or inciting the commission of, an offence falling within paragraph (a) or (b) above.

KEYNOTE

A person charged in any proceedings is not compellable by virtue of subs. (2) or (2A) to give evidence (s. 80(4)).

The Marriage (Same Sex Couples) Act 2013 extended marriage to same-sex couples and the Partnership (Opposite-sex Couples) Regulations 2019 extended civil partnership to opposite-sex couples.

The Marriage and Civil Partnership (Minimum Age) Act 2022 has amended the Marriage Act 1949 and Civil Partnership Act 2004 whereby a person cannot get married or enter into a civil partnership until they have attained 18 years of age (ss. 1 and 3 respectively).

There is no requirement to tell a wife that she was not a compellable witness against her husband before interviewing her about a crime of which her husband was suspected. A statement obtained from the wife in such circumstances could be admitted in evidence even though the wife refused to give evidence against her husband, provided it did not lead to an injustice (*R* v *L* [2008] EWCA Crim 973). However, the prosecution's hand is likely to be strengthened if it were shown that she was told that there was no obligation for her to make a statement (*R* v *Horsnell* [2012] EWCA Crim 227).

A person who is no longer married or in a civil partnership with the accused is compellable to give evidence as if they had never been married or been in a civil partnership (Police and Criminal Evidence Act 1984, s. 80(5) and (5A)). The person must have been divorced, or where it was a voidable marriage this must have been annulled.

Cohabitees are not afforded the same concessions as a spouse or civil partner and are both competent and compellable to give evidence (see *R* v *Pearce* [2001] EWCA Crim 2834 and *R* v *Suski* [2016] EWCA Crim 24).

2.3.7.6 Child Witnesses

Children acting as witnesses in criminal proceedings may be sworn for the purpose of giving evidence on oath if they have attained the age of 14 (s. 55(2) of the Youth Justice and Criminal Evidence Act 1999). This statutory provision requires that no witness under the age of 14 is to be sworn.

Witnesses of 14 or over are only eligible to be sworn if they understand the solemnity of a criminal trial and that by taking the oath they are responsible for telling the truth. The witness shall, if he/she is able to give *intelligible testimony*, be presumed to have sufficient appreciation of those matters if no evidence tending to show the contrary is adduced (s. 55(3)). Whether a witness is able to give *intelligible testimony* may be determined by expert evidence (s. 55(6)), or where the court consider the witness is able to understand questions put to him/her and give answers to them which can be understood (s. 55(8)).

The 1999 Act provides that a person *of any* age who is competent to give evidence, but by virtue of s. 55(2) is not permitted to be sworn, may give unsworn evidence (s. 56(1) and (2)). A child under the age of four years could still be a competent witness as long as he/she displays such competence throughout the whole of his/her evidence (*R* v *P* [2006] EWCA Crim 3).

2.3.7.7 Issues of Age

The time at which a person attains a particular age expressed in years shall be the commencement of the relevant anniversary of the date of his/her birth (s. 9(1) of the Family Law Act 1969).

Section 150 of the Magistrates' Courts Act 1980 states:

> (4) Where the age of any person at any time is material for the purposes of any provision of this Act regulating the powers of a magistrates' court, his age at the material time shall be deemed to be or to have been that which appears to the court after considering any available evidence to be or to have been his age at that time.

KEYNOTE

A birth certificate is usually accepted as evidence of age. A statement from a person present at the birth may be useful in difficult cases. If a certificate of birth is produced to prove age, evidence must also be provided to positively identify the person as the person named in the certificate (*R* v *Rogers* (1914) 10 Cr App R 276).

In *R* v *Viazani* (1867) 31 JP 260, it was held that where the statement of an accused as to his/her age is in conflict with his/her appearance the statement of the accused may be disregarded.

2.3.7.8 Witnesses with a Disorder or Disability of the Mind

As with child witnesses, the law in relation to witnesses with a disorder or disability of the mind is contained in s. 55 of the Youth Justice and Criminal Evidence Act 1999.

In determining whether such a witness is competent to give *intelligible testimony*, expert evidence is allowed, or the court may consider whether the witness is able to understand questions put to him/her and give answers to them which can be understood.

Clearly, there is no inherent reason why a person suffering from a disorder or disability of the mind would not make a reliable witness. In *R* v *Barratt* [1996] Crim LR 495, a witness was suffering from a psychiatric condition and the court considered that her evidence was as reliable as that of any other witness save for certain aspects affected by her condition. The videotaped interview of a witness suffering from Alzheimer's disease was admitted in evidence where she was deemed unfit to attend trial (*R* v *Ali Sed* [2004] EWCA Crim 1294).

2.3.7.9 Witness Anonymity

The Coroners and Justice Act 2009, provides for witness anonymity orders and s. 86 of the Act states:

(1) In this Chapter a 'witness anonymity order' is an order made by a court that requires such specified measures to be taken in relation to a witness in criminal proceedings as the court considers appropriate to ensure that the identity of the witness is not disclosed in or in connection with the proceedings.

KEYNOTE

A 'witness anonymity order' may only be granted on the application of the prosecutor or defendant if the following three conditions, contained in s. 88, are satisfied:

- Condition A: the order is necessary to protect the safety of the witness, or another person, or the prevention of serious damage to property or to prevent real harm to the public interest;
- Condition B: having regard to all the circumstances, the taking of these measures would be consistent with the defendant receiving a fair trial; and
- Condition C: it is in the interests of justice that the witness ought to testify and the witness would not testify without the order being made, and there would be real harm to the public interest if the witness were to testify without the proposed order being made.

2.3.8 Directions for Live Links in Criminal Proceedings

Witnesses will ordinarily give their evidence from the witness box. However, there are occasions where evidence may be given through a live audio or video link.

2.3.8.1 Criminal Justice Act 2003

The Criminal Justice Act 2003, s. 51 states:

Directions for live links in criminal proceedings

(1) The court may, by a direction, require or permit a person to take part in eligible criminal proceedings through—
   (a) a live audio link, or
   (b) a live video link.

KEYNOTE

'Eligible criminal proceedings' include a preliminary hearing, a summary trial and a trial on indictment or any other trial in the Crown Court for an offence (s. 51(3)).

The court may give a direction requiring or permitting a person who is outside England and Wales (whether in the United Kingdom or elsewhere) to take part in eligible criminal proceedings through a live audio link or a live video link (s. 52(1)(c)).

A person who takes part in eligible criminal proceedings in accordance with a direction under s. 51 is to be treated as present in court for the purposes of those proceedings (s. 52A(2)).

In deciding whether to give a direction, the court must consider all the circumstances of the case, including the importance of the witness's evidence to the proceedings. It must also consider whether the direction might tend to inhibit any party to the proceedings from effectively testing the witness's evidence and the arrangements that would or could be put in place for members of the public to see or hear the proceedings as conducted in accordance with the direction (s. 56(6)).

In *R (On the Application of DPP)* v *Redbridge Youth Court* [2001] EWHC 209 (Admin), it was held that there was no presumption of using a television link under any legislative provision and its use had to be justified in displacing the general rule that a witness should give evidence in the presence of the defendant.

A court has no inherent power to permit evidence to be given by telephone, even with the consent of the parties (*R* v *Hampson* [2012] EWCA Crim 1807).

A statement made on oath by a witness outside the United Kingdom and given in evidence through a live audio link or a live video link in accordance with a direction under s. 51 is to be treated for the purposes of s. 1 of the Perjury Act 1911 (see ***General Police Duties*****, para. 3.14.2)** as having been made in the proceedings in which it is given in evidence (s. 52A(5)).

2.3.9 Special Measures

The Youth Justice and Criminal Evidence Act 1999 contains a range of measures designed to help young, disabled, vulnerable or intimidated witnesses to give evidence in criminal proceedings.

2.3.9.1 Eligible Witnesses

The Youth Justice and Criminal Evidence Act 1999 provides that both prosecution and defence witnesses are eligible for special measures, and the categories of eligibility include:

- all witnesses under the age of 18 at the time of the hearing or video recording (s. 16(1)(a));
- vulnerable witnesses who are affected by a mental disorder, impairment of intelligence and social functioning (s. 16(2)(a));
- vulnerable witnesses who are affected by physical disability or disorder (s. 16(2)(b));
- witnesses in fear or distress about testifying (s.17(2));
- any witness to a 'relevant offence', currently defined to include homicide offences and other offences involving a firearm or knife (s. 17(5)–(7), sch. 1A);
- adult victims of domestic violence who are vulnerable or intimidated;
- adult complainants of sexual offences (as defined by s. 62 of the 1999 Act), human trafficking offences (s. 59A of the Sexual Offences Act 2003 or s. 4 of the Asylum and Immigration (Treatment of Claimants, etc.) Act 2004), indecent photographs of children offences (s. 1 of the Protection of Children Act 1978 (take, permit to be taken or publish etc. such a photograph), s. 160 of the Criminal Justice Act 1988 (possession of such a photograph)), slavery and trafficking offences (ss. 1 and 2 of the Modern Slavery Act 2015) and an offence of domestic abuse under the Domestic Abuse Act 2021.

KEYNOTE

While the primary rule is that all witnesses under the age of 18, regardless of the nature of the offence charged, are eligible for their evidence to be given by video interview and the use of live link, this does not prohibit a child witness who wishes to testify in court (ss. 21 and 22).

Regulation 2 of the Special Measures for Child Witnesses (Sexual Offences) Regulations 2013 (SI 2013/2971) amended the 1999 Act so that a complainant of a relevant offence whose age is uncertain will be presumed to be under the age of 18 if there are reasons to believe that person is under the age of 18. The effect is that a complainant to whom the presumption applies will be eligible for 'special measures' under s. 16. This provision also applies to a victim of human trafficking who is believed to be under 18 (s. 51 of the Modern Slavery Act 2015).

In relation to the category 'any witness to a "relevant offence" involving a firearm, offensive weapon or knife', the 'relevant offence' is an offence specified in sch. 1A to the 1999 Act that includes murder, manslaughter, wounding, assault etc. All witnesses involved in such cases, including police officers, are automatically eligible for a special measures direction unless they decline (s. 17(5)).

Generally, special measures directions in the case of vulnerable and intimidated witnesses apply to proceedings in relation to anti-social behaviour injunctions (s. 16 of the Anti-social Behaviour, Crime and Policing Act 2014) and criminal behaviour orders (s. 31 of the 2014 Act).

2.3.9.2 Special Measures Directions

There is a range of measures available to the court provided by the 1999 Act to help a witness or defendant to give evidence or otherwise participate, and these include:

- screening the witness from seeing the defendant (s. 23);
- allowing a witness to give evidence by live link, accompanied by a supporter (s. 24);
- hearing a witness's evidence in private in a sex offence case, a trafficking for exploitation case, or where there is a fear the witness may be intimidated (s. 25);
- dispensing with the wearing of wigs and gowns (s. 26);
- admitting video recording of evidence-in-chief (s. 27);
- admitting video recording of cross-examination and re-examination (s. 28);
- questioning a witness through an intermediary in the case of a young or incapacitated witness (s. 29);
- provision of aids to communication for a young or incapacitated witness (s. 30);
- an investigation anonymity order or a witness anonymity order (s. 86 of the Coroners and Justice Act 2009);
- an offence under s. 75A of the Serious Crime Act 2015 (strangulation or suffocation) in a case involving the carrying of a firearm or knife.

KEYNOTE

Failure to provide special measures may result in a conviction being overturned as in the case of *R* v *Pringle* [2019] EWCA 1722, where a defendant identified as having a number of communication difficulties was not permitted to have an intermediary.

The wide range of special measures has not altered the overall responsibility of the court for the fairness of the trial. The court is expected to deal with any communication problems faced by any witness or defendant as part of the ordinary control of the judicial process (*R* v *Cox* [2012] EWCA Crim 549).

Special measures principles apply to child defendants as witnesses in the same way as they apply to any other vulnerable witness (*R* v *Grant-Murray* [2017] EWCA Crim 1228).

2.3.10 Refreshing Memory

The Criminal Justice Act 2003 provides for the use of documents and transcripts by witnesses to refresh their memory.

Section 139 of the 2003 Act states:

(1) A person giving oral evidence in criminal proceedings about any matter may, at any stage in the course of doing so, refresh his memory of it from a document made or verified by him at an earlier time if—
   (a) he states in his oral evidence that the document records his recollection of the matter at that earlier time, and
   (b) his recollection of the matter is likely to have been significantly better at that time than it is at the time of his oral evidence.

(2) Where—
   (a) a person giving oral evidence in criminal proceedings about any matter has previously given an oral account, of which a sound recording was made, and he states in that evidence that the account represented his recollection of the matter at that time,
   (b) his recollection of the matter is likely to have been significantly better at the time of the previous account than it is at the time of his oral evidence, and
   (c) a transcript has been made of the sound recording,

   he may, at any stage in the course of giving his evidence, refresh his memory of the matter from that transcript.

KEYNOTE

In relation to the condition set out in s. 139(1)(b), ultimately it is a matter for the assessment of the judge, whatever the witness's view of the matter (*R* v *Chinn*) [2012] EWCA Crim 501).

For the purposes of s. 139, a 'document means anything in which information of any description is recorded, but not including any recording of sounds of moving images' (s. 140). However, under common law a document includes a tape recording (*R* v *Bailey* [2001] All ER (D) 185 (Mar)). In the case of video recordings, witnesses are entitled to and should view the interview before trial to refresh their memory but not immediately before giving evidence (*R* v *R* [2010] EWCA Crim 2469).

The fact that the witness refreshed his/her memory from a document or transcript before going into the witness box does not affect the presumption contained within s. 139.

The Court of Appeal made clear that training or coaching witnesses in relation to a forthcoming criminal trial is prohibited (*R* v *Momodou: R* v *Limani* [2005] EWCA Crim 177).

2.3.11 Victims of Crime Code of Practice

The Code of Practice for Victims of Crime in England and Wales (April 2021), published by the Ministry of Justice pursuant to s. 33 of the Domestic Violence, Crime and Victims Act 2004, sets out the services and a minimum standard for these services that must be provided to victims by organisations (service providers), such as the police. This is done through the provision of 12 rights, which include the right to be able to understand and to be understood (Right 1) and the right to be provided with information when reporting a crime (Right 3).

Right 7 provides for a Victim Personal Statement where a victim may explain in their own words how a crime has affected them, whether physically, emotionally, financially or in any other way. This statement is considered by the judge or magistrate when determining what sentence the defendant should receive and may also help in providing additional support for the victim. Additionally, a bereaved close relative may also make a Victim Personal Statement. A business may make an Impact Statement for Business, allowing the business to explain how a crime has affected it, such as direct financial loss, operational disruption or reputational damage. Police officers are required to inform victims of the scheme, and a statement may be made or updated at any time prior to the disposal of the case. The decision about whether or not to make a statement is entirely for the victim.

The Code also provides enhanced rights for victims who are considered vulnerable or intimidated, are victims of the most serious crime or have been persistently targeted.

These statements are limited to expressing the effect of particular crimes upon a particular community and should not be used as character assassination of offenders (*R* v *Skelton* [2015] 1 Cr App R (S) 265 (34)).

2.3.12 Oaths and Affirmations

It is the general rule that every witness who gives evidence must be sworn, that is, take the oath or make an affirmation.

The manner in which the oath is administered is provided by s. 1 of the Oaths Act 1978. This requires the witness to hold the New Testament (Old Testament in the case of a Jew) in his uplifted hand and repeat, after the person administering the oath, the words 'I swear by Almighty God that . . .', followed by the oath prescribed by law.

Where the witness is neither a Christian nor a Jew he/she can object to taking the oath in the prescribed manner. Alternatively, the witness may affirm or take an oath upon a holy book appropriate to his/her religion or belief. For example, Hindus are sworn on the Vedas and Muslims are sworn on the Koran (*R* v *Morgan* (1764) 1 Leach 54).

An affirmation may be made by a witness who objects to being sworn or where his/her request for an alternative form of oath is not reasonably practicable and would delay or inconvenience the proceedings (s. 5 of the 1978 Act). The witness repeats after the person administering the affirmation, the words 'I [name] do solemnly, sincerely and truly declare and affirm', followed by the words of the oath prescribed by law (s. 6 of the 1978 Act).

Children may give unsworn evidence (Youth Justice and Criminal Evidence Act 1999, s. 55), and witnesses merely producing a document need not be sworn (*Perry* v *Gibson* (1834) 1 A & E 48).

2.3.13 Examination-in-Chief

The party who calls a witness (prosecution or defence) is entitled to examine the witness by asking questions with a view to providing evidence which is favourable to that party's case. This is known as 'examination-in-chief'.

All witnesses are examined in chief with one exception: where the prosecution determine not to examine their witness in chief but allow the witness to be cross-examined by the defence. This is common in the case of police officers whose evidence-in-chief will be identical. Consequently, one police officer can give the evidence-in-chief but other officers involved may be required for cross-examination by the defence.

2.3.14 Cross-examination

Under Article 6(3)(d) of the European Convention on Human Rights, everyone charged with a criminal offence shall be entitled:

> to examine or have examined witnesses against him and to obtain the attendance and examination of witnesses on his behalf under the same conditions as witnesses against him . . .

Cross-examination is the process by which one party may ask questions of the other party's witnesses. This examination is usually focused on either undermining their evidence or supporting that of the party's own witnesses. In *R* v *Shah* [2010] EWCA Crim 2326, a trial was held to be unfair if the defence were not afforded the opportunity to cross-examine key witnesses, where either through gross incompetence or as a deliberate act by the prosecution the witnesses were not present in court.

2.3.14.1 Protection of Complainants from Cross-examination

The Youth Justice and Criminal Evidence Act 1999, ss. 34 to 39, protect three categories of witness from cross-examination by an accused person.

Section 34 Complainants in proceedings for sexual offences

No person charged with a sexual offence may in any criminal proceedings cross-examine in person a witness who is the complainant, either—

- (a) in connection with that offence, or
- (b) in connection with any other offence (of whatever nature) with which that person is charged in the proceedings.

Section 35 Child complainants and other child witnesses

(1) No person charged with an offence to which this section applies may in any criminal proceedings cross-examine in person a protected witness, either—
- (a) in connection with that offence, or
- (b) in connection with any other offence (of whatever nature) with which that person is charged in the proceedings.

(2) For the purposes of subsection (1) a 'protected witness' is a witness who—
- (a) either is the complainant or is alleged to have been a witness to the commission of the offence to which this section applies, and
- (b) either is a child or falls to be cross-examined after giving evidence in chief (whether wholly or in part)—
  - (i) by means of a video recording made (for the purposes of section 27) at a time when the witness was a child, or
  - (ii) in any other way at any such time.

Section 36 Direction prohibiting accused from cross-examining particular witness

(1) This section applies where, in a case where neither of sections 34 and 35 operates to prevent an accused in any criminal proceedings from cross-examining a witness in person—
- (a) the prosecutor makes an application for the court to give a direction under this section in relation to the witness, or
- (b) the court of its own motion raises the issue whether such a direction should be given.

(2) If it appears to the court—
- (a) that the quality of evidence given by the witness on cross-examination—
  - (i) is likely to be diminished if the cross-examination (or further cross-examination) is conducted by the accused in person, and
  - (ii) would be likely to be improved if a direction were given under this section, and
- (b) that it would not be contrary to the interests of justice to give such a direction,

the court may give a direction prohibiting the accused from cross-examining (or further cross-examining) the witness in person.

KEYNOTE

The sections to which s. 35 apply are: any of ss. 33 to 36 of the Sexual Offences Act 1956; the Protection of Children Act 1978; part 1 of the Sexual Offences Act 2003 or any relevant superseded enactment; ss. 1 and 2 of the Modern Slavery Act 2015; kidnapping, false imprisonment or an offence under s. 1 or 2 of the Child Abduction Act 1984; any offence under s. 1 of the Children and Young Persons Act 1933; any offence (not within any of the preceding paragraphs) which involves an assault on, or injury or a threat of injury to, any person.

The restrictions on cross-examination of a vulnerable young witness are appropriate provided the defence case is understood and the jury are advised of any disadvantage caused to the defence (*R* v *Wills* [2011] EWCA Crim 1938 and *R* v *E* [2011] EWCA Crim 3028).

2.3.14.2 Cross-examination of Witnesses about Previous Sexual Behaviour

The Youth Justice and Criminal Evidence Act 1999 provides that where a person is charged with a sexual offence no evidence may be adduced and no questions asked in cross-examination by or on behalf of an accused about any sexual behaviour of the complainant (s. 41(1)).

'Sexual behaviour' means any sexual behaviour or other sexual experience, whether or not involving any accused or other person, but excluding anything alleged to have taken place which is the subject matter of the charge against the accused (s. 42(1)(c)). It may refer to acts or events of a sexual character, as opposed to the existence of a relationship, acquaintanceship or familiarity. The phrases are wide enough to embrace the viewing of pornography, or sexually charged messaging over a live internet connection or answering questions in a sexually implicit quiz (*R* v *Ben-Rejab* [2011] EWCA Crim 1136). However, in *R* v *T* [2021] EWCA Crim 318, it was held that evidence or questioning about the complainant's sexual behaviour which involves speculation or is simply irrelevant to any issues in the case is inadmissible. The provisions of the 1999 Act recognise that to allow victims of sexual offences to be harassed unfairly by questions about their previous sexual experiences is unjust to them and bad for society, because if victims are afraid to complain then the guilty may escape justice.

Provision is made for limited occasions where an accused may be allowed to cross-examine the complainant about their sexual behaviour (s. 41(2) and (3)).

2.4 Exclusion of Admissible Evidence

2.4.1 Introduction

In ensuring that a person has a fair trial, the court may exclude evidence, *even though the evidence itself is admissible*. In certain circumstances, the court may exclude any evidence and has additional powers in relation to evidence obtained by confession. The courts' powers to exclude evidence come generally from s. 78 of the Police and Criminal Evidence Act 1984 and specifically in relation to confession evidence from s. 76(2) of that Act, although the courts also have common law powers to exclude evidence.

2.4.2 Confessions

Where the suspect initially confesses to the offence, he/she may still plead not guilty, alleging that the confession was obtained by oppression and/or in circumstances that would render it unreliable or that it should be excluded as having been unfairly obtained. The courts are concerned with the reliability of evidence and often regard confessions as the least reliable way to prove a person's involvement in an offence.

A confession, which is defined by s. 82 of the Police and Criminal Evidence Act 1984 (see later), is an out-of-court statement made by a person and therefore falls into the category of evidence known as 'hearsay' evidence. Hearsay evidence is inadmissible unless it falls within one of the statutory or common law exceptions.

Confessions are such an exceptional category and are admissible in evidence as outlined in s. 76(1) of the 1984 Act. However, evidence of confession may be excluded by a court under either s. 76(2) or 78 of the 1984 Act.

Section 76 of the Police and Criminal Evidence Act 1984 states:

(1) In any proceedings a confession made by an accused person may be given in evidence against him in so far as it is relevant to any matter in issue in the proceedings and is not excluded by the court in pursuance of this section.

A 'confession' is defined by s. 82 of the 1984 Act, which states:

(1) In this Part of this Act—'confession' includes any statement wholly or partly adverse to the person who made it, whether made to a person in authority or not and whether made in words or otherwise;

KEYNOTE

A confession, therefore, is a positive action by the person making it. The person must use words or some other method of communication (e.g. nodding his/her head to a question, or a video tape of the suspect taking police to a murder weapon). Therefore confessions do not include silence by a person (although this may be relevant to special warnings, **see chapter 2.8**). It could include a filmed re-enactment of the crime (*Li Shu-Ling* v *The Queen* [1989] AC 270).

The confession does not have to be a pure statement of guilt and can include the answers to questions asked in interview which are adverse to the defendant. In *R* v *Z* [2003] EWCA Crim 191, the Court of Appeal considered the meaning of 'confession' for the purposes of the Police and Criminal Evidence Act 1984 in light of the Human Rights Act 1998. The court held that the decision as to whether or not a statement was a confession was to be made at the time it was sought to give the statement in evidence as opposed to at the time the statement was made by the person.

Section 76A (which makes provisions for exclusion similar to those under s. 76) states that so long as it has not been excluded by the court, that in any proceedings where a confession was made by one accused person it may be given in evidence for another person charged in the same proceedings (a co-accused). The key part of this subsection is that the co-accused must be 'charged in the same proceedings': for instance, in *R* v *Finch* [2007] EWCA Crim 36, where one suspect pleaded guilty the House of Lords held that he was no longer a person charged or accused in the trial; accordingly, s. 76A of the 1984 Act did not apply and what he said to the police was not admissible in the trial of the other defendant.

2.4.2.1 The Exclusion of Confession Evidence

Section 76(2) of the Police and Criminal Evidence Act 1984 gives the courts a responsibility to exclude confessions where they have been obtained by oppression (s. 76(2)(a)), or where the court considers that they are unreliable (s. 76(2)(b)). There is also a general power (under s. 78 of the 1984 Act and at common law) to exclude any evidence that the court considers would be detrimental to the fairness of the trial if allowed, which can also be applicable to the exclusion of confessions. Once the defence raises the issue of oppression and/or unreliability, it is for the prosecution to prove that the confession was not obtained in such circumstances (*R* v *Allen* [2001] EWCA Crim 1607).

2.4.2.2 Exclusion under Section 76 PACE

Section 76 of the Police and Criminal Evidence Act 1984 states:

> (2) If, in any proceedings where the prosecution proposes to give in evidence a confession made by an accused person, it is represented to the court that the confession was or may have been obtained—
> (a) by oppression of the person who made it; or
> (b) in consequence of anything said or done which was likely, in the circumstances existing at the time, to render unreliable any confession which might be made by him in consequence thereof,
>
> the court shall not allow the confession to be given in evidence against him except in so far as the prosecution proves to the court beyond reasonable doubt that the confession (notwithstanding that it may be true) was not obtained as aforesaid.

2.4.2.3 Oppression

Under s. 76(2)(a) a court is under a duty to exclude a confession where it has been, or may have been, obtained by the oppression of the person making the confession. This means that there must be some link between the oppressive behaviour and the confession. So for instance, if the confession was made before the oppressive behaviour, this would not justify exclusion under this subsection (it may, however, justify exclusion under the general power of the courts). Where a confession has been obtained by oppression, any later confession obtained properly may also be excluded from evidence (*R* v *Ismail* [1990] Crim LR 109). It does not matter whether or not the confession is true; the issue under s. 76(2)(a) is how the person has been treated and whether any mistreatment led, or might have led, the person to make the confession. This issue is of particular importance in the interviewing of suspects. In looking at this, the courts seem to take into account the nature of the person being interviewed. It was said in *R* v *Gowan* [1982] Crim LR 821 that hardened criminals must expect vigorous police interrogation.

2.4.2.4 What is Oppression?

In s. 76(8) of the Police and Criminal Evidence Act 1984, 'oppression' includes torture, inhuman or degrading treatment and the use or threat of violence (whether or not amounting to torture).

KEYNOTE

In *R* v *Fulling* [1987] QB 426, the Court of Appeal held that oppression is:

> [The] exercise of authority or power in a burdensome, harsh or wrongful manner; unjust or cruel treatment of subjects, inferiors etc, or the imposition of unreasonable or unjust burdens.

In *Fulling*, the court also drew attention to a quotation which exemplifies the meaning of the term: 'There is not a word in our language that expresses more detestable wickedness than oppression.'

It is suggested by some commentators that oppression involves some kind of impropriety on the part of the police, which might be suggested by a deliberate failure to follow the PACE Codes of Practice, although a failure to follow the Codes is not of itself an automatic reason for excluding evidence. Given that the courts have occasionally excluded evidence even where the relevant Code of Practice has been followed, the converse does not appear to be true and it is possible that a court might conclude that treatment had been 'oppressive' under all the circumstances even though the Codes of Practice had been followed.

The oppression must have been against the person who makes the confession.

When the defence raise the issue of oppression, it will be for the prosecution to show beyond reasonable doubt (*R* v *Miller* (1993) 97 Cr App R 99) that this was not the case. For these reasons (as well as those of professional ethics) it is of great importance to comply with the PACE Codes of Practice. It is also important to keep records of how a case is investigated, together with the reasons for taking decisions during the course of the investigation so that the prosecution can present a case which demonstrates that there was no oppressive or improper conduct in obtaining the confession.

It is a question of fact on each occasion whether a person's treatment was oppressive and whether there was any link between that person's treatment and his/her decision to make the confession. It might be possible for the defence to use evidence against officers involved in the case who have allegedly 'mistreated' suspects in other cases (*R* v *Twitchell* [2000] 1 Cr App R 373; *Charlton* v *R* [2016] EWCA Crim 52).

It will be for the prosecution to satisfy the judge that the confession was made voluntarily; even where the confession is admissible a jury would still need to be directed that they should disregard the confession if they considered that it was or may have been obtained by oppression or in consequence of anything said or done that was likely to render it unreliable (*R* v *Mushtaq* [2005] UKHL 25).

The legislation itself gives little guidance as to what will amount to oppression. For this reason it is necessary to look at the case law. Below are examples where the courts have held that the treatment of a person was 'oppressive':

- A person who was on the border of being vulnerable because of a mental health condition or mental disorder admitted the offence after denying it over 300 times because of the bullying manner of the questioning (*R* v *Paris* (1993) 97 Cr App R 99). This case does not mean that interviewers cannot go over the same point several times or even suggest to the interviewee that he/she is lying. However, *Paris* does suggest that this should be done in moderation and not to the point where it becomes oppressive.
- A person confessed but had been kept in custody longer than the court felt was justified and therefore unlawfully (*R* v *Davison* [1988] Crim LR 442).
- The suspect was wrongly informed that he/she had been recognised when this was not true (*R* v *Heron* (1993), unreported).
- There was a failure to have an appropriate adult present (*R* v *Silcott* (1991) *The Times*, 9 December).

- The defendant was a choir master and the police had told him that if he did not make a statement they would have to interview all the members of the choir and this could disclose other offences on his part (*R* v *Howden-Simpson* [1991] Crim LR 49).
- A confession was obtained where the person was being held without access to a solicitor (*Barbera* v *Spain* (1989) 11 EHRR 360).
- Interviews had extended over a three-hour period and were conducted in a manner that was persistent, aggressive and calculated to get a conviction as opposed to necessarily getting to the truth (*R* v *Ridley* (1999) 17 December, unreported). The court went on to comment that the manner in which the interviews were conducted was to be deplored and was an exploitation of a naive man by methods which were unacceptable and prejudiced the fair conduct of the trial.
- A person had been kept in custody for 14 hours, had been interviewed four times before confessing and had been refused any visits from family (*R* v *Silcott* [1987] Crim LR 765).

2.4.2.5 Unreliability

Under s. 76(2)(b) a court is under a duty to exclude a confession where it is, has been or may have been obtained in consequence of anything which was likely, in the circumstances that existed at the time, to render it unreliable.

When looking at whether a confession is reliable, the court will consider the circumstances as they actually were at the time and not as they were believed to be. For instance, if it was believed that a suspect was in a fit state to be interviewed but it later transpires that he/she was medically unfit, there is likely to be some doubt as to whether a confession made at that time is reliable. (The belief of the officers at the time of acting, however, may be relevant to any disciplinary matters.)

For instance, in *R* v *Walker* [1998] Crim LR 211 the court held that the defendant's mental state may be taken into account when considering the surrounding circumstances, regardless of whether it was known to the police. The prosecution bore the burden of proof to show that the confession was admissible. The court went further and said that s. 76(2)(b) was not restricted in its application to use by the police of oppression. It was not necessary to show that the confession was unreliable by reference to the old common law test of 'threat or inducement'. A successful submission under s. 76(2)(b) does not require a breach of a Code of Practice.

Once again, it is for the prosecution to show (beyond reasonable doubt) that the confession is reliable once the question of unreliability has been raised by the defence.

In *R* v *Fulling* [1987] QB 426 it was suggested that questioning had been:

> ... by its nature, duration, or other attendant circumstances (including the fact of custody) excites hopes (such as the hope of release) or fears, or so affects the mind of the subject that his will crumbles and he speaks when otherwise he would have stayed silent.

Thus, the circumstances of a case can affect the reliability of the accused's statement.

A confession volunteered without anything being said or done cannot fall foul of s. 76(2)(b). Where an appropriate adult was the unwilling recipient of unsolicited confessions by an accused where nothing was said or done by the adult or anyone else, then it was unlikely to render the confession unreliable (*R* v *Ward* [2018] EWCA Crim 1464).

2.4.2.6 What is Unreliable?

It is a question of fact on each occasion whether the reliability of a person's confession is in question as a result of something said or done. Below are examples where the courts have held that a confession was unreliable:

- No caution was given to the suspect, the suspect was not asked if he wanted his solicitor present and was not shown the note of the interview (*R* v *Trussler* [1998] Crim LR 446).

- The PACE Codes of Practice were flagrantly breached (*R* v *Delaney* (1989) 88 Cr App R 338). Not all breaches of PACE will lead to evidence being excluded (*Lariba* v *R* [2015] EWCA Crim 4878).
- A suspect who had just vomited was interviewed (any medical condition could affect the reliability of a confession; if in doubt the person should be examined by a doctor) (*R* v *McGovern* (1991) 92 Cr App R 228).
- The appropriate adult had a low IQ and was unable to assist the detained person (*R* v *Silcott*).
- In a case where the suspect was a vulnerable person, the fact that he/she confessed to the offence without an appropriate adult being called made the confession unreliable. The court found that had the adult been present, a solicitor would in all probability have been instructed and there was a realistic likelihood that the suspect would not have made any admissions (*R* v *W* [2010] EWCA Crim 2799).
- It was suggested to a suspect of a sexual assault that it would be better for him/her to receive treatment than go to prison (*R* v *Delaney*).
- An offer of bail was made subject to the suspect admitting the offence or, conversely, the suspect was told that he/she would be kept in custody until he/she admitted the offence (*R* v *Barry* (1992) 95 Cr App R 384).
- Psychiatric evidence suggested that the suspect suffered from a severe personality disorder and that her admissions in her interview were unreliable (*R* v *Walker* [1998] Crim LR 211).
- A suspect had been forcibly overcome, and a confession was obtained in response to a question designed to elicit details of the offence from him without any prior caution having been administered (*R* v *Allen* [2001] EWCA Crim 1607).
- The promise not to involve the police held out by a shop manager to an employee suspected of stealing gave rise to the inference that anything said in consequence was likely to be unreliable (*R* v *Roberts* [2011] EWCA Crim 2974).

2.4.2.7 Effect of Excluding Confessions

Often further evidence is obtained after a person makes a confession. If a court excludes all or any part of a confession, then this may impact on the value of the additional evidence obtained by the prosecution.

While the additional evidence obtained after a confession may be admissible, much of the value of the evidence may be lost because s. 76(5) of the 1984 Act prevents the prosecution from linking the discovery of the additional evidence to any confession which has been excluded.

If the additional evidence cannot be linked to the confession, then it might not be possible to link the evidence to the suspect (and the evidence may be excluded under s. 78 of the 1984 Act or at common law).

EXAMPLE

In the case of a murder, if a suspect confesses to the murder and tells the investigators where he/she has hidden the murder weapon, this would be good evidence that the person committed the offence. If the confession is excluded then, although evidence can be given that the weapon found is in fact the murder weapon, it will not be possible to show any connection between the suspect and the weapon. Therefore, unless there is some other evidence to link the weapon to the suspect (e.g. DNA or fingerprint evidence), the case may fail. The reason is that it would not be possible to say that the police went to the location where the weapon was hidden without at least implying that the suspect had indicated that it was there when interviewed. All that can be said is that the weapon was found at the particular location, which could be accessible to any number of people.

Section 76(4) of the Police and Criminal Evidence Act 1984 provides that the exclusion of such additional evidence is not affected by the exclusion of the confession. Even where a confession is excluded, it may still be admissible for other matters such as the fact that the accused speaks in a certain way or writes or expresses him/herself in a particular fashion. In such a case, it would only be that part of the confession which is necessary to prove the point that will be admissible. Once again, this illustrates the point that evidence is often only admissible for a specific purpose.

2.4.3 Exclusion of Evidence Generally

The courts in England and Wales can exclude any evidence under certain circumstances. Those circumstances will usually be concerned with the way in which the evidence has been obtained or with the potential effect of allowing it to be adduced at trial.

2.4.3.1 Confessions by Mentally Handicapped Persons

Section 77 of the Police and Criminal Evidence Act 1984 states:

> (1) Without prejudice to the general duty of the court at a trial on indictment with a jury to direct the jury on any matter on which it appears to the court appropriate to do so, where at such a trial—
> (a) the case against the accused depends wholly or substantially on a confession by him; and
> (b) the court is satisfied—
> (i) that he is mentally handicapped; and
> (ii) that the confession was not made in the presence of an independent person,
> the court shall warn the jury that there is special need for caution before convicting the accused in reliance on the confession, and shall explain that the need arises because of the circumstances mentioned in paragraphs (a) and (b) above.

KEYNOTE

Section 77 of the Police and Criminal Evidence Act 1984 provides additional safeguards for those who suffer from a 'mental handicap'. This is defined as being in 'a state of arrested or incomplete development of mind which includes significant impairment of intelligence and social functioning' (s. 77(3)).

The test is an objective one. The court should consider medical evidence as to the actual mental condition of the suspect. The disorder must be of a type which might render a suspect's confession unreliable and there must be a significant deviation from the norm. In addition, there must be a history of making admissions, which point toward or explain the abnormality of mind suffered by the suspect and are not solely based on a history given by the suspect.

2.4.3.2 Exclusion of Unfair Evidence

Section 78 of the Police and Criminal Evidence Act 1984 states:

> (1) In any proceedings the court may refuse to allow evidence on which the prosecution proposes to rely to be given if it appears to the court that, having regard to all the circumstances, including the circumstances in which the evidence was obtained, the admission of the evidence would have such an adverse effect on the fairness of the proceedings that the court ought not to admit it.
> (2) Nothing in this section shall prejudice any rule of law requiring a court to exclude evidence.

KEYNOTE

Section 78 is wider than s. 76 and applies to all evidence that the prosecution intend to produce in court.

When applying s. 78, the courts will look at the fairness of allowing the evidence to be admitted against the defendant.

The mere fact that evidence might exert a significant adverse impact upon a jury is not a reason to exclude it under s. 78 and were it otherwise a great deal of incriminating evidence would never be admitted (*R* v *Hunter* [2021] EWCA Crim 1785).

Compliance with the Codes of Practice is vital. In *Batley* v *DPP* (1998) *The Times*, 5 March, the court said that where steps required by the Codes were not observed and where material was entered as evidence without those checks which formed an important aspect of the case, there was a real risk to the fairness of the proceedings against the defendant. This must be balanced against *R* v *Parris* (1989) 89 Cr App R 68, where the court held that a breach of the Codes is not an automatic exclusion of evidence. It is important to note that the court may take account of any changes to the Codes of Practice (even when changed after the person was in police detention) on the basis that the new Code reflects what is considered to be fair (*R* v *Word* (1994) 98 Cr App R 337).

In *R* v *Samuel* [1988] QB 615 the court stated that it is undesirable to attempt any general guidance as to the way in which a judge's discretion under s. 78 should be exercised. It is a question of fact in each case and, while s. 76 requires links with the treatment of the person spoken to, the only issue under s. 78 is whether it would be unfair to admit the evidence in court. *Stanesby* v *DPP* [2012] EWHC 1320 (Admin) is a case that supports this position; this was a drink-drive procedure where the defendant told the custody sergeant that he was taking medication for depression, which should have triggered an appropriate adult being called (Code C1.4). The court held that each case had to be determined on its facts; the breath test had been properly administered, by persons acting in good faith, to somebody who appeared to understand, and in fact did understand, what was required of him; even if an appropriate adult had attended it would not have made any difference to the administration of the breath test. Under s. 78, admission of the breath test results would not have such an adverse effect on the fairness of the proceedings that they should be excluded.

2.4.3.3 Evidence Which will be Excluded

It is therefore difficult to give specific guidance, but the following are examples of evidence that has been excluded:

- Evidence of a driver being over the prescribed limit where the officer did not suspect that the driver had alcohol in his/her body.
- Some cases of 'entrapment' where the court is not satisfied that the person would have committed such an offence had it not been for the action of the police/customs officers. The court may look to see whether the person was pressurised into committing the offence/providing information or whether, by some ruse, the person was given an opportunity of so doing (*R* v *De Silva* [2002] EWCA Crim 2673).
- Informing the suspect and his/her solicitor that the suspect's fingerprints had been found on items at the scene of the offence when this was not true (*R* v *Mason* [1988] 1 WLR 139).
- Undercover operations where the officers failed to record conversations in accordance with the PACE Codes of Practice.
- Failure by custody officers to inform a detained person of his/her rights.
- Interviewing a suspect without informing the person of his/her rights.
- Failing to provide the detained person with adequate meals.
- 'Off the record' interviews that were not recorded as required by the PACE Codes of Practice.
- Failing to make a contemporaneous note of a conversation.
- Failing to get an interpreter or appropriate adult.

- Interviewing a person suffering from schizophrenia without an appropriate adult being present (*R* v *Aspinall* [1999] 2 Cr App R 115).
- Identification of a suspect by police officers who had seen the person after he had been arrested and in handcuffs (*R* v *Bazil* (1996) 6 April, unreported).
- Failing to inform a suspect arrested in respect of one offence that it was proposed to question him/her in respect of another more serious offence or failing to ensure that he/she was aware of the true nature of the investigation (*R* v *Kirk* [2000] 1 WLR 567).

2.4.3.4 Exclusion at Common Law

Section 82(3) of the Police and Criminal Evidence Act 1984 retained the courts' common law power to exclude evidence at its discretion (as to which, see *R* v *Sang* [1980] AC 402). For evidence to be excluded at common law the court will not so much concern itself with *how* evidence is obtained, but rather the *effect* that the evidence will have at trial. The court can exclude evidence at common law where the prejudicial effect of the evidence on the defendant greatly outweighs its probative value.

In these cases, the courts are looking at the trial process itself, as opposed to the investigation, and therefore this power has less impact on how investigations should be conducted.

2.4.4 Entrapment

The issue of entrapment falls into two categories: that is to say, trying to obtain evidence relating to offences that have already been committed; and those cases where evidence is obtained of offences yet to be committed.

In relation to investigations concerning offences already committed, the House of Lords in *R* v *Sang* [1980] AC 402 held that:

> Save with regard to admissions and confessions and generally with regard to evidence obtained from the accused after commission of the offence, [the judge] has no discretion to refuse to admit relevant admissible evidence on the ground that it was obtained by improper or unfair means. The court is not concerned with how it was obtained. It is no ground for the exercise of discretion to exclude that the evidence was obtained as the result of the activities of an *agent provocateur*.

(This is now subject to s. 78 of the 1984 Act but the principle still applies.)

In *R* v *Bailey* [1993] 3 All ER 513, the Court of Appeal held that recordings of incriminating conversations between defendants who, after they had been charged, had been tricked into sharing a bugged police cell were admissible in evidence. The two men, who had remained silent during police interviews, were charged with conspiracy to commit robberies. Although there was some evidence incriminating the appellants, the police needed more evidence and obtained permission to install listening equipment in a remand cell. The men were remanded into police custody to take part in identification parades. The police, to allay suspicion about the cell being bugged, acted out a charade whereby they pretended that they did not wish to put both men in the same cell but that it was being forced on them by an uncooperative custody officer. The suspects were fooled by the officers' play-acting and embarked on conversations which contained a number of admissions.

2.4.4.1 Undercover Operations

One of the arguments often raised by defendants who are caught by undercover officers is that they were induced or pressurised into committing the offence by the officers and, as a result, they should not be prosecuted or the evidence of the officer(s) should be excluded.

In *R* v *Loosely; Attorney-General's Reference (No. 3 of 2000)* [2001] UKHL 53, the House of Lords took the chance to set out the legal position in relation to these issues. Their lordships held that it is both unfair and an abuse of process if a person is incited (the predecessor of encouraging or assisting an offence (**see *Crime*, chapter 1.3**)), or pressurised by an undercover officer into committing a crime which the person would otherwise not have committed. If, however, the police officer(s) did no more than present a person with an 'unexceptional opportunity' to commit a criminal offence and the person took that opportunity, this would not amount to such an abuse of process.

In *Ridgeway* v *The Queen* (1995) 184 CLR 19, the court stated that:

> The State can justify the use of entrapment techniques to induce the commission of an offence only when the inducement is consistent with the ordinary temptations and stratagems that are likely to be encountered in the course of criminal activity. That may mean that some degree of deception, importunity and even threats on the part of the authorities may be acceptable. But once the State goes beyond the ordinary, it is likely to increase the incidence of crime by artificial means.

An example of such an 'unexceptional opportunity' can be seen in *R* v *Breen* [2001] EWCA Crim 1213, where police officers had attended the suspect's address unannounced and asked for 'blow'. The suspect gave the police his mobile telephone number and they returned the following day and were supplied with £20 worth of cannabis resin. The officers were invited to return at any time and they were supplied with drugs on subsequent visits. The Court of Appeal held that the judge had been entitled to find that the undercover officers had done no more than give the appellants an opportunity to break the law, of which each of them freely took advantage.

In *Edwards* v *United Kingdom* (2005) 40 EHRR 24, the European Court of Human Rights restated the rights of defendants who are to be prosecuted on the basis of evidence obtained by undercover officers, and highlighted the tensions between protecting the sensitive sources of that evidence while affording the defendant a fair trial.

- It is not acceptable for the 'State' (police officers or other agents) to lure its citizens into committing acts that are against the law and then to prosecute those citizens for doing so—this amounts to entrapment, a misuse of power and abuse of the courts' process.
- If police officers acted only as 'detectives' and 'passive observers' of criminal activity that was to take place anyway, there would be no problem in drawing the line between what is allowable and what is not.
- However, some offences need a degree of active involvement by the police if those offences are to be successfully prosecuted. In such cases, the police officers themselves become the reporters and witnesses of the offence as well as the investigators.
- The yardstick for judging the activities of the police in this regard is to ask whether the officers' conduct preceding the offence was no more than might have been expected from others in the circumstances. That is, did they do no more than give the defendant the 'unexceptional opportunity' to commit a crime as described above? If the answer is 'yes', the consequences below are not relevant. If the answer is 'no', there are several potential consequences for any subsequent trial.

The trial judge's task in such cases is to distinguish between legitimate crime detection and illegitimate crime creation (*R* v *Byrne* [2003] EWCA Crim 1073).

- The greater the inducement or persistence by the officers—the more readily the courts will conclude that they have overstepped the line.
- The greater the degree of intrusiveness into the 'target's' life—the closer the courts will scrutinise the 'proportionality' of the operation.
- The courts will also look at the defendant's personal circumstances including vulnerability and experience. What might be insignificant in terms of an inducement to one person may not be seen as so insignificant in relation to another.

Where an accused planned to kill his estranged wife, before encouraging a friend and an undercover police officer to join him in the plan, even though their presence made the plan possible, it was held that it did not amount to entrapment (*R* v *Winter* [2007] EWCA Crim 3493).

In *R* v *Jones* [2007] EWCA Crim 1118, after graffiti had been found in the toilets of trains and stations seeking girls of 8–13 years old for sex, offering payment and leaving a contact number, a police officer posed as a 12-year-old girl. Several texts were shared between the undercover officer and the defendant, some of which were of an explicit sexual nature. The Court of Appeal held that the police did not incite or instigate a crime but merely provided an opportunity for the defendant to commit an offence of inciting sexual activity with a child under 13.

This is an area where the substantive criminal law overlaps with evidence and procedure. Evidential factors to consider in running an operation that involves forms of entrapment include:

- The nature of the offence, as some offences are difficult to detect otherwise. Therefore, the more difficult the offence is to detect without intrusive inducement from the police, the more such intrusion will be justifiable.
- What suspicion officers have that an offence of that kind would be committed in the locality, for example, the setting-up of a van containing cigarettes to see if someone took the opportunity to steal them (*Williams and O'Hare* v *DPP* [1993] 3 All ER 365). 'If the trick had been the individual enterprise of a policeman in an area where such crime was not suspected to be prevalent, it would have been an abuse of State power' (Lord Hoffmann in *Attorney-General's Reference (No. 3 of 2000)* [2001] UKHL 53).

In *Nottingham City Council* v *Amin* (2000) 1 WLR 1071, Lord Bingham of Cornhill CJ suggested the test as:

> On the one hand it has been recognised as deeply offensive to ordinary notions of fairness if a defendant were to be convicted and punished for committing a crime which he only committed because he had been incited, instigated, persuaded, pressurised or wheedled into committing it by a law enforcement officer. On the other hand it has been recognised that law enforcement agencies have a general duty to the public to enforce the law and it has been regarded as unobjectionable if a law enforcement officer gives a defendant an opportunity to break the law, of which the defendant freely takes advantage, in circumstances where it appears that the defendant would have behaved in the same way if the opportunity had been offered by anyone else.

2.4.4.2 Consequences

The potential consequences are as follows:

- Courts have a general discretion to exclude evidence under the Police and Criminal Evidence Act 1984, s. 78.
- Courts also have a common law power to stay (discontinue) proceedings and order the release of a defendant where it becomes apparent that there has been a serious abuse of power by the State (*R* v *Horseferry Road Magistrates' Court, ex parte Bennett* [1994] 1 AC 42).
- Courts also have a general duty to consider the fairness of any defendant's trial under Article 6 of the European Convention on Human Rights. However, it should be noted that violations of Article 8 (right to privacy) will not by themselves usually give rise to exclusion of any evidence obtained as a result (*PG* v *United Kingdom* (2008) 46 EHRR 51).

2.5 Disclosure of Evidence
Criminal Procedure and Investigation Act 1996 and Code of Practice

A thick grey line down the margin denotes text that is an extract of the Code itself (i.e. the actual wording of the legislation). This material is examinable for both Sergeants and Inspectors.

2.5.1 Introduction

During 2017, there were a number of high-profile cases that collapsed due to failures in the management of the disclosure of material by the police, attracting considerable adverse comment and risking public confidence. Also during 2017, Her Majesty's Inspectorate of Constabulary (HMIC), in collaboration with Her Majesty's Crown Prosecution Service Inspectorate (HMCPSI) published their report: 'Making it fair—a joint inspection of the disclosure of unused material in volume Crown Court cases'. This inspection identified a number of issues which are contributing to widespread failures across the board by both police and prosecutors. Additionally, in November 2018 the Attorney General's Review of the efficiency and effectiveness of disclosure in the criminal justice system highlighted significant concerns with the culture around disclosure, engagement between prosecutors, investigators and defence practitioners, and the challenge of the exponential increase in digital data. The A-G's Review made a series of practical recommendations, which included earlier engagement between the prosecution and defence, harnessing the use of technology and culture change.

Disclosure can be grouped under two main areas: the material the prosecution will use in court to prove the case against the defendant, and all other material not forming part of the prosecution case which might have a bearing on the decision the court makes.

The Criminal Procedure and Investigations Act 1996 (the 1996 Act) is made up of seven parts. It is the first two parts which are of interest to the police:

- part I sets out the procedures for disclosure and the effects of failing to comply with the Act; and
- part II sets out the duties of police officers in relation to the disclosure provisions.

The 1996 Act introduced a Code of Practice which sets out the manner in which police officers are to record, retain and reveal to the prosecutor material obtained in a criminal investigation and which may be relevant to the investigation, and related matters. The Code assumes that the defence have already been informed of the details of the prosecution case and is included within this chapter. In addition to the Code of Practice, this chapter also makes reference to the Attorney-General's Guidelines on Disclosure for Investigators, Prosecutors and Defence Practitioners (referred to in this chapter as the A-G's Guidelines); as well as the CPS Disclosure Manual. The Codes of Practice and the A-G's Guidelines have both been updated as of December 2020. *R* v *Gohil and Preko* [2018] EWCA Crim 140 highlighted the importance of the essential need for coordination between investigators, prosecutors and independent counsel with their separate roles.

The 2013 Protocol and Good Practice Model Disclosure of Information in cases of alleged child abuse and linked criminal and care directions hearings is another source of guidance. This protocol applies to cases involving criminal investigations into alleged child abuse (child victims who were aged 17 and under at the time of the alleged offending) and/or Family Court proceedings concerning a child (aged 17 and under).

2.5.2 Failure to Comply

Compliance with the rules of disclosure, by both the defence and prosecution, is essential if the 1996 Act is to have any real value. First, in cases where the defence are obliged to make disclosure to the prosecution, failure to do so may lead to the court or jury drawing such inferences as appear proper in deciding the guilt or innocence of the accused (s. 11(5) of the 1996 Act). Should the prosecution fail to comply with their obligations then an accused does not have to make defence disclosure and no such inference can be made. Secondly, failure by the prosecution to comply with the rules could lead to the court staying the proceedings on the grounds that there has been an abuse of process (s. 10). It could also lead to an action for damages or such other relief as the court sees fit under the Human Rights Act 1998, particularly in relation to Article 6 of the European Convention on Human Rights and the right to a fair trial. Additionally, where the prosecution have not made disclosure on time or fully, a stay on the proceedings or a further adjournment is possible. Even if there has been a failure to comply with disclosure the case will not automatically be stayed and therefore any failings should be brought to the attention of the CPS so that the matter can be considered. In *R (On the Application of Ebrahim)* v *Feltham Magistrates' Court* [2001] EWHC Admin 130, the court stated that:

> It must be remembered that it is commonplace in a criminal trial for the defendant to rely on holes in the prosecution case. If in such a case, there is sufficient credible evidence, apart from the missing evidence, which, if believed, would justify safe conviction then the trial should proceed, leaving the defendant to seek to persuade the jury or magistrates not to convict because evidence that might otherwise have been available was not before the court through no fault of the defendant.

Further guidance was provided in *R* v *Brooks* [2004] EWCA Crim 3537, a case where the prosecution failed to comply with the disclosure requirements. The Court of Appeal held that if the court was satisfied that the prosecution had deliberately withheld evidence from the court or frustrated the defence, the court did have the power to stay the prosecution. If the court was not so satisfied it would consider whether, despite all that had gone wrong, a fair trial was possible.

Failure to disclose may result in convictions being overturned; for instance in *R* v *Poole* [2003] EWCA Crim 1753, the Court of Appeal overturned convictions for murder because the non-disclosure of prosecution evidence influenced the jury's assessment of the reliability of the evidence of a key eye-witness. In this case, the witness gave an account that was false in a material particular. However, the police did not follow up those inconsistencies and they failed to inform the CPS that his evidence was unreliable.

The level of disclosure that is required will be a question of fact in each case. In *Filmer* v *DPP* [2006] EWHC 3450 (Admin), the court held that the extent of disclosure required from the prosecution depends on the evidence and issue in a particular case. The prosecution are required to provide sufficient disclosure to enable a defendant to present his/her case. The court went on to say that this has to be the approach otherwise the prosecution would have to second guess every question the defence may want to ask (this is where the defence disclosure becomes relevant, **see para. 2.5.11.1**).

2.5.3 Disclosing Initial Details of the Prosecution Case

This refers to the material that the defence are entitled to have in order to consider whether to plead guilty or not guilty. In some cases, it is not a question of whether the defendant committed the crime but whether the prosecution are in a position to prove the offence and, in order to consider this, the defence are unlikely to agree to plead or decide on the mode of trial without knowing the strength of the prosecution case. It is clearly in the public interest that guilty pleas are entered or indicated as soon as possible (*R* v *Calderdale Magistrates' Court, ex parte Donahue* [2001] Crim LR 141) and often this cannot be achieved unless advanced information has been provided. The need to know as early as possible whether a defendant is going to plead not guilty can be particularly important as there are time limits by which the courts have to set trials and committals. Often these can be delayed because the prosecution have not complied with their disclosure duties.

Ensuring that all defendants receive copies of any initial details of the prosecution case (or any later disclosure) is also important. In *R* v *Tompkins* [2005] EWCA Crim 3035, the court held that where there has been non-disclosure at the time a plea had been entered, a defendant who had pleaded guilty should not in any way be in a worse position than a defendant who had pleaded not guilty.

2.5.3.1 Obligations on Prosecution Regarding Disclosing the Initial Details of the Prosecution Case

In the magistrates' court, Part 8 of the Criminal Procedure Rules 2020 provides that where the offence is one that can be tried in a magistrates' court the prosecutor must provide initial details of the prosecution case to the court and the defendant as soon as practicable, and in any event no later than the beginning of the day of the first hearing. These initial details must include (r. 8.3):

(a) where, immediately before the first hearing in the magistrates' court, the defendant was in police custody for the offence charged—
   (i) a summary of the circumstances of the offence, and
   (ii) the defendant's criminal record, if any;
(b) where paragraph (a) does not apply—
   (i) a summary of the circumstances of the offence,
   (ii) any account given by the defendant in interview, whether contained in that summary or in another document,
   (iii) any written witness statement or exhibit that the prosecutor then has available and considers material to plea, or to the allocation of the case for trial, or to sentence,
   (iv) the defendant's criminal record, if any, and
   (v) any available statement of the effect of the offence on a victim, a victim's family or others.

For trials at the Crown Court, the defence will receive the majority of the prosecution case through the disclosure of witness statements or depositions. If the prosecution wish to use any additional evidence after committal they must serve this on the defence.

It is suggested that Article 6 of the European Convention on Human Rights supports the need to provide initial details of the prosecution case to the defence in all cases and that this should be done as soon as possible. Article 6(3)(a) states that a person is:

> ... to be informed promptly ... and in detail, of the nature and cause of the accusation against him;

Article 6(3)(b) states that an accused is entitled to:

> ... have adequate time ... for the preparation of his defence.

However, the point concerning initial information in summary cases was considered in *R* v *Stratford Justices, ex parte Imbert* [1999] 2 Cr App R 276, where the court gave its opinion that Article 6 does not give an absolute right to pre-trial disclosure; it will be a question of whether the defendant can have a fair trial. Clearly, it will be easier to satisfy this test where initial information has been provided to the defence. This information might also include the following and so consideration should be had to providing this material to the prosecutor so that he/she can forward it to the defence where appropriate (ensuring that the addresses and other details of witnesses and victims are protected):

- a copy of the custody record;
- copies of any interview tape(s);
- a copy of any first descriptions where relevant;
- significant information that might affect a bail decision or enable the defence to contest the allocation hearing (A-G's Guidelines, para. 78 and CPIA Code, para. 6.5);
- any material which is relevant to sentence (e.g. information which might mitigate the seriousness of the offence or assist the accused to lay blame in whole or in part upon a co-accused or another person);
- statements and/or a summary of the prosecution cases;
- a copy of any video evidence.

(For the actual disclosure that must be provided to the prosecutor in order to allow the defence to prepare their case, **see para. 2.5.9.**)

Where a person has made several statements but all the relevant evidence for the prosecution case is contained in one statement, it is only that one statement which needs to be disclosed. In order to comply with disclosing the initial details of the prosecution case, the defence needs to be either given a copy of the document or allowed to inspect the document (or a copy of it). In *R* v *Lane and Lane* [2011] EWCA Crim 2745, one of the witnesses refused to put incriminating evidence into his statement due to fear of repercussions. The police had notified the prosecution of the witness's increased knowledge, but the prosecution failed to notify the defence that the statement had been a partial account. The Court of Appeal held that the statement was untruthful as it did not disclose all the information that it should have done. The witness should have been told to make a full statement or he should have been abandoned as a witness, but he should never have been allowed to make a partial statement.

The following sections set out the Disclosure Code of Practice issued under the Criminal Procedure and Investigations Act 1996; the latest Code came into effect on 31 December 2020.

2.5.4 Disclosure Code of Practice—1 Introduction

1.1 This Code of Practice applies in respect of criminal investigations conducted by police officers which begin on or after the day on which this Code comes into effect. Persons other than police officers who are charged with the duty of conducting an investigation as defined in the Act are to have regard to the relevant provisions of the Code, and should take these into account in applying their own operating procedures.

1.2 This Code does not apply to persons who are not charged with the duty of conducting an investigation as defined in the Act.

1.3 Nothing in this Code applies to material intercepted in obedience to a warrant issued under section 2 of the Interception of Communications Act 1985 or section 5 of the Regulation of Investigatory Powers Act 2000, or to any copy of that material as defined in section 10 of the 1985 Act or section 15 of the 2000 Act and by sections of the Investigatory Powers Act 2016.

1.4 This Code extends only to England and Wales.

2.5.4.1 **KEYNOTE**

Aims of the 1996 Act

The aim of the disclosure rules within the Criminal Procedure and Investigations Act 1996 is to make sure that a defendant gets a fair trial and speeds up the whole trial process. This was confirmed by *R* v *Stratford Justices, ex parte Imbert* [1999] 2 Cr App R 276, where the court said that the legislation was to try to ensure that nothing which might assist the defence was kept from the accused.

The Act creates an initial duty on the prosecution to disclose with a continuing duty to disclose until the accused is acquitted or convicted or the prosecutor decides not to proceed with the case.

The following diagram, which is taken from para. 16 of the A-G's Guidelines, illustrates how material that forms part of an investigation may be categorised and consequently treated.

The prosecution must, from the start, consider any material that might undermine the prosecution case or assist the defence (s. 3 of the 1996 Act). It is submitted that this requires the prosecution to consider in

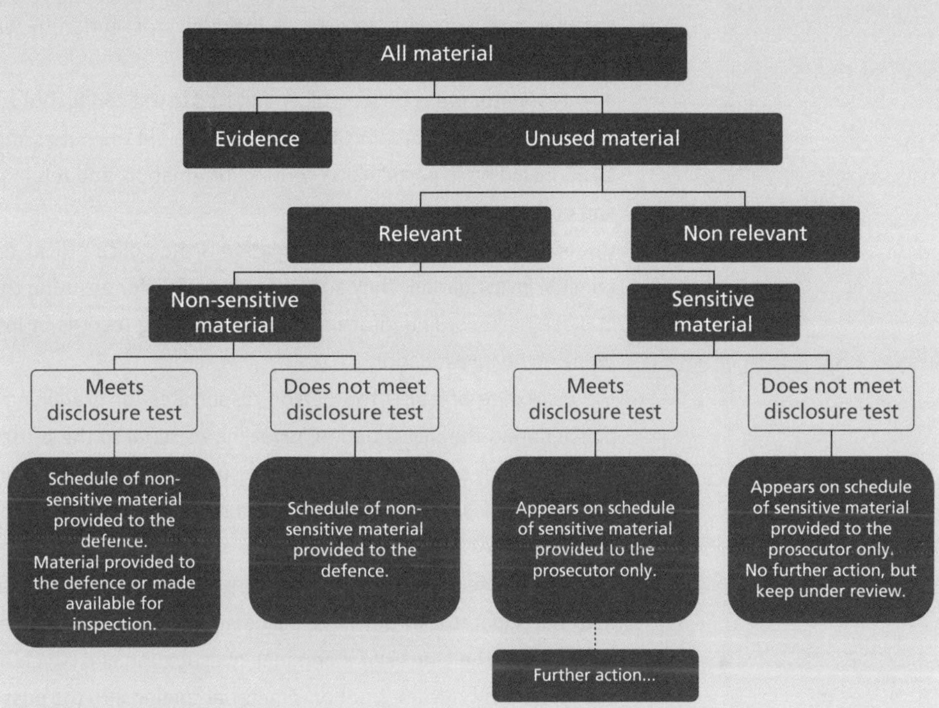

more detail the types of defence that might be used at trial. Once the prosecution have provided their initial disclosure the defence in some cases are obliged to provide a defence statement and in other cases this is optional (see para. 2.5.11.1). Once the defence have provided their defence statement it may provide greater focus to the prosecution as to what other unused material may need to be disclosed.

While the duty of disclosure is placed on the prosecutor, the police have a responsibility to assist in this process. It is therefore vital that police officers understand, not only the statutory requirements made of them, but also the extent of their role within the whole disclosure process.

The HMIC report found that police are routinely failing to comply with guidance and requirements when completing and recording data, such as the non-sensitive disclosure schedule (known as MG6C). Many officers submitted schedules that had missing or deficient data and were often ignorant of processes behind sensitive material, such as information for warrants. The inspection found that in 33 per cent of cases the disclosure officer's report, the MG6E, was either not supplied at all or was wholly inadequate. It is the responsibility of the disclosure officer to comply with the disclosure rules, but it is suggested there is also a supervisory responsibility as well.

2.5.5 **Disclosure Code of Practice—2 Definitions**

2.1 In this Code:

- *a criminal investigation* is an investigation conducted by police officers with a view to it being ascertained whether a person should be charged with an offence, or whether a person charged with an offence is guilty of it. This will include:
  - investigations into crimes that have been committed;
  - investigations whose purpose is to ascertain whether a crime has been committed, with a view to the possible institution of criminal proceedings; and
  - investigations which begin in the belief that a crime may be committed, for example when the police keep premises or individuals under observation for a period of time, with a view to the possible institution of criminal proceedings;
- charging a person with an offence includes prosecution by way of summons or postal requisition;
- *an investigator* is any police officer involved in the conduct of a criminal investigation. All investigators have a responsibility for carrying out the duties imposed on them under this Code, including in particular recording information, and retaining records of information and other material;
- the *officer in charge of an investigation* is the police officer responsible for directing a criminal investigation. They are also responsible for ensuring that proper procedures are in place for recording information, and retaining records of information and other material, in the investigation;
- the *disclosure officer* is the person responsible for examining material retained by the police during the investigation; revealing material to the prosecutor during the investigation and any criminal proceedings resulting from it, and certifying that they have done this; and disclosing material to the accused at the request of the prosecutor;
- the *prosecutor* is the authority responsible for the conduct, on behalf of the Crown, of criminal proceedings resulting from a specific criminal investigation;
- *material* is material of any kind, including information and objects, which is obtained or inspected in the course of a criminal investigation and which may be relevant to the investigation. This includes not only material coming into the possession of the investigator (such as documents seized in the course of searching premises) but also material generated by them (such as interview records);
- *sensitive material* is material, the disclosure of which, the disclosure officer believes, would give rise to a real risk of serious prejudice to an important public interest;
- references to *prosecution disclosure* are to the duty of the prosecutor under sections 3 and 7A of the Act to disclose material which is in their possession or which they have inspected in pursuance of this Code, and which might reasonably be considered capable of undermining the case against the accused, or of assisting the case for the accused;
- references to the disclosure of material to a person accused of an offence include references to the disclosure of material to his legal representative;
- references to police officers and to the chief officer of police include those employed in a police force as defined in section 3(3) of the Prosecution of Offences Act 1985.

2.5.5.1 **KEYNOTE**

Criminal Investigation

Section 1 of the Criminal Procedure and Investigations Act 1996 defines in which type of cases the disclosure provisions apply. In reality, this applies to all cases other than those where the defendant pleads guilty at the magistrates' court. These rules only apply where no criminal investigation into the alleged offence took place before 1 April 1997. If an investigation began before 1 April 1997, then it will be necessary to refer to the common law rules; however, NPCC has stated that the 1996 Act should be followed in all cases when considering disclosure. For those investigations that started after 4 April 2005, the amendments introduced by the Criminal Justice Act 2003 will apply.

Some guidance is given by the case of *R* v *Uxbridge Magistrates' Court, ex parte Patel* (2000) 164 JP 209, as to the time an investigation begins. There it was said that the phrase 'criminal investigation' in s. 1(3) of the 1996 Act means that a criminal investigation could begin into an offence before it was committed. This could be so in a surveillance case or where a series of offences was committed, some before and some after the appointed day. Whether in any given case that was the correct view would be a question of fact for the court to determine.

Section 1 also defines a criminal investigation and states:

(4) For the purposes of this section a criminal investigation is an investigation which police officers or other persons have a duty to conduct with a view to it being ascertained—

(a) whether a person should be charged with an offence, or
(b) whether a person charged with an offence is guilty of it.

Consequently, this part of the Act also applies to other people, besides the police, who carry out investigations where they have a duty to ascertain whether criminal offences have been committed (e.g. National Crime Agency, HM Revenue and Customs, Department for Work and Pensions investigators). It does not apply to those whose primary responsibility does not relate to criminal offences (e.g. local authorities and schools).

2.5.5.2 **KEYNOTE**

Disclosure Officer

A disclosure officer can be a police officer or civilian. If not appointed at the start of an investigation, a disclosure officer must be appointed in sufficient time to be able to prepare the unused material schedules for inclusion in the full file submitted to the CPS (CPS Disclosure Manual, chapter 3).

2.5.5.3 **KEYNOTE**

Prosecutor

This role is defined by s. 2(3) of the 1996 Act as being 'any person acting as prosecutor whether an individual or a body'. In other words, the person who will be taking the case to court. On most occasions, this will be the CPS. It would also apply to the Serious Fraud Office or the Data Protection Registrar. In the case of private prosecutions, the prosecutor is obliged to comply with the disclosure provisions of the 1996 Act but does not have to comply with the Code of Practice. The prosecutor is responsible for ensuring that initial disclosure is made to the defence as well as any further disclosure as required under the continuing duty to disclose. The prosecutor should also be available to advise the OIC, disclosure officer and investigators on matters relating to the relevance of material recorded and retained by police, sensitive material and any other disclosure issues that might arise.

Should there need to be an application to the court to withhold material because of public interest (see para. 2.5.9.3), this will be done through the prosecutor.

A more detailed explanation of the roles and responsibilities of the prosecutor are set out in the CPS Disclosure Manual.

2.5.5.4 **KEYNOTE**

Relevant Material

The material will be relevant whether or not it is beneficial to the prosecution case, weakens the prosecution case or assists the defence case. It is not only material that will become 'evidence' in the case that should be considered; any information, record or thing which may have a bearing on the case can be material for the purposes of disclosure. The way in which evidence has been obtained may in itself be relevant.

As restated in the 2017 HMIC inspection, disclosure of unused material is a key component of the investigative and prosecution process. It should be considered at the point where a criminal investigation commences, continue at the point of charge, and be at the forefront as the case progresses and at every subsequent court hearing. Every unused item that is retained by police and considered relevant to an investigation should be reviewed to ascertain whether its existence is capable of undermining the prosecution or assisting the defence case. If either factor applies, unless certain restrictions apply, it must be disclosed to the defence.

What is relevant to the offence is once again a question of fact, and will not include everything. In *DPP* v *Metten* (1999) 22 January, unreported, it was claimed that the constables who had arrested the defendant had known the identities of potential witnesses to the arrest and these had not been disclosed. The court said that this was not relevant to the case as it did not fall within the definition of an investigation in s. 2(1) of the 1996 Act in that it concerned the time of arrest, and not what happened at the time the offence was committed. Paragraphs 5.4 and 5.5 of the Code give guidance on items that might be considered to be relevant material in a case.

Relevant material may relate to the credibility of witnesses, such as previous convictions, the fact that they have a grudge against the defendant, or where a witness is subsequently shown to be unreliable (*R* v *Dunn* [2016] EWCA Crim 1392). It might even include the weather conditions for the day if relevant to the issue of identification. It may include information that house-to-house inquiries were made and that no one witnessed anything.

Particularly at the early stages of an investigation (sometimes not until the defence statement is provided outlining the defence case), it may not be possible to know whether material is relevant. If in doubt, it should be recorded and placed on the appropriate schedule of unused material. Throughout the case, investigators and all others involved should continually review the material in the light of the investigation.

Material includes information given orally. Where relevant material is not recorded in any way, it will need to be reduced into a suitable form (CPS Disclosure Manual, chapter 4).

2.5.6 Disclosure Code of Practice—3 General Responsibilities

3.1 The functions of the investigator, the officer in charge of an investigation and the disclosure officer are separate. Whether they are undertaken by one, two or more persons will depend on the complexity of the case and the administrative arrangements within each police force. Where they are undertaken by more than one person, close consultation between them is essential to the effective performance of the duties imposed by this code.

3.2 In any criminal investigation, one or more deputy disclosure officers may be appointed to assist the disclosure officer, and a deputy disclosure officer may perform any function of a disclosure officer as defined in paragraph 2.1.

3.3 The chief officer of police for each police force is responsible for putting in place arrangements to ensure that in every investigation the identity of the officer in charge of an investigation and the disclosure officer is recorded. The chief officer of police for each police force shall ensure that disclosure officers and deputy disclosure officers have sufficient skills and authority, commensurate with the complexity of the investigation, to discharge their functions effectively. An individual must not be appointed as disclosure officer, or continue in that role, if that is likely to result in a conflict of interest, for instance, if the disclosure officer is the victim of the alleged crime which is the subject of the investigation. The advice of a more senior officer must always be sought if there is doubt as to whether a conflict of interest precludes an individual acting as disclosure officer. If thereafter the doubt remains, the advice of a prosecutor should be sought.

3.4 The officer in charge of an investigation may delegate tasks to another investigator, to civilians employed by the police force, or to other persons participating in the investigation under arrangements for joint investigations, but they remain responsible for ensuring that these have been carried out and for accounting for any general policies followed in the investigation. In particular, it is an essential part of their duties to ensure that all material which may be relevant to an investigation is retained, and either made available to the disclosure officer or (in exceptional circumstances) revealed directly to the prosecutor.

3.5 In conducting an investigation, the investigator should pursue all reasonable lines of inquiry, whether these point towards or away from the suspect. What is reasonable in each case will depend on the particular circumstances. It is a matter for the investigator, with the assistance of the prosecutor if required, to decide what constitutes a reasonable line of inquiry in each case.

3.6 If the officer in charge of an investigation believes that other persons may be in possession of material that may be relevant to the investigation, and if this has not been obtained under paragraph 3.5 above, they should ask the disclosure officer to inform them of the existence of the investigation and to invite them to retain the material in case they receive a request for its disclosure. The disclosure officer should inform the prosecutor that they may have such material. However, the officer in charge of an investigation is not required to make speculative enquiries of other persons; there must be some reason to believe that they may have relevant material. That reason may come from information provided to the police by the accused or from other inquiries made or from some other source.

3.7 If, during a criminal investigation, the officer in charge of an investigation or disclosure officer for any reason no longer has responsibility for the functions falling to them, either their supervisor or the police officer in charge of criminal investigations for the police force concerned must assign someone else to assume that responsibility. That person's identity must be recorded, as with those initially responsible for these functions in each investigation.

2.5.6.1 **KEYNOTE**

General Responsibility of the Disclosure Officer

The disclosure officer creates the link between the investigation team and the prosecutor (CPS) and is therefore very important to the disclosure process. For investigations carried out by the police, generally speaking there is no restriction on who performs this role; however, they must be suitably trained and experienced. The role and responsibility of the disclosure officer are set out in the CPS Disclosure Manual, chapter 3:

- examine, inspect, view or listen to all relevant material that has been retained by the investigator and that does not form part of the prosecution case;
- create schedules that fully describe the material;
- identify all material which satisfies the disclosure test using the MG6E;
- submit the schedules and copies of disclosable material to the prosecutor;
- at the same time, supply to the prosecutor a copy of material falling into any of the categories described in para. 7.3 of the Code and copies of all documents required to be routinely revealed and which have not previously been revealed to the prosecutor;
- consult with and allow the prosecutor to inspect the retained material;
- review the schedules and the retained material continually, particularly after the defence statement has been received, identify to the prosecutor material that satisfies the disclosure test using the MG6E and supply a copy of any such material not already provided;
- schedule and reveal to the prosecutor any relevant additional unused material pursuant to the continuing duty of disclosure;
- certify that all retained material has been revealed to the prosecutor in accordance with the Code;
- where the prosecutor requests the disclosure officer to disclose any material to the accused, give the accused a copy of the material or allow the accused to inspect it.

As stated at the start of this keynote the disclosure officer has a responsibility to communicate effectively with the prosecutor ensuring that all the schedules are completed properly and all material is examined to satisfy themselves that there is no further material that should be brought to the attention of the prosecutor.

2.5.6.2

KEYNOTE

Reasonable Lines of Inquiry

An officer who is classed as an investigator must pursue all reasonable lines of inquiry (Code, para. 3.5) and having done so retain all material which is relevant to the case (**see para. 2.5.8.1**), whether or not it is helpful to the prosecution (Code, para. 5.1). Failure to do so could lead to a miscarriage of justice. In *R* v *Poole* [2003] EWCA Crim 1753, Y provided a statement to police in a murder case. It transpired that N had been with Y at the relevant time and this cast doubt over Y's evidence. The police did not follow up the inconsistencies. The Court of Appeal held that the failure to disclose N's evidence was a material irregularity which in part led to a successful appeal by the defendant. The investigator also has a responsibility to identify material that could be sensitive and bring this to the attention of the CPS. This need to be proactive was reinforced in *R* v *Joof* [2012] EWCA Crim 1475 where the court held that the responsibilities imposed by the Criminal Procedure and Investigations Act 1996 and the A-G's Guidelines could not be circumvented by not making inquiries.

An officer who believed that a person might have information which might undermine the prosecution case or assist the defence could not decline to make inquiries in order to avoid the need to disclose what might be said. Where material is identified steps must be taken to record and retain the material. For information recorded on computers, see 'Digital Guidance', chapter 30 of the CPS Disclosure Manual and Annex A to the A-G's Guidelines.

In *R* v *Khalime Shah* [2002] EWCA Crim 1623, the court observed that decisions as to whether or not to investigate are essentially matters for the police in accordance with the judgement of the investigating officer; the court will always be reluctant to intervene and suggest a line of inquiry that has not been conducted. 'We want to make it clear that it was never the intention, as we understand it, of these provisions in some way that the defence could obtain a piece of information and then by sending it to the prosecution place upon them a duty to investigate matters, in the hope that in some speculative way, it might produce further information that would assist the defence case.' It is suggested that the rationale not to follow a line of inquiry should be recorded.

2.5.6.3

KEYNOTE

Pre-charge Engagement with Suspects or their Legal Advisors

In some investigations it may be appropriate for the officer in charge of the investigation to seek engagement with the defence at the pre-charge stage. This is likely to be where it is possible that such engagement will lead to the defence volunteering additional information which may assist in identifying new lines of inquiry. Pre-charge engagement in these circumstances refers to voluntary engagement between the parties to an investigation after the first PACE interview, and before any suspect has been formally charged. Pre-charge engagement is a voluntary process and it may be terminated at any time. It does not refer to engagement between the parties to an investigation by way of further PACE interviews (A-G's Guidelines, paras 25, 26 and B3). Annex B of the A-G's Guideline sets out the process for any such pre-charge engagement.

Pre-charge engagement may take place whenever it is agreed between the parties that it may assist the investigation. The engagement should not, however, be considered a replacement to a further interview with a suspect. Investigators and prosecutors should be conscious that adverse inferences under s. 34 of the Criminal Justice and Public Order Act 1994 are not available at trial where a suspect failed to mention a fact when asked about a matter in pre-charge engagement.

This engagement may, among other things, involve:

a. Giving the suspect the opportunity to comment on any proposed further lines of inquiry.
b. Ascertaining whether the suspect can identify any other lines of inquiry.
c. Asking whether the suspect is aware of, or can provide access to, digital material that has a bearing on the allegation.
d. Discussing ways to overcome barriers to obtaining potential evidence, such as revealing encryption keys.
e. Agreeing any key word searches of digital material that the suspect would like carried out.
f. Obtaining a suspect's consent to access medical records.

g. The suspect identifying and providing contact details of any potential witnesses.
h. Clarifying whether any expert or forensic evidence is agreed and, if not, whether the suspect's representatives intend to instruct their own expert, including timescales for this.

Depending on the circumstances, it may be appropriate for an investigator, the prosecutor, the suspect's representative or an unrepresented suspect to initiate pre-charge engagement. Where a suspect is not yet represented, an investigator should take care to ensure that the suspect understands their right to legal advice before the pre-charge engagement process commences. Sufficient time should be given to enable a suspect to access this advice if they wish to do so.

When referring a case to a prosecutor, the investigator should inform the prosecutor if any pre-charge engagement has already taken place and should indicate if they believe pre-charge engagement would benefit the case. It should also be noted that the prosecutor may advise the investigator to initiate and carry out pre-charge engagement, or do so themselves (A-G's Guidelines, Appendix B).

2.5.6.4 **KEYNOTE**

Material that Undermines the Prosecution Case

Material that undermines the prosecution test will consist mainly of material which raises question marks over the strength of the prosecution case, the value of evidence given by witnesses and issues relating to identification. If officers feel that the material is not relevant to the prosecution case but may be useful to the defence in cross-examination, it may well come within the category of material which undermines the prosecution case. In *Tucker* v *CPS* [2008] EWCA Crim 3063, the prosecution did not reveal to the defence a record containing important information as to a possible motive for a witness lying about the defendant's involvement in the offence. This led to the conviction being overturned. It was clearly material that undermined the prosecution case as it raised questions over the value of the witness's evidence. By s. 3 of the CPIA 1996, the disclosure test will be satisfied where material might reasonably be considered capable of undermining the case for the prosecution against the accused, or of assisting the case for the accused and prosecutors should resolve any doubts in favour of disclosure (*Akle and Bond* v *The Crown* [2021] EWCA Crim 1879).

Disclosure of previous convictions and other matters that might affect the credibility of a witness may 'undermine the prosecution case' as it may limit the value of the witness's testimony. This factor may not be apparent at the time but may come to light after the initial disclosure, such as where it becomes known that the witness has a grudge against the defendant. This is one reason why the 1996 Act requires the decision as to whether material undermines the prosecution case to be continuously monitored throughout the case.

In *R (On the Application of Ebrahim)* v *Feltham Magistrates' Court* [2001] EWHC Admin 130, the court stated that the extent of the investigation should be proportionate to the seriousness of the matter being investigated. What is reasonable in a case may well depend on such factors as the staff and resources available, the seriousness of the case, the strength of evidence against the suspect and the nature of the line of inquiry to be pursued. If in doubt it is suggested that the CPS is contacted for guidance.

Paragraph 5.16 of the CPS Disclosure Manual makes important observations concerning negative results: when making inquiries, 'negative results can sometimes be as significant to an investigation as positive ones'. It is impossible to define precisely when a negative result may be significant, as every case is different. However, it will include the result of any inquiry that differs from what might be expected, given the prevailing circumstances. Not only must material or information which points towards a fact or an individual be retained, but also that which casts doubt on the suspect's guilt, or implicates another person. Examples of negative information include:

- a CCTV camera that did not record the crime/location/suspect in a manner which is consistent with the prosecution case (the fact that a CCTV camera did not function or have videotape loaded will not usually be considered relevant negative information);
- where a number of people present at a particular location at the particular time that an offence is alleged to have taken place state that they saw nothing unusual;
- where a finger-mark from a crime scene cannot be identified as belonging to a known suspect;
- any other failure to match a crime scene sample with one taken from the accused.

2.5.6.5

KEYNOTE

Complaints against Police Officers Involved in a Case

Not only might the credibility of witnesses undermine the prosecution case, but so too might complaints against officers involved in the case, together with any occasions where officers have not been believed in court in the past. In these cases, it will be necessary to decide whether this information should be disclosed to the defence and, if disclosed, in how much detail. This question is probably best answered by the following extract from advice given to prosecutors by the DPP:

> It is, of course, necessary in the first instance for the police to bring such matters to the notice of the prosecutor, but it is submitted that the prosecutor should have a greater element of discretion than with the disclosure of previous convictions. With convictions against prosecution witnesses, disclosure normally follows, whereas in relation to disciplinary findings regard should be had to the nature of the finding and its likely relevance to the matters in issue. Findings which involve some element of dishonesty should invariably be disclosed, while matters such as disobedience to orders, neglect of duty and discreditable conduct will often have no relevance to the officer's veracity or the guilt or otherwise of a defendant. Certainly, there should be no duty on the prosecution to disclose details of unsubstantiated complaints even though this is a popular type of inquiry from some defence representatives. The imposition of such a duty would only encourage the making of false complaints in the hope that they might be used to discredit an officer in the future.

Professional Standards Departments (PSDs) have final responsibility for the value judgement on whether information relating to misconduct of police officers should be revealed to the prosecutor. This decision must be made on a case-by-case basis; guidance may be sought from the prosecutor. Responsibility to reveal relevant misconduct findings, or criminal convictions or cautions, rests with the police officer concerned. The officer, assisted by the PSD, should ensure that there is a sufficient level of detail on the MG6B to enable the CPS to make an informed decision about disclosure of the information in the proceedings in question (CPS Disclosure Manual, chapter 18).

Some guidance is given by the courts. In *R* v *Edwards* [1991] 1 WLR 207, the court held that a disciplinary finding and reprimand of a DCI for countersigning interview notes which had been wrongly re-written in another case should have been disclosed to the defence. *R* v *Guney* [1998] 2 Cr App R 242 followed Edwards. In *Guney*, six police officers went to the defendant's home with a warrant to search for drugs. Three of the officers had formerly been members of a squad which had been subject to 'considerable internal police interest'. The court held that the defence were not entitled to be informed of every occasion when any officer had given evidence 'unsuccessfully' or whenever allegations were made against him/her. In this case, the information should have been disclosed. The court went on to say that the records available to the CPS should include transcripts of any decisions of the Court of Appeal Criminal Division where convictions were quashed because of the misconduct or lack of veracity of identified police officers as well as cases stopped by the trial judge or discontinued on the same basis. The systematic collection of such material was preferable to the existing haphazard arrangement.

If in doubt advice should be sought from the CPS.

2.5.6.6

KEYNOTE

Third Party Material

Third party material can be considered in two categories:

(a) that which is or has been in the possession of the police or which has been inspected by the police;
(b) all other material not falling under (a).

Material which falls into the first category is covered by the same rules of disclosure as any other material the police have. Where police do not have material that they believe may be relevant to the case, para. 3.6 of the Code provides direction.

In the vast majority of cases the third party will make the material available to the investigating officer. However, there may be occasions where the third party refuses to hand over the material and/or allow it to be examined.

If the OIC, the investigator or the disclosure officer believes that a third party holds material that may be relevant to the investigation, that person or body should be told of the investigation. They should be alerted to the need to preserve relevant material. Consideration should be given as to whether it is appropriate to seek access to the material and, if so, steps should be taken to obtain such material. It will be important to do so if the material or information is likely to undermine the prosecution case, or to assist a known defence. A letter should be sent to the third party together with the explanatory leaflet provided in the CPS Disclosure Manual at Annex B.

Where access to the material is declined or refused by the third party and it is believed that it is reasonable to seek production of the material before a suspect is charged, the investigator should consider making an application under sch. 1 to the Police and Criminal Evidence Act 1984 (special procedure material) (CPS Disclosure Manual, chapter 5).

Where the suspect has been charged and the third party refuses to produce the material, application will have to be made to the court for a witness summons. In the magistrates' court this is covered by s. 97 of the Magistrates' Courts Act 1980 and in the Crown Court it is covered by ss. 2(2) and 2A to 2D of the Criminal Procedure (Attendance of Witnesses) Act 1965. The third party may still wish to resist the requirement to produce the material and the point was considered in *R* v *Brushett* [2001] Crim LR 471 (this was a case that concerned Social Services Department files relating to a children's home). The court considered a number of earlier cases and established some central principles as follows:

- To be material evidence documents must be not only relevant to the issues arising in the criminal proceedings, but also documents admissible as such in evidence.
- Documents which are desired merely for the purpose of possible cross-examination are not admissible in evidence and, thus, are not material for the purposes of s. 97.
- Whoever seeks production of documents must satisfy the justices with some evidence that the documents are 'likely to be material' in the sense indicated, likelihood for this purpose involving a real possibility, although not necessarily a probability.
- It is not sufficient that the applicant merely wants to find out whether or not the third party has such material documents. This procedure must not be used as a disguised attempt to obtain discovery.
- Where social services documents are supplied to the prosecution, the prosecution should retain control of such material as part of the disclosure regime. That is envisaged by the rules. It cannot be acceptable to return material to social services to avoid the obligations arising under the rules. In any event, the obligation would arise in relation to the notes taken and retained.
- The obligation laid on the prosecution by statute and rules cannot be avoided by a third party making an agreement with the prosecution that the prosecution will abrogate any duties laid upon it by either common law or statute.
- If circumstances arise where it would be unjust not to allow disclosure of certain other material, so a defendant would not receive a fair trial in the sense that he/she could not establish his innocence where he/she might otherwise do so, then that material must be disclosed.
- The fact that the prosecution have knowledge of the third party material may be a relevant factor to allow the defence access.
- Material concerning false allegations in the past may be relevant material (*R* v *Bourimech* [2002] EWCA Crim 2089).
- If the disputed material might prove the defendant's innocence or avoid a miscarriage of justice, the weight came down resoundingly in favour of disclosing it (*R* v *Reading Justices, ex parte Berkshire County Council* (1996) 1 Cr App R 239).

In *R* v *Alibhai* [2004] EWCA Crim 681, the Court of Appeal held that under the Criminal Procedure and Investigations Act 1996 the prosecutor was only under a duty to disclose material in the hands of third parties if that material had come into the prosecutor's hands and the prosecutor was of the opinion that such material undermined the case. However, the A-G's Guidelines went further by requiring a prosecutor to take steps pursuing third party disclosure if there was a suspicion that documents would be detrimental to the prosecution or of assistance to the defence. However, in such circumstances, the prosecutor enjoyed a margin of consideration as to what steps were appropriate. The provisions for disclosure are not intended to create duties for third parties to follow. The disclosure duties under the 1996 Act were created in respect of material that the prosecution or the police had and which the prosecution had inspected. Material was not prosecution material unless it was held by the investigator or by the disclosure officer (*DPP* v *Wood and McGillicuddy* [2006] EWHC 32 (Admin)).

The A-G's Guidelines also deal with materials held by third parties (including government agencies) in paras 26–53.

The CPIA Code and A-G's Guidelines make clear the obligation on the investigator to pursue all reasonable lines of inquiry in relation to material held by third parties within the UK. Paragraphs 31–3 deal with cases where a government department or another Crown body has material that may be relevant to an issue in the case. Paragraphs 38–44 deal with other domestic bodies that have material or information which might be relevant to the case, such as a local authority, social services department, hospital, doctor, school, provider of forensic services or CCTV operator.

Crown servants have a duty to support the administration of justice and should take reasonable steps to identify and consider such material. If access is denied to relevant material, the investigator or prosecutor should consider the reasons given by the government department or Crown body and what, if any, further steps might be taken to obtain the material. The final decision on further steps rests with the prosecutor. However, other third parties have no obligation under the CPIA 1996 to reveal material to investigators or prosecutors. There is also no duty on the third party to retain material which may be relevant to the investigation and, in some circumstances, the third party may not be aware of the investigation or prosecution. If access to the material is refused and, despite the reasons given for refusal of access, it is still believed that it is reasonable to seek production of the material or information and that the requirements of a witness summons are satisfied (or any other relevant power), then the prosecutor or investigator should apply for the summons causing a representative of the third party to produce the material to court (A-G's Guidelines, paras 40 and 41).

The obligations under the CPIA Code to pursue all reasonable lines of inquiry apply to material held overseas. Where it appears that there is relevant material, the prosecutor must take reasonable steps to obtain it, either informally or making use of the powers contained in the Crime (International Co-operation) Act 2003 and any international conventions. There is no absolute duty on the prosecutor to disclose relevant material held overseas by entities not subject to the jurisdiction of the courts in England and Wales. However, consideration should be given to whether the type of material believed to be held can be provided to the defence (A-G's Guidelines, paras 45–53).

In all cases of material held by third parties, where appropriate the defence should be informed of the steps taken to obtain material and the results of the line of inquiry (A-G's Guidelines, paras 37, 44 and 53).

2.5.7 Disclosure Code of Practice—4 Recording of Information

4.1 If material which may be relevant to the investigation consists of information which is not recorded in any form, the officer in charge of an investigation must ensure that it is recorded in a durable or retrievable form.

4.2 Where it is not practicable to retain the initial record of information because it forms part of a larger record which is to be destroyed, its contents should be transferred as a true record to a durable and more easily-stored form before that happens.

4.3 Negative information is often relevant to an investigation. If it may be relevant it must be recorded. An example might be a number of people present in a particular place at a particular time who state that they saw nothing unusual.

4.4 Where information which may be relevant is obtained, it must be recorded at the time it is obtained or as soon as practicable after that time. This includes, for example, information obtained in house-to-house enquiries, although the requirement to record information promptly does not require an investigator to take a statement from a potential witness where it would not otherwise be taken.

2.5.7.1 **KEYNOTE**

Contemporaneous Records

The need for contemporaneous records is also required under the Police and Criminal Evidence Act 1984 and if not complied with could affect the admissibility of important evidence (s. 78 of the 1984 Act).

2.5.8

Disclosure Code of Practice—5 Retention of Material

(a) Duty to retain material

5.1 The investigator must retain material obtained in a criminal investigation which may be relevant to the investigation. Material may be photographed, video-recorded, captured digitally or otherwise retained in the form of a copy rather than the original at any time, if the original is perishable; the original was supplied to the investigator rather than generated by them and is to be returned to its owner; or the retention of a copy rather than the original is reasonable in all the circumstances.

5.2 Where material has been seized in the exercise of the powers of seizure conferred by the Police and Criminal Evidence Act 1984, the duty to retain it under this Code is subject to the provisions on the retention of seized material in section 22 of that Act.

5.3 If the officer in charge of an investigation becomes aware as a result of developments in the case that material previously examined but not retained (because it was not thought to be relevant) may now be relevant to the investigation, they should, wherever practicable, take steps to obtain it or ensure that it is retained for further inspection or for production in court if required.

5.4 The duty to retain material includes in particular the duty to retain material falling into the following categories:

- Records which are derived from tapes or recordings of telephone messages (for example, 999 calls) containing descriptions of an alleged offence or offender;
- Any incident logs relating to the allegation;
- Contemporaneous records of the incident, such as:
  - crime reports and crime report forms;
  - an investigation log;
  - any record or note made by an investigator (including police notebook entries and other handwritten notes) on which they later make a statement or which relates to contact with suspects, victims or witnesses;
  - an account of an incident or information relevant to an incident noted by an investigator in manuscript or electronically;
  - records of actions carried out by officers (such as house-to-house interviews, CCTV or forensic enquiries) noted by a police officer in manuscript or electronically;
  - CCTV footage, or other imagery, of the incident in action;
- The defendant's custody record or voluntary attendance record;
- Any previous accounts made by a complainant or any other witnesses;
- Interview records (written records, or audio or video tapes, of interviews with actual or potential witnesses or suspects);
- Any material casting doubt on the reliability of a witness e.g. relevant previous convictions and relevant cautions of any prosecution witnesses and any co accused;
- Final versions of witness statements (and draft versions where their content differs from the final version), including any exhibits mentioned (unless these have been returned to their owner on the understanding that they will be produced in court if required);
- Material relating to other suspects in the investigation;
- Communications between the police and experts such as forensic scientists, reports of work carried out by experts, and schedules of scientific material prepared by the expert for the investigator, for the purposes of criminal proceedings;
- Records of the first description of a suspect by each potential witness who purports to identify or describe the suspect, whether or not the description differs from that of subsequent descriptions by that or other witnesses.

5.5 The duty to retain material, where it may be relevant to the investigation, also includes in particular the duty to retain any material which may satisfy the test for prosecution disclosure in the Act, such as:

- information provided by an accused person which indicates an explanation for the offence with which they have been charged;
- any material casting doubt on the reliability of a confession;
- any material casting doubt on the reliability of a prosecution witness.

5.6 The duty to retain material falling into these categories does not extend to items which are purely ancillary to such material and possess no independent significance (for example, duplicate copies of records or reports).

(b) Length of time for which material is to be retained

5.7 All material which may be relevant to the investigation must be retained until a decision is taken whether to institute proceedings against a person for an offence.

5.8 If a criminal investigation results in proceedings being instituted, all material which may be relevant must be retained at least until the accused is acquitted or convicted or the prosecutor decides not to proceed with the case.

5.9 Where the accused is convicted, all material which may be relevant must be retained at least until:

- the convicted person is released from custody, or discharged from hospital, in cases where the court imposes a custodial sentence or a hospital order;
- six months from the date of conviction, in all other cases.

If the court imposes a custodial sentence or hospital order and the convicted person is released from custody or discharged from hospital earlier than six months from the date of conviction, all material which may be relevant must be retained at least until six months from the date of conviction.

5.10 If an appeal against conviction is in progress when the release or discharge occurs, or at the end of the period of six months specified in paragraph 5.9, all material which may be relevant must be retained until the appeal is determined. Similarly, if the Criminal Cases Review Commission is considering an application at that point in time, all material which may be relevant must be retained at least until the Commission decides not to refer the case to the Court.

2.5.8.1 **KEYNOTE**

Retention of Material

In order to disclose material to the defence, there is a need first to find it and secondly to retain it. Retention of material applies to documents and other evidence, including digital media. Failure to retain material could lead to the prosecution losing the case, particularly where the court considers that its absence will lead to the defendant not being able to receive a fair trial (Article 6 of the European Convention on Human Rights). In *Mouat* v *DPP* [2001] EWHC Admin 130, the defendant had been charged with speeding. Police officers had recorded a video of the defendant driving at speed and had shown the video to the defendant prior to charge but had later recorded over it. The defendant contended that he had been intimidated by the unmarked police car being driven only inches from his rear bumper. The policy of the force was to keep videos for 28 days, unless they recorded an offence, in which case they were kept for 12 months. The court held that the police were under a duty to retain the video tapes at least until the end of the suspended enforcement period, during which time the defendant was entitled to consider whether he wished to contest his liability in court.

In deciding what material should be retained in an investigation, consideration should be given to any force orders, what powers there are to seize and retain the said material, as well as the Disclosure Code and the A-G's Guidelines. Where an investigator discovers material that is relevant to the case, he/she must record that information or retain the material (Code, para. 5.1).

When deciding if the material should be retained the A-G's Guidelines provide that:

> The investigator should also exercise considerable caution in reaching that conclusion. The investigator should be particularly mindful of the fact that some investigations continue over some time. Material that is incapable of impact may change over time and it may not be possible to foresee what the issues in the case will be.
>
> (A-G's Guidelines, para. 23)

It is important to note that the material itself does not have to be admissible in court for it to undermine the prosecution case. This point was made in *R* v *Preston* [1994] 2 AC 130, where it was said that:

> In the first place, the fact that an item of information cannot be put in evidence by a party does not mean that it is worthless. Often, the train of inquiry which leads to the discovery of evidence which is admissible at a trial may include an item which is not admissible, and this may apply, although less frequently, to the defence as well as the prosecution.

If, during the lifetime of a case, the OIC becomes aware that material which has been examined during the course of an investigation, but not retained, becomes relevant as a result of new developments, para. 5.3 of the Code will apply. That officer should take steps to recover the material wherever practicable, or ensure that it is preserved by the person in possession of it (CPS Disclosure Manual, chapter 5).

In some of these cases the investigation may well have started some time before the defendant became a suspect. In such cases all the material from the investigation/operation would have to be reviewed to see if it is relevant to the defence case. In cases where there is a surveillance operation or observation point, it may be that the details of the observation point and the surveillance techniques would not be revealed but it would be necessary to retain material generating from it (**see para. 2.5.9.3**).

2.5.8.2 **KEYNOTE**

CCTV

The likelihood of an incident being caught on CCTV can be quite strong, which raises the question as to the responsibility of the police to investigate the possibility of there being a recording and retaining the recording tape. This point was considered in *R (On the Application of Ebrahim)* v *Feltham Magistrates' Court* [2001] EWHC Admin 130. These cases related to the obliteration of video evidence. In coming to its judgment, the court considered a number of previous decisions where the police were not required to retain CCTV evidence. The general question for the court was whether the prosecution had been under a duty to obtain or retain video evidence. If there was no such duty, the prosecution could not have abused the process of the court simply because the material was no longer available, i.e. it was a reasonable line of inquiry (as to whether they were under a duty to obtain the evidence, **see para. 2.5.6.2**). *Ebrahim* shows that CCTV footage does not necessarily have to be retained in all cases. *R* v *Dobson* [2001] EWCA Crim 1606 followed *Ebrahim*. Dobson had been convicted of arson with intent to endanger life, his defence being that he was elsewhere at the time. There had been a strong possibility that the route that Dobson claimed to have taken would have been covered by CCTV but it would have depended on which side of the road he had been using and which way the cameras were pointing at the time. Dobson's solicitors had not asked for the tapes to be preserved at interview and the police confirmed that the possibility of investigating the tapes had been overlooked. The tapes had been overwritten after 31 days. In following the principles set down in *Ebrahim*, the police, by their own admissions, had failed in their duty to obtain and retain the relevant footage. While there was plainly a degree of prejudice in Dobson being deprived of the opportunity of checking the footage in the hope that it supported his case, that prejudice was held not to have seriously prejudiced his case given the uncertainty of the likelihood that it would assist and the fact that Dobson had equally been in a position to appreciate the possible existence and significance of the tapes. The fact that there was no suggestion of malice or intentional omission by the police was also an important consideration for the court.

2.5.9 Disclosure Code of Practice—6 Preparation of Material for Prosecutor

(a) Schedules of unused material

6.1 The officer in charge of the investigation, the disclosure officer or an investigator may seek advice from the prosecutor about whether any particular item of material may be relevant to the investigation.

6.2 Material which may be relevant to an investigation and has been retained in accordance with this code, and which the disclosure officer believes will not form part of the prosecution case, must be listed on the appropriate schedule of unused material.

6.3 The disclosure officer must ensure that the appropriate schedule of unused material is prepared in the following circumstances:

- the accused is charged with an offence which is triable only on indictment;
- the accused is charged with an offence which is triable either way, and it is considered that the case is likely to be tried on indictment;
- the accused is charged with an either-way offence that is likely to remain in the magistrates' court, and it is considered that they are likely to plead not guilty;
- the accused is charged with a summary offence and it is considered that they are likely to plead not guilty.

6.4 Where, however, the accused is charged with a summary offence or an either-way offence, and it is considered that they are likely to plead guilty (e.g. because they have admitted the offence), a schedule is not required unless a not guilty plea is subsequently entered or indicated.

6.5 Irrespective of the anticipated plea, the Common Law test for disclosure requires material to be disclosed if there is material known to the disclosure officer that might assist the defence with the early preparation of their case or at a bail hearing (for example, a key prosecution witness has relevant previous convictions or a witness has withdrawn their statement). A note must be made on the case summary for the prosecutor of any such material, which must be revealed to the prosecutor who will review it and consider whether it is disclosable. Where there is no such material, a certificate to that effect must be completed.

6.6 Material in the following list (which where it exists will have been retained or recorded in accordance with paragraph 5.4) is likely to include information which meets the test for prosecution disclosure. This material must therefore, subject to the exception at 6.4 above, be scheduled and provided to the prosecutor. In reviewing this material, disclosure officers and prosecutors are to start with a presumption that it is likely to meet the disclosure test, although the material will need to be carefully considered and the disclosure test applied before a decision is made:

a) records which are derived from tapes or recordings of telephone messages (for example 999 calls) containing descriptions of an alleged offence or offender;
b) any incident logs relating to the allegation;
c) contemporaneous records of the incident, such as:
   - crime reports and crime report forms;
   - an investigation log;
   - any record or note made by an investigator (including police notebook entries and other handwritten notes) on which they later make a statement or which relates to contact with suspects, victims or witnesses;
   - an account of an incident or information relevant to an incident noted by an investigator in manuscript or electronically;
   - records of actions carried out by officers (such as house-to-house interviews, CCTV or forensic enquiries) noted by a police officer in manuscript or electronically;
   - CCTV footage, or other imagery, of the incident in action;
d) the defendant's custody record or voluntary attendance record;
e) any previous accounts made by a complainant or by any other witnesses;

f) interview records (written records, or audio or video tapes, of interviews with actual or potential witnesses or suspects);

g) any material casting doubt on the reliability of a witness e. g. relevant previous convictions and relevant cautions of any prosecution witnesses and any co-accused.

This material must be listed on the schedule by the disclosure officer in addition to all other material which may be relevant to an investigation; it is likely that some of this material will need to be redacted (see 6.12).

(b) Way in which material is to be listed on schedule

6.7 Material which the disclosure officer does not believe is sensitive must be listed on a schedule of non-sensitive material, which must include a statement that the disclosure officer does not believe the material is sensitive. Where there is sensitive unused material, see para 6.13 below.

6.8 The disclosure officer should ensure, subject to paras 6.10–6.11 below, that each item of material is listed separately on the schedule, and is numbered consecutively (which may include numbering by volume and sub-volume).

6.9 The description of each item should make clear the nature of the item and should contain sufficient detail to enable the prosecutor to decide whether they need to inspect the material before deciding whether or not it should be disclosed.

6.10 In some investigations it may be disproportionate to list each item of material separately. These may be listed in a block or blocks and described by quantity and generic title.

6.11 Even if some material is listed in a block, the disclosure officer must ensure that any items among that material which might satisfy the test for prosecution disclosure are listed and described individually.

(c) Redaction of sensitive material

6.12 The disclosure officer should redact any sensitive information contained in material that is likely to satisfy the test for prosecution disclosure. The disclosure officer should also redact any personal, confidential information in material that is to be disclosed. Such could include a person's date of birth, address, email address and phone number.

6.13 Any material which is believed to be sensitive must be listed on a schedule of sensitive material. If there is no sensitive material, the disclosure officer must record this fact on a schedule of sensitive material, or otherwise so indicate.

6.14 Subject to paragraph 6.15 below, the disclosure officer must list on a sensitive schedule any material the disclosure of which they believe would give rise to a real risk of serious prejudice to an important public interest, and the reason for that belief. The schedule must include a statement that the disclosure officer believes the material is sensitive. Depending on the circumstances, examples of such material may include the following among others:

- material relating to national security;
- material received from the intelligence and security agencies;
- material relating to intelligence from foreign sources which reveals sensitive intelligence gathering methods;
- material given in confidence;
- material relating to the identity or activities of informants, or undercover police officers, or witnesses, or other persons supplying information to the police who may be in danger if their identities are revealed;
- material revealing the location of any premises or other place used for police surveillance, or the identity of any person allowing a police officer to use them for surveillance;
- material revealing, either directly or indirectly, techniques and methods relied upon by a police officer in the course of a criminal investigation, for example covert surveillance techniques, or other methods of detecting crime;

- material whose disclosure might facilitate the commission of other offences or hinder the prevention and detection of crime;
- material upon the strength of which search warrants were obtained;
- material containing details of persons taking part in identification parades;
- material supplied to an investigator during a criminal investigation which has been generated by an official of a body concerned with the regulation or supervision of bodies corporate or of persons engaged in financial activities, or which has been generated by a person retained by such a body;
- material supplied to an investigator during a criminal investigation which relates to a child or young person and which has been generated by a local authority social services department, an Area Child Protection Committee or other party contacted by an investigator during the investigation;
- material relating to the private life of a witness.

6.15 In exceptional circumstances, where an investigator considers that material is so sensitive that its revelation to the prosecutor by means of an entry on the sensitive schedule is inappropriate, the existence of the material must be revealed to the prosecutor separately. This will apply only where compromising the material would be likely to lead directly to the loss of life, or directly threaten national security.

6.16 In such circumstances, the responsibility for informing the prosecutor lies with the investigator who knows the detail of the sensitive material. The investigator should act as soon as is reasonably practicable after the file containing the prosecution case is sent to the prosecutor. The investigator must also ensure that the prosecutor is able to inspect the material so that they can assess whether it is disclosable and, if so, whether it needs to be brought before a court for a ruling on disclosure.

2.5.9.1 **KEYNOTE**

Initial Disclosure

Under s. 3 of the 1996 Act, all previously undisclosed material that might undermine the prosecution case must be disclosed to the defence. If there is no such material, then the accused must be given a written statement to that effect. This applies to all material in possession of the police or that has been inspected under the provisions of the Disclosure Code of Practice. This therefore requires the disclosure officer to know what material exists and what material has already been made available to the defence. The court in *Grant* [2015] EWCA Crim 1815 stated that there is corporate knowledge implied by the possession of the relevant information that falls to be disclosed by any arm of the prosecution; the courts will expect the disclosure officer to be aware of any material held or inspected by other officers in the case.

In magistrates' courts there is now a streamlined procedure in summary cases that are expected to end in a guilty plea, so that a schedule of unused material need not be served in such cases, but that the prosecution should perform its obligations at common law (as set out in *R* v *DPP, ex parte Lee*, see para. 2.5.10.2) and provide written confirmation that it has been done.

The prosecution only have to disclose material relevant to the prosecution in question. For instance, surveillance logs concerning another matter would not need to be disclosed (*R* v *Dennis* (2000) 13 April, unreported).

In deciding whether material satisfies the disclosure test, consideration should include:

a. The use that might be made of it in cross-examination;
b. Its capacity to support submissions that could lead to:
    i. The exclusion of evidence;
    ii. A stay of proceedings, where the material is required to allow a proper application to be made;
    iii. A court or tribunal finding that any public authority had acted incompatibly with the accused's rights under the European Convention of Human Rights;
c. Its capacity to suggest an explanation or partial explanation of the accused's actions;
d. Its capacity to undermine the reliability or credibility of a prosecution witness;
e. The capacity of the material to have a bearing on scientific or medical evidence in the case.

Material should not be viewed in isolation as, whilst items taken alone may not be reasonably considered capable of undermining the prosecution case or assisting the case for the accused, several items together can have that effect.

(A-G's Guidelines, paras 84 and 86)

It is up to the prosecutor to decide on the format in which material is disclosed to the accused. If material is to be copied, s. 3(3) of the 1996 Act leaves open the question of whether this should be done by the prosecutor or by the police. The prosecutor must also provide the defence with a schedule of all non-sensitive material (s. 4(2) of the 1996 Act). This includes all other information in police possession, or material that has been examined by the police other than 'sensitive material' (this is disclosed to the prosecutor separately). 'Sensitive material' is material which it is not in the public interest to disclose. At this stage, the defence are not entitled to inspect items on the schedule that have not been disclosed (s. 3(6) and (7)).

Material must not be disclosed to the extent that the court concludes that it is not in the public interest to disclose it and orders accordingly or it is material whose disclosure is prohibited by s. 17 of the Regulation of Investigatory Powers Act 2000 unless it falls within the exception provided by s. 18 of the Act.

2.5.9.2 **KEYNOTE**

Completing the Schedules

It is important that the schedules themselves are completed fully. Guidance is given by paras 6.8 to 6.11 of the Code and in detail in the CPS Disclosure Manual, chapters 6 to 8. Where appropriate, use should be made of the block listing provisions in para. 6.10 of the Code. It may not be practicable to list each item of material separately. If so, these may be listed in a block and described by quantity and generic title (A-G's Guidelines, para. A50). The disclosure officer should keep a copy of the schedules sent to the prosecutor, in case there are any queries that need to be resolved and to assist in keeping track of the items listed should the schedules need to be updated (CPS Disclosure Manual, chapter 6).

The following items should also be considered when deciding on initial disclosure in cases where the disclosure is in the public interest (that is where they are not 'sensitive material'):

- records of previous convictions and cautions for prosecution witnesses;
- any other information which casts doubt on the reliability of a prosecution witness or on the accuracy of any prosecution evidence;
- any motives for the making of false allegations by a prosecution witness;
- any material which may have a bearing on the admissibility of any prosecution evidence;
- the fact that a witness has sought, been offered or received a reward;
- any material that might go to the credibility of a prosecution witness;
- any information which may cast doubt on the reliability of a confession. Any item which relates to the accused's mental or physical health, his intellectual capacity, or to any ill-treatment which the accused may have suffered when in the investigator's custody is likely to have the potential for casting doubt on the reliability of a purported confession;
- information that a person other than the accused was or might have been responsible or which points to another person whether charged or not (including a co-accused) having involvement in the commission of the offence (CPS Disclosure Manual, chapter 10).

The disclosure officer should be mindful of the need to demonstrate that he/she has taken all reasonable steps should it transpire that full disclosure had not been made.

The prosecutor is required to advise the disclosure officer of any items on the MG6C that should properly be on the MG6D and vice versa; any apparent omissions or amendments required; insufficient or unclear descriptions of items or where there is a failure to provide schedules at all. In circumstances where the schedules are inadequate, the prosecutor will return them with a target date for resubmission. The disclosure officer must take all necessary remedial action and provide properly completed schedules to the prosecutor. Failure to do so may result in the matter being raised with a senior officer. There may be occasions where schedules need to be edited; the Codes place responsibility for keeping them accurate and up to date on the disclosure officer. The disclosure officer must provide different certifications in the course of the disclosure process, to cover:

- revelation of all relevant retained material;
- whether material satisfies the disclosure test; and
- whether material satisfies the disclosure test following a defence statement as part of the continuing duty.

The case against each accused must be considered and certified separately (CPS Disclosure Manual, chapter 10).

2.5.9.3 **KEYNOTE**

Sensitive Material

This is material which the disclosure officer believes it is not in the public interest to disclose. While the general principle that governs the 1996 Act and Article 6 of the European Convention is that material should not be withheld from the defence, sensitive material is an exception to this. In *Van Mechelen* v *Netherlands* (1998) 25 EHRR 647, the court stated that in some cases it may be necessary to withhold certain evidence from the defence so as to preserve the fundamental rights of another individual or to safeguard an important public interest. However, only such measures restricting the rights of the defence which are strictly necessary are permissible under Article 6. It should be noted that the court did recognise that the entitlement of disclosure of relevant evidence was not an absolute right but could only be restricted as was strictly necessary. In *R* v *Keane* [1994] 1 WLR 746, Lord Taylor CJ stated that 'the judge should carry out a balancing exercise, having regard both to the weight of the public interest in non-disclosure and to the importance of the documents to the issues of interest, present and potential, to the defence, and if the disputed material might prove a defendant's innocence or avoid a miscarriage of justice, the balance came down resoundingly in favour of disclosure'.

Decisions as to what should be withheld from the defence are a matter for the court and, where necessary, an application to withhold the material must be made to the court (*R* v *Ward* [1993] 1 WLR 619). The application of public interest immunity was considered by the House of Lords in *R* v *H* [2004] UKHL 3. In this case, the defendants were charged with conspiracy to supply a Class A drug following a covert police investigation, and sought disclosure of material held by the prosecution relating to the investigation. The prosecution resisted the disclosure on grounds of public interest immunity. The court held that if the material did not weaken the prosecution case or strengthen the defence, there would be no requirement to disclose it. Once material is considered to be sensitive then it should be disclosed only if the public interest application fails (unless abandoning the case is considered more appropriate); before such action is taken there must be consultation between the CPS (Unit Head or above) and police (ACC or above). Such material is not as wide as it seems; for instance it does not mean evidence which might harm the prosecution case. This category is limited and the Code of Practice, at para. 6.12, gives a number of examples of such material. It will be for the disclosure officer to decide what material, if any, falls into this category; guidance is provided in chapters 13 and 34 of the CPS Disclosure Manual.

Paragraph 6.14 of the Code provides examples of sensitive material. Many of these items are included within the common law principles of public interest immunity. The case law in this area will still apply to decisions regarding the disclosure of such material. These groups are not exclusive and the areas most likely to apply will be those concerning the protection of intelligence and intelligence methods. In any consideration as to what should be withheld, the provisions of part II of the Regulation of Investigatory Powers Act 2000 should be referred to. Part II of the Act will make provision, not only for the gathering and recording of intelligence, but also disclosure of any material gained and methods used. Claims to withhold material may be made by parties other than the prosecutor (who would do so on behalf of the police). In some cases, the relevant minister or the Attorney-General may intervene to claim immunity. Alternatively, the claim to immunity may be made by the party seeking to withhold the evidence, either on its own initiative or at the request of the relevant government department.

Guidance is also provided in para. 115 of the A-G's Guidelines: even where an application is made to the court to withhold material a prosecutor should aim to disclose as much of the material as he/she properly can (by giving the defence redacted or edited copies of summaries).

In deciding whether material attracts public interest immunity the court will have to be satisfied that the material in no way helps the defence or undermines the prosecution case. Where the material related to secret or confidential systems it should not be revealed as this would aid serious criminal enterprise in the future (*R* v *Templar* [2003] EWCA Crim 3186).

Where police consider that material should not be disclosed due to its sensitive nature, the CPS Disclosure Manual, chapter 10 should be followed. This states that in order to assist the prosecutor to decide how to deal with sensitive material which the investigator believes may meet the disclosure test, he/she should provide detailed information dealing with the following issues:

- the reasons why the material is said to be sensitive;
- the degree of sensitivity said to attach to the material, i.e. why it is considered that disclosure will create a real risk of serious prejudice to an important public interest;
- the consequences of revealing to the defence:
  - the material itself,
  - the category of the material,
  - the fact that an application is being made;
- the apparent significance of the material to the issues in the trial;
- the involvement of any third parties in bringing the material to the attention of the police;
- where the material is likely to be the subject of an order for disclosure, what police views are regarding continuance of the prosecution;
- whether it is possible to disclose the material without compromising its sensitivity.

In applications for public interest immunity, the CPS has an obligation to ensure that all such material is in its possession and the police have a duty to pass the material on (*R* v *Menga and Marshalleck* [1998] Crim LR 58).

Care must be taken to safeguard material that is sensitive and keep it separate from other material because if the material subject to a public interest immunity order for non-disclosure is inadvertently disclosed by the prosecution to lawyers for the defendants, those lawyers cannot be ordered not to further disseminate that material to any third party, including their own clients (*R* v *G* [2004] EWCA Crim 1368).

The investigator also has a responsibility to identify material that could be sensitive and bring this to the attention of the CPS. Where material is identified steps must be taken to record and retain the material. For information recorded on computers, see 'Digital guidance', chapter 30 of the CPS Disclosure Manual and Annex A to the A-G's Guidelines.

2.5.9.4 **KEYNOTE**

Informants

The courts recognise the need to protect the identity of informants to ensure that the supply of information about criminal activities does not dry up and to ensure the informants' own safety. However, there may be occasions where if the case is to continue the identity of an informant will have to be disclosed.

This is particularly so where there is a suggestion that an informant has participated in the events constituting, surrounding or following the crime; the judge must consider whether this role so impinges on an issue of interest to the defence, present or potential, as to make disclosure necessary (*R* v *Turner* [1995] 1 WLR 264).

The need to disclose details of informants has been considered by the Court of Appeal in two cases. The first case, *R* v *Denton* [2002] EWCA Crim 272, concerned a defendant who was a police informer. The defendant was charged with murder and alleged that he had been told by his police handlers not to tell his lawyers about his status. The court held that there was no duty for the Crown to disclose to the defence, or to seek a ruling from the judge, as to any information regarding an accused being a police informer. On any common sense view, the material had already been disclosed to the defendant, and the Crown had no duty to supply the defendant with information with which he was already familiar. This last point may also be relevant to other situations. The second case, *R* v *Dervish* [2001] EWCA Crim 2789, concerned an undercover operation that was commenced after an informant gave information. The court held in this case that the public interest in protecting the identification of an informant had to be balanced against the right of the defendant to a fair trial; if there was material that might assist the defence, the necessity for the defendant to have a fair trial would outweigh the other interests in the case and the material would have to be disclosed or the prosecution discontinued. There had been no such material in this case. In *R* v *Edwards (formerly Steadman)* [2012] EWCA Crim 5, a murder case, the prosecution failed to disclose the fact that they were seeking one of the witness's registration as an informant, and that this witness was willing to give information if he did not receive any additional custodial sentence in respect of the offences with which he had been charged. The court stated that these were factors which should have been made available to the jury in deciding the credibility of the witness. However, in the circumstances of the case, even with full and proper disclosure, the task of assessing this witness's reliability would have changed neither the landscape of the trial nor the jury's deliberations upon the evidence. The circumstantial case was compelling, and the verdict was safe.

Where an informant who has participated in the crime is called to give evidence at the trial there would have to be very strong reasons for this fact not to be disclosed (*R* v *Patel* [2001] EWCA Crim 2505).

There are strong links between the principles of informants and undercover police officers. In *R* v *Barkshire* [2011] EWCA Crim 1885, the Court of Appeal, upholding the appeal, held that recordings and the statement of an undercover police officer contained information which assisted the defence. They showed that the undercover officer had been involved in activities which went much further than the authorisation that he had been given. They appeared to show him as an enthusiastic supporter of criminal activity, arguably, as an agent provocateur. Further, the recordings supported the defendant's contentions that their intended activities were directed to the saving of life and avoidance of injury, and that they proposed to conduct the occupation in a careful and proportionate manner. This material was pertinent to a potential submission of abuse of process by way of entrapment and in any event had the capacity to support B's defence.

2.5.9.5 **KEYNOTE**

Observation Points and the *Johnson* Ruling

R v *Rankine* [1986] 2 WLR 1075, considering previous cases, stated that it was the rule that police officers should not be required to disclose sources of their information, whether those sources were paid informers or public-spirited citizens, subject to a discretion to admit to avoid a miscarriage of justice and that observation posts were included in this rule.

In *R* v *Johnson* [1988] 1 WLR 1377, the appellant was convicted of supplying drugs. The only evidence against him was given by police officers, who testified that, while stationed in private premises in a known drug-dealing locality, they had observed him selling drugs. The defence applied to cross-examine the officers on the exact location of the observation posts, in order to test what they could see, having regard to the layout of the street and the objects in it. In the jury's absence, the prosecution called evidence as to the difficulty of obtaining assistance from the public, and the desire of the occupiers, who were also occupiers at the time of the offence, that their names and addresses should not be disclosed because they feared for their safety.

The judge ruled that the exact location of the premises need not be revealed. The appeal was dismissed; although the conduct of the defence was to some extent affected by the restraints placed on it, this led to no injustice. The jury were well aware of the restraints, and were most carefully directed about the very special care they had to give to any disadvantage they may have brought to the defence. *Johnson* was applied and approved in *R* v *Hewitt* (1992) 95 Cr App R 81 (see also *R* v *Grimes* [1994] Crim LR 213).

In *Johnson*, Watkins LJ at pp. 1385–6 gave the following guidance as to the minimum evidential requirements needed if disclosure is to be protected:

a) The police officer in charge of the observations to be conducted, no one of lower rank than a sergeant should usually be acceptable for this purpose, must be able to testify that beforehand he visited all observation places to be used and ascertained the attitude of occupiers of premises, not only to the use to be made of them, but to the possible disclosure thereafter of the use made and facts which could lead to the identification of the premises thereafter and of the occupiers. He may of course in addition inform the court of difficulties, if any, usually encountered in the particular locality of obtaining assistance from the public.

b) A police officer of no lower rank than a chief inspector must be able to testify that immediately prior to the trial he visited the places used for observations, the results of which it is proposed to give in evidence, and ascertained whether the occupiers are the same as when the observations took place and whether they are or are not, what the attitude of those occupiers is to the possible disclosure of the use previously made of the premises and of facts which could lead at the trial to identification of premises and occupiers.

Such evidence will of course be given in the absence of the jury when the application to exclude the material evidence is made. The judge should explain to the jury, as this judge did, when summing up or at some appropriate time before that, the effect of his ruling to exclude, if he so rules.

The guidelines in *Johnson* do not require a threat of violence before protection can be afforded to the occupier of an observation post; it suffices that the occupier is in fear of harassment (*Blake* v *DPP* (1993) 97 Cr App R 169).

This extended the rules established in *R* v *Rankine* [1986] QB 861 and is based on the protection of the owner or occupier of the premises, and not on the identity of the observation post. Thus, where officers have witnessed the commission of an offence as part of a surveillance operation conducted from an unmarked police vehicle, information relating to the surveillance and the colour, make and model of the vehicle should not be withheld (*R* v *Brown and Daley* (1988) 87 Cr App R 52).

2.5.10 Disclosure Code of Practice—7 Revelation of Material to Prosecutor

7.1 Where cases have been charged on the Full Code Test and it is anticipated that the defendant will plead not guilty, the disclosure officer should provide the schedules concerning unused material to the prosecutor at the point of charge (for police charged cases) or prior to charge (for CPS charged cases).

7.2 In all other cases the disclosure officer must provide the schedules as soon as possible after a not guilty plea has been either indicated or entered.

7.3 The disclosure officer should draw the attention of the prosecutor to any material an investigator has retained (including material to which paragraph 6.15 applies) which it is considered may satisfy the test for prosecution disclosure in the Act, explaining the reasons for coming to that view.

7.4 The disclosure officer must give the prosecutor a copy of any such material (unless it has already been supplied as part of the file containing the material for the prosecution case), together with any material which falls into the following categories:
- information provided by an accused person which indicates an explanation for the offence with which they have been charged;
- any material casting doubt on the reliability of a confession;
- any material casting doubt on the reliability of a prosecution witness

7.5 The disclosure officer must give the prosecutor a copy of any material which has been scheduled in accordance with paragraph 6.6, indicating whether it is, or is not, considered to satisfy the test for prosecution disclosure, and in either case explaining the reasons for coming to that view.

7.6 The disclosure officer must comply with a request from the prosecutor to be allowed to inspect material which has not already been copied to them. If the prosecutor asks to be provided with a copy of such material it should be provided, except where (having consulted the officer in charge of the investigation) the disclosure officer believes that the material is too sensitive to be copied and can only be inspected.

7.7 If material consists of information which is recorded other than in writing, whether it should be given to the prosecutor in its original form as a whole, or by way of relevant extracts recorded in the same form, or in the form of a transcript, is a matter for agreement between the disclosure officer and the prosecutor.

2.5.10.1 **KEYNOTE**

What Satisfies the Test for Prosecution Disclosure

Paragraphs 7.3 to 7.4 of the Code create a catch-all provision and presumably require the disclosure officer to make inquiries of the other investigating officers who have been involved in the case to ensure that all material is included.

However, what needs to be disclosed should be balanced by the A-G's Guidelines:

> A fair trial does not require consideration of irrelevant material. It does not require irrelevant material to be obtained or reviewed. It should not involve spurious applications or arguments which aim to divert the trial process from examining the real issues before the court.
>
> The statutory disclosure regime does not require the prosecutor to make available to the accused either neutral material or material which is adverse to the accused.... [P]rosecutors should not disclose material which they are not required to, as this would overburden the participants in the trial process, divert attention away from the relevant issues and may lead to unjustifiable delays. Disclosure should be completed in a thinking manner, in light of the issues in the case, and not simply as a schedule completing exercise.
>
> Defence statements are an integral part of the statutory disclosure regime. A defence statement should help to focus the attention of the prosecutor, court and co-defendants on the relevant issues in order to identify material which may meet the test for disclosure.
>
> (A-G's Guidelines, paras 3, 4 and 121)

There will occasionally be cases where the police investigation has been intelligence-led; there may be a deputy disclosure officer appointed just to deal with intelligence material which, by its very nature, is likely to be sensitive (**see para. 2.5.9.3**). Where there are a number of disclosure officers assigned to a case, there should be a lead disclosure officer who is the focus for inquiries and whose responsibility it is to ensure that the investigator's disclosure obligations are complied with. Where appropriate, regular case conferences and other meetings should be held to ensure prosecutors are apprised of all relevant developments in investigations. Full records should be kept of such meetings (A-G's Guidelines, para. 10).

It should be noted that where material is available to police from a particular source, e.g. local authority records, a decision that some of the material is relevant does not mean that it all has to be disclosed. This point was reinforced by the case of *R* v *Abbott* [2003] EWCA Crim 350, where the Court of Appeal held that the defendant was not entitled to blanket disclosure of all the files.

2.5.10.2 **KEYNOTE**

Time Period for Initial Disclosure

While there are provisions to set specific time periods by which initial disclosure must be met, none currently exist. Until such time, disclosure at this stage must be made as soon as practicable after the duty arises.

In *R* v *Bourimech* [2002] EWCA Crim 2089, the defendant sought disclosure following the service of his defence statement of a previous crime report made by the victim. One day before the trial was scheduled to begin, the crime report relating to that incident was served among other papers on the defence. This report escaped the notice of the defence until the final day of the trial. The court held that the defect in disclosure amounted to unfairness in the proceedings and the court could not be confident that if the victim had been cross-examined in relation to the previous allegation the jury might not have found the witness to be credible.

In most jury trial cases, prosecution disclosure can wait until after committal without jeopardising the defendant's right to a fair trial. However, in all cases the prosecutor must always be alive to the need to make disclosure of material that should be disclosed at an earlier stage (*R* v *DPP, ex parte Lee* [1999] 1 WLR 1950). Examples include:

- previous convictions of a complainant or a deceased if that information could reasonably be expected to assist the defence when applying for bail;
- material that might enable a defendant to make an application to stay the proceedings as an abuse of process;
- material that might enable a defendant to submit that he/she should only be sent for trial on a lesser charge, or perhaps that he/she should not be sent for trial at all;

- depending on what the defendant chooses to reveal about his/her case at this early stage, material that would enable the defendant and his/her legal advisers to make preparations for trial that would be significantly less effective if disclosure were delayed; for example, names of eye-witnesses whom the prosecution did not intend to use.

It should be noted that any disclosure by the prosecution prior to the application hearing would not normally exceed that required by s. 3 of the 1996 Act.

2.5.11 Disclosure Code of Practice—8 Subsequent Action by Disclosure Officer

8.1 At the time when a schedule of non-sensitive material is prepared, the disclosure officer may not know exactly what material will form the case against the accused. In addition, the prosecutor may not have given advice about the likely relevance of particular items of material. Once these matters have been determined, the disclosure officer must give the prosecutor, where necessary, an amended schedule listing any additional material:

- which may be relevant to the investigation,
- which does not form part of the case against the accused,
- which is not already listed on the schedule, and
- which they believe is not sensitive,

unless they are informed in writing by the prosecutor that the prosecutor intends to disclose the material to the defence.

8.2 Section 7A of the Act imposes a continuing duty on the prosecutor, for the duration of criminal proceedings against the accused, to disclose material which satisfies the test for disclosure (subject to public interest considerations). To enable this to be done, any new material coming to light should be treated in the same way as the earlier material.

8.3 In particular, after a defence statement has been given, or details of the issues in dispute have been recorded on the Preparation for Effective Trial form or the Plea and Trial Preparation Hearing form, the disclosure officer must look again at the material which has been retained and must draw the attention of the prosecutor to any material which might reasonably be considered capable of undermining the case for the prosecution against the accused or of assisting the case for the accused; and must reveal it to them in accordance with paragraphs 7.4 and 7.5 above.

2.5.11.1 **KEYNOTE**

Disclosure by the Defence

The duty on the defence to make disclosure only arises after the prosecution has made the initial disclosure (s. 5(1) of the 1996 Act). This duty falls into two categories: compulsory and voluntary. The disclosure required by the defence is limited to material that they intend to use at trial.

The defence statement should set out the nature of the defendant's defence, including any particular defences on which he/she intends to rely and particulars of the matters of fact on which the defendant intends to rely; this means the defence will need to disclose a factual narrative of their case. In addition, those issues, relevant to the case, which the accused disputes with the prosecution must be set out with reasons. The defence statement must indicate any point of law (including any point as to the admissibility of evidence or an abuse of process) which the defendant wishes to raise, and any authority on which he/she intends to rely for that purpose (s. 6A of the 1996 Act). This requirement to give reasons is intended to stop the defence going on a 'fishing expedition' to speculatively look at material in order to find some kind of defence.

Where the defence case involves an alibi, the statement must give details of the alibi, including the name and address of any alibi witness. In cases where there are co-accused, there is no duty to disclose this information to the other defendants, although this could be done voluntarily.

An alibi for the purposes of the defence statement is defined as evidence tending to show that by reason of the presence of the accused at a particular place or in a particular area at a particular time, he/she was not, or was unlikely to have been, at the place where the offence is alleged to have been committed at the time of its alleged commission. Where this applies, the defence must provide details including the name, address and date of birth of any witness the accused believes is able to give evidence in support of the alibi, or as many of those details as are known to the accused when the statement is given. Where such details are not known, the statement must include any information in the accused's possession which might be of material assistance in identifying or finding any such witness (s. 6A(2) of the 1996 Act).

The defence must also give to the court and the prosecutor notice of any other witnesses other than the defendant who will be called to give evidence. If any other witness is to be called then the name, address and date of birth of each such proposed witness, or as many of those details as are known to the accused must be provided. If any of this information is not available the defence must provide any information in their possession which might be of material assistance in identifying or finding any such proposed witness (s. 6C of the 1996 Act), see para. 2.5.11.7.

There may be occasions where the defence statement is allowed to be used in cross-examination when it is alleged that the defendant has changed his/her defence or in re-examination to rebut a suggestion of recent invention (*R* v *Lowe* [2003] EWCA Crim 3182).

2.5.11.2 **KEYNOTE**

Compulsory Disclosure by Defence (s. 5)

In proceedings before the Crown Court, where the prosecutor has provided initial disclosure, or purported to, the accused must serve a defence statement on the prosecutor and the court. The accused must also provide details of any witnesses he/she intends to call at the trial. Where there are other accused in the proceedings and the court so orders, the accused must also give a defence statement to each of the other accused specified by the court, and a request for a copy of the defence statement may be made by any co-accused.

Once a defence statement has been provided (whether compulsorily or voluntarily), the prosecution must disclose any prosecution material that:

- might be reasonably expected to assist the accused's defence; and
- has not already been disclosed.

It will be a question of fact whether material in police possession might be reasonably expected to assist the defence case. If the court feels that material that was not disclosed would to any reasonable person have been expected to help the defence case, the case may fail.

The defence statement is likely to point the prosecution to other lines of inquiry. The disclosure officer should share the information with any deputy disclosure officer and the officer in charge of the investigation. Further investigation in these circumstances should be considered and reasonable lines of inquiry followed (CPS Disclosure Manual, chapter 15).

If there is no additional material to be disclosed then the prosecutor must give a written statement to this effect. It is not the responsibility of the prosecutor or the police to examine material held by third parties which the defence have stated they wish to examine (the defence can request this from the third party or apply for a witness summons). However, there may be occasions where matters disclosed in the defence statement lead investigators to look at material held by third parties as it might impact on the prosecution case. This stage of the disclosure process may require further inquiries prompted by the defence statement. The result of those inquiries may then have to be disclosed because it either undermines the prosecution case or it assists the accused's defence.

2.5.11.3

KEYNOTE

Voluntary Disclosure by Accused (s. 6)

In the magistrates' court, the accused is not obliged to serve a defence statement but may choose to do so, in which case the statutory provisions apply. However, it is a mandatory requirement for the accused to provide details of their witnesses. The purpose of s. 6 of the 1996 Act is to allow the defence, in cases where the case is being tried summarily as a not guilty plea, to obtain further disclosure from the prosecution after the initial disclosure. This is only likely to happen where:

- the defence are not satisfied with the material disclosed at the initial disclosure stage or where they wish to examine items listed in the schedule of non-sensitive material;
- the defence wish to show the strength of their case in order to persuade the prosecution not to proceed.

If the defence decide to make a defence statement they must comply with the same conditions imposed on compulsory defence disclosure.

2.5.11.4

KEYNOTE

Time Period for the Defence Statement

Once the prosecution provides the initial disclosure, the defence have 14 days in respect of summary proceedings, or 28 days in respect of Crown Court proceedings within which the accused in criminal proceedings must give: a compulsory defence statement under s. 5 of the Act; a voluntary defence statement under s. 6 of the Act; or a notice of his/her intention to call any person, other than him/herself, as a witness at trial under s. 6C of the Act (Alibi witness). The court can only grant an extension if satisfied that the accused could not reasonably have given a defence statement or given notification within the relevant period. There is no limit on the number of days by which the relevant period may be extended or the number of applications for extensions that may be made (Criminal Procedure and Investigations Act 1996 (Defence Disclosure Time Limits) Regulations 2011 (SI 2011/209)).

2.5.11.5

KEYNOTE

Effect of Failure in Defence Disclosure

If the defence fail to give a defence statement under s. 5 or, where a defence statement is provided, they:

- are outside the time limits;
- set out inconsistent defences in a defence statement or at trial put forward a different defence; or
- at trial adduce evidence in support of an alibi without having given particulars of the alibi in a defence statement, or call a witness in support of an alibi without providing details of the witness or information that might help trace the witness;

then the following sanctions may apply:

- the court or, with the leave of the court, any other party may make such comment as appears appropriate;
- the court or jury may draw such inferences as appear proper in deciding whether the accused is guilty of the offence concerned (but there must also be other evidence to convict the defendant);
- even if the defence serve the defence statement outside the time limits, the prosecution must still consider the impact of the statement in terms of the need for any further disclosure (*Murphy* v *DPP* [2006] EWHC 1753 (Admin)).

2.5.11.6

KEYNOTE

Continuing Duty of Prosecutor to Disclose (s. 7A)

Section 7A places a continuing duty on the prosecutor at any time between the initial disclosure and the accused being acquitted or convicted or the prosecutor deciding not to proceed with the case concerned, to keep under review the question of further disclosure. In considering the need for further disclosure, the prosecutor must consider whether material might reasonably be considered capable of undermining the case for the prosecution against the accused or of assisting the case for the accused. If there is any such material, it must be disclosed to the accused as soon as is reasonably practicable. Consideration of what might need to be disclosed could change depending on the state of affairs at that time (including the case for the prosecution as it then stands) and so should be reviewed on a continuing basis (s. 7A(4)).

In *R* v *Tyrell* [2004] EWCA Crim 3279 this responsibility was clearly outlined. The court held that there was an obligation to consider whether there was any material in the hands of the prosecution which might undermine the case against the applicants or might reasonably be expected to assist the disclosed defences. In addition, the Crown had to consider whether there was any material which might be relevant to an issue which might feature in the trial; this clearly required a continuing duty. In this case, the court found that disclosure had been considered many times as the case progressed in relation to a variety of issues as they arose and ensured a fair trial.

Material must not be disclosed to the extent that the court concludes that it is not in the public interest to disclose it and orders accordingly or it is material whose disclosure is prohibited by s. 17 of the Regulation of Investigatory Powers Act 2000.

There is a duty on the prosecution to continue to review the disclosure of prosecution material right up until the case is completed (acquittal, conviction or discontinuance of the case).

In *R (Nunn)* v *CC of Suffolk Police* [2015] AC 225, the court stated that there can be no doubt that if the police or prosecution come into possession, after the appellate process is exhausted, of something new which might afford arguable grounds for contending that the conviction was unsafe, it is their duty to disclose it to the convicted defendant. Simple examples might include a new (and credible) confession by someone else, or the discovery, incidentally to a different investigation, of a pattern, or of evidence, which throws doubt on the original conviction. Sometimes such material may appear unexpectedly and adventitiously; in other cases it may be the result of a re-opening by the police of the inquiry. In either case, the new material is likely to be unknown to the convicted defendant unless disclosed to him. In all such cases, there is a clear obligation to disclose it (para. 138 of the A-G's Guidelines). The court also considered the A-G's Guidelines at para. 137 that prosecutors must consider disclosing in the interests of justice any material relevant to sentence, such as information not known to the defendant which might assist him in placing his role in the offence in the correct context vis-à-vis other offenders. There is also a common law duty post-conviction and pending appeal '... to disclose to the defendant any material which comes to light and might cast doubt on the safety of the conviction' (*R* v *Gohil and Preko* [2018] EWCA Crim 140).

If the defence are not satisfied that the prosecution have disclosed all they should have, s. 8 of the 1996 Act allows for the defence to apply to the court for further disclosure.

2.5.11.7

KEYNOTE

Interviewing Defence Witnesses or Alibi Witnesses

Section 21A of the Criminal Procedure and Investigations Act 1996 introduced a Code of Practice for Arranging and Conducting Interviews of Witnesses Notified by the Accused. The Code sets out guidance that police officers and other persons charged with investigating offences must follow if they arrange or conduct interviews of proposed witnesses whose details are disclosed to the prosecution under the 1996 Act. These are set out below:

Arrangement of the interview

Information to be provided to the witness before any interview may take place

3.1 If an investigator wishes to interview a witness, the witness must be asked whether he consents to being interviewed and informed that:

- an interview is being requested following his identification by the accused as a proposed witness under section 6A(2) or section 6C of the Act,
- he is not obliged to attend the proposed interview,
- he is entitled to be accompanied by a solicitor at the interview (but nothing in this Code of Practice creates any duty on the part of the Legal Services Commission to provide funding for any such attendance), and
- a record will be made of the interview and he will subsequently be sent a copy of the record.

3.2 If the witness consents to being interviewed, the witness must be asked:

- whether he wishes to have a solicitor present at the interview,
- whether he consents to a solicitor attending the interview on behalf of the accused, as an observer, and
- whether he consents to a copy of the record being sent to the accused. If he does not consent, the witness must be informed that the effect of disclosure requirements in criminal proceedings may nevertheless require the prosecution to disclose the record to the accused (and any co-accused) in the course of the proceedings.

Information to be provided to the accused before any interview may take place

4.1 The investigator must notify the accused or, if the accused is legally represented in the proceedings, the accused's representatives:

- that the investigator requested an interview with the witness,
- whether the witness consented to the interview, and
- if the witness consented to the interview, whether the witness also consented to a solicitor attending the interview on behalf of the accused, as an observer.

4.2 If the accused is not legally represented in the proceedings, and if the witness consents to a solicitor attending the interview on behalf of the accused, the accused must be offered the opportunity, a reasonable time before the interview is held, to appoint a solicitor to attend it.

Identification of the date, time and venue for the interview

5 The investigator must nominate a reasonable date, time and venue for the interview and notify the witness of them and any subsequent changes to them.

Notification to the accused's solicitor of the date, time and venue of the interview

6 If the witness has consented to the presence of the accused's solicitor, the accused's solicitor must be notified that the interview is taking place, invited to observe, and provided with reasonable notice of the date, time and venue of the interview and any subsequent changes.

Conduct of the interview

The investigator conducting the interview

7 The identity of the investigator conducting the interview must be recorded. That person must have sufficient skills and authority, commensurate with the complexity of the investigation, to discharge his functions effectively. That person must not conduct the interview if that is likely to result in a conflict of interest, for instance, if that person is the victim of the alleged crime which is the subject of the proceedings. The advice of a more senior officer must always be sought if there is doubt as to whether a conflict of interest precludes an individual conducting the interview. If thereafter the doubt remains, the advice of a prosecutor must be sought.

Attendance of the accused's solicitor

8.1 The accused's solicitor may only attend the interview if the witness has consented to his presence as an observer. Provided that the accused's solicitor was given reasonable notice of the date, time and place of the interview, the fact that the accused's solicitor is not present will not prevent the interview from being conducted. If the witness at any time withdraws consent to the accused's solicitor being present at the interview, the interview may continue without the presence of the accused's solicitor.

8.2 The accused's solicitor may attend only as an observer.

Attendance of the witness's solicitor

9 Where a witness has indicated that he wishes to appoint a solicitor to be present, that solicitor must be permitted to attend the interview.

Attendance of any other appropriate person

10 A witness under the age of 18 or a witness who is mentally disordered or otherwise mentally vulnerable must be interviewed in the presence of an appropriate person.

Recording of the interview

11.1 An accurate record must be made of the interview, whether it takes place at a police station or elsewhere. The record must be made, where practicable, by audio recording or by visual recording with sound, or otherwise in writing. Any written record must be made and completed during the interview, unless this would not be practicable or would interfere with the conduct of the interview, and must constitute either a verbatim record of what has been said or, failing this, an account of the interview which adequately and accurately summarises it. If a written record is not made during the interview it must be made as soon as practicable after its completion. Written interview records must be timed and signed by the maker.

11.2 A copy of the record must be given, within a reasonable time of the interview, to:

(a) the witness, and

(b) if the witness consents, to the accused or the accused's solicitor.

2.5.12

Disclosure Code of Practice—9 Certification by Disclosure Officer

9.1 The disclosure officer must certify to the prosecutor that to the best of their knowledge and belief, all relevant material which has been retained and made available to them has been revealed to the prosecutor in accordance with this Code. They must sign and date the disclosure officer certificate. It will be necessary to certify not only at the time when the schedule and accompanying material is submitted to the prosecutor, and when relevant material which has been retained is reconsidered after the accused has given a defence statement, but also whenever a schedule is otherwise given or material is otherwise revealed to the prosecutor.

2.5.13

Disclosure Code of Practice—10 Disclosure of Material to Accused

10.1 A prosecutor must review the schedules of unused material provided by the disclosure officer and endorse the schedule to indicate whether each item of material does or does not meet the test for disclosure. If any of the material does meet the test for disclosure, the prosecutor should record the reason for this decision.

10.2 A prosecutor must additionally review any material provided by the disclosure officer under paragraph 6.6 (material likely to meet the test for disclosure). The prosecutor must endorse the schedule to indicate whether the material does or does not meet the test for disclosure, and must record the reason for the decision.

10.3 When a prosecutor provides material to the defence in accordance with the obligation under section 3 or section 7A of the Criminal Procedure and Investigations Act 1996, the prosecutor must at the same time provide the schedule of non-sensitive material to the defence.

10.4 Other than early disclosure under Common Law, in the magistrates' court the schedule (and any relevant unused material to be disclosed under it) must be disclosed to the accused either:

- at the hearing where a not guilty plea is entered, or
- as soon as possible following a formal indication from the accused or representative that a not guilty plea will be entered at the hearing.

In the Crown Court, initial disclosure should if possible be served prior to the Plea and Trial Preparation Hearing (PTPH). Where this has not been done, it should be served as soon as possible after that hearing and in accordance with any direction made by the Court.

10.5 If material has been copied to the prosecutor, and it is to be disclosed, whether it is disclosed by the prosecutor or the disclosure officer is a matter of agreement between the two of them.

10.6 If material has not already been copied to the prosecutor, and they request its disclosure to the accused on the ground that:

- it satisfies the test for prosecution disclosure, or
- the court has ordered its disclosure after considering an application from the accused, the disclosure officer must disclose it to the accused.

10.7 The disclosure officer must disclose material to the accused either by giving them a copy or by allowing them to inspect it. If the accused person asks for a copy of any material which they have been allowed to inspect, the disclosure officer must supply it, unless in the opinion of the disclosure officer that is either not practicable (for example because the material consists of an object which cannot be copied, or because the volume of material is so great), or not desirable (for example because the material is a statement by a child witness in relation to a sexual offence).

10.8 If material which the accused has been allowed to inspect consists of information which is recorded other than in writing, whether it should be given to the accused in its original form or in the form of a transcript is a matter for the discretion of the disclosure officer. If the material is transcribed, the disclosure officer must ensure that the transcript is certified to the accused as a true record of the material which has been transcribed.

10.9 If a court concludes that an item of sensitive material satisfies the prosecution disclosure test and that the interests of the defence outweigh the public interest in withholding disclosure, it will be necessary to disclose the material if the case is to proceed. This does not mean that sensitive documents must always be disclosed in their original form: for example, the court may agree that sensitive details still requiring protection should be blocked out, or that documents may be summarised, or that the prosecutor may make an admission about the substance of the material under section 10 of the Criminal Justice Act 1967.

2.5.13.1 **KEYNOTE**

Disclosing Material to the Defence

The court can order disclosure of material which the prosecution contend is sensitive. In such cases, it may be appropriate to seek guidance on whether to disclose the material or offer no evidence, thereby protecting the sensitive material or the source of that material (e.g. where informants or surveillance techniques are involved).

Forces may have instructions as to providing further copies when requested by the defence in relation to procedures and costs. It is suggested that where copies are provided, some proof of delivery should be obtained.

2.5.13.2 **KEYNOTE**

Disclosure of Statements in Cases of Complaints against the Police

Statements made by witnesses during an investigation of a complaint against a police officer are disclosable; however, the timing of the disclosure may be controlled. In *R* v *Police Complaints Authority, ex parte Green* [2002] EWCA Civ 389, the Court of Appeal stated that there is no requirement to disclose witness statements to eye-witness complainants during the course of an investigation. The evidence of such complainants could be contaminated and, therefore, disclosure would risk hindering or frustrating the very purpose of the investigation. A complainant's legitimate interests were appropriately and adequately safeguarded by his/her right to a thorough and independent investigation, to contribute to the evidence, to be kept informed of the progress of the investigation and to be given reasoned conclusions on completion of the investigation. However, a complainant had no right to participate in the investigation as though he/she were supervising it. The general rule was that complainants, whether victims or next of kin, were not entitled to the disclosure of witness statements used in the course of a police investigation until its conclusion at the earliest.

Police complaints and disciplinary files may also fall within sensitive material that does not have to be disclosed (*Halford* v *Sharples* [1992] 1 WLR 736). This would not apply to written complaints against the police prompting investigations or the actual statements obtained during the investigations, although immunity may be claimed in the case of a particular document by reason of its contents (*R* v *Chief Constable of the West Midlands Police, ex parte Wiley* [1995] 1 AC 274). However, the working papers and reports prepared by the investigating officers do form a class which is entitled to immunity and therefore production of such material should be ordered only where the public interest in disclosure of their contents outweighs the public interest in preserving confidentiality (*Taylor* v *Anderton* [1995] 1 WLR 447).

2.5.13.3 **KEYNOTE**

Confidentiality

The defence may only use material disclosed to them under the 1996 Act for purposes related to the defence case; any other use will be a contempt of court. Once evidence has been given in open court, however, the material is available for other purposes.

2.6 Detention and Treatment of Persons by Police Officers

A thick grey line down the margin denotes text that is an extract of the PACE Code itself (i.e. the actual wording of the legislation). This material is examinable for both Sergeants and Inspectors.

2.6.1 Introduction

The law dealing with persons who have been arrested and the manner in which they must be dealt with is primarily contained in the Police and Criminal Evidence Act 1984 (hereafter referred to as 'PACE84') and the PACE Code of Practice for the detention, treatment and questioning of persons by Police Officers (hereafter referred to as 'Code C').

This chapter uses the elements of Code C dealing with the detention and treatment of persons by police officers as a framework to explain this area of the syllabus and incorporates relevant law within the keynotes where appropriate. As some sections of Code C deal with the questioning of suspects, they are included in **chapter 2.8** (the chapter dealing with Interviews).

This chapter regularly refers to terms such as 'custody officer', 'designated person', 'designated police station' and 'police detention' so it is useful to examine what those terms mean before examining PACE84 and Code C in greater detail.

2.6.2 Custody Officer

The custody officer is responsible for the reception and treatment of prisoners detained at the police station. Custody officers act independently of those conducting the investigation, thereby ensuring the welfare and rights of the detained person (s. 36(5) PACE84).

Section 36 requires that one or more custody officers must be appointed for each designated police station. However, in *Vince* v *Chief Constable of Dorset* [1993] 1 WLR 415, it was held that a chief constable was under a duty to appoint one custody officer for each designated police station and had a discretionary power to appoint more than one, but this duty did not go so far as to require a sufficient number to ensure that the functions of custody officer were always performed by them. The provision of the facility of a custody officer must be reasonable. Section 36(3) states that a custody officer must be an officer of at least the rank of sergeant. However, s. 36(4) allows officers of any rank to perform the functions of custody officer at a designated police station if a custody officer is not readily available to perform them. The effect of s. 36(3) and (4) is that the practice of allowing officers of any other rank to perform the role of custody officer where a sergeant (*who has no other role to perform*) is in the police station must therefore be unlawful. Should a decision be made to use acting sergeants or untrained custody officers, this may lead to a claim in negligence by the officer or the detained person where there is a breach of the Codes or someone is injured as a result of the failure to manage the custody suite effectively. It could also lead to a prosecution under health and safety legislation.

For cases where arrested people are taken to a non-designated police station, s. 36(7) states that an officer of any rank not involved in the investigation should perform the role of custody officer. If no such person is at the station, the arresting officer (or any other officer involved in the investigation) or the officer that released him/her under s. 30A PACE84 (bail prior to being taken to a police station) should perform the role. In these cases, an officer of at least the rank of inspector at a designated police station must be informed. It is suggested that once informed, that officer should consider the circumstances of the detained person.

Where a custody officer feels that he/she is unable to comply with the minimum standards of detention as required by PACE84, it is suggested that he/she should draw this to the attention of the line manager and/or the superintendent responsible for the custody suite. Custody officers should be mindful of Article 5 of the European Convention on Human Rights in considering whether they are able to manage the number of detained persons in their custody to ensure that their detention is not longer than needed.

2.6.3 Designated Person

Sections 38 and 39 of the Police Reform Act 2002 allow the chief officer of police of any police force to designate a relevant employee as either or both of the following:

- a community support officer;
- a policing support officer.

The chief officer of police shall not designate a person unless he/she is satisfied that the person is a suitable person to carry out the functions for which he/she is designated, is capable of effectively carrying out those functions and has received adequate training in the carrying out of those functions and in the exercise and performance of the powers and duties of a designated officer.

The powers and duties that may be conferred or imposed on a community support officer or a policing support officer include any power or duty of a constable, *except* the following powers and functions:

- any power or duty of a constable to make an arrest;
- any power or duty of a constable to stop and search an individual or a vehicle or other thing;
- the power of a constable, under s. 36(4) PACE84, to perform the functions of a custody officer at a designated police station if a custody officer is not readily available to perform them;
- any power that is exercisable only by a constable of a particular rank.

Where powers have been given to a community support officer or police support officer they can be used within their police force area or in such areas outside their police area as set out by the chief officer of the force. Where any of the powers allow for the use of reasonable force when exercised by a police constable, a designated person has the same entitlement to use reasonable force as a constable.

KEYNOTE

Not all designated officers have the same range of powers so it is important to know what powers a particular designated officer has been given and therefore what his/her role will be. Of particular relevance are the roles of investigating officer, detention officer and escort officer.

Investigating Officers

- To act as the supervisor of any access to seized material to which a person is entitled, to supervise the taking of a photograph of seized material or to photograph it him/herself.
- Power for the custody officer to transfer to a designated officer responsibility for a detainee. This power includes a duty for the person investigating the offence, once the detainee is returned to the custody of the custody officer, to report back to the custody officer on how the Codes were complied with.
- To question an arrested person under ss. 36 and 37 of the Criminal Justice and Public Order Act 1994 about facts which may be attributable to the person's participation in an offence. The designated person may also give the suspect the necessary warning about the capacity of a court to draw inferences from a failure to give a satisfactory account in response to questioning.

Detention Officers

- Powers to search detained persons, to take fingerprints and certain samples without consent and to take photographs.
- To require certain defined categories of persons who have been convicted, cautioned, reprimanded or warned in relation to recordable offences to attend a police station to have their fingerprints taken.
- To carry out non-intimate searches of persons detained at police stations or elsewhere and to seize items found during such searches.
- To carry out searches and examinations in order to determine the identity of persons detained at police stations. Identifying marks found during such processes may be photographed.
- To carry out intimate searches in the same very limited circumstances that are applicable to constables.
- To take fingerprints without consent in the same circumstances that a constable can.
- To take non-intimate samples without consent and to inform the person from whom the sample is to be taken of any necessary authorisation by a senior officer and of the grounds for that authorisation.
- To require certain defined categories of persons who have been charged with or convicted of recordable offences to attend a police station to have a sample taken.
- To inform a person that intimate samples taken from him/her may be the subject of a speculative search (i.e. this will satisfy the requirement that the person must be informed that the sample will be the subject of a speculative search).
- To photograph detained persons in the same way that constables can.

Escort Officers

- To transport arrested persons to police stations and escort detained persons from one police station to another or between police stations and other locations specified by the custody officer.
- To carry out the duty of taking a person arrested by a constable to a police station as soon as practicable.
- With the authority of the custody officer, to escort detainees between police stations or between police stations and other specified locations.
- To conduct non-intimate searches of the detainee; and to seize or retain, or cause to be seized or retained, anything found on such a search (restrictions on power to seize personal effects are the same as for police officers, as is the requirement that the search be carried out by a member of the same sex).

Note that not all support staff will be designated for the purposes of the Police Reform Act 2002 and non-designated staff *will not* have the additional powers as outlined above.

2.6.4 Designated Police Station

Section 30 PACE84 requires that a person who has been arrested at a place other than a police station must be taken to a police station *as soon as practicable* after arrest, unless the arrested person has been released prior to arrival at the police station (s. 30A PACE84 allows a constable to release a person who is under arrest, **see para. 2.2.2**). PACE84 requires that those who will be detained (or who are likely to be detained) for more than six hours must go to a 'designated' police station (s. 30(2)). A designated police station is one that has enough facilities for the purpose of detaining arrested people. Section 35 requires the chief officer of police to designate sufficient police stations to deal with detained arrested persons. It is for the chief officer to decide which stations are to be designated stations and these details are then published. Police stations can be designated permanently or for any specified periods provided that they are not designated for part of a day.

2.6.5 Police Detention

'Police detention' is defined by s. 118 PACE84 which states:

> (2) Subject to subsection (2A) a person is in police detention for the purposes of this Act if—
> (a) he has been taken to a police station after being arrested for an offence or after being arrested under section 41 of the Terrorism Act 2000, or
> (b) he is arrested at a police station after attending voluntarily at the station or accompanying a constable to it, and is detained there or is detained elsewhere in the charge of a constable, except that a person who is at a court after being charged is not in police detention for those purposes.
> (2A) Where a person is in another's lawful custody by virtue of paragraph 34(1) or 35(3) of Schedule 4 to the Police Reform Act 2002, he shall be treated as in police detention.

Paragraph 34(1) of sch. 4 to the Police Reform Act 2002 relates to designated escort officers taking an arrested person to a police station; para. 35(3) deals with a designated escort officer transferring a detainee from one police station to another.

2.6.6 Code C—1 General

1.0 The powers and procedures in this Code must be used fairly, responsibly, with respect for the people to whom they apply and without unlawful discrimination. Under the Equality Act 2010, section 149 (Public sector Equality Duty), police forces must, in carrying out their functions, have due regard to the need to eliminate unlawful discrimination, harassment, victimisation and any other conduct which is prohibited by that Act, to advance equality of opportunity between people who share a relevant protected characteristic and people who do not share it, and to foster good relations between those persons. The Equality Act also makes it unlawful for police officers to discriminate against, harass or victimise any person on the grounds of the 'protected characteristics' of age, disability, gender reassignment, race, religion or belief, sex and sexual orientation, marriage and civil partnership, pregnancy and maternity, when using their powers.

KEYNOTE

Although certain sections of this Code apply specifically to people in custody at police stations, a person who attends a police station or other location voluntarily to assist with an investigation should be treated with no less consideration, e.g. offered or allowed refreshments at appropriate times, and enjoy an absolute right to obtain legal advice or communicate with anyone outside the police station or other location (see Code C, paras 3.21 and 3.22).

1.1 All persons in custody must be dealt with expeditiously, and released as soon as the need for detention no longer applies.

1.1A A custody officer must perform the functions in this Code as soon as practicable. A custody officer will not be in breach of this Code if delay is justifiable and reasonable steps are taken to prevent unnecessary delay. The custody record shall show when a delay has occurred and the reason.

KEYNOTE

Paragraph 1.1A is intended to cover delays which may occur in processing detainees, e.g. if a large number of suspects are brought into the station simultaneously to be placed in custody, or interview rooms are all being used, or perhaps there are difficulties contacting an appropriate adult, solicitor or interpreter. However, if that delay was not 'justified', it could lead to actions for unlawful detention and false imprisonment, and any evidence obtained as a result may be held to be inadmissible (*Roberts* v *Chief Constable of Cheshire Constabulary* [1999] 1 WLR 662).

1.2 This Code of Practice must be readily available at all police stations for consultation by:

- police officers;
- police staff;
- detained persons;
- members of the public.

1.3 The provisions of this Code:

- include the *Annexes*
- do not include the *Notes for Guidance* which form guidance to police officers and others about its application and interpretation.

1.4 If at any time an officer has any reason to suspect that a person of any age may be vulnerable (see *paragraph 1.13(d)*), in the absence of clear evidence to dispel that suspicion, that person shall be treated as such for the purposes of this Code and to establish whether any such reason may exist in relation to a person suspected of committing an offence (see *paragraph 10.1*), the custody officer in the case of a detained person, or the officer investigating the offence in the case of a person who has not been arrested or detained, shall take, or cause to be taken, (see *paragraph 3.5*) the following action:

(a) reasonable enquiries shall be made to ascertain what information is available that is relevant to any of the factors described in *paragraph 1.13(d)* as indicating that the person may be vulnerable might apply;

(b) a record shall be made describing whether any of those factors appear to apply and provide any reason to suspect that the person may be vulnerable or (as the case may be) may not be vulnerable; and

(c) the record mentioned in sub-paragraph (b) shall be made available to be taken into account by police officers, police staff and any others who, in accordance with the provisions of this or any other Code, are required or entitled to communicate with the person in question. This would include any solicitor, appropriate adult and health care professional and is particularly relevant to communication by telephone or by means of a live link (see *paragraphs 12.9A* (interviews), *13.12* (interpretation), and *15.3C*, *15.11A*, *15.11B*, *15.11C* and *15.11D* (reviews and extension of detention)).

KEYNOTE

A person may be vulnerable as a result of having a mental health condition or mental disorder. Similarly, simply because an individual does not have, or is not known to have, any such condition or disorder does not mean that they are not vulnerable for the purposes of this Code. It is therefore important that the custody officer in the case of a detained person or the officer investigating the offence in the case of a person who has not been arrested or detained, as appropriate, considers on a case-by-case basis, whether any of the factors described in para. 1.13(d) might apply to the person in question. In doing so, the officer must take into account the particular circumstances of the individual and how the nature of the investigation might affect them and bear in mind that juveniles, by virtue of their age, will always require an appropriate adult.

For the purposes of para 1.4(a), examples of relevant information that may be available include:

- the behaviour of the adult or juvenile;
- the mental health and capacity of the adult or juvenile;
- what the adult or juvenile says about themselves;
- information from relatives and friends of the adult or juvenile;
- information from police officers and staff and from police records;
- information from health and social care (including liaison and diversion services) and other professionals who know, or have had previous contact with, the individual and may be able to contribute to assessing their need for help and support from an appropriate adult. This includes contacts and assessments arranged by the police or at the request of the individual or (as applicable) their appropriate adult or solicitor.

The Mental Health Act 1983 Code of Practice at page 26 describes the range of clinically recognised conditions which can fall with the meaning of mental disorder for the purpose of para. 1.13(d).

When a person is under the influence of drink and/or drugs, it is not intended that they are to be treated as vulnerable and requiring an appropriate adult for the purpose of para. 1.4 unless other information indicates that any of the factors described in para. 1.13(d) may apply to that person. When the person has recovered from the effects of drink and/or drugs, they should be reassessed in accordance with para. 1.4. See para. 15.4A for application to live link.

1.5 Anyone who appears to be under 18, shall, in the absence of clear evidence that they are older be treated as a juvenile for the purposes of this Code and any other Code.

KEYNOTE

Paragraph 1.5 reflects the statutory definition of 'arrested juvenile' in s. 37(15) PACE84. This section was amended by s. 42 of the Criminal Justice and Courts Act 2015 with effect from 26 October 2015, and includes anyone who appears to be under the age of 18. This definition applies for the purposes of the detention and bail provisions in ss. 34 to 51 PACE84. With effect from 3 April 2017, amendments made by the Policing and Crime Act 2017 require persons under the age of 18 to be treated as juveniles for the purposes of all other provisions of PACE84 and the Codes.

1.5A *Not used.*

1.6 If a person appears to be blind, seriously visually impaired, deaf, unable to read or speak or has difficulty orally because of a speech impediment, they shall be treated as such for the purposes of this Code in the absence of clear evidence to the contrary.

1.7 The appropriate adult' means, in the case of a:

(a) juvenile:

(i) the parent, guardian or, if the juvenile is in the care of a local authority or voluntary organisation, a person representing that authority or organisation,

KEYNOTE

A person, including a parent or guardian, should not be an appropriate adult if he/she is:

- suspected of involvement in the offence;
- the victim;
- a witness;
- involved in the investigation; or
- has received admissions prior to attending to act as the appropriate adult.

If a juvenile's parent is estranged from the juvenile, he/she should not be asked to act as the appropriate adult if the juvenile expressly and specifically objects to his/her presence.

(ii) a social worker of a local authority;

KEYNOTE

If a juvenile admits an offence to, or in the presence of, a social worker or member of a youth offending team other than during the time that person is acting as the juvenile's appropriate adult, another appropriate adult should be appointed in the interest of fairness.

(iii) failing these, some other responsible adult aged 18 or over who is *not*:
- a police officer;
- employed by the police;
- under the direction or control of the chief officer of a police force; or
- a person who provides services under contractual arrangements (but without being employed by the chief officer of a police force), to assist that force in relation to the discharge of its chief officer's functions, whether or not they are on duty at the time.

(b) a person who is vulnerable (see *paragraph 1.4*):

(i) a relative, guardian or other person responsible for their care or custody;

(ii) someone experienced in dealing with vulnerable people but who is *not*:
- a police officer;
- employed by the police;
- under the direction or control of the chief officer of a police force; or
- a person who provides services under contractual arrangements (but without being employed by the chief officer of a police force), to assist that force in relation to the discharge of its chief officer's functions, whether or not they are on duty at the time;

(iii) failing these, some other responsible adult aged 18 or over other than a person described in the bullet points in *sub-paragraph (b)(ii)* above.

KEYNOTE

In the case of someone who is vulnerable, it may be more satisfactory if the appropriate adult is someone experienced or trained in their care rather than a relative lacking such qualifications. But if the person prefers a relative to a better qualified stranger or objects to a particular person their wishes should, if practicable, be respected.

An appropriate adult who is not a parent or guardian in the case of a juvenile, or a relative, guardian or carer in the case of a vulnerable person, must be independent of the police as their role is to safeguard the person's rights and entitlements. Additionally, a solicitor or independent custody visitor who is present at the police station and acting in that capacity may not be the appropriate adult.

1.7A The role of the appropriate adult is to safeguard the rights, entitlements and welfare of juveniles and vulnerable persons (see *paragraphs 1.4* and *1.5*) to whom the provisions of this and any other Code of Practice apply. For this reason, the appropriate adult is expected, amongst other things, to:

- support, advise and assist them when, in accordance with this Code or any other Code of Practice, they are given or asked to provide information or participate in any procedure;
- observe whether the police are acting properly and fairly to respect their rights and entitlements, and inform an officer of the rank of inspector or above if they consider that they are not;
- assist them to communicate with the police whilst respecting their right to say nothing unless they want to as set out in the terms of the caution (see *paragraphs 10.5* and *10.6*);
- help them to understand their rights and ensure that those rights are protected and respected (see *paragraphs 3.15, 3.17, 6.5A* and *11.17*).

KEYNOTE

Appropriate Adults—General

In *R* v *Aspinall* [1999] 2 Cr App R 115, the Court of Appeal emphasised the importance of appropriate adults. There it was held that an appropriate adult played a significant role in respect of a vulnerable person whose condition rendered him/her liable to provide information which was unreliable, misleading or self-incriminating.

A detainee should always be given an opportunity, when an appropriate adult is called to the police station, to consult privately with a solicitor in the appropriate adult's absence if he/she wants. An appropriate adult is not subject to legal privilege.

The custody officer must remind the appropriate adult and detainee about the right to legal advice and record any reasons for waiving it in accordance with s. 6.

While an appropriate adult should be given access to a juvenile in police detention, this does not mean that he/she has free access to the custody area. In *Butcher* v *DPP* [2003] EWHC 580 (Admin), the custody officer physically escorted the detainee's appropriate adult from the custody suite as she had entered it without being invited and had been verbally abusive and aggressive. The court held that the custody sergeant had not detained the appropriate adult, but had merely used reasonable force to remove her in order to maintain the operational effectiveness of the custody suite. The court held that the custody sergeant was entitled to ask her to leave and to use reasonable force when she failed to comply with that request.

It is also important to consider the welfare of the appropriate adult. This is demonstrated by the case of *Leach* v *Chief Constable of Gloucestershire Constabulary* [1999] 1 WLR 1421. Here L was asked by a police officer to attend police interviews of a murder suspect who was also thought to be mentally disordered, as an 'appropriate adult' per the requirement of the Codes. She was told only that the suspect was a 52-year-old male, and was not informed of the nature of the case. The suspect was in fact Frederick West, who was being questioned in connection with murders committed in particularly harrowing and traumatic circumstances. For many weeks L acted as an appropriate adult, accompanying the officer and suspect to murder scenes, and on many occasions being left alone in a locked cell with the suspect. She claimed to be suffering from post-traumatic stress and psychological injury as well as a stroke as a result of her experiences. The Court of Appeal said that the Fred West case was notorious among modern crimes and it was foreseeable that psychiatric harm might arise. While there was no requirement to in such cases, counselling or trained help should be offered.

1.8 If this Code requires a person be given certain information, they do not have to be given it if at the time they are incapable of understanding what is said, are violent or may become violent or in urgent need of medical attention, but they must be given it as soon as practicable.

1.9 References to a custody officer include any police officer who, for the time being, is performing the functions of a custody officer.

1.9A When this Code requires the prior authority or agreement of an officer of at least inspector or superintendent rank, that authority may be given by a sergeant or chief inspector authorised to perform the functions of the higher rank under the Police and Criminal Evidence Act 1984 (PACE), section 107.

1.10 Subject to *paragraph 1.12*, this Code applies to people in custody at police stations in England and Wales, whether or not they have been arrested, and to those removed to a police station as a place of safety under the Mental Health Act 1983, sections 135 and 136, as amended by the Policing and Crime Act 2017 (see *paragraph 3.16*). *Section 15* applies solely to people in police detention, e.g. those brought to a police station under arrest or arrested at a police station for an offence after going there voluntarily.

1.11 No part of this Code applies to a detained person:

(a) to whom PACE Code H applies because:

- they are detained following arrest under section 41 of the Terrorism Act 2000 (TACT) and not charged; or
- an authorisation has been given under section 22 of the Counter-Terrorism Act 2008 (CTACT) (post-charge questioning of terrorist suspects) to interview them.

(b) to whom the Code of Practice issued under paragraph 6 of Schedule 14 to TACT applies because they are detained for examination under Schedule 7 to TACT.

1.12 This Code does not apply to people in custody:

(i) arrested by officers under the Criminal Justice and Public Order Act 1994, section 136(2) on warrants issued in Scotland, or arrested or detained without warrant under section 137(2) by officers from a police force in Scotland. In these cases, police powers and duties and the person's rights and entitlements whilst at a police station in England or Wales are the same as those in Scotland;

(ii) arrested under the Immigration and Asylum Act 1999, section 142(3) in order to have their fingerprints taken;

(iii) whose detention has been authorised under Schedules 2 or 3 to the Immigration Act 1971 or section 62 of the Nationality, Immigration and Asylum Act 2002;

(iv) who are convicted or remanded prisoners held in police cells on behalf of the Prison Service under the Imprisonment (Temporary Provisions) Act 1980;

(v) *Not used.*

(vi) detained for searches under stop and search powers except as required by Code A.

The provisions on conditions of detention and treatment in *sections 8* and *9* must be considered as the minimum standards of treatment for such detainees.

1.13 In this Code:

(a) 'designated person' means a person other than a police officer, who has specified powers and duties conferred or imposed on them by designation under section 38 or 39 of the Police Reform Act 2002;

(b) reference to a police officer includes a designated person acting in the exercise or performance of the powers and duties conferred or imposed on them by their designation;

(c) if there is doubt as to whether the person should be treated, or continue to be treated, as being male or female in the case of:

(i) a search or other procedure to which this Code applies which may only be carried out or observed by a person of the *same sex* as the detainee; or

(ii) any other procedure which requires action to be taken or information to be given that depends on whether the person is to be treated as being male or female;

then the gender of the detainee and other parties concerned should be established and recorded in line with Annex L of this Code.

(d) 'vulnerable' applies to any person who, because of a mental health condition or mental disorder:

(i) may have difficulty understanding or communicating effectively about the full implications for them of any procedures and processes connected with:

- their arrest and detention; or (as the case may be)
- their voluntary attendance at a police station or their presence elsewhere (see *paragraph 3.21*), for the purpose of a voluntary interview; and
- the exercise of their rights and entitlements

(ii) does not appear to understand the significance of what they are told, of questions they are asked or of their replies:

(iii) appears to be particularly prone to:

- becoming confused and unclear about their position;
- providing unreliable, misleading or incriminating information without knowing or wishing to do so;
- accepting or acting on suggestions from others without consciously knowing or wishing to do so; or
- readily agreeing to suggestions or proposals without any protest or question.

(e) 'Live link' means

(i) for the purpose of *paragraph 12.9A*; an arrangement by means of which the *interviewing officer* who is not present at the police station where the detainee is held, is able to see and hear, and to be seen and heard by, the detainee concerned, the detainee's solicitor, appropriate adult and interpreter (as applicable) and the officer who has custody of that detainee.

(ii) for the purpose of *paragraph 15.9A*; an arrangement by means of which the *review officer* who is not present at the police station where the detainee is held, is able to see and hear, and to be seen and heard by, the detainee concerned and the detainee's solicitor, appropriate adult and interpreter (as applicable). The use of live link for decisions about detention under *section 45A of PACE* is subject to regulations made by the Secretary of State being in force.

(iii) for the purpose of *paragraph 15.11A*; an arrangement by means of which the *authorising officer* who is not present at the police station where the detainee is held, is able to see and hear, and to be seen and heard by, the detainee concerned and the detainee's solicitor, appropriate adult and interpreter (as applicable).

(iv) for the purpose of *paragraph 15.11C*; an arrangement by means of which the *detainee* when not present in the court where the hearing is being held, is able to see and hear, and to be seen and heard by, the court during the hearing.

Note: Chief officers must be satisfied that live link used in their force area for the above purposes provides for accurate and secure communication between the detainee, the detainee's solicitor, appropriate adult and interpreter (as applicable). This includes ensuring that at any time during which the live link is being used: a person cannot see, hear or otherwise obtain access to any such communications unless so authorised or allowed by the custody officer or, in the case of an interview, the interviewer and that as applicable, the confidentiality of any private consultation between a suspect and their solicitor and appropriate adult is maintained.

KEYNOTE

For the purpose of the provisions of PACE84 that allow a live link to be used, any impairment of the detainee's eyesight or hearing is to be disregarded. This means that if a detainee's eyesight or hearing is impaired, the arrangements which would be needed to ensure effective communication if all parties were physically present in the same location, for example using sign language, would apply to the live link arrangements.

1.14 Designated persons are entitled to use reasonable force as follows:

(a) when exercising a power conferred on them which allows a police officer exercising that power to use reasonable force, a designated person has the same entitlement to use force; and

(b) at other times when carrying out duties conferred or imposed on them that also entitle them to use reasonable force, for example:

- when at a police station carrying out the duty to keep detainees for whom they are responsible under control and to assist any police officer or designated person to keep any detainee under control and to prevent their escape;
- when securing, or assisting any police officer or designated person in securing, the detention of a person at a police station;
- when escorting, or assisting any police officer or designated person in escorting, a detainee within a police station;
- for the purpose of saving life or limb;
- or preventing serious damage to property.

1.15 Nothing in this Code prevents the custody officer, or other police officer or designated person (see *paragraph 1.13(a)*) given custody of the detainee by the custody officer, from allowing another person (see *(a)* and *(b)* below) to carry out individual procedures or tasks at the police station if the law allows. However, the officer or designated person given custody remains responsible for making sure the procedures and tasks are carried out correctly in accordance with the Codes of Practice (see *paragraph 3.5*). The other person who is allowed to carry out the procedures or tasks must be someone who *at that time*, is:

(a) under the direction and control of the chief officer of the force responsible for the police station in question; or

(b) providing services under contractual arrangements (but without being employed by the chief officer the police force), to assist a police force in relation to the discharge of its chief officer's functions.

1.16 Designated persons and others mentioned in *sub-paragraphs (a)* and *(b)* of *paragraph 1.15*, must have regard to any relevant provisions of the Codes of Practice.

1.17 In any provision of this or any other Code which allows or requires police officers or police staff to make a record in their report book, the reference to report book shall include any official report book or electronic recording device issued to them that enables the record in question to be made and dealt with in accordance with that provision. References in this and any other Code to written records, forms and signatures include electronic records and forms and electronic confirmation that identifies the person making the record or completing the form.

Chief officers must be satisfied as to the integrity and security of the devices, records and forms to which this *paragraph* applies and that use of those devices, records and forms satisfies relevant data protection legislation.

2.6.7 Code C—2 Custody Records

2.1A When a person:

- is brought to a police station under arrest
- is arrested at the police station having attended there voluntarily or
- attends a police station to answer bail they must be brought before the custody officer as soon as practicable after their arrival at the station or if applicable, following their arrest after attending the police station voluntarily.

This applies to both designated and non-designated police stations. A person is deemed to be 'at a police station' for these purposes if they are within the boundary of any building or enclosed yard which forms part of that police station.

2.1 A separate custody record must be opened as soon as practicable for each person brought to a police station under arrest or arrested at the station having gone there voluntarily or attending a police station in answer to street bail. All information recorded under this Code must be recorded as soon as practicable in the custody record unless otherwise specified. Any audio or video recording made in the custody area is not part of the custody record.

2.2 If any action requires the authority of an officer of a specified rank, subject to *paragraph 2.6A*, their name and rank must be noted in the custody record.

2.3 The custody officer is responsible for the custody record's accuracy and completeness and for making sure the record or copy of the record accompanies a detainee if they are transferred to another police station. The record shall show the:

- time and reason for transfer;
- time a person is released from detention.

2.3A If a person is arrested and taken to a police station as a result of a search in the exercise of any stop and search power to which PACE Code A (Stop and search) or the 'search powers code' issued under TACT applies, the officer carrying out the search is responsible for ensuring that the record of that stop and search is made as part of the person's custody record. The custody officer must then ensure that the person is asked if they want a copy of the search record and if they do, that they are given a copy as soon as practicable. The person's entitlement to a copy of the search record which is made as part of their custody record is in addition to, and does not affect, their entitlement to a copy of their custody record or any other provisions of *section 2* (Custody records) of this Code. (See Code A, *paragraph 4.2B* and the TACT search powers code *paragraph 5.3.5*).

2.4 The detainee's solicitor and appropriate adult must be permitted to inspect the whole of the detainee's custody record as soon as practicable after their arrival at the station and at any other time on request, whilst the person is detained. This includes the following specific records relating to the reasons for the detainee's arrest and detention and the offence concerned, to which *paragraph 3.1(b)* refers:

(a) The information about the circumstances and reasons for the detainee's arrest as recorded in the custody record in accordance with *paragraph 4.3 of Code G*. This applies to any further offences for which the detainee is arrested whilst in custody;

(b) The record of the grounds for each authorisation to keep the person in custody. The authorisations to which this applies are the same as those described at items *(i)(a)* to *(d)* in the table in *paragraph 2* of *Annex M* of this Code.

Access to the records in sub-paragraphs (a) and (b) is in addition to the requirements in *paragraphs 3.4(b), 11.1A, 15.0, 15.7A(c)* and *16.7A* to make certain documents and materials available and to provide information about the offence and the reasons for arrest and detention.

Access to the custody record for the purposes of this paragraph must be arranged and agreed with the custody officer and may not unreasonably interfere with the custody officer's duties. A record shall be made when access is allowed and whether it includes the records described in *sub-paragraphs (a)* and *(b)* above.

2.4A When a detainee leaves police detention or is taken before a court they, their legal representative or appropriate adult shall be given, on request, a copy of the custody record as soon as practicable. This entitlement lasts for 12 months after release.

2.5 The detainee, appropriate adult or legal representative shall be permitted to inspect the original custody record after the detainee has left police detention provided they give reasonable notice of their request. Any such inspection shall be noted in the custody record.

2.6 Subject to *paragraph 2.6A*, all entries in custody records must be timed and signed by the maker. Records entered on computer shall be timed and contain the operator's identification.

2.6A Nothing in this Code requires the identity of officers or other police staff to be recorded or disclosed:

(a) *Not used.*

(b) if the officer or police staff reasonably believe recording or disclosing their name might put them in danger.

In these cases, they shall use their warrant or other identification numbers and the name of their police station.

KEYNOTE

The purpose of using warrant or identification numbers instead of names referred to in Code C, para. 2.6A is to protect those involved in serious organised crime investigations or arrests of particularly violent suspects when there is reliable information that those arrested or their associates may threaten or cause harm to those involved. In cases of doubt, an officer of inspector rank or above should be consulted.

2.7 The fact and time of any detainee's refusal to sign a custody record, when asked in accordance with this Code, must be recorded.

2.6.8

Code C—3 Initial Action

(A) Detained persons—normal procedure

3.1 When a person is brought to a police station under arrest or arrested at the station having gone there voluntarily, the custody officer must make sure the person is told clearly about:

(a) the following continuing rights, which may be exercised at any stage during the period in custody:
   (i) their right to consult privately with a solicitor and that free independent legal advice is available as in *section 6*;
   (ii) their right to have someone informed of their arrest as in *section 5*;
   (iii) their right to consult the Codes of Practice; and
   (iv) if applicable, their right to interpretation and translation (see *paragraph 3.12*) and their right to communicate with their High Commission, Embassy or Consulate (see *paragraph 3.12A*).

(b) their right to be informed about the offence and (as the case may be) any further offences for which they are arrested whilst in custody and why they have been arrested and detained in accordance with *paragraphs 2.4, 3.4(a)* and *11.1A* of this Code and *paragraph 3.3* of *Code G*.

KEYNOTE

The right to consult the Codes of Practice does not entitle the person concerned to delay unreasonably any necessary investigative or administrative action whilst they do so. Examples of action which need not be delayed unreasonably include:

- procedures requiring the provision of breath, blood or urine specimens under the Road Traffic Act 1988 or the Transport and Works Act 1992;
- searching detainees at the police station;
- taking fingerprints, footwear impressions or non-intimate samples without consent for evidential purposes.

3.2 The detainee must also be given a written notice, which contains information:

(a) to allow them to exercise their rights by setting out:
   (i) their rights under *paragraph 3.1, paragraph 3.12* and *3.12A*;
   (ii) the arrangements for obtaining legal advice, see *section 6*;
   (iii) their right to a copy of the custody record as in *paragraph 2.4A*;
   (iv) their right to remain silent as set out in the caution in the terms prescribed in *section 10*;
   (v) their right to have access to materials and documents which are essential to effectively challenging the lawfulness of their arrest and detention for any offence and (as the case may be) any further offences for which they are arrested whilst in custody, in accordance with *paragraphs 3.4(b), 15.0, 15.7A(c)* and *16.7A* of this Code;
   (vi) the maximum period for which they may be kept in police detention without being charged, when detention must be reviewed and when release is required;
   (vii) their right to medical assistance in accordance with *section 9* of this Code; (viii) their right, if they are prosecuted, to have access to the evidence in the case before their trial in accordance with the Criminal Procedure and Investigations Act 1996, the Attorney General's Guidelines on Disclosure, the common law and the Criminal Procedure Rules; and

(b) briefly setting out their other entitlements while in custody, by:
   (i) mentioning:
      ~ the provisions relating to the conduct of interviews;
      ~ the circumstances in which an appropriate adult should be available to assist the detainee and their statutory rights to make representations whenever the need for their detention is reviewed;
   (ii) listing the entitlements in this Code, concerning;
      ~ reasonable standards of physical comfort;
      ~ adequate food and drink;

- access to toilets and washing facilities, clothing, medical attention, and exercise when practicable.
- personal needs relating to health, hygiene and welfare concerning the provision of menstrual and any other health, hygiene and welfare products needed by the detainee in question and speaking about these in private to a member of the custody staff (see *paragraphs 9.3A* and *9.3B*).

3.2A The detainee must be given an opportunity to read the notice and shall be asked to sign the custody record to acknowledge receipt of the notice. Any refusal to sign must be recorded on the custody record.

3.3 *Not used.*

3.3A An 'easy read' illustrated version should also be provided if available.

3.4 (a) The custody officer shall:

- record the offence(s) that the detainee has been arrested for and the reason(s) for the arrest on the custody record. See *paragraph 10.3 and Code G paragraphs 2.2 and 4.3*;
- note on the custody record any comment the detainee makes in relation to the arresting officer's account but shall not invite comment. If the arresting officer is not physically present when the detainee is brought to a police station, the arresting officer's account must be made available to the custody officer remotely or by a third party on the arresting officer's behalf. If the custody officer authorises a person's detention, subject to *paragraph 1.8*, that officer must record the grounds for detention in the detainee's presence and at the same time, inform them of the grounds. The detainee must be informed of the grounds for their detention before they are questioned about any offence;
- note any comment the detainee makes in respect of the decision to detain them but shall not invite comment;
- not put specific questions to the detainee regarding their involvement in any offence, nor in respect of any comments they may make in response to the arresting officer's account or the decision to place them in detention. Such an exchange is likely to constitute an interview as in *paragraph 11.1A* and require the associated safeguards in *section 11*.

Note: This *sub-paragraph* also applies to any further offences and grounds for detention which come to light whilst the person is detained.

See *paragraph 11.13* in respect of unsolicited comments.

KEYNOTE

Detention of Person under Arrest

The power to detain a person under arrest at a police station is derived from s. 37 PACE84 which states:

(1) Where—
  (a) a person is arrested for an offence—
    (i) without a warrant; or
    (ii) under a warrant not endorsed for bail,
  (b) [repealed],

the custody officer at each police station where he is detained after his arrest shall determine whether he has before him sufficient evidence to charge that person with the offence for which he was arrested and may detain him at the police station for such period as is necessary to enable him to do so.

(2) If—
  (a) the custody officer ('C') determines that C does not have such evidence before C, and
  (b) the pre-conditions for bail are satisfied, the person arrested must be released on bail (subject to subsection (3)).

(2A) If—
  (a) the custody officer ('C') determines that C does not have such evidence before C, and
  (b) the pre-conditions for bail are not satisfied,

the person arrested must be released without bail (subject to subsection (3)).

(3) If the custody officer has reasonable grounds for believing that the person's detention without being charged is necessary to secure or preserve evidence relating to an offence for which the person is under arrest or to obtain such evidence by questioning the person he may authorise the person arrested to be kept in police detention.

(4) Where a custody officer authorises a person who has not been charged to be kept in police detention, he shall, as soon as is practicable, make a written record of the grounds for the detention.

(5) Subject to subsection (6) below, the written record shall be made in the presence of the person arrested who shall at that time be informed by the custody officer of the grounds for his detention.

(6) Subsection (5) above shall not apply where the person arrested is, at the time when the written record is made—

(a) incapable of understanding what is said to him;

(b) violent or likely to become violent; or

(c) in urgent need of medical attention.

Having heard the details of and grounds for the arrest, the custody officer must decide whether or not there are reasons which justify authorising that person's detention. Some commentators have suggested that it is also the role of the custody officer to establish that the arrest itself was lawful. While good practice, the custody officer's duty is confined to acting in accordance with the requirements set out in s. 37 PACE84. These duties do not include considering whether the arrest was lawful unless this is relevant to the main question of whether there is sufficient evidence to charge the suspect. The view is supported by the decision of the Divisional Court in *DPP* v *L* [1999] Crim LR 752, where the court held that there was no express or implied requirement imposing a duty on a custody officer to inquire into the legality of an arrest and in that case the custody officer was therefore entitled to assume that it was lawful. A subsequent finding that the arrest was unlawful did not invalidate the decision of the custody officer to hold the person in custody. However, where the custody officer is aware that the arrest is unlawful, he/she will need to consider whether continued detention is justifiable.

The mere fact that a person needs to be interviewed about the offence is not of itself justification for authorising detention. The question that has to be asked is whether the person can be bailed prior to the interview or even bailed before being taken to the police station (s. 30A PACE84). Factors which might be relevant in making this decision include:

- whether the person may interfere with witnesses;
- whether he/she is likely to return if bailed;
- where there is more than one suspect, that they would have an opportunity to confer before their interviews;
- whether there is outstanding property;
- whether the person's name and address are verified.

The fact that the officers and any legal representative will be ready to start the interview shortly may also be relevant when making this decision.

Where initial suspicion rests on several people, it may be appropriate to hold all suspects until they all are interviewed before deciding whether there is enough evidence to warrant a charge against any of them. Detention for questioning where there are reasonable grounds for suspecting that an offence has been committed is lawful so long as the suspicion has not been dispelled in the interim and the questioning is not unnecessarily delayed (*Clarke* v *Chief Constable of North Wales* [2000] All ER (D) 477).

(b) Documents and materials which are essential to effectively challenging the lawfulness of the detainee's arrest and detention must be made available to the detainee or their solicitor. Documents and materials will be 'essential' for this purpose if they are capable of undermining the reasons and grounds which make the detainee's arrest and detention *necessary*. The decision about whether particular documents or materials must be made available for the purpose of this requirement therefore rests with the custody officer who determines whether detention is necessary, in consultation with the investigating officer who has the knowledge of the documents and materials in a particular case necessary to inform that decision. A note should be made in the detainee's custody record of the *fact* that documents or materials have been made available under this sub-paragraph and when. The investigating officer should make a separate note of what is made available and how it is made available in a particular case. This sub-paragraph also applies (with modifications) for the purposes of *sections 15 (Reviews and extensions of detention)* and *16 (Charging detained persons)*. See *paragraphs 15.0* and *16.7A*.

KEYNOTE

For the purposes of para. 3.4(b) (and also para. 15.0 of this Code), investigating officers are responsible for bringing to the attention of the officer who is responsible for authorising the suspect's detention or (as the case may be) continued detention (before or after charge), any documents and materials in their possession or control which appear to undermine the need to keep the suspect in custody. In accordance with Part IV of PACE84, this officer will be either the custody officer, the officer reviewing the need for detention before or after charge (s. 40) or the officer considering the need to extend detention without charge from 24 to 36 hours (s. 42) who is then responsible for determining which, if any, of those documents and materials are capable of undermining the need to detain the suspect and must therefore be made available to the suspect or their solicitor.

It is not the case that documents need to be copied and provided to the suspect or their solicitor; the way in which documents and materials are 'made available' is a matter for the investigating officer to determine on a case-by-case basis and having regard to the nature and volume of the documents and materials involved. For example, they may be made available by supplying a copy or allowing supervised access to view. However, for view-only access, it will be necessary to demonstrate that sufficient time is allowed for the suspect and solicitor to view and consider the documents and materials in question. It is suggested that a record should be made of what material was provided.

3.5 The custody officer or other custody staff as directed by the custody officer shall:

(a) ask the detainee whether at this time, they:

(i) would like legal advice, see *paragraph 6.5*;

(ii) want someone informed of their detention, see *section 5*;

(b) ask the detainee to sign the custody record to confirm their decisions in respect of (*a*);

(c) determine whether the detainee:

(i) is, or might be, in need of medical treatment or attention, see *section 9*;

(ii) is a juvenile and/or vulnerable and therefore requires an appropriate adult (see *paragraphs 1.4*, *1.5*, and *3.15*);

(iia) wishes to speak in private with a member of the custody staff who may be of the same sex about any matter concerning their personal needs relating to health, hygiene and welfare (see *paragraph 9.3A*);

(iii) requires:

- help to check documentation (see *paragraphs 3.20*);
- an interpreter (see *paragraph 3.12*).

(ca) if the detainee is a female aged 18 or over, ask if they require or are likely to require any menstrual products whilst they are in custody (see *paragraph 9.3B*). For girls under 18, see *paragraph 3.20A*;

(d) record the decision and actions taken as applicable in respect of (*c*) and (*ca*).

Where any duties under this paragraph have been carried out by custody staff at the direction of the custody officer, the outcomes shall, as soon as practicable, be reported to the custody officer who retains overall responsibility for the detainee's care and treatment and ensuring that it complies with this Code.

KEYNOTE

A custody officer or other officer who, in accordance with this Code, allows or directs the carrying out of any task or action relating to a detainee's care, treatment, rights and entitlements to another officer or any other person, must be satisfied that the officer or person concerned is suitable, trained and competent to carry out the task or action in question.

3.6 When the needs mentioned in *paragraph 3.5(c)* are being determined, the custody officer is responsible for initiating an assessment to consider whether the detainee is likely to present specific risks to custody staff, any individual who may have contact with detainee (e.g. legal advisers, medical staff) or themselves. This risk assessment must include the taking of reasonable steps to establish the detainee's identity and to obtain information about the detainee that is relevant to their safe custody, security and welfare and risks to others. Such assessments should therefore always include a check on the Police National Computer (PNC), to be carried out as soon as practicable, to identify any risks that have been highlighted in relation to the detainee. Although such assessments are primarily the custody officer's responsibility, it may be necessary for them to consult and involve others, e.g. the arresting officer or an appropriate healthcare professional, see *paragraph 9.13*. Other records held by or on behalf of the police and other UK law enforcement authorities that might provide information relevant to the detainee's safe custody, security and welfare and risk to others and to confirming their identity should also be checked. Reasons for delaying the initiation or completion of the assessment must be recorded.

3.7 Chief officers should ensure that arrangements for proper and effective risk assessments required by *paragraph 3.6* are implemented in respect of all detainees at police stations in their area.

3.8 Risk assessments must follow a structured process which clearly defines the categories of risk to be considered and the results must be incorporated in the detainee's custody record. The custody officer is responsible for making sure those responsible for the detainee's custody are appropriately briefed about the risks. If no specific risks are identified by the assessment, that should be noted in the custody record. See *paragraph 9.14*.

3.8A The content of any risk assessment and any analysis of the level of risk relating to the person's detention is not required to be shown or provided to the detainee or any person acting on behalf of the detainee. But information should not be withheld from any person acting on the detainee's behalf, for example, an appropriate adult, solicitor or interpreter, if to do so might put that person at risk.

3.9 The custody officer is responsible for implementing the response to any specific risk assessment, e.g.:

- reducing opportunities for self harm;
- calling an appropriate healthcare professional;
- increasing levels of monitoring or observation;
- reducing the risk to those who come into contact with the detainee.

3.10 Risk assessment is an ongoing process and assessments must always be subject to review if circumstances change.

3.11 If video cameras are installed in the custody area, notices shall be prominently displayed showing cameras are in use. Any request to have video cameras switched off shall be refused.

(B) Detained persons—special groups

3.12 If the detainee appears to be someone who does not speak or understand English or who has a hearing or speech impediment, the custody officer must ensure:

(a) that without delay, arrangements (*see paragraph 13.1ZA*) are made for the detainee to have the assistance of an interpreter in the action under *paragraphs 3.1* to *3.5*. If the person appears to have a hearing or speech impediment, the reference to 'interpreter' includes appropriate assistance necessary to comply with *paragraphs 3.1* to *3.5*. See *paragraph 13.1C* if the detainee is in Wales. See *section 13*;

(b) that in addition to the continuing rights set out in *paragraph 3.1(a)(i)* to *(iv)*, the detainee is told clearly about their right to interpretation and translation;

(c) that the written notice given to the detainee in accordance with *paragraph 3.2* is in a language the detainee understands and includes the right to interpretation and translation together with information about the provisions in *section 13* and *Annex M*, which explain how the right applies; and

(d) that if the translation of the notice is not available, the information in the notice is given through an interpreter and a written translation provided without undue delay.

3.12A If the detainee is a citizen of an independent Commonwealth country or a national of a foreign country, including the Republic of Ireland, the custody officer must ensure that in addition to the continuing rights set out in *paragraph 3.1(a)(i)* to *(iv)*, they are informed as soon as practicable about their rights of communication with their High Commission, Embassy or Consulate set out in *section 7*. This right must be included in the written notice given to the detainee in accordance with *paragraph 3.2*.

3.13 If the detainee is a juvenile, the custody officer must, if it is practicable, ascertain the identity of a person responsible for their welfare. That person:

- may be:
  - ~ the parent or guardian;
  - ~ if the juvenile is in local authority or voluntary organisation care, or is otherwise being looked after under the Children Act 1989, a person appointed by that authority or organisation to have responsibility for the juvenile's welfare;
  - ~ any other person who has, for the time being, assumed responsibility for the juvenile's welfare.
- must be informed as soon as practicable that the juvenile has been arrested, why they have been arrested and where they are detained. This right is in addition to the juvenile's right in *section 5* not to be held incommunicado.

KEYNOTE

If the juvenile is in local authority or voluntary organisation care but living with their parents or other adults responsible for their welfare, although there is no legal obligation to inform them, they should normally be contacted, as well as the authority or organisation unless they are suspected of involvement in the offence concerned. Even if the juvenile is not living with their parents, consideration should be given to informing them.

3.14 If a juvenile is known to be subject to a court order under which a person or organisation is given any degree of statutory responsibility to supervise or otherwise monitor them, reasonable steps must also be taken to notify that person or organisation (the 'responsible officer'). The responsible officer will normally be a member of a Youth Offending Team, except for a curfew order which involves electronic monitoring when the contractor providing the monitoring will normally be the responsible officer.

3.15 If the detainee is a juvenile or a vulnerable person, the custody officer must, as soon as practicable, ensure that:

- the detainee is informed of the decision that an appropriate adult is required and the reason for that decision (see *paragraph 3.5(c)(ii)* and; the detainee is advised:
  - ~ of the duties of the appropriate adult as described in *paragraph 1.7A*; and
  - ~ that they can consult privately with the appropriate adult at any time.
- the appropriate adult, who in the case of a juvenile may or may not be a person responsible for their welfare, as in *paragraph 3.13*, is informed of:
  - ~ the grounds for their detention;
  - ~ their whereabouts; and
- the attendance of the appropriate adult at the police station to see the detainee is secured.

3.16 It is imperative that a person detained under the Mental Health Act 1983, section 135 or 136, be assessed as soon as possible within the permitted period of detention specified in that Act. A police station may only be used as a place of safety in accordance with The Mental Health Act 1983 (Places of Safety) Regulations 2017. If that assessment is to take place at the police station, an approved mental health professional and a registered medical practitioner shall be called to the station as soon as possible to carry it out. The appropriate adult has no role in the assessment process and their presence is not required. Once the detainee has been assessed and suitable arrangements made for their treatment or care, they can no longer be detained under section 135 or 136. A detainee must be immediately discharged from detention if a registered medical practitioner, having examined them, concludes they are not mentally disordered within the meaning of the Act.

3.17 If the appropriate adult is:

- already at the police station, the provisions of *paragraphs 3.1* to *3.5* must be complied with in the appropriate adult's presence;
- not at the station when these provisions are complied with, they must be complied with again in the presence of the appropriate adult when they arrive, and a copy of the notice given to the detainee in accordance with *paragraph 3.2*, shall also be given to the appropriate adult.

3.17A The custody officer must ensure that at the time the copy of the notice is given to the appropriate adult, or as soon as practicable thereafter, the appropriate adult is advised of the duties of the appropriate adult as described in *paragraph 1.7A*.

3.18 *Not used.*

3.19 If the detainee, or appropriate adult on the detainee's behalf, asks for a solicitor to be called to give legal advice, the provisions of *section 6* apply (see *paragraph 6.5A*).

KEYNOTE

The purpose of the provisions at para. 3.19 (and also para. 6.5A) is to protect the rights of juvenile and vulnerable persons who may not understand the significance of what is said to them. They should always be given an opportunity, when an appropriate adult is called to the police station, to consult privately with a solicitor in the absence of the appropriate adult if they wish.

3.20 If the detainee is blind, seriously visually impaired or unable to read, the custody officer shall make sure their solicitor, relative, appropriate adult or some other person likely to take an interest in them and not involved in the investigation is available to help check any documentation. When this Code requires written consent or signing the person assisting may be asked to sign instead, if the detainee prefers. This paragraph does not require an appropriate adult to be called solely to assist in checking and signing documentation for a person who is not a juvenile, or is not vulnerable (see *paragraph 3.15*).

3.20A The Children and Young Persons Act 1933, section 31, requires that arrangements must be made for ensuring that a girl under the age of 18, while detained in a police station, is under the care of a woman. The custody officer must ensure that the woman under whose care the girl is, makes the enquiries and provides the information concerning personal needs relating to their health, hygiene and welfare described in *paragraph 9.3A* and menstrual products described in *paragraph 9.3B*. The section also requires that arrangements must be made for preventing any person under 18, while being detained in a police station, from associating with an adult charged with any offence, unless that adult is a relative or the adult is jointly charged with the same offence as the person under 18.

(C) Detained persons—Documentation

3.20B The grounds for a person's detention shall be recorded, in the person's presence if practicable. See *paragraph 1.8*.

3.20C Action taken under *paragraphs 3.12* to *3.20A* shall be recorded.

KEYNOTE

It is suggested that the custody officer record all the reasons for authorising the person's detention as it may be necessary in any criminal or civil proceedings. Indeed, it will be difficult for the custody officer to explain his/her decision without such information.

(D) Persons attending a police station or elsewhere voluntarily

3.21 Anybody attending a police station or other location (see *paragraph 3.22*) voluntarily to assist police with the investigation of an offence may leave at will unless arrested. The person may only be prevented from leaving at will if their arrest on suspicion of committing the offence is necessary in accordance with Code G.

KEYNOTE

The treatment of people who attend police stations voluntarily to assist the police with their investigations is dealt with by s. 29 PACE84 (see *General Police Duties*, para. 3.3.10).

An interviewer who is not sure, or has any doubt, about whether a place or location elsewhere than a police station is suitable for carrying out a voluntary interview, particularly in the case of a juvenile or vulnerable person, should consult an officer of the rank of sergeant or above for advice.

Although certain sections of this Code apply specifically to people in custody at police stations, a person who attends a police station or other location voluntarily to assist with an investigation should be treated with no less consideration, e.g. offered or allowed refreshments at appropriate times, and enjoy an absolute right to obtain legal advice or communicate with anyone outside the police station or other location.

This Code does not affect the principle that all citizens have a duty to help police officers to prevent crime and discover offenders. This is a civic rather than a legal duty; but when police officers are trying to discover whether, or by whom, offences have been committed, they are entitled to question any person from whom they think useful information can be obtained, subject to the restrictions imposed by this Code. A person's declaration that they are unwilling to reply does not alter this entitlement.

Action if arrest becomes necessary

(a) If during a person's voluntary attendance at a police station or other location it is decided for any reason that their arrest is necessary, they must:
- be informed at once that they are under arrest and of the grounds and reasons as required by *Code G*, and
- be brought before the custody officer at the police station where they are arrested or (as the case may be) at the police station to which they are taken after being arrested elsewhere. The custody officer is then responsible for making sure that a custody record is opened and that they are notified of their rights in the same way as other detainees as required by this Code.

KEYNOTE

If an officer forms a view that the person should be arrested at the police station for the purpose of interview and informs the custody officer of this view, the custody officer can authorise detention for the interview and is entitled to assume that the arrest by the officer is lawful (*Al-Fayed* v *Metropolitan Police Commissioner* [2004] EWCA Civ 1579).

Information to be given when arranging a voluntary interview:

(b) If the suspect's arrest is not necessary but they are cautioned as required in *section 10*, the person who, after describing the nature and circumstances of the suspected offence, gives the caution must at the same time, inform them that they are not under arrest and that they are not obliged to remain at the station or other location (see *paragraph 3.22*). The rights, entitlements and safeguards that apply to the conduct and recording of interviews with suspects are not diminished simply because the interview is arranged on a voluntary basis. For the purpose of arranging a voluntary interview the duty of the interviewer reflects that of the custody officer with regard to detained suspects. As a result:
   (i) the requirement in *paragraph 3.5(c)(ii)* to determine whether a detained suspect requires an appropriate adult, help to check documentation or an interpreter shall apply equally to a suspect who has not been arrested; and
   (ii) the suspect must not be asked to give their informed consent to be interviewed until *after* they have been informed of the rights, entitlements and safeguards that apply to voluntary interviews. These are set out in *paragraph 3.21A* and the interviewer is responsible for ensuring that the suspect is so informed and for explaining these rights, entitlements and safeguards.

3.21A The interviewer must inform the suspect that the purpose of the voluntary interview is to question them to obtain evidence about their involvement or suspected involvement in the offence(s) described when they were cautioned and told that they were not under arrest. The interviewer shall then inform the suspect that the following matters will apply if they agree to the voluntary interview proceeding:

(a) Their right to information about the offence(s) in question by providing sufficient information to enable them to understand the nature of any such offence(s) and why they are suspected of committing it. This is in order to allow for the effective exercise of the rights of the defence as required by *paragraph 11.1A*. It applies whether or not they ask for legal advice and includes any further offences that come to light and are pointed out during the voluntary interview and for which they are cautioned.

(b) Their right to free legal advice by:
   (i) explaining that they may obtain free and independent legal advice if they want it, and that this includes the right to speak with a solicitor on the telephone and to have the solicitor present during the interview;
   (ii) asking if they want legal advice and recording their reply; and
   (iii) if the person requests advice, securing its provision before the interview by contacting the Defence Solicitor Call Centre and explaining that the time and place of the interview will be arranged to enable them to obtain advice and that the interview will be delayed until they have received the advice unless, in accordance with *paragraph 6.6(c)* (Nominated solicitor not available and duty solicitor declined) or *paragraph 6.6(d)* (Change of mind), an officer of the rank of inspector or above agrees to the interview proceeding; or
   (iv) if the person declines to exercise the right, asking them why and recording any reasons given.

Note: When explaining the right to legal advice and the arrangements, the interviewer must take care not to indicate, except to answer a direct question, that the time taken to arrange and complete the voluntary interview might be reduced if:

- the suspect does not ask for legal advice or does not want a solicitor present when they are interviewed; or
- the suspect asks for legal advice or (as the case may be) asks for a solicitor to be present when they are interviewed, but changes their mind and agrees to be interviewed without waiting for a solicitor.

(c) Their right, if in accordance with *paragraph 3.5(c)(ii)* the interviewer determines:
   (i) that they are a juvenile or are vulnerable; or
   (ii) that they need help to check documentation (see *paragraph 3.20*), to have the appropriate adult present or (as the case may be) to have the necessary help to check documentation; and that the interview will be delayed until the presence of the appropriate adult or the necessary help, is secured.

(d) If they are a juvenile or vulnerable and do not want legal advice, their appropriate adult has the right to ask for a solicitor to attend if this would be in their best interests and the appropriate adult must be so informed. In this case, action to secure the provision of advice if so requested by their appropriate adult will be taken without delay in the same way as if requested by the person (see *sub-paragraph (b)(iii))*. However, they cannot be forced to see the solicitor if they are adamant that they do not wish to do so (see *paragraphs 3.19* and *6.5A*).

(e) Their right to an interpreter, if in accordance with, *paragraphs 3.5(c)(ii)* and *3.12*, the interviewer determines that they require an interpreter and that if they require an interpreter, making the necessary arrangements in accordance with *paragraph 13.1ZA* and that the interview will be delayed to make the arrangements.

(f) That interview will be arranged for a time and location (see *paragraph 3.22*) that enables:
   (i) the suspect's rights described above to be fully respected; and
   (ii) the whole of the interview to be recorded using an authorised recording device in accordance with Code E (Code of Practice on Audio recording of interviews with suspects) or (as the case may be) Code F (Code of Practice on visual recording with sound of interviews with suspects); and

(g) That their agreement to take part in the interview also signifies their agreement for that interview to be audio-recorded or (as the case may be) visually recorded with sound.

3.21B The provision by the interviewer of factual information described in *paragraph 3.21A* and, if asked by the suspect, further such information, does not constitute an interview for the purpose of this Code and *when that information is provided*:

(a) the interviewer must remind the suspect about the caution as required in *section 10* but must not *invite* comment about the offence or put specific questions to the suspect regarding their involvement in any offence, nor in respect of any comments they may make when given the information. Such an exchange is itself likely to constitute an interview as in *paragraph 11.1A* and require the associated interview safeguards in *section 11*.

(b) Any comment the suspect makes when the information is given which might be relevant to the offence, must be recorded and dealt with in accordance with *paragraph 11.13*.

(c) The suspect must be given a notice summarising the matters described in *paragraph 3.21A* and which includes the arrangements for obtaining legal advice. If a specific notice is not available, the notice given to detained suspects with references to detention-specific requirements and information redacted, may be used.

(d) For juvenile and vulnerable suspects (see *paragraphs 1.4* and *1.5*):
   (i) the information must be provided or (as the case may be) provided again, together with the notice, in the presence of the appropriate adult;
   (ii) if cautioned in the absence of the appropriate adult, the caution must be repeated in the appropriate adult's presence (see *paragraph 10.12*);
   (iii) the suspect must be informed of the decision that an appropriate is required and the reason (see *paragraph 3.5(c)(ii)*;
   (iv) the suspect *and* the appropriate adult shall be advised:
      - that the duties of the appropriate adult include giving advice and assistance in accordance with *paragraphs 1.7A* and *11.17*;
      - and that they can consult privately at any time.

(v) their informed agreement to be interviewed voluntarily must be sought and given in the *presence* of the appropriate adult and for a juvenile, the agreement of a parent or guardian of the juvenile is also required.

3.22 If the other location mentioned in *paragraph 3.21* is any place or premises for which the interviewer requires the person's informed consent to remain, for example, the person's home, then the references that the person is 'not obliged to remain' and that they 'may leave at will' mean that the person may also withdraw their consent and require the interviewer to leave.

Commencement of voluntary interview—general

3.22A Before asking the suspect any questions about their involvement in the offence they are suspected of committing, the interviewing officer must ask them to confirm that they agree to the interview proceeding. This confirmation shall be recorded in the interview record made in accordance with section 11 of this Code (written record) or Code E or Code F.

Documentation

3.22B Action taken under *paragraphs 3.21A* to *3.21B* shall be recorded. The record shall include the date time and place the action was taken, who was present and anything said to or by the suspect and to or by those present.

3.22 *Not used.*

3.23 *Not used.*

(E) Persons answering street bail

3.25 When a person is answering street bail, the custody officer should link any documentation held in relation to arrest with the custody record. Any further action shall be recorded on the custody record in accordance with *paragraphs 3.20B* and *3.20C* above.

(F) Requirements for suspects to be informed of certain rights

3.26 The provisions of this section identify the information which must be given to suspects who have been cautioned in accordance with *section 10 of this Code* according to whether or not they have been arrested and detained. It includes information required by *EU Directive 2012/13* on the right to information in criminal proceedings. If a complaint is made by or on behalf of such a suspect that the information and (as the case may be) access to records and documents has not been provided as required, the matter shall be reported to an inspector to deal with as a complaint for the purposes of *paragraph 9.2*, or *paragraph 12.9* if the challenge is made during an interview. This would include, for example:

(a) in the case of a detained suspect:
- not informing them of their rights (see *paragraph 3.1*);
- not giving them a copy of the Notice (see *paragraph 3.2(a)*);
- not providing an opportunity to read the notice (see *paragraph 3.2A*);
- not providing the required information (see *paragraphs 3.2(a)*, *3.12(b)* and, *3.12A*;
- not allowing access to the custody record (see *paragraph 2.4*);
- not providing a translation of the Notice (see *paragraph 3.12(c)* and *(d)*); and

(b) in the case of a suspect who is not detained:
- not informing them of their rights or providing the required information (see *paragraph 3.21(b)* to *3.21B*).

KEYNOTE

If the person is arrested on a warrant, any directions given by the court in the warrant must be followed. Consideration can always be given to contacting the court to get a variation on the conditions of the warrant. If the warrant was issued for the arrest of a person who has not yet been charged or summonsed for an offence, he/she should be dealt with as any other person arrested for an offence without warrant unless there are any additional directions on the warrant that must be followed.

Where a person who has been bailed under s. 37(7)(a) in order that the DPP can make a case disposal decision answers his/her bail or is arrested for failing to return on bail, detention can only be authorised to allow him/her to be further bailed under s. 37D PACE84 or in order that he/she can be charged or cautioned for offences connected with the original bail. If the person is not in a fit state to be dealt with he/she may be kept in police detention until he/she is (s. 37D PACE84).

2.6.9

Code C—4 Detainee's Property

(A) Action

4.1 The custody officer is responsible for:

(a) ascertaining what property a detainee:

(i) has with them when they come to the police station, whether on:

- arrest or re-detention on answering to bail;
- commitment to prison custody on the order or sentence of a court;
- lodgement at the police station with a view to their production in court from prison custody;
- transfer from detention at another station or hospital;
- detention under the Mental Health Act 1983, section 135 or 136;
- remand into police custody on the authority of a court.

(ii) might have acquired for an unlawful or harmful purpose while in custody;

(b) the safekeeping of any property taken from a detainee which remains at the police station.

The custody officer may search the detainee or authorise their being searched to the extent they consider necessary, provided a search of intimate parts of the body or involving the removal of more than outer clothing is only made as in *Annex A*. A search may only be carried out by an officer of the same sex as the detainee. See *Annex L*.

KEYNOTE

Section 54 PACE84 provides a custody officer with a power to search, seize and retain items which have been found during the search of a detained person.

Section 54 PACE84 states:

(1) The custody officer at a police station shall ascertain everything which a person has with him when he is—

(a) brought to the station after being arrested elsewhere or after being committed to custody by an order or sentence of a court; or

(b) arrested at the station or detained there, as a person falling within section 34(7), under section 37 above or as a person to whom section 46ZA(4) or (5) applies.

(2) The custody officer may record or cause to be recorded all or any of the things which he ascertains under subsection (1).

(2A) In the case of an arrested person, any such record may be made as part of his custody record.

(3) Subject to subsection (4) below, a custody officer may seize and retain any such thing or cause any such thing to be seized and retained.

(4) Clothes and personal effects may only be seized if the custody officer—

(a) believes that the person from whom they are seized may use them—

(i) to cause physical injury to himself or any other person;

(ii) to damage property;

(iii) to interfere with evidence; or

(iv) to assist him to escape; or

(b) has reasonable grounds for believing that they may be evidence relating to an offence.

(5) Where anything is seized, the person from whom it is seized shall be told the reason for the seizure unless he is—

(a) violent or likely to become violent; or

(b) incapable of understanding what is said to him.

(6) Subject to subsection (7) below, a person may be searched if the custody officer considers it necessary to enable him to carry out his duty under subsection (1) above and to the extent that the custody officer considers necessary for that purpose.

(6A) A person who is in custody at a police station or is in police detention otherwise than at a police station may at any time be searched in order to ascertain whether he has with him anything which he could use for any of the purposes specified in subsection (4)(a) above.

(6B) Subject to subsection (6C) below, a constable may seize and retain, or cause to be seized and retained, anything found on such a search.

(6C) A constable may only seize clothes and personal effects in the circumstances specified in subsection (4) above.

(7) An intimate search may not be conducted under this section.

(8) A search under this section shall be carried out by a constable.

(9) The constable carrying out a search shall be of the same sex as the person searched.

Reasonable force may be used (s. 117 PACE84).

Not all detained persons need to be searched; s. 54(1) and para. 4.1 require a detainee to be searched when it is clear the custody officer will have continuing duties in relation to that detainee or when that detainee's behaviour or offence makes an inventory appropriate. They do not require every detainee to be searched, e.g. if it is clear that a person will only be detained for a short period and is not to be placed in a cell, the custody officer may decide not to search him/her. In such a case, the custody record will be endorsed 'not searched', para. 4.4 will not apply, and the detainee will be invited to sign the entry. If the detainee refuses, the custody officer will be obliged to ascertain what property he/she has in accordance with para. 4.1.

4.2 Subject to *paragraph 4.3A*, detainees may retain clothing and personal effects at their own risk unless the custody officer considers they may use them to cause harm to themselves or others, interfere with evidence, damage property, effect an escape or they are needed as evidence. In this event the custody officer may withhold such articles as they consider necessary and must tell the detainee why.

4.3 Personal effects are those items a detainee may lawfully need, use or refer to while in detention but do not include cash and other items of value.

4.3A For the purposes of *paragraph 4.2*, the reference to clothing and personal effects shall be treated as including menstrual and any other health, hygiene and welfare products needed by the detainee in question (see *paragraphs 9.3A* and *9.3B*) and a decision to withhold any such products must be subject to a further specific risk assessment.

(B) Documentation

4.4 It is a matter for the custody officer to determine whether a record should be made of the property a detained person has with him or had taken from him on arrest. Any record made is not required to be kept as part of the custody record but the custody record should be noted as to where such a record exists and that record shall be treated as being part of the custody record for the purpose of this and any other Code of Practice (see *paragraphs 2.4*, *2.4A* and *2.5*). Whenever a record is made the detainee shall be allowed to check and sign the record of property as correct. Any refusal to sign shall be recorded.

KEYNOTE

Where property by virtue of its nature, quantity or size in the detainee's possession at the time of arrest has not been brought to the police station the custody officer is not required to record this on the custody record.

Only items of clothing worn by the detained person which have been withheld need to be recorded on the custody record.

Paragraph 4.4 does not require items of clothing worn by the person to be recorded unless withheld by the custody officer as in para. 4.2.

4.5 If a detainee is not allowed to keep any article of clothing or personal effects, the reason must be recorded.

KEYNOTE

The Search

The custody officer may authorise a constable to search a detained person, or may search the detained person him/herself in order to ascertain what property the detained person has with him/her (s. 54(6)). It should be noted that the custody officer must first authorise any search and the extent of the search (which will be to the extent the custody officer considers necessary to comply with his/her duty); officers *should not* search a person until this authority has been given. There are three levels to which searches can be conducted:

- routine searches that do not involve the removal of more than the detained person's outer clothing (this includes shoes and socks);
- strip searches (see Code C, Annex A, paras 9 to 12);
- intimate searches (see Code C, Annex A, paras 1 to 8).

A custody officer can authorise a routine search and/or a strip search but an intimate search can only be authorised by an officer of the rank of inspector or above.

Force standing orders are not an automatic right to search all detained persons (*Brazil* v *Chief Constable of Surrey* [1983] 1 WLR 1155).

2.6.10

Code C—5 Right not to be Held Incommunicado

(A) Action

5.1 Subject to *paragraph 5.7B*, any person arrested and held in custody at a police station or other premises may, on request, have one person known to them or likely to take an interest in their welfare informed at public expense of their whereabouts as soon as practicable. If the person cannot be contacted the detainee may choose up to two alternatives. If they cannot be contacted, the person in charge of detention or the investigation has discretion to allow further attempts until the information has been conveyed.

KEYNOTE

If the detainee does not know anyone to contact for advice or support or cannot contact a friend or relative, the custody officer should bear in mind any local voluntary bodies or other organisations which might be able to help. Paragraph 6.1 applies if legal advice is required.

In some circumstances it may not be appropriate to use the telephone to disclose information under paras 5.1 and 5.5.

5.2 The exercise of the above right in respect of each person nominated may be delayed only in accordance with *Annex B*.

5.3 The above right may be exercised each time a detainee is taken to another police station.

5.4 If the detainee agrees, they may at the custody officer's discretion, receive visits from friends, family or others likely to take an interest in their welfare, or in whose welfare the detainee has an interest.

KEYNOTE

At the custody officer's discretion and subject to the detainee's consent, visits should be allowed when possible, subject to having sufficient personnel to supervise a visit and any possible hindrance to the investigation.

5.5 If a friend, relative or person with an interest in the detainee's welfare enquires about their whereabouts, this information shall be given if the suspect agrees and *Annex B* does not apply.

5.6 The detainee shall be given writing materials, on request, and allowed to telephone one person for a reasonable time. Either or both of these privileges may be denied or delayed if an officer of inspector rank or above considers sending a letter or making a telephone call may result in any of the consequences in:

(a) *Annex B paragraphs 1* and *2* and the person is detained in connection with an indictable offence;

(b) *Not used.*

Nothing in this paragraph permits the restriction or denial of the rights in *paragraphs 5.1* and *6.1*.

KEYNOTE

A person may request an interpreter to interpret a telephone call or translate a letter.

The telephone call at para. 5.6 is in addition to any communication under paras 5.1 and 6.1.

5.7 Before any letter or message is sent, or telephone call made, the detainee shall be informed that what they say in any letter, call or message (other than in a communication to a solicitor) may be read or listened to and may be given in evidence. A telephone call may be terminated if it is being abused. The costs can be at public expense at the custody officer's discretion.

5.7A Any delay or denial of the rights in this section should be proportionate and should last no longer than necessary

5.7B In the case of a person in police custody for specific purposes and periods in accordance with a direction under the *Crime (Sentences) Act 1997, Schedule 1* (productions from prison etc.), the exercise of the rights in this section shall be subject to any additional conditions specified in the direction for the purpose of regulating the detainee's contact and communication with others whilst in police custody.

(B) Documentation

5.8 A record must be kept of any:

(a) request made under this section and the action taken;

(b) letters, messages or telephone calls made or received or visit received;

(c) refusal by the detainee to have information about them given to an outside enquirer.

The detainee must be asked to countersign the record accordingly and any refusal recorded.

KEYNOTE

Section 5 of Code C relates to the law contained in s. 56 PACE84 setting out the right a person has to have someone informed of their arrest and location.

2.6.11 **Code C—6 Right to Legal Advice**

(A) Action

6.1 Unless *Annex B* applies, all detainees must be informed that they may at any time consult and communicate privately with a solicitor, whether in person, in writing or by telephone, and that free independent legal advice is available.

KEYNOTE

Section 6 of Code C relates to the law contained in s. 58 of PACE84 setting out the right a person has to legal advice.

A detainee has a right to free legal advice and to be represented by a solicitor. An explanation of the arrangements which enable detainees to obtain legal advice is given below. An outline of these arrangements is also included in the Notice of Rights and Entitlements given to detainees in accordance with para. 3.2. The arrangements also apply, with appropriate modifications, to persons attending a police station or other location (see para. 3.22) voluntarily who are cautioned prior to being interviewed. See para. 3.21. When a detainee asks for free legal advice, the Defence Solicitor Call Centre (DSCC) must be informed of the request. Free legal advice will be limited to telephone advice provided by the Criminal Defence Service Direct (CDS Direct) if a detainee is:

- detained for a non-imprisonable offence;
- arrested on a bench warrant for failing to appear and being held for production at court (except where the solicitor has clear documentary evidence available that would result in the client being released from custody);
- arrested for drink driving (driving/in charge with excess alcohol, failing to provide a specimen, driving/in charge whilst unfit through drink); or
- detained in relation to breach of police or court bail conditions

unless one or more exceptions apply, in which case the DSCC should arrange for advice to be given by a solicitor at the police station, for example:

- the police want to interview the detainee or carry out an eye-witness identification procedure;
- the detainee needs an appropriate adult;
- the detainee is unable to communicate over the telephone;
- the detainee alleges serious misconduct by the police;
- the investigation includes another offence not included in the list;
- the solicitor to be assigned is already at the police station.

When free advice is not limited to telephone advice, detainees can ask for free advice from a solicitor they know or if they do not know a solicitor or the solicitor they know cannot be contacted, from the duty solicitor.

To arrange free legal advice, the police should telephone the DSCC. The call centre will decide whether legal advice should be limited to telephone advice from CDS Direct or whether a solicitor known to the detainee or the duty solicitor should speak to the detainee.

When detainees want to pay for legal advice themselves:

- the DSCC will contact a solicitor of their choice on their behalf;
- they may, when free advice is only available by telephone from CDS Direct, still speak to a solicitor of their choice on the telephone for advice, but the solicitor would not be paid by legal aid and may ask the person to pay for the advice;
- they should be given an opportunity to consult a specific solicitor or another solicitor from that solicitor's firm. If this solicitor is not available, they may choose up to two alternatives. If these alternatives are not available, the custody officer has discretion to allow further attempts until a solicitor has been contacted and agreed to provide advice;
- they are entitled to a private consultation with their chosen solicitor on the telephone or the solicitor may decide to come to the police station;
- if their chosen solicitor cannot be contacted, the DSCC may still be called to arrange free legal advice.

Apart from carrying out duties necessary to implement these arrangements, an officer must not advise the suspect about any particular firm of solicitors.

Whenever a detainee exercises his/her right to legal advice by consulting or communicating with a solicitor, he/she must be allowed to do so in private. This right to consult or communicate in private is fundamental. If the requirement for privacy is compromised because what is said or written by the detainee or solicitor for the purpose of giving and receiving legal advice is overheard, listened to or read by others without the informed consent of the detainee, the right will effectively have been denied. When a detainee chooses to speak to a solicitor on the telephone, he/she should be allowed to do so in private unless this is impractical because of the design and layout of the custody area or the location of telephones. However, the normal expectation should be that facilities will be available, unless they are being used, at all police stations to enable detainees to speak in private to a solicitor either face to face or over the telephone.

6.2 *Not used.*

6.3 A poster advertising the right to legal advice must be prominently displayed in the charging area of every police station.

KEYNOTE

A poster or posters of the right to legal advice containing translations into Welsh, the main minority ethnic languages and the principal European languages should be displayed wherever they are likely to be helpful and it is practicable to do so.

6.4 No police officer should, at any time, do or say anything with the intention of dissuading any person who is entitled to legal advice in accordance with this Code, whether or not they have been arrested and are detained, from obtaining legal advice.

KEYNOTE

No police officer or police staff shall indicate to any suspect, except to answer a direct question, that the period for which he/she is liable to be detained, or if not detained, the time taken to complete the interview, might be reduced:

- if the suspect does not ask for legal advice or does not want a solicitor present when he/she is interviewed; or
- if he/she has asked for legal advice or (as the case may be) asked for a solicitor to be present when he/she is interviewed but changes his/her mind and agrees to be interviewed without waiting for a solicitor.

6.5 The exercise of the right of access to legal advice may be delayed only as in *Annex B*. Whenever legal advice is requested, and unless *Annex B* applies, the custody officer must act without delay to secure the provision of such advice. If the detainee has the right to speak to a solicitor in person but declines to exercise the right the officer should point out that the right includes the right to speak with a solicitor on the telephone. If the detainee continues to waive this right, or a detainee whose right to free legal advice is limited to telephone advice from the Criminal Defence Service (CDS) Direct declines to exercise that right, the officer should ask them why and any reasons should be recorded on the custody record or the interview record as appropriate. Reminders of the right to legal advice must be given as in *paragraphs 3.5, 11.2, 15.4, 16.4, 16.5, 2B of Annex A, 3 of Annex K* and *5 of Annex M* of this Code and Code D, *paragraphs 3.17(ii)* and *6.3*. Once it is clear a detainee does not want to speak to a solicitor in person or by telephone they should cease to be asked their reasons.

KEYNOTE

A detainee has a right to free legal advice and to be represented by a solicitor. A detainee is not obliged to give reasons for declining legal advice and should not be pressed to do so.

6.5A In the case of a person who is a juvenile or is vulnerable, an appropriate adult should consider whether legal advice from a solicitor is required. If such a detained person wants to exercise the right to legal advice, the appropriate action should be taken and should not be delayed until the appropriate adult arrives. If the person indicates that they do not want legal advice, the appropriate adult has the right to ask for a solicitor to attend if this would be in the best interests of the person and must be so informed. In this case, action to secure the provision of advice if so requested by the appropriate adult shall be taken without delay in the same way as when requested by the person. However, the person cannot be forced to see the solicitor if they are adamant that they do not wish to do so.

6.6 A detainee who wants legal advice may not be interviewed or continue to be interviewed until they have received such advice unless:

(a) *Annex B* applies, when the restriction on drawing adverse inferences from silence in *Annex C* will apply because the detainee is not allowed an opportunity to consult a solicitor; or

(b) an officer of superintendent rank or above has reasonable grounds for believing that:

(i) the consequent delay might:

- lead to interference with, or harm to, evidence connected with an offence;
- lead to interference with, or physical harm to, other people;
- lead to serious loss of, or damage to, property;
- lead to alerting other people suspected of having committed an offence but not yet arrested for it;
- hinder the recovery of property obtained in consequence of the commission of an offence.

(ii) when a solicitor, including a duty solicitor, has been contacted and has agreed to attend, awaiting their arrival would cause unreasonable delay to the process of investigation.

Note: In these cases the restriction on drawing adverse inferences from silence in *Annex C* will apply because the detainee is not allowed an opportunity to consult a solicitor.

(c) the solicitor the detainee has nominated or selected from a list:

(i) cannot be contacted;

(ii) has previously indicated they do not wish to be contacted; or

(iii) having been contacted, has declined to attend; and

- the detainee has been advised of the Duty Solicitor Scheme but has declined to ask for the duty solicitor;
- in these circumstances the interview may be started or continued without further delay provided an officer of inspector rank or above has agreed to the interview proceeding.

Note: The restriction on drawing adverse inferences from silence in *Annex C* will not apply because the detainee is allowed an opportunity to consult the duty solicitor;

(d) the detainee changes their mind about wanting legal advice or (as the case may be) about wanting a solicitor present at the interview and states that they no longer wish to speak to a solicitor. In these circumstances, the interview may be started or continued without delay provided that:

(i) an officer of inspector rank or above:

- speaks to the detainee to enquire about the reasons for their change of mind, and
- makes, or directs the making of, reasonable efforts to ascertain the solicitor's expected time of arrival and to inform the solicitor that the suspect has stated that they wish to change their mind and the reason (if given);

(ii) the detainee's reason for their change of mind (if given) and the outcome of the action in (i) are recorded in the custody record;

(iii) the detainee, after being informed of the outcome of the action in (i) above, confirms in writing that they want the interview to proceed without speaking or further speaking to a solicitor or (as the case may be) without a solicitor being present and do not wish to wait for a solicitor by signing an entry to this effect in the custody record;

(iv) an officer of inspector rank or above is satisfied that it is proper for the interview to proceed in these circumstances and:

- gives authority in writing for the interview to proceed and, if the authority is not recorded in the custody record, the officer must ensure that the custody record shows the date and time of the authority and where it is recorded, and
- takes, or directs the taking of, reasonable steps to inform the solicitor that the authority has been given and the time when the interview is expected to commence and records or causes to be recorded, the outcome of this action in the custody record.

(v) When the interview starts and the interviewer reminds the suspect of their right to legal advice (see *paragraph 11.2*, Code E *paragraph 4.5* and Code F *paragraph 4.5*), the interviewer shall then ensure that the following is recorded in the written interview record or the interview record made in accordance with Code E or F:

- confirmation that the detainee has changed their mind about wanting legal advice or (as the case may be) about wanting a solicitor present and the reasons for it if given;
- the fact that authority for the interview to proceed has been given and, subject to *paragraph 2.6A*, the name of the authorising officer;
- that if the solicitor arrives at the station before the interview is completed, the detainee will be so informed without delay and *a break will be taken* to allow them to speak to the solicitor if they wish, unless *paragraph 6.6(a)* applies, and
- that at any time during the interview, the detainee may again ask for legal advice and that if they do, a break will be taken to allow them to speak to the solicitor, unless *paragraph 6.6(a), (b), or (c)* applies.

Note: In these circumstances, the restriction on drawing adverse inferences from silence in *Annex C* will not apply because the detainee is allowed an opportunity to consult a solicitor if they wish.

KEYNOTE

In considering if para. 6.6(b) applies, the officer should, if practicable, ask the solicitor for an estimate of how long it will take to come to the station and relate this to the time detention is permitted, the time of day (i.e. whether the rest period under para. 12.2 is imminent) and the requirements of other investigations. If the solicitor is on their way or is to set off immediately, it will not normally be appropriate to begin an interview before they arrive. If it appears necessary to begin an interview before the solicitor's arrival, they should be given an indication of how long the police would be able to wait before para. 6.6(b) applies so there is an opportunity to make arrangements for someone else to provide legal advice.

Subject to the constraints of Annex B, a solicitor may advise more than one client in an investigation if he/she wishes. Any question of a conflict of interest is for the solicitor under his/her professional code of conduct. If, however, waiting for a solicitor to give advice to one client may lead to unreasonable delay to the interview with another, the provisions of para. 6.6(b) may apply.

6.7 If *paragraph 6.6(a)* applies, where the reason for authorising the delay ceases to apply, there may be no further delay in permitting the exercise of the right in the absence of a further authorisation unless *paragraph 6.6(b), (c)* or *(d)* applies. If *paragraph 6.6(b)(i)* applies, once sufficient information has been obtained to avert the risk, questioning must cease until the detainee has received legal advice unless *paragraph 6.6(a), (b)(ii), (c)* or *(d)* applies.

6.8 A detainee who has been permitted to consult a solicitor shall be entitled on request to have the solicitor present when they are interviewed unless one of the exceptions in *paragraph 6.6* applies.

6.9 The solicitor may only be required to leave the interview if their conduct is such that the interviewer is unable properly to put questions to the suspect.

KEYNOTE

The solicitor's only role in the police station is to protect and advance the legal rights of his/her client. On occasions, this may require the solicitor to give advice which has the effect of the client avoiding giving evidence which strengthens a prosecution case. The solicitor may intervene in order to seek clarification, challenge an improper question to the client or the manner in which it is put, advise the client not to reply to particular questions or if he/she wishes to give the client further legal advice. Paragraph 6.9 only applies if the solicitor's approach or conduct prevents or unreasonably obstructs proper questions being put to the suspect or the suspect's response being recorded. Examples of unacceptable conduct include answering questions on a suspect's behalf or providing written replies for the suspect to quote.

An officer who takes the decision to exclude a solicitor must be in a position to satisfy the court that the decision was properly made. In order to do this, he/she may need to witness what is happening.

6.10 If the interviewer considers a solicitor is acting in such a way, they will stop the interview and consult an officer not below superintendent rank, if one is readily available, and otherwise an officer not below inspector rank not connected with the investigation. After speaking to the solicitor, the officer consulted will decide if the interview should continue in the presence of that solicitor. If they decide it should not, the suspect will be given the opportunity to consult another solicitor before the interview continues and that solicitor given an opportunity to be present at the interview.

6.11 The removal of a solicitor from an interview is a serious step and, if it occurs, the officer of superintendent rank or above who took the decision will consider if the incident should be reported to the Solicitors Regulatory Authority. If the decision to remove the solicitor has been taken by an officer below superintendent rank, the facts must be reported to an officer of superintendent rank or above, who will similarly consider whether a report to the Solicitors Regulatory Authority would be appropriate. When the solicitor concerned is a duty solicitor, the report should be both to the Solicitors Regulatory Authority and to the Legal Aid Agency.

6.12 'Solicitor' in this Code means:

- a solicitor who holds a current practising certificate;
- an accredited or probationary representative included on the register of representatives maintained by the Legal Aid Agency.

6.12A An accredited or probationary representative sent to provide advice by, and on behalf of, a solicitor shall be admitted to the police station for this purpose unless an officer of inspector rank or above considers such a visit will hinder the investigation and directs otherwise. Hindering the investigation does not include giving proper legal advice to a detainee. Once admitted to the police station, *paragraphs 6.6* to *6.10* apply.

6.13 In exercising their discretion under *paragraph 6.12A*, the officer should take into account in particular:

- whether:
  - ~ the identity and status of an accredited or probationary representative have been satisfactorily established;
  - ~ they are of suitable character to provide legal advice, e.g. a person with a criminal record is unlikely to be suitable unless the conviction was for a minor offence and not recent.

- any other matters in any written letter of authorisation provided by the solicitor on whose behalf the person is attending the police station.

KEYNOTE

If an officer of at least inspector rank considers that a particular solicitor or firm of solicitors is persistently sending probationary representatives who are unsuited to provide legal advice, he/she should inform an officer of at least superintendent rank, who may wish to take the matter up with the Solicitors Regulation Authority.

6.14 If the inspector refuses access to an accredited or probationary representative or a decision is taken that such a person should not be permitted to remain at an interview, the inspector must notify the solicitor on whose behalf the representative was acting and give them an opportunity to make alternative arrangements. The detainee must be informed and the custody record noted.

6.15 If a solicitor arrives at the station to see a particular person, that person must, unless *Annex B* applies, be so informed whether or not they are being interviewed and asked if they would like to see the solicitor. This applies even if the detainee has declined legal advice or, having requested it, subsequently agreed to be interviewed without receiving advice. The solicitor's attendance and the detainee's decision must be noted in the custody record.

(B) Documentation

6.16 Any request for legal advice and the action taken shall be recorded.

6.17 A record shall be made in the interview record if a detainee asks for legal advice and an interview is begun either in the absence of a solicitor or their representative, or they have been required to leave an interview.

2.6.12 Code C—7 Citizens of Independent Commonwealth Countries or Foreign Nationals

(A) Action

7.1 A detainee who is a citizen of an independent Commonwealth country or a national of a foreign country, including the Republic of Ireland, has the right, upon request, to communicate at any time with the appropriate High Commission, Embassy or Consulate. That detainee must be informed as soon as practicable of this right and asked if they want to have their High Commission, Embassy or Consulate told of their whereabouts and the grounds for their detention. Such a request should be acted upon as soon as practicable.

7.2 A detainee who is a citizen of a country with which a bilateral consular convention or agreement is in force requiring notification of arrest must also be informed that subject to *paragraph 7.4*, notification of their arrest will be sent to the appropriate High Commission, Embassy or Consulate as soon as practicable, whether or not they request it. A list of the countries to which this requirement currently applies and contact details for the relevant High Commissions, Embassies and Consulates can be obtained from the Consular Directorate of the Foreign and Commonwealth Office (FCO) as follows:

- from the FCO web pages:
  - *https://gov.uk/government/publications/table-of-consular-conventions-and-mandatory-notification-obligations*, and
  - *https://www.gov.uk/government/publications/foreign-embassies-in-the-uk*
- by telephone to 020 7008 3100,
- by email to *fcocorrespondence@fco.gov.uk*.
- by letter to the Foreign and Commonwealth Office, King Charles Street, London, SW1A 2AH.

7.3 Consular officers may, if the detainee agrees, visit one of their nationals in police detention to talk to them and, if required, to arrange for legal advice. Such visits shall take place out of the hearing of a police officer.

7.4 Notwithstanding the provisions of consular conventions, if the detainee claims that they are a refugee or have applied or intend to apply for asylum, the custody officer must ensure that UK Visas and Immigration (UKVI) (formerly the UK Border Agency) is informed as soon as practicable of the claim. UKVI will then determine whether compliance with relevant international obligations requires notification of the arrest to be sent and will inform the custody officer as to what action police need to take.

(B) Documentation

7.5 A record shall be made:

- when a detainee is informed of their rights under this section and of any requirement in paragraph 7.2;
- of any communications with a High Commission, Embassy or Consulate, and
- of any communications with UKVI about a detainee's claim to be a refugee or to be seeking asylum and the resulting action taken by police.

KEYNOTE

The exercise of the rights in this section may not be interfered with even where Code C, Annex B applies, i.e. the right to communicate with the High Commission, Embassy, Consulate, etc. must be granted even in cases where other rights (such as delay in notification of arrest) are delayed in accordance with PACE84.

2.6.13

Code C—8 Conditions of Detention

(A) Action

8.1 So far as it is practicable, not more than one detainee should be detained in each cell.

8.2 Cells in use must be adequately heated, cleaned and ventilated. They must be adequately lit, subject to such dimming as is compatible with safety and security to allow people detained overnight to sleep. No additional restraints shall be used within a locked cell unless absolutely necessary and then only restraint equipment, approved for use in that force by the chief officer, which is reasonable and necessary in the circumstances having regard to the detainee's demeanour and with a view to ensuring their safety and the safety of others. If a detainee is deaf or a vulnerable person, particular care must be taken when deciding whether to use any form of approved restraints.

8.3 Blankets, mattresses, pillows and other bedding supplied shall be of a reasonable standard and in a clean and sanitary condition.

KEYNOTE

The provisions in para. 8.3 (and para. 8.6) are of particular importance in the case of a person likely to be detained for an extended period. In deciding whether to allow meals to be supplied by family or friends, the custody officer is entitled to take account of the risk of items being concealed in any food or package and the officer's duties and responsibilities under food-handling legislation.

8.4 Access to toilet and washing facilities must be provided. This must take account of the dignity of the detainee.

KEYNOTE

In cells subject to CCTV monitoring, privacy in the toilet area should be ensured by any appropriate means and detainees should be made aware of this when they are placed in the cell. If a detainee, or appropriate adult on their behalf, expresses doubts about the effectiveness of the means used, reasonable steps should be taken to allay those doubts, for example, by explaining or demonstrating the means used.

8.5 If it is necessary to remove a detainee's clothes for the purposes of investigation, for hygiene, health reasons or cleaning, removal shall be conducted with proper regard to the dignity, sensitivity and vulnerability of the detainee and replacement clothing of a reasonable standard of comfort and cleanliness shall be provided. A detainee may not be interviewed unless adequate clothing has been offered.

KEYNOTE

In *Pile* v *Chief Constable of Merseyside Police* [2020] EWHC 2472 (QB), a claim was made arguing that the police should not have removed the clothing of the claimant who, having been arrested for the offence of being drunk and disorderly, had vomited over her own clothing when unconscious in a police cell. The court stated that it was necessary to remove the claimant's clothing for hygiene and health reasons and that a failure to do so would have amounted to a breach of the Code.

8.6 At least two light meals and one main meal should be offered in any 24-hour period. Drinks should be provided at meal times and upon reasonable request between meals. Whenever necessary, advice shall be sought from the appropriate healthcare professional, on medical and dietary matters. As far as practicable, meals provided shall offer a varied diet and meet any specific dietary needs or religious beliefs the detainee may have. The detainee may, at the custody officer's discretion, have meals supplied by their family or friends at their expense.

KEYNOTE

Meals should, so far as practicable, be offered at recognised meal times, or at other times that take account of when the detainee last had a meal.

8.7 Brief outdoor exercise shall be offered daily if practicable.

8.8 A juvenile shall not be placed in a police cell unless no other secure accommodation is available and the custody officer considers it is not practicable to supervise them if they are not placed in a cell or that a cell provides more comfortable accommodation than other secure accommodation in the station. A juvenile may not be placed in a cell with a detained adult.

(B) Documentation

8.9 A record must be kept of replacement clothing and meals offered.

8.10 If a juvenile is placed in a cell, the reason must be recorded.

8.11 The use of any restraints on a detainee whilst in a cell, the reasons for it and, if appropriate, the arrangements for enhanced supervision of the detainee whilst so restrained, shall be recorded. See *paragraph 3.9*.

2.6.14 Code C—9 Care and Treatment of Detained Persons

(A) General

9.1 Nothing in this section prevents the police from calling an appropriate healthcare professional to examine a detainee for the purposes of obtaining evidence relating to any offence in which the detainee is suspected of being involved.

KEYNOTE

A 'health care professional' means a clinically qualified person working within the scope of practice as determined by his/her relevant professional body. Whether a health care professional is 'appropriate' depends on the circumstances of the duties he/she carries out at the time.

9.2 If a complaint is made by, or on behalf of, a detainee about their treatment since their arrest, or it comes to notice that a detainee may have been treated improperly, a report must be made as soon as practicable to an officer of inspector rank or above not connected with the investigation. If the matter concerns a possible assault or the possibility of the unnecessary or unreasonable use of force, an appropriate healthcare professional must also be called as soon as practicable.

9.3 Subject to *paragraph 9.6* in the case of a person to whom The Mental Health Act 1983 (Places of Safety) Regulations 2017 apply, detainees should be visited at least every hour. If no reasonably foreseeable risk was identified in a risk assessment, see *paragraphs 3.6* to *3.10*, there is no need to wake a sleeping detainee. Those suspected of being under the influence of drink or drugs or both or of having swallowed drugs, or whose level of consciousness causes concern must, subject to any clinical directions given by the appropriate healthcare professional, see *paragraph 9.13*:

- be visited and roused at least every half hour;
- have their condition assessed as in *Annex H*;
- and clinical treatment arranged if appropriate.

KEYNOTE

Whenever possible, juveniles and vulnerable detainees should be visited more frequently.

A detainee who appears drunk or behaves abnormally may be suffering from illness, the effects of drugs or may have sustained injury, particularly a head injury which is not apparent. A detainee needing or dependent on certain drugs, including alcohol, may experience harmful effects within a short time of being deprived of his/her supply. In these circumstances, when there is any doubt, police should always act urgently to call an appropriate health care professional or an ambulance.

Paragraph 9.3 also applies to a person in police custody by order of a magistrates' court under the Criminal Justice Act 1988, s. 152 (as amended by the Drugs Act 2005, s. 8) to facilitate the recovery of evidence after being charged with drug possession or drug trafficking and suspected of having swallowed drugs. In the case of the health care needs of a person who has swallowed drugs, the custody officer, subject to any clinical directions, should consider the necessity for rousing every half hour. This does not negate the need for regular visiting of the suspect in the cell.

The purpose of recording a person's responses when attempting to rouse them using the procedure in Annex H is to enable any change in the individual's consciousness level to be noted and clinical treatment arranged if appropriate.

9.3A As soon as practicable after arrival at the police station, each detainee must be given an opportunity to speak in private with a member of the custody staff who if they wish, may be of the same sex as the detainee (see *paragraph 1.13(c)*), about any matter concerning the detainee's personal needs relating to their health, hygiene and welfare that might affect or concern them whilst in custody. If the detainee wishes to take this opportunity, the necessary arrangements shall be made as soon as practicable. In the case of a juvenile or vulnerable person, the appropriate adult must be involved in accordance with *paragraph 3.17* and in the case of a girl under 18, see *paragraph 3.20A*.

KEYNOTE

Matters concerning personal needs to which para. 9.3A applies include any requirement for menstrual products, incontinence products and colostomy appliances, where these needs have not previously been identified (see para. 3.5(c)). It also enables adult women to speak in private to a female officer about their requirements for menstrual products if they decline to respond to the more direct enquiry envisaged under para. 9.3B. This contact should be facilitated at any time, where possible.

9.3B Each female detainee aged 18 or over shall be asked in private if possible and at the earliest opportunity, if they require or are likely to require any menstrual products whilst they are in custody. They must also be told that they will be provided free of charge and that replacement products are available. At the custody officer's discretion, detainees may have menstrual products supplied by their family or friends at their expense. For girls under 18, see *paragraph 3.20A*.

9.4 When arrangements are made to secure clinical attention for a detainee, the custody officer must make sure all relevant information which might assist in the treatment of the detainee's condition is made available to the responsible healthcare professional. This applies whether or not the healthcare professional asks for such information. Any officer or police staff with relevant information must inform the custody officer as soon as practicable.

(B) Clinical treatment and attention

9.5 The custody officer must make sure a detainee receives appropriate clinical attention as soon as reasonably practicable if the person:
- (a) appears to be suffering from physical illness; or
- (b) is injured; or
- (c) appears to be suffering from a mental disorder; or
- (d) appears to need clinical attention.

KEYNOTE

Paragraph 9.5 does not apply to minor ailments or injuries which do not need attention. However, all such ailments or injuries must be recorded in the custody record and any doubt must be resolved in favour of calling the appropriate health care professional.

9.5A This applies even if the detainee makes no request for clinical attention and whether or not they have already received clinical attention elsewhere. If the need for attention appears urgent, e.g. when indicated as in *Annex H*, the nearest available healthcare professional or an ambulance must be called immediately.

9.5B The custody officer must also consider the need for clinical attention in relation to those suffering the effects of alcohol or drugs.

9.6 *Paragraph 9.5* is not meant to prevent or delay the transfer to a hospital if necessary of a person detained under the Mental Health Act 1983, sections 135 and 136, as amended by the Policing and Crime Act 2017. When an assessment under that Act is to take place at a police station (see *paragraph 3.16*) the custody officer must also ensure that in accordance with *The Mental Health Act 1983 (Places of Safety) Regulations 2017*, a health professional is present and available to the person throughout the period they are detained at the police station and that at the welfare of the detainee is checked by the health professional at least once every thirty minutes and any appropriate action for the care and treatment of the detainee taken.

9.7 If it appears to the custody officer, or they are told, that a person brought to a station under arrest may be suffering from an infectious disease or condition, the custody officer must take reasonable steps to safeguard the health of the detainee and others at the station. In deciding what action to take, advice must be sought from an appropriate healthcare professional. The custody officer has discretion to isolate the person and their property until clinical directions have been obtained.

KEYNOTE

It is important to respect a person's right to privacy, and information about his/her health must be kept confidential and only disclosed with his/her consent or in accordance with clinical advice when it is necessary to protect the detainee's health or that of others who come into contact with him/her.

9.8 If a detainee requests a clinical examination, an appropriate healthcare professional must be called as soon as practicable to assess the detainee's clinical needs. If a safe and appropriate care plan cannot be provided, the appropriate healthcare professional's advice must be sought. The detainee may also be examined by a medical practitioner of their choice at their expense.

9.9 If a detainee is required to take or apply any medication in compliance with clinical directions prescribed before their detention, the custody officer must consult the appropriate healthcare professional before the use of the medication. Subject to the restrictions in *paragraph 9.10*, the custody officer is responsible for the safekeeping of any medication and for making sure the detainee is given the opportunity to take or apply prescribed or approved medication. Any such consultation and its outcome shall be noted in the custody record.

9.10 No police officer may administer or supervise the self-administration of medically prescribed controlled drugs of the types and forms listed in the Misuse of Drugs Regulations 2001, Schedule 2 or 3. A detainee may only self-administer such drugs under the personal supervision of the registered medical practitioner authorising their use or other appropriate healthcare professional. The custody officer may supervise the self-administration of, or authorise other custody staff to supervise the self-administration of, drugs listed in Schedule 4 or 5 if the officer has consulted the appropriate healthcare professional authorising their use and both are satisfied self-administration will not expose the detainee, police officers or anyone else to the risk of harm or injury.

9.11 When appropriate healthcare professionals administer drugs or authorise the use of other medications, supervise their self-administration or consult with the custody officer about allowing self-administration of drugs listed in Schedule 4 or 5, it must be within current medicines legislation and the scope of practice as determined by their relevant statutory regulatory body.

9.12 If a detainee has in their possession, or claims to need, medication relating to a heart condition, diabetes, epilepsy or a condition of comparable potential seriousness then, even though *paragraph 9.5* may not apply, the advice of the appropriate healthcare professional must be obtained.

9.13 Whenever the appropriate healthcare professional is called in accordance with this section to examine or treat a detainee, the custody officer shall ask for their opinion about:

- any risks or problems which police need to take into account when making decisions about the detainee's continued detention;
- when to carry out an interview if applicable; and

- the need for safeguards.

9.14 When clinical directions are given by the appropriate healthcare professional, whether orally or in writing, and the custody officer has any doubts or is in any way uncertain about any aspect of the directions, the custody officer shall ask for clarification. It is particularly important that directions concerning the frequency of visits are clear, precise and capable of being implemented.

KEYNOTE

The custody officer should always seek to clarify directions that the detainee requires constant observation or supervision and should ask the appropriate health care professional to explain precisely what action needs to be taken to implement such directions.

(C) Documentation

9.15 A record must be made in the custody record of:

(a) the arrangements made for an examination by an appropriate healthcare professional under *paragraph 9.2* and of any complaint reported under that paragraph together with any relevant remarks by the custody officer;

(b) any arrangements made in accordance with *paragraph 9.5*;

(c) any request for a clinical examination under *paragraph 9.8* and any arrangements made in response;

(d) the injury, ailment, condition or other reason which made it necessary to make the arrangements in (*a*) to (*c*);

(e) any clinical directions and advice, including any further clarifications, given to police by a healthcare professional concerning the care and treatment of the detainee in connection with any of the arrangements made in (*a*) to (*c*);

(f) if applicable, the responses received when attempting to rouse a person using the procedure in *Annex H*.

9.16 If a healthcare professional does not record their clinical findings in the custody record, the record must show where they are recorded. However, information which is necessary to custody staff to ensure the effective ongoing care and well being of the detainee must be recorded openly in the custody record, see *paragraph 3.8* and *Annex G, paragraph 7*.

KEYNOTE

A solicitor or appropriate adult must be permitted to consult a detainee's custody record as soon as practicable after his/her arrival at the station and at any other time while the person is detained (Code C, para. 2.4). Therefore details required to be included in the custody record concerning the detainee's injuries and ailments will be accessible to both the solicitor and appropriate adult. However, paras 9.15 and 9.16 do not require any information about the cause of any injury, ailment or condition to be recorded on the custody record if it appears capable of providing evidence of an offence.

9.17 Subject to the requirements of *Section 4*, the custody record shall include:

- a record of all medication a detainee has in their possession on arrival at the police station;
- a note of any such medication they claim to need but do not have with them.

Code C—10 Cautions [see chapter 2.8]

Code C—11 Interviews—General [see chapter 2.8]

Code C—12 Interviews in Police Stations [see chapter 2.8]

2.6.15

Code C—13 Interpreters

(A) General

13.1 Chief officers are responsible for making arrangements (see *paragraph 13.1ZA*) to provide appropriately qualified independent persons to act as interpreters and to provide translations of essential documents for:

(a) detained suspects who, in accordance with *paragraph 3.5(c)(ii)*, the custody officer has determined require an interpreter, and

(b) suspects who are not under arrest but are cautioned as in section 10 who, in accordance with *paragraph 3.21(b)*, the interviewer has determined require an interpreter. In these cases, the responsibilities of the custody officer are, if appropriate, assigned to the interviewer. An interviewer who has any doubts about whether and what arrangements for an interpreter must be made or about how the provisions of this section should be applied to a suspect who is not under arrest should seek advice from an officer of the rank of sergeant or above.

If the suspect has a hearing or speech impediment, references to 'interpreter' and 'interpretation' in this Code include arrangements for appropriate assistance necessary to establish effective communication with that person. See *paragraph 13.1C* below if the person is in Wales.

13.1ZA References in *paragraph 13.1* above and elsewhere in this Code (see *paragraphs 3.12(a), 13.2, 13.2A, 13.5, 13.6, 13.9, 13.10, 13.10A, 13.10D* and *13.11 below* and in any other Code, to making arrangements for an interpreter to assist a suspect, mean making arrangements for the interpreter to be *physically* present in the same location as the suspect *unless* the provisions in *paragraph 13.12* below, and Part 1 of *Annex N*, allow live-link interpretation to be used.

13.1A The arrangements *must* comply with the minimum requirements set out in *Directive 2010/64/EU* of the European Parliament and of the Council of 20 October 2010 on the right to interpretation and translation in criminal proceedings. The provisions *of this* Code implement the requirements for those to whom this Code applies. These requirements include the following:

- That the arrangements made and the quality of interpretation and translation provided shall be sufficient to '*safeguard the fairness of the proceedings, in particular by ensuring that suspected or accused persons have knowledge of the cases against them and are able to exercise their right of defence*'. This term which is used by the Directive means that the suspect must be able to understand their position and be able to communicate effectively with police officers, interviewers, solicitors and appropriate adults as provided for by this and any other Code in the same way as a suspect who can speak and understand English and who does not have a hearing or speech impediment and who would therefore not require an interpreter. See *paragraphs 13.12* to *13.14* and *Annex N* for application to live-link interpretation.
- The provision of a written translation of all documents considered essential for the person to exercise their right of defence and to '*safeguard the fairness of the proceedings*' as described above. For the purposes of this Code, this includes any decision to authorise a person to be detained and details of any offence(s) with

which the person has been charged or for which they have been told they may be prosecuted, see *Annex M*.

- Procedures to help determine:
  - whether a suspect can speak and understand English and needs the assistance of an interpreter, see *paragraph 13.1*; and
  - whether another interpreter should be arranged or another translation should be provided when a suspect complains about the quality of either or both, see *paragraphs 13.10A* and *13.10C*.

KEYNOTE

Chief officers have discretion when determining the individuals or organisations they use to provide interpretation and translation services for their forces, provided that these services are compatible with the requirements of the Directive of the European Parliament and of the Council.

A procedure for determining whether a person needs an interpreter might involve a telephone interpreter service or using cue cards or similar visual aids which enable detainees to indicate their ability to speak and understand English and their preferred language. This could be confirmed through an interpreter who could also assess the extent to which the person can speak and understand English.

There should also be a procedure for determining whether suspects who require an interpreter require assistance in accordance with para. 3.20 to help them check and if applicable sign any documentation.

13.1B All reasonable attempts should be made to make the suspect understand that interpretation and translation will be provided at public expense.

13.1C With regard to persons in Wales, nothing in this or any other Code affects the application of the Welsh Language Schemes produced by police and crime commissioners in Wales in accordance with the Welsh Language Act 1993. See *paragraphs 3.12 and 13.1*.

(B) Interviewing suspects—foreign languages

13.2 Unless *paragraphs 11.1 or 11.18(c)* apply, a suspect who for the purposes of this Code requires an interpreter because they do not appear to speak or understand English (see *paragraphs 3.5(c)(ii)* and *3.12*) must not be interviewed unless arrangements are made for a person capable of interpreting to assist the suspect to understand and communicate.

13.2A If a person who is a juvenile or a vulnerable person is interviewed and the person acting as the appropriate adult does not appear to speak or understand English, arrangements must be made for an interpreter to assist communication between the person, the appropriate adult and the interviewer, unless the interview is urgent and *paragraphs 11.1 or 11.18(c)* apply.

13.3 When a written record of the interview is made (see *paragraph 11.7*), the interviewer shall make sure the interpreter makes a note of the interview at the time in the person's language for use in the event of the interpreter being called to give evidence, and certifies its accuracy. The interviewer should allow sufficient time for the interpreter to note each question and answer after each is put, given and interpreted. The person should be allowed to read the record or have it read to them and sign it as correct or indicate the respects in which they consider it inaccurate. If an audio or visual record of the interview is made, the arrangements in Code E or F shall apply. *See paragraphs 13.12* to *13.14* and *Annex N* for application to live-link interpretation.

13.4 In the case of a person making a statement under caution (see *Annex D*) to a police officer or other police staff in a language other than English:

(a) the interpreter shall record the statement in the language it is made;

(b) the person shall be invited to sign it;

(c) an official English translation shall be made in due course. See *paragraphs 13.12* to *13.14* and *Annex N* for application to live-link interpretation.

(C) Interviewing suspects who have a hearing or speech impediment

13.5 Unless *paragraphs 11.1 or 11.18(c)* (urgent interviews) apply, a suspect who for the purposes of this Code requires an interpreter or other appropriate assistance to enable effective communication with them because they appear to have a hearing or speech impediment (see *paragraphs 3.5(c)(ii)* and *3.12*) must not be interviewed without arrangements having been made to provide an independent person capable of interpreting or of providing other appropriate assistance.

13.6 An interpreter should also be arranged if a person who is a juvenile or who is mentally disordered or mentally vulnerable is interviewed and the person who is present as the appropriate adult, appears to have a hearing or speech impediment, unless the interview is urgent and *paragraphs 11.1 or 11.18(c)* apply.

13.7 If a written record of the interview is made, the interviewer shall make sure the interpreter is allowed to read the record and certify its accuracy in the event of the interpreter being called to give evidence. If an audio or visual recording is made, the arrangements in Code E or F apply.

See *paragraphs 13.12* to *13.14* and *Annex N* for application to live-link interpretation.

(D) Additional rules for detained persons

13.8 *Not used.*

13.9 If *paragraph 6.1* applies and the detainee cannot communicate with the solicitor because of language, hearing or speech difficulties, arrangements must be made for an interpreter to enable communication. A police officer or any other police staff may not be used for this purpose.

13.10 After the custody officer has determined that a detainee requires an interpreter (see *paragraph 3.5(c)(ii)*) and following the initial action in *paragraphs 3.1 to 3.5*, arrangements must also be made for an interpreter to:

- explain the grounds and reasons for any authorisation for their *continued* detention, before or after charge and any information about the authorisation given to them by the authorising officer and which is recorded in the custody record. See *paragraphs 15.3, 15.4* and *15.16(a)* and *(b)*;
- to provide interpretation at the magistrates' court for the hearing of an application for a warrant of further detention or any extension or further extension of such warrant to explain any grounds and reasons for the application and any information about the authorisation of their further detention given to them by the court (see PACE, sections 43 and 44 and *paragraphs 15.2* and *15.16(c)*); and
- explain any offence with which the detainee is charged or for which they are informed they may be prosecuted and any other information about the offence given to them by or on behalf of the custody officer, see *paragraphs 16.1* and *16.3*.

13.10A If a detainee complains that they are not satisfied with the quality of interpretation, the custody officer or (as the case may be) the interviewer, is responsible for deciding whether to make arrangements for a different interpreter in accordance with the procedures set out in the arrangements made by the chief officer, see *paragraph 13.1A*.

(E) Translations of essential documents

13.10B Written translations, oral translations and oral summaries of essential documents in a language the detainee understands shall be provided in accordance with Annex M (Translations of documents and records).

13.10C If a detainee complains that they are not satisfied with the quality of the translation, the custody officer or (as the case may be) the interviewer, is responsible for deciding whether a further translation should be provided in accordance with the procedures set out in the arrangements made by the chief officer, see *paragraph 13.1A*.

(F) Decisions not to provide interpretation and translation

13.10D If a suspect challenges a decision:

- made by the custody officer or (as the case may be) by the interviewer, in accordance with this Code (see *paragraphs 3.5(c)(ii)* and *3.21(b)*) that they do not require an interpreter, or
- made in accordance with *paragraphs 13.10A, 13.10B* or *13.10C* not to make arrangements to provide a different interpreter or another translation or not to translate a requested document,

the matter shall be reported to an inspector to deal with as a complaint for the purposes of *paragraph 9.2* or *paragraph 12.9* if the challenge is made during an interview.

(G) Documentation

13.11 The following must be recorded in the custody record or, as applicable, the interview record:

(a) Action taken to arrange for an interpreter, including the live-link requirements in *Annex N* as applicable;

(b) Action taken when a detainee is not satisfied about the standard of interpretation or translation provided, see *paragraphs 13.10A* and *13.10C*;

(c) When an urgent interview is carried out in accordance with *paragraph 13.2* or *13.5* in the absence of an interpreter;

(d) When a detainee has been assisted by an interpreter for the purpose of providing or being given information or being interviewed;

(e) Action taken in accordance with *Annex M* when:

- a written translation of an essential document is provided;
- an oral translation or oral summary of an essential document is provided instead of a written translation and the authorising officer's reason(s) why this would not prejudice the fairness of the proceedings (see *Annex M, paragraph 3*);
- a suspect waives their right to a translation of an essential document (see *Annex M, paragraph 4*);
- when representations that a document which is not included in the table is essential and that a translation should be provided are refused and the reason for the refusal (see *Annex M, paragraph 8*).

(H) Live-link interpretation

13.12 In this section and in *Annex N*, 'live-link interpretation' means an arrangement to enable communication between the suspect and an interpreter who is not *physically* present with the suspect. The arrangement must ensure that anything said by any person in the suspect's presence and hearing can be interpreted in the same way as if the interpreter was physically present at that time. The communication must be by audio *and* visual means for the purpose of an interview, and for all other purposes it may be *either*; by audio and visual means, or by audio means *only*, as follows:

(a) Audio and visual communication

This applies for the purposes of an interview conducted and recorded in accordance with Code E (Audio recording) or Code F (Visual recording) and during that interview, live link interpretation must *enable*:

(i) the suspect, the interviewer, solicitor, appropriate adult and any other person *physically* present with the suspect at any time during the interview and an interpreter who is not *physically* present, to *see* and *hear* each other; and

(ii) the interview to be conducted and recorded in accordance with the provisions of Codes C, E and F, subject to the modifications in *Part 2 of Annex N.*

(b) Audio and visual or audio without visual communication

This applies to communication for the purposes of any provision of this or any other Code except as described in (a), which requires or permits information to be given to, sought from, or provided by a suspect, whether orally or in writing, which would include communication between the suspect and their solicitor and/or appropriate adult, and for these cases, live link interpretation must:

(i) *enable* the suspect, the person giving or seeking that information, any other person *physically* present with the suspect at that time and an interpreter who is not so present, to either *see* and *hear* each other, or to *hear without seeing* each other (for example by using a telephone); and

(ii) enable that information to be given to, sought from, or provided by, the suspect in accordance with the provisions of this or any other Code that apply to that information, as modified for the purposes of the live-link, by *Part 2 of Annex N.*

13.12A The requirement in *sub-paragraphs 13.12(a)(ii)* and *(b)(ii)*, that live-link interpretation must enable compliance with the relevant provisions of the Codes C, E and F, means that the arrangements must provide for any written or electronic record of what the suspect says in their own language which is made by the interpreter, to be securely transmitted without delay so that the suspect can be invited to read, check and if appropriate, sign or otherwise confirm that the record is correct or make corrections to the record.

KEYNOTE

The requirement mentioned in para. 13.12A means that certain elements of Codes C, E and F require modification. The precise details of those modifications can be found in Part 2 of Annex N.

13.13 Chief officers must be satisfied that live-link interpretation used in their force area for the purposes of *paragraphs 3.12(a)* and *(b)*, provides for accurate and secure communication with the suspect. This includes ensuring that at any time during which live link interpretation is being used: a person cannot see, hear or otherwise obtain access to any communications between the suspect and interpreter or communicate with the suspect or interpreter unless so authorised or allowed by the custody officer or, in the case of an interview, the interviewer and that as applicable, the confidentiality of any private consultation between a suspect and their solicitor and appropriate adult (see *paragraphs 13.2A, 13.6* and *13.9*) is maintained. See *Annex N paragraph 4.*

2.6.16 Code C—14 Questioning—Special Restrictions

14.1 If a person is arrested by one police force on behalf of another and the lawful period of detention in respect of that offence has not yet commenced in accordance with PACE, section 41 no questions may be put to them about the offence while they are in transit between the forces except to clarify any voluntary statement they make.

14.2 If a person is in police detention at a hospital they may not be questioned without the agreement of a responsible doctor.

KEYNOTE

If questioning takes place at a hospital under para. 14.2, or on the way to or from a hospital, the period of questioning concerned counts towards the total period of detention permitted.

2.6.17 **Limits on Period of Detention without Charge**

The total maximum period for which a person can be kept in police detention without being charged is 96 hours (this is sometimes referred to as the 'PACE clock').

The face of the 96-hour PACE clock can be divided into three sections:

- 0 to 24 hours—the basic period of detention authorised by the custody officer;
- beyond 24 hours and up to 36 hours—continued detention authorised by an officer of the rank of superintendent or above (s. 42);
- beyond 36 hours and up to 96 hours—continued detention by way of a warrant of further detention authorised by a magistrates' court (ss. 43 and 44).

2.6.17.1 **Relevant Time**

What starts the PACE clock ticking is 'relevant time'. Provisions in relation to relevant time are set out in s. 41(2)–(5) PACE84 which states:

(2) The time from which the period of detention of a person is to be calculated (in this Act referred to as 'the relevant time')—
  (a) in the case of a person to whom this paragraph applies, shall be—
    (i) the time at which that person arrives at the relevant police station; or
    (ii) the time 24 hours after the time of that person's arrest,
    whichever is the earlier;
  (b) in the case of a person arrested outside England and Wales, shall be—
    (i) the time at which that person arrives at the first police station to which he is taken in the police area in England or Wales in which the offence for which he was arrested is being investigated; or
    (ii) the time 24 hours after the time of that person's entry into England and Wales,
    whichever is the earlier;
  (c) in the case of a person who—
    (i) attends voluntarily at a police station; or
    (ii) accompanies a constable to a police station without having been arrested,
    and is arrested at the police station, the time of his arrest;
  (ca) in the case of a person who attends a police station to answer to bail granted under section 30A, the time he arrives at the police station;
  (d) in any other case, except where subsection (5) below applies, shall be the time at which the person arrested arrives at the first police station to which he is taken after his arrest.

(3) Subsection (2)(a) above applies to a person if—
  (a) his arrest is sought in one police area in England and Wales;
  (b) he is arrested in another police area; and
  (c) he is not questioned in the area in which he is arrested in order to obtain evidence in relation to an offence for which he is arrested;
  and in sub-paragraph (i) of that paragraph 'the relevant police station' means the first police station to which he is taken in the police area in which his arrest was sought.

(4) Subsection (2) above shall have effect in relation to a person arrested under section 31 above as if every reference in it to his arrest or his being arrested were a reference to his arrest or his being arrested for the offence for which he was originally arrested.

(5) If—
  (a) a person is in police detention in a police area in England and Wales ('the first area'); and
  (b) his arrest for an offence is sought in some other police area in England and Wales ('the second area'); and
  (c) he is taken to the second area for the purposes of investigating that offence, without being questioned in the first area in order to obtain evidence in relation to it,
  the relevant time shall be—
    (i) the time 24 hours after he leaves the place where he is detained in the first area; or
    (ii) the time at which he arrives at the first police station to which he is taken in the second area,
  whichever is the earlier.

KEYNOTE

At a Police Station

Code C (para. 2.1A) states that a person is deemed to be 'at a police station' if they are within the boundary of any building or enclosed yard which forms part of that police station.

Relevant Time Scenarios

Generally, 'relevant time' will be the time at which the detained person arrives at the relevant police station, or the time of arrest, *whichever is the earlier*. That said, s. 41 sets out a number of relevant time scenarios that require consideration alongside those that will be more frequently encountered. To assist understanding of the issues associated with s. 41(2)–(5), West Midlands Police and Greater Manchester Police have been used as examples in the following scenarios.

Scenario 1—s. 41(2)(a)

X is arrested in the West Midlands Police area and taken to a police station in the West Midlands Police area.

Relevant time starts when X arrives at the West Midlands police station or 24 hours after X's arrest—*whichever is the earlier.*

Scenario 2—s. 41(2)(b)

X is wanted for an offence by West Midlands Police. X is arrested in Glasgow (Scotland) and transported to the West Midlands area.

Relevant time starts when X arrives at the first police station in the West Midlands area or 24 hours after X crossed the border into England—*whichever is the earlier.*

Scenario 3—s. 41(2)(c)

X is arrested after voluntarily attending a police station (with or without an accompanying officer).

Relevant time starts at the time of X's arrest.

Scenario 4—s. 41(2)(ca)

X attends a police station to answer s. 30A bail.

Relevant time starts at the time X arrives at the police station to which the notice of bail states he/she must attend.

Scenario 5—s. 41(3)

X is wanted by West Midlands Police and is arrested in Manchester (by Greater Manchester Police) for the offence committed in the West Midlands.

Relevant time starts when X arrives at the first police station in the West Midlands area or 24 hours after X's arrest—*whichever is the earlier.*

Note that in Scenario 5, if X is questioned whilst in custody in the Greater Manchester force area *in order to obtain evidence* in relation to the West Midlands offence, then relevant time starts when X first arrived at the police station in the Greater Manchester force area.

Scenario 6—s. 41(5)

X is wanted by West Midlands Police. X is arrested in Manchester (by Greater Manchester Police) for an offence committed in Manchester. X has been dealt with for the Greater Manchester offence.

Relevant time, for the West Midlands offence, starts when X arrives at the first police station in the West Midlands area or 24 hours after X leaves the station where X was detained in Manchester—*whichever is the earlier.*

Note that in Scenario 6, if X is questioned whilst in custody in the Greater Manchester force area *in order to obtain evidence* in relation to the West Midlands offence, then relevant time starts when X first arrived at the police station in the Greater Manchester force area.

Scenario 7—s. 41(2)(d)

Section 41(2)(d) is a 'fail-safe' option—if none of the previous scenarios fit the circumstances, s. 41(2)(d) applies. For example, X commits a s. 18 wounding and is arrested at the scene of the offence. X was injured during the commission of the offence and requires hospital treatment so is taken directly to hospital. Treatment at the hospital takes some time and X is released 30 hours later—at this point he is taken to a police station. At no time whilst going to, at or coming from the hospital was X questioned in order to obtain evidence in relation to the s. 18 wounding. Scenarios 1 to 6 do not therefore apply, s. 41(2)(d)—relevant time starts when X arrives at the first police station to which he is taken after his arrest.

2.6.17.2 Relevant Time and Hospital Treatment

Section 41(6) PACE84 states that if a person *in police detention* (**see para 2.6.5**) is removed to hospital for medical treatment, the time at hospital and the period spent travelling to and from the hospital *does not* count towards the relevant time unless the person is asked questions for the purpose of obtaining evidence about an offence. Where questioning takes place, this period *would* count towards the relevant time and therefore the custody officer must be informed of it. Note that in the circumstances of Scenario 7 (above), X was never in *police detention* so s. 41(6) is not applicable to X's situation.

'Medical treatment' encompasses psychiatric/mental state assessment, examination and interview (*In the matter of an application by XX for Habeas Corpus* v *CCC of PSNI* [2019] NIQB 31).

2.6.17.3 Relevant Time and Bail

Stopping and Re-starting the PACE Clock

Relevant time relates to the actual time spent *in police detention*. This means that every time the person is bailed subject to a duty to attend at a police station (s. 47(4) PACE84), the PACE clock stops (as they are released from police detention). The PACE clock will restart when the person answers their bail at the police station as at this point they are returning to police detention (s. 47(6) PACE84). This will also be the case when they are arrested under s. 47(6A) PACE84 for failing to answer police bail or breaching a condition of police bail. For example, if X had been arrested and bailed with a duty to appear at a police station having spent five hours in police detention, the PACE clock stops at five hours when X is bailed. When X answers bail at the police station, the PACE clock restarts from five hours (there would be 19 hours remaining of the basic period of detention).

Suspending the PACE Clock

The Police, Crime, Sentencing and Courts Act 2022 inserted s. 46(6A) into PACE84 stating:

> (6A) Where a person has been arrested under section 46A above (other than in a case within subsection (1ZA) or (1ZB) of that section) the period of 3 hours beginning with the time at which the person arrives at a police station following the arrest is not to be included as part of any period of police detention which falls to be calculated in relation to the person under this Part of this Act.

This provides that where a person has been arrested under s. 46A, the PACE clock is suspended for three hours. This is designed to ensure that the PACE clock is not run down as a result of an individual repeatedly breaching bail conditions, helping to ensure that the time taken to deal with the arrest does not have a detrimental impact on future time that may be required to, for example, interview the person. For example, X is bailed with a duty to appear at police station having spent 20 hours in police detention. This would mean that if X complies with the duty then when X answers bail there would be four hours remaining of the basic period of detention. X does not comply and is arrested under s. 46A for failing to answer police bail. X arrives at a police station at 1 pm. Rather than the PACE clock restarting and the basic period of detention running out at 5 pm, X's PACE clock is suspended for three hours until 4 pm when the PACE clock restarts—this would mean that X's 24-hour basic period of detention would finish at 8 pm.

Re-arrest = Reset the PACE Clock

Section 47 PACE84 states:

> (7) Where a person who was released on bail under this Part subject to a duty to attend at a police station is re-arrested, the provisions of this Part of this Act shall apply to him/her as they apply to a person arrested for the first time but this subsection does not apply to a person who is arrested under section 46A above or has attended a police station in accordance with the grant of bail (and who accordingly is deemed by section 34(7) above to have been arrested for an offence).

For example, X is arrested in connection with an offence of robbery and is released on bail with a duty to appear at a police station having spent 10 hours in police detention. The PACE clock stops (as per s. 47(6)) and if X answers bail at the appointed time and place the PACE clock would restart (with 14 hours remaining of the basic detention time). Six days after X was bailed, new evidence connecting X to the robbery (in this example, we shall say DNA evidence and evidence from an eye-witness which was not available at the time of X's original arrest) is produced. As a result of this new evidence being discovered, X is re-arrested in connection with the robbery and taken to a police station. X has not been arrested under s. 46A and is not at the police station in accordance with the grant of bail and consequently, the PACE clock is reset to 0 hours and the basic period of detention starts at this time.

2.6.17.4 The Existence of a Warrant

In *Henderson* v *Chief Constable of Cleveland* [2001] EWCA Civ 335, the court considered the policy of not executing a default warrant for non-payment of a fine issued by a magistrates' court until after other matters for which the person had been detained were completed. The court held that, once a warrant was executed, there was a requirement to follow the directions of the warrant. The police, however, had discretion as to when to execute the warrant, but the discretion must be exercised reasonably. In such cases, if the warrant is executed immediately, the direction on the warrant tells officers to take the person before the next available court, an action which could interfere with the investigation. If *Henderson* is followed, there is no requirement to execute the warrant straight away and the other matters can be dealt with before the requirement to produce the person at court under the warrant applies.

2.6.18 Code C—15 Reviews and Extensions of Detention

(A) Persons detained under PACE

15.0 The requirement in *paragraph 3.4(b)* that documents and materials essential to challenging the lawfulness of the detainee's arrest and detention must be made available to the detainee or their solicitor, applies for the purposes of this section as follows:

(a) The officer reviewing the need for detention without charge (*PACE, section 40*), or (as the case may be) the officer considering the need to extend detention without charge from 24 to 36 hours (*PACE, section 42*), is responsible, in consultation with the investigating officer, for deciding which documents and materials are essential and must be made available.

(b) When *paragraph 15.7A* applies (application for a warrant of further detention or extension of such a warrant), the officer making the application is responsible for deciding which documents and materials are essential and must be made available before the hearing.

15.1 The review officer is responsible under PACE, section 40 for periodically determining if a person's detention, before or after charge, continues to be necessary. This requirement continues throughout the detention period and, except when a telephone or a live link is used in accordance with *paragraphs 15.9* to *15.11C*, the review officer must be present at the police station holding the detainee.

KEYNOTE

The Review Officer

The 'review officer' for the purposes of ss. 40, 40A and 45A PACE84 means, in the case of a person arrested but not charged, an officer of at least inspector rank not directly involved in the investigation and, if a person has been arrested and charged, the custody officer (s. 40(1)).

Timing of the Review

Section 40 sets out the times when reviews must be conducted:

> (3) Subject to subsection (4) ...
> (a) the first review shall be not later than six hours after the detention was first authorised;
> (b) the second review shall be not later than nine hours after the first;
> (c) subsequent reviews shall be at intervals of not more than nine hours.

The first review must be made within six hours of the custody officer *authorising detention* (this, it must be remembered, *is not* the time from which the 'PACE clock' starts, i.e. the 'relevant time', but the time at which the custody officer *authorised detention*). Thereafter, each review must be made within nine hours of the last review.

The periods set out in s. 40(3) are the maximum periods that a review can be left; should the review officer wish to review before this time for operational reasons, etc. the review could be brought forward.

The detainee need not be woken for the review. However, if the detainee is likely to be asleep, e.g. during a period of rest, at the latest time a review or authorisation to extend detention may take place, the officer should, if the legal obligations and time constraints permit, bring forward the procedure to allow the detainee to make representations. A detainee not asleep during the review must be present when the grounds for his/her continued detention are recorded and must at the same time be informed of those grounds unless the review officer considers that the person is incapable of understanding what is said, is violent or likely to become violent or is in urgent need of medical attention (see also para. 15.7).

Postponing the Review

> (4) A review may be postponed—
> (a) if, having regard to all the circumstances prevailing at the latest time for it specified in subsection (3) above, it is not practicable to carry out the review at that time;
> (b) without prejudice to the generality of paragraph (a) above—
> (i) if at that time the person in detention is being questioned by a police officer and the review officer is satisfied that an interruption of the questioning for the purpose of carrying out the review would prejudice the investigation in connection with which he is being questioned; or
> (ii) if at that time no review officer is readily available.

If the review is delayed, then it must still be conducted as soon as practicable after the latest time specified in subsection (3) above (s. 40(5)).

Section 40(6) states that 'if a review is carried out after postponement under subsection (4) above, the fact that it was so carried out shall not affect any requirement of this section as to the time at which any subsequent review is to be carried out'. What this means is that the timing of subsequent reviews is unaffected by a postponement. For example, if the first review of a detained person was due at 3.15 pm and was delayed until 4 pm, the second review would have to be conducted no later than 12.15 am and not 1 am. When the review is conducted, the review officer does not have to authorise detention for the full nine-hour period; he/she could decide that the case should be reviewed again within a shorter period and the review decision would reflect this.

The review officer shall record the reasons for any postponement of the review in the custody record (s. 40(7)).

In *Roberts* v *Chief Constable of Cheshire Constabulary* [1999] 1 WLR 662, the claimant had been detained at 11.25 pm. His detention was not reviewed by an inspector until 7.45 am the next morning (8 hours 20 minutes after his detention had been authorised). The Court of Appeal held that under s. 40(1)(b) PACE84, a review of his detention should have been carried out by an officer of the rank of inspector or above six hours after detention was first authorized (5.25 am). Section 34(1) was mandatory and provided that a person must not be kept in police detention except in accordance with the relevant provisions of the Act. Therefore, the respondent's detention had been unlawful unless some event occurred to have made it lawful. The court made it clear that PACE84 existed in order to ensure that members of the public were not detained except in certain defined circumstances. In the absence of a review, the time spent in detention between 5.25 am and 7.45 am, meant that for that period the defendant's detention was unlawful and amounted to a false imprisonment.

Review Considerations

When reviewing the detention of a person the review officer goes through the same process as the custody officer did when detention was first authorised (s. 40(8) and s. 37(1)–(6)), namely by asking:

- Is there sufficient evidence to charge? If 'yes', charge or release the person with or without bail. If 'no', then:
- Is detention necessary in order to secure or preserve evidence or is it necessary to detain the person in order to obtain such evidence by questioning him/her? If 'yes', authorise continued detention. If 'no', release the person with or without bail.

In cases where it has been decided that a person should be charged but he/she has been detained because he/she is not in a fit state to be charged (s. 37(9)), the review officer must determine whether the person is yet in a fit state. If the detainee is in a fit state, the custody officer should be informed that the person should be charged or released. If the detainee is not in a fit state, detention can be authorised for a further period (s. 40(9)).

Non-statutory Reviews

The detention of persons in police custody not subject to the statutory review requirement in para. 15.1 should still be reviewed periodically as a matter of good practice. Such reviews can be carried out by an officer of the rank of sergeant or above. The purpose of such reviews is to check that the particular power under which a detainee is held continues to apply, any associated conditions are complied with, and to make sure that appropriate action is taken to deal with any changes. This includes the detainee's prompt release when the power no longer applies, or his/her transfer if the power requires the detainee be taken elsewhere as soon as the necessary arrangements are made. Examples include persons:

- arrested on warrant because they failed to answer bail to appear at court;
- arrested under the Bail Act 1976, s. 7(3) for breaching a condition of bail granted after charge;
- in police custody for specific purposes and periods under the Crime (Sentences) Act 1997, sch. 1;
- convicted or remand prisoners, held in police stations on behalf of the Prison Service under the Imprisonment (Temporary Provisions) Act 1980, s. 6;
- being detained to prevent them causing a breach of the peace;
- detained at police stations on behalf of Immigration Enforcement (formerly the UK Immigration Service);
- detained by order of a magistrates' court under the Criminal Justice Act 1988, s. 152 (as amended by the Drugs Act 2005, s. 8) to facilitate the recovery of evidence after being charged with drug possession or drug trafficking and suspected of having swallowed drugs.

The detention of persons remanded into police detention by order of a court under the Magistrates' Courts Act 1980, s. 128 is subject to a statutory requirement to review that detention. This is to make sure that the detainee is taken back to court no later than the end of the period authorised by the court or when the need for his/her detention by police ceases, whichever is the sooner.

15.2 Under PACE, section 42, an officer of superintendent rank or above who is responsible for the station holding the detainee may give authority any time after the second review to extend the maximum period the person may be detained without charge by up to 12 hours. Except when a live link is used as in *paragraph 15.11A*, the superintendent must be present at the station holding the detainee. Further detention without charge may be authorised only by a magistrates' court in accordance with PACE, sections 43 and 44 and unless the court has given a live link direction as in *paragraph 15.11B*, the detainee must be brought before the court for the hearing.

KEYNOTE

Authorisation of Continued Detention

Under s. 42 PACE84, detention can be authorised beyond 24 hours and up to a maximum of 36 hours from the relevant time.

Section 42 of PACE84 states:

(1) Where a police officer of the rank of superintendent or above who is responsible for the police station at which a person is detained has reasonable grounds for believing that—
   (a) the detention of that person without charge is necessary to secure or preserve evidence relating to an offence for which he is under arrest or to obtain such evidence by questioning him;
   (b) an offence for which he is under arrest is an indictable offence; and
   (c) the investigation is being conducted diligently and expeditiously, he may authorise the keeping of that person in police detention for a period expiring at or before 36 hours after the relevant time.

The reference to the officer 'responsible for the police station at which a person is detained', and in para. 15.2, the officer 'responsible for the station holding the detainee', includes a superintendent or above who, in accordance with their force operational policy or police regulations, is given that responsibility on a temporary basis whilst the appointed long-term holder is off duty or otherwise unavailable.

The grounds for this continuing detention are the same as those when the custody officer made the initial decision to detain, with the additional requirements that the case has been conducted diligently and expeditiously. To be able to satisfy the superintendent or above of this, it will be necessary for the custody record to be available for inspection and also details of what inquiries have been made and evidence that the investigation has been moving at a pace that will enable the superintendent or above to conclude that the inquiries should not already have been completed.

If the authorising officer considers that there is sufficient evidence to charge, he/she cannot authorise further detention beyond 24 hours unless the detained person is in custody for another indictable offence for which further detention can be authorised (*R* v *Samuel* [1988] QB 615).

Although the authorising officer can authorise detention up to a maximum of 36 hours from the 'relevant time' of detention, the period can be shorter than this. It can then be further authorised by that officer or any other officer of the rank of superintendent or above who is responsible for the station at which the person is detained to allow the period to be further extended up to the maximum 36-hour period (s. 42(2)).

If it is proposed to transfer a detained person from one police area to another for the purpose of investigating the offences for which he/she is detained, the authorising officer may take into consideration the period it will take to get to the other police area when deciding whether detention can go beyond 24 hours (s. 42(3)).

15.2A An authorisation under section 42(1) of PACE extends the maximum period of detention permitted before charge for indictable offences from 24 hours to 36 hours. Detaining a juvenile or vulnerable person for longer than 24 hours will be dependent on the circumstances of the case and with regard to the person's:

(a) special vulnerability;
(b) the legal obligation to provide an opportunity for representations to be made prior to a decision about extending detention;
(c) the need to consult and consider the views of any appropriate adult; and
(d) any alternatives to police custody.

15.3 Before deciding whether to authorise continued detention the officer responsible under *paragraph 15.1* or *15.2* shall give an opportunity to make representations about the detention to:

(a) the detainee, unless in the case of a review as in *paragraph 15.1*, the detainee is asleep;

(b) the detainee's solicitor if available at the time; and

(c) the appropriate adult if available at the time.

KEYNOTE

In relation to the detainee's solicitor or appropriate adult being 'available' to make representations, this includes being contactable in time to enable him/her to make representations remotely by telephone or other electronic means or in person by attending the station. Reasonable efforts should therefore be made to give the solicitor and appropriate adult sufficient notice of the time the decision is expected to be made so that they can make themselves available.

15.3A Other people having an interest in the detainee's welfare may also make representations at the authorising officer's discretion.

15.3B Subject to *paragraph 15.10*, the representations may be made orally in person or by telephone or in writing. The authorising officer may, however, refuse to hear oral representations from the detainee if the officer considers them unfit to make representations because of their condition or behaviour.

15.3C The decision on whether the review takes place in person or by telephone or by video conferencing is a matter for the review officer. In determining the form the review may take, the review officer must always take full account of the needs of the person in custody. The benefits of carrying out a review in person should always be considered, based on the individual circumstances of each case with specific additional consideration if the person is:

(a) a juvenile (and the age of the juvenile); or

(b) a vulnerable person; or

(c) in need of medical attention for other than routine minor ailments; or

(d) subject to presentational or community issues around their detention.

See *paragraph 1.4(c)*.

15.4 Before conducting a review or determining whether to extend the maximum period of detention without charge, the officer responsible must make sure the detainee is reminded of their entitlement to free legal advice, see *paragraph 6.5*, unless in the case of a review the person is asleep. When determining whether to extend the maximum period of detention without charge, it should also be pointed out that for the purposes of *paragraph 15.2*, the superintendent or (as the case may be) the court, responsible for authorising any such extension, will not be able to use a live link unless the detainee has received legal advice on the use of the live link (see *paragraphs 15.11A(ii)* and *15.11C(ii)*) and given consent to its use (see *paragraphs 15.11A(iii)* and *15.11C(iii)*. The detainee must also be given information about how the live link is used.

15.4A Following sections 45ZA and 45ZB of PACE, when the reminder and information concerning legal advice and about the use of the live link is given and the detainee's consent is sought, the presence of an appropriate adult is required if the detainee in question is a juvenile (see *paragraph 1.5*) or is a *vulnerable adult* by virtue of being a person aged 18 or over who, because of a mental disorder established in accordance *paragraphs 1.4* and *1.13(d)* or for <u>*any other reason*</u> (see *paragraph 15.4B*), may have difficulty understanding the purpose of:

(a) an authorisation under section 42 of PACE or anything that occurs in connection with a decision whether to give it (see *paragraphs 15.2* and *15.2A*); or

(b) a court hearing under section 43 or 44 of PACE or what occurs at the hearing it (see *paragraphs 15.2* and *15.7A*).

15.4B For the purpose of using a live link in accordance with sections 45ZA and 45ZB of PACE to authorise detention without charge (see *paragraphs 15.11A* and *15.11C*), the reference to '*any other reason*' would extend to difficulties in understanding the purposes mentioned in *paragraph 15.4A* that might arise if the person happened to be under the influence of drink or drugs at the time the live link is to be used. This does not however apply for the purposes of *paragraphs 1.4* and *1.13(d)*.

15.5 If, after considering any representations, the review officer under *paragraph 15.1* decides to keep the detainee in detention or the superintendent under *paragraph 15.2* extends the maximum period for which they may be detained without charge, then any comment made by the detainee shall be recorded. If applicable, the officer shall be informed of the comment as soon as practicable. See also *paragraphs 11.4* and *11.13*.

15.6 No officer shall put specific questions to the detainee:

- regarding their involvement in any offence;
- or in respect of any comment they may make:
  - ~ when given the opportunity to make representations; or
  - ~ in response to a decision to keep them in detention or extend the maximum period of detention.

Such an exchange could constitute an interview as in *paragraph 11.1A* and would be subject to the associated safeguards in *section 11* and, in respect of a person who has been charged, *paragraph 16.5*. See also *paragraph 11.13*.

15.7 A detainee who is asleep at a review, see *paragraph 15.1*, and whose continued detention is authorised must be informed about the decision and reason as soon as practicable after waking.

15.7A When an application is made to a magistrates' court under PACE, section 43 for a warrant of further detention to extend detention without charge of a person arrested for an *indictable offence*, or under section 44, to extend or further extend that warrant, the detainee:

(a) must, unless the court has given a live link direction as in *paragraph 15.11C*, be brought to court for the hearing of the application;

(b) is entitled to be legally represented if they wish, in which case, *Annex B* cannot apply; and

(c) must be given a copy of the information which supports the application and states:

(i) the nature of the offence for which the person to whom the application relates has been arrested;

(ii) the general nature of the evidence on which the person was arrested;

(iii) what inquiries about the offence have been made and what further inquiries are proposed;

(iv) the reasons for believing continued detention is necessary for the purposes of the further inquiries;

Note: A warrant of further detention can only be issued or extended if the court has reasonable grounds for believing that the person's further detention is necessary for the purpose of obtaining evidence of an indictable offence for which the person has been arrested and that the investigation is being conducted diligently and expeditiously.

See *paragraph 15.0(b)*.

KEYNOTE

Warrants of Further Detention

A warrant of further detention (under s. 43 PACE84), is granted by a magistrates' court. Initially, the magistrates can issue a warrant of further detention for a period of up to 36 hours (taking the overall period of detention to 72 hours from the relevant time (s. 42(12))).

Section 43 PACE84 states:

(1) Where, on an application on oath made by a constable and supported by an information, a magistrates' court is satisfied that there are reasonable grounds for believing that the further detention of the person to whom the application relates is justified, it may issue a warrant of further detention authorising the keeping of that person in police detention.

Section 43(3) provides that the detained person is entitled to be legally represented (also mentioned in para. 15.7A). If the person is not legally represented but then requests legal representation at court, the case must be adjourned to allow representation (s. 43(3)). Should the detained person choose to be legally represented at court, and thereby try to delay the police investigation, s. 43(3)(b) allows the person to be taken back into police detention during the adjournment.

Warrants of Further Detention: Timing of the Application

An application to a magistrates' court under PACE84, s. 43 (for a warrant of further detention) or 44 (for an extension of a warrant of detention) should be made between 10 am and 9 pm, and if possible during normal court hours. It will not usually be practicable to arrange for a court to sit specially outside the hours of 10 am to 9 pm. If it appears that a special sitting may be needed outside normal court hours but between 10 am and 9 pm, the clerk to the justices should be given notice and informed of this possibility, while the court is sitting if possible.

The application for the warrant can be made at any time, *even before a superintendent's review has been carried out.* Section 43(5) allows the application to be made:

(a) at any time before the expiry of 36 hours after the relevant time; or
(b) in a case where—
  (i) it is not practicable for the magistrates' court to which the application will be made to sit at the expiry of 36 hours after the relevant time; but
  (ii) the court will sit during the 6 hours following that period,
  at any time before the expiry of the said 6 hours.

There are dangers in applying outside the 36-hour period as if the court feels that it would have been reasonable to make the application within the 36-hour period it must refuse the application for the warrant regardless of the merits of the case (s. 43(7)). In *R* v *Slough Justices, ex parte Stirling* [1987] Crim LR 576, the 36-hour period expired at 12.53 pm. The case was not heard by the justices until 2.45 pm. The Divisional Court held that the police should have made their application between 10.30 am and 11.30 am, even though this was before the 36-hour time limit had been reached.

If the court is not satisfied that there are reasonable grounds for believing that further detention is justified, the court may either refuse the application or adjourn the hearing until such time as it specifies up to the end of the 36-hour period of detention (s. 43(8)).

If the application is refused, the person must be charged or released with or without bail at the expiry of the current permissible period of detention (s. 43(15)).

If the application is made within the 36-hour period and it is refused, it does not mean that the person must be released straight away. Section 43(16) allows the person to be detained until the end of the current detention period (24 hours or 36 hours). The benefit of an early application has to be set against the risk that, once the court has refused an application, it is not allowed to hear any further applications for a warrant of further detention unless new evidence has come to light since the application was refused (s. 43(17)).

Extension of Warrants of Further Detention

An extension of a warrant of further detention (under s. 44 PACE84) is granted by a magistrates' court in the same way a warrant of further detention is granted under s. 43 with the exception that the application must be made before the expiry of the extension given in the previous warrant. The extension period shall not be longer than 36 hours or end later than 96 hours after the relevant time (s. 44(3)).

15.8 *Not used.*

(B) Review of detention by telephone and live link facilities

15.9 PACE, section 40A provides that the officer responsible under section 40 for reviewing the detention of a person who has not been charged, need not attend the police station holding the detainee and may carry out the review by telephone.

15.9A PACE, section 45A(2) provides that the officer responsible under section 40 for reviewing the detention of a person who has not been charged, need not attend the police station holding the detainee and may carry out the review using a live link. See *paragraph 1.13(e)(ii)*.

15.9B A telephone review is not permitted where facilities for review by live link exist and it is practicable to use them.

15.9C The review officer can decide at any stage that a telephone review or review by live link should be terminated and that the review will be conducted in person. The reasons for doing so should be noted in the custody record.

KEYNOTE

The provisions of s. 40A PACE84 allowing telephone reviews or live link do not apply to reviews of detention after charge by the custody officer. When use of a live link is not required, they allow the use of a telephone to carry out a review of detention before charge.

15.10 When a review is carried out by telephone or by live link facilities, an officer at the station holding the detainee shall be required by the review officer to fulfil that officer's obligations under PACE section 40 and this Code by:

(a) making any record connected with the review in the detainee's custody record;
(b) if applicable, making the record in (*a*) in the presence of the detainee; and
(c) for a review by telephone, giving the detainee information about the review.

15.11 When a review is carried out by telephone or by live link facilities, the requirement in *paragraph 15.3* will be satisfied:

(a) if facilities exist for the immediate transmission of written representations to the review officer, e.g. fax or email message, by allowing those who are given the opportunity to make representations, to make their representations:
  (i) orally by telephone or (as the case may be) by means of the live link; or
  (ii) in writing using the facilities for the immediate transmission of written representations; and
(b) in all other cases, by allowing those who are given the opportunity to make representations, to make their representations orally by telephone or by means of the live link.

(C) Authorisation to extend detention using live link (sections 45ZA and 45ZB)

15.11A For the purpose of *paragraphs 15.2* and *15.2A*, a superintendent who is not present at the police station where the detainee is being held but who has access to the use of a live link (see *paragraph 1.13(e)(iii)*) may, using that live link, give authority to extend the maximum period of detention permitted before charge, if, and only if, the following conditions are satisfied:

(i) the custody officer considers that the use of the live link is appropriate;
(ii) the detainee in question has requested and received legal advice on the use of the live link (see *paragraph 15.4*).
(iii) the detainee has given their consent to the live link being used (see *paragraph 15.11D*)

KEYNOTE

In considering whether the use of the live link is appropriate (paras 15.11A, 15.11B and 15.11C) in the case of a juvenile or vulnerable person, the custody officer and the superintendent should have regard to the detainee's ability to understand the purpose of the authorisation or (as the case may be) the court hearing, and be satisfied that the suspect is able to take part effectively in the process (see para. 1.4(c)). The appropriate adult should always be involved.

15.11B When a live link is used:

(a) the authorising superintendent shall, with regard to any record connected with the authorisation which PACE, section 42 and this Code require to be made by the authorising officer, require an officer at the station holding the detainee to make that record in the detainee's custody record;

(b) the requirement in *paragraph 15.3* (allowing opportunity to make representations) will be satisfied:

(i) if facilities exist for the immediate transmission of written representations to the authorising officer, e.g. fax or email message, by allowing those who are given the opportunity to make representations, to make their representations:

- in writing by means of those facilities or
- orally by means of the live link; or

(ii) in all other cases, by allowing those who are given the opportunity to make representations, to make their representations orally by means of the live link.

(c) The authorising officer can decide at any stage to terminate the live link and attend the police station where the detainee is held to carry out the procedure in person. The reasons for doing so should be noted in the custody record.

15.11C For the purpose of *paragraph 15.7A* and the hearing of an application to a magistrates' court under PACE, section 43 for a warrant of further detention to extend detention without charge of a person arrested for an *indictable offence*, or under PACE, section 44, to extend or further extend that warrant, the magistrates' court may give a direction that a live link (see *paragraph 1.13(e)(iv)*) be used for the purposes of the hearing if, and only if, the following conditions are satisfied:

(i) the custody officer considers that the use of the live link for the purpose of the hearing is appropriate;

(ii) the detainee in question has requested and received legal advice on the use of the live link (see *paragraph 15.4*);

(iii) the detainee has given their consent to the live link being used (see *paragraph 15.11D*); and

(iv) it is not contrary to the interests of justice to give the direction.

15.11D References in *paragraphs 15.11A(iii)* and *15.11C(iii)* to the consent of the detainee mean:

(a) if detainee is aged 18 or over, the consent of that detainee;

(b) if the detainee is aged 14 and under 18, the consent of the detainee *and* their parent or guardian; and

(c) if the detainee is aged under 14, the consent of their parent or guardian.

15.11E The consent described in *paragraph 15.11D* will only be valid if:

(i) in the case of a detainee aged 18 or over who is a *vulnerable adult* as described in *paragraph 15.4A*), information about how the live link is used *and* the reminder about their right to legal advice mentioned in *paragraph 15.4* and their consent, are given in the *presence of the appropriate adult*; and

(ii) in the case of a *juvenile*:

- if information about how the live link is used *and* the reminder about their right to legal advice mentioned in *paragraph 15.4* are given in the *presence of the appropriate adult* (who may or may not be their parent or guardian); and

- if the juvenile is aged 14 or over, their consent is given in the *presence of the appropriate adult* (who may or may not be their parent or guardian).

Note: If the juvenile is aged under 14, the consent of their parent or guardian is sufficient in its own right.

KEYNOTE

For the purpose of paras 15.11D and 15.11E, the consent required from a parent or guardian may, for a juvenile in the care of a local authority or voluntary organisation, be given by that authority or organisation. In the case of a juvenile, nothing in paras 15.11D and 15.11E require the parent, guardian or representative of a local authority or voluntary organisation to be present with the juvenile to give their consent, unless they are acting as the appropriate adult. However, it is important that the parent, guardian or representative of a local authority or voluntary organisation who is not present is fully informed before being asked to consent. They must be given the same information as that given to the juvenile and the appropriate adult in accordance with para. 15.11E. They must also be allowed to speak to the juvenile and the appropriate adult if they wish. Provided the consent is fully informed and is not withdrawn, it may be obtained at any time before the live link is used.

(D) Documentation

15.12 It is the officer's responsibility to make sure all reminders given under *paragraph 15.4* are noted in the custody record.

15.13 The grounds for, and extent of, any delay in conducting a review shall be recorded.

15.14 When a review is carried out by telephone or video conferencing facilities, a record shall be made of:

(a) the reason the review officer did not attend the station holding the detainee;

(b) the place the review officer was;

(c) the method representations, oral or written, were made to the review officer, see *paragraph 15.11*.

15.15 Any written representations shall be retained.

15.16 A record shall be made as soon as practicable of:

(a) the outcome of each review of detention before or after charge, and if *paragraph 15.7* applies, of when the person was informed and by whom;

(b) the outcome of any determination under PACE, section 42 by a superintendent whether to extend the maximum period of detention without charge beyond 24 hours from the relevant time. If an authorisation is given, the record shall state the number of hours and minutes by which the detention period is extended or further extended.

(c) the outcome of each application under PACE, section 43, for a warrant of further detention or under section 44, for an extension or further extension of that warrant. If a warrant for further detention is granted under section 43 or extended or further extended under 44, the record shall state the detention period authorised by the warrant and the date and time it was granted or (as the case may be) the period by which the warrant is extended or further extended.

Note: Any period during which a person is released on bail does not count towards the maximum period of detention without charge allowed under PACE, sections 41 to 44.

2.6.19 Code C—16 Charging Detained Persons

(A) Action

16.1 When the officer in charge of the investigation reasonably believes there is sufficient evidence to provide a realistic prospect of conviction for the offence (see *paragraph 11.6*), they shall without delay, and subject to the following qualification, inform the custody officer who will be responsible for considering whether the detainee should be charged. When a person is detained in respect of more than one offence it is permissible to delay informing the custody officer until the above conditions are satisfied in respect of all the offences, but see *paragraph 11.6.* If the detainee is a juvenile or a vulnerable person, any resulting action shall be taken in the presence of the appropriate adult if they are present at the time.

KEYNOTE

The custody officer must take into account alternatives to prosecution under the Crime and Disorder Act 1998 applicable to persons under 18 (youth cautions and youth conditional cautions), and in national guidance on the cautioning of offenders applicable to persons aged 18 and over (**see para. 2.6.20**).

If the custody officer decides there is sufficient evidence to charge the detained person, that person shall be charged or, if not charged, released in relation to that matter as set out in s. 37(7)–(8) PACE84 which states:

(7) Subject to section 41(7) below [expiry of 24 hours after the relevant time], if the custody officer determines that he has before him sufficient evidence to charge the person arrested with the offence for which he was arrested, the person arrested—
- (a) shall be—
  - (i) released without charge and on bail, or
  - (ii) kept in police detention, for the purpose of enabling the Director of Public Prosecutions to make a decision under section 37B below,
- (b) shall be released—
  - (i) without charge and
  - (ii) if the pre-conditions for bail are satisfied, on bail, but not for the purpose mentioned in paragraph (a),
- (c) shall be released—
  - (i) without charge and
  - (ii) if the pre-conditions for bail are not satisfied, without bail, or
- (d) shall be charged.

(7A) The decision as to how a person is to be dealt with under subsection (7) above shall be that of the custody officer.

(7B) Where a person is released under subsection (7)(a) above, it shall be the duty of the custody officer to inform him that he is being released or (as the case may be) detained, to enable the Director of Public Prosecutions to make a decision under section 37B below.

(8) Where—
- (a) a person is released under subsection (7)(b) or (c) above; and
- (b) at the time of his release a decision whether he should be prosecuted for the offence for which he was arrested has not been taken,

it shall be the duty of the custody officer so to inform him/her.

Where there is sufficient evidence to charge, a delay in bringing charges may be seen to be unreasonable under Article 6 of the European Convention on Human Rights (*D* v *HM Advocate* [2000] HRLR 389).

In deciding whether there is sufficient evidence to charge for the purposes of authorising detention or when a person's detention is reviewed, where there is a conflict between the detained person's account and victims' or witnesses' accounts, it is reasonable to be in possession of at least one witness statement in the English language before preferring charges (*R (On the Application of Wiles)* v *Chief Constable of Hertfordshire* [2002] EWHC 387 (Admin)). There is no breach of PACE84 in keeping the detained person in police detention while a statement is translated.

Under s. 37(9) PACE84, release can be delayed if the person is not in a fit state to be released (e.g. he/she is drunk) until he/she is fit.

16.1A Where guidance issued by the Director of Public Prosecutions under PACE, section 37A is in force the custody officer must comply with that Guidance in deciding how to act in dealing with the detainee.

KEYNOTE

Under s. 37A PACE84, guidance has been issued to enable custody officers to decide whether there is sufficient evidence to charge and for which offences the police may charge without reference to the CPS. Where in accordance with the guidance the case is referred to the CPS for decision, the custody officer should ensure that an officer involved in the investigation sends to the CPS such information as is specified in the guidance. A detained person should not be kept in custody just for the sole purpose of seeking advice from the CPS as to what offences the offender should be charged with (*R (On the Application of G)* v *Chief Constable of West Yorkshire Police and DPP* [2008] EWCA Civ 28).

When a person is arrested under the provisions of the Criminal Justice Act 2003 which allow a person to be re-tried after being acquitted of a serious offence which is a qualifying offence specified in sch. 5 to that Act and not precluded from further prosecution by virtue of s. 75(3) of that Act, the detention provisions of PACE84 are modified and make an officer of the rank of superintendent or above who has not been directly involved in the investigation responsible for determining whether the evidence is sufficient to charge.

16.1B Where in compliance with the DPP's Guidance the custody officer decides that the case should be immediately referred to the CPS to make the charging decision, consultation should take place with a Crown Prosecutor as soon as is reasonably practicable. Where the Crown Prosecutor is unable to make the charging decision on the information available at that time, the detainee may be released without charge and on bail (with conditions if necessary) under section 37(7)(a). In such circumstances, the detainee should be informed that they are being released to enable the Director of Public Prosecutions to make a decision under section 37B.

KEYNOTE

Section 37B of the Police and Criminal Evidence Act 1984 states:

(1) Where a person is dealt with under section 37(7)(a) above, an officer involved in the investigation of the offence shall, as soon as is practicable, send to the Director of Public Prosecutions such information as may be specified in guidance under section 37A above.

(2) The Director of Public Prosecutions shall decide whether there is sufficient evidence to charge the person with an offence.

(3) If he decides that there is sufficient evidence to charge the person with an offence, he shall decide—
  (a) whether or not the person should be charged and, if so, the offence with which he should be charged, and
  (b) whether or not the person should be given a caution and, if so, the offence in respect of which he should be given a caution.

(4) The Director of Public Prosecutions shall give notice of his decision to an officer involved in the investigation of the offence.

(4A) Notice under subsection (4) above shall be in writing, but in the case of a person kept in police detention under section 37(7)(a) above it may be given orally in the first instance and confirmed in writing subsequently.

(5) If his decision is—
  (a) that there is not sufficient evidence to charge the person with an offence, or
  (b) that there is sufficient evidence to charge the person with an offence but that the person should not be charged with an offence or given a caution in respect of an offence,

a custody officer shall give the person notice in writing that he is not to be prosecuted.

Where a person has been bailed under s. 37(7)(a) with or without bail conditions, the CPS must be consulted in order to determine what case disposal decision will be made (this may itself require further inquiries to gather further evidence).

The prosecutor will decide whether there is sufficient evidence to charge or caution the person and shall give written notice of the decision to an officer involved in the investigation of the details of the offence. This decision must be followed (s. 37B(6)) if the decision was for the person to be cautioned (this includes conditional cautions), and if the person refuses, or for some other reason a caution cannot be given, he/she must be charged with the offence (s. 37B(7)).

In cases where the prosecutor decides that there is not sufficient evidence to charge the person with an offence, or that there is sufficient evidence to charge the person with an offence but that the person should not be charged with an offence or given a caution in respect of an offence, the custody officer must inform the person in writing of the decision. Similarly the person must be informed of those cases where there is insufficient evidence to charge him/her, but if further evidence or information comes to light in the future the case may be reconsidered under the Code for Crown Prosecutors.

In cases where further time is needed to obtain evidence or for the prosecutor to make a case disposal decision, the person can be further bailed. In these cases, the custody officer must give the person notice in writing.

16.2 When a detainee is charged with or informed they may be prosecuted for an offence, they shall, unless the restriction on drawing adverse inferences from silence applies, see *Annex C*, be cautioned as follows:

'You do not have to say anything. But it may harm your defence if you do not mention now something which you later rely on in court. Anything you do say may be given in evidence.'

Where the use of the Welsh Language is appropriate, a constable may provide the caution directly in Welsh in the following terms:

'Does dim rhaid i chi ddweud dim byd. Ond gall niweidio eich amddiffyniad os ŋa fyddwch chi'n sôn, yn awr, am rywbeth y byddwch chi'n dibynnu arno nes ymlaen yn y llys. Gall unrhyw beth yr ydych yn ei ddweud gael ei roi fel tystiolaeth.'

Annex C, paragraph 2 sets out the alternative terms of the caution to be used when the restriction on drawing adverse inferences from silence applies.

16.3 When a detainee is charged they shall be given a written notice showing particulars of the offence and, subject to *paragraph 2.6A*, the officer's name and the case reference number. As far as possible the particulars of the charge shall be stated in simple terms, but they shall also show the precise offence in law with which the detainee is charged. The notice shall begin:

'You are charged with the offence(s) shown below.' Followed by the caution.

If the detainee is a juvenile, mentally disordered or otherwise mentally vulnerable, a copy of the notice should also be given to the appropriate adult.

16.4 If, after a detainee has been charged with or informed they may be prosecuted for an offence, an officer wants to tell them about any written statement or interview with another person relating to such an offence, the detainee shall either be handed a true copy of the written statement or the content of the interview record brought to their attention. Nothing shall be done to invite any reply or comment except to:

(a) caution the detainee, 'You do not have to say anything, but anything you do say may be given in evidence.';

Where the use of the Welsh Language is appropriate, caution the detainee in the following terms:

'Does dim rhaid i chi ddweud dim byd, ond gall unrhyw beth yr ydych yn ei ddweud gael ei roi fel tystiolaeth.'

and

(b) remind the detainee about their right to legal advice.

16.4A If the detainee:

- cannot read, the document may be read to them;
- is a juvenile, mentally disordered or otherwise mentally vulnerable, the appropriate adult shall also be given a copy, or the interview record shall be brought to their attention.

16.5 A detainee may not be interviewed about an offence after they have been charged with, or informed they may be prosecuted for it, unless the interview is necessary:

- to prevent or minimise harm or loss to some other person, or the public
- to clear up an ambiguity in a previous answer or statement
- in the interests of justice for the detainee to have put to them, and have an opportunity to comment on, information concerning the offence which has come to light since they were charged or informed they might be prosecuted.

Before any such interview, the interviewer shall:

(a) caution the detainee, 'You do not have to say anything, but anything you do say may be given in evidence.'

Where the use of the Welsh Language is appropriate, the interviewer shall caution the detainee: 'Does dim rhaid i chi ddweud dim byd, ond gall unrhyw beth yr ydych yn ei ddweud gael ei roi fel tystiolaeth.'

(b) remind the detainee about their right to legal advice.

KEYNOTE

There is no power under PACE84 to detain a person and delay action under paras 16.2 to 16.5 solely to await the arrival of the appropriate adult. Reasonable efforts should therefore be made to give the appropriate adult sufficient notice of the time the decision (charge etc.) is to be implemented so that he/she can be present. If the appropriate adult is not, or cannot be, present at that time, the detainee should be released on bail to return for the decision to be implemented when the adult is present, unless the custody officer determines that the absence of the appropriate adult makes the detainee unsuitable for bail for this purpose. After charge, bail cannot be refused, or release on bail delayed, simply because an appropriate adult is not available, unless the absence of that adult provides the custody officer with the necessary grounds to authorise detention after charge under s. 38 PACE84.

16.6 The provisions of *paragraphs 16.2* to *16.5* must be complied with in the appropriate adult's presence if they are already at the police station. If they are not at the police station then these provisions must be complied with again in their presence when they arrive unless the detainee has been released.

16.7 When a juvenile is charged with an offence and the custody officer authorises their continued detention after charge, the custody officer must make arrangements for the juvenile to be taken into the care of a local authority to be detained pending appearance in court *unless* the custody officer certifies in accordance with PACE, section 38(6), that:

(a) for any juvenile; it is impracticable to do so and the reasons why it is impracticable must be set out in the certificate that must be produced to the court; or,

(b) in the case of a juvenile of at least 12 years old, no secure accommodation is available and other accommodation would not be adequate to protect the public from serious harm from that juvenile.

Note: Chief officers should ensure that the operation of these provisions at police stations in their areas is subject to supervision and monitoring by an officer of the rank of inspector or above.

KEYNOTE

Except as in para. 16.7, neither a juvenile's behaviour nor the nature of the offence provides grounds for the custody officer to decide it is impracticable to arrange the juvenile's transfer to local authority care. Impracticability concerns the transport and travel requirements and the lack of secure accommodation which is provided for the purposes of restricting liberty does not make it impracticable to transfer the juvenile. Rather, 'impracticable' should be taken to mean that exceptional circumstances render movement of the child impossible or that the juvenile is due at court in such a short space of time that transfer would deprive them of rest or cause them to miss a court appearance. When the reason for not transferring the juvenile is an imminent court appearance, details of the travelling and court appearance times which justify the decision should be included in the certificate. The availability of secure accommodation is only a factor in relation to a juvenile aged 12 or over when other local authority accommodation would not be adequate to protect the public from serious harm from them. The obligation to transfer a juvenile to local authority accommodation applies as much to a juvenile charged during the daytime as to a juvenile to be held overnight, subject to a requirement to bring the juvenile before a court under PACE, s. 46.

16.7A The requirement in *paragraph 3.4(b)* that documents and materials essential to effectively challenging the lawfulness of the detainee's arrest and detention must be made available to the detainee and, if they are represented, their solicitor, applies for the purposes of this section and a person's detention after charge. This means that the custody officer making the bail decision (*PACE, section 38*) or reviewing the need for detention after charge (*PACE, section 40*), is responsible for determining what, if any, documents or materials are essential and must be made available to the detainee or their solicitor.

(B) Documentation

16.8 A record shall be made of anything a detainee says when charged.

16.9 Any questions put in an interview after charge and answers given relating to the offence shall be recorded in full during the interview on forms for that purpose and the record signed by the detainee or, if they refuse, by the interviewer and any third parties present. If the questions are audibly recorded or visually recorded the arrangements in Code E or F apply.

16.10 If arrangements for a juvenile's transfer into local authority care as in *paragraph 16.7* are not made, the custody officer must record the reasons in a certificate which must be produced before the court with the juvenile.

2.6.20 Cautions as a Means of Disposal

In dealing with any offence committed by a person, the police have a range of options:

- no further action;
- community resolution;
- caution;
- conditional caution; or
- charge.

There are occasions where a person for whom there is sufficient evidence to charge with an offence may be cautioned for it as an alternative method of disposing with the case (usually involving low-level offending). There are four different types of caution which can be separated into two groups using the age of the person cautioned as the determining factor:

Cautions—Aged Under 18	Cautions—Aged 18 or Over
Youth cautions	Simple cautions
Youth conditional cautions	Adult conditional cautions

2.6.20.1 Youth Cautions and Simple Cautions

The Ministry of Justice Guidance regarding the decision-making processes and administration of youth cautions and simple cautions is lengthy and a reproduction of such detail is beyond the scope of this Manual; however, a brief summary of the youth caution and simple caution framework is presented below:

	Youth Caution	Simple Caution
Relevant age?	Person aged 10 to 17	Person aged 18 or over
Administered when?	the offender admits the offence + there is sufficient evidence to charge the offender with the offence + not in the public interest to prosecute	
Who decides if a caution is suitable?	If the offence is summary only or triable either way, the police. If the offence is indicatable only, the case should be referred to the CPS for a decision	
Who delivers the caution?	A police officer (preferably in uniform) who has been given appropriate training	The custody officer or other suitably trained person
Where is the caution delivered?	May take place on Youth Offending Team (YOT) premises where police officers in the YOT are responsible for delivering cautions or other suitable location	May be administered in a police station, court building or other suitable location
Unsuitable location for delivery?	In the street or the individual's home	

KEYNOTE

Consent to the Caution

If a youth caution is to be given, the 'consent' of the young person concerned *is not required* as it is up to the police to decide appropriate disposal.

However, a simple caution can only be given if the person to be cautioned *agrees to accept it*. Therefore, it is important that the full implications of accepting a simple caution (e.g. the fact that a simple caution forms part of an offender's criminal record, a record will be retained by the police for future use and it may also be referred to in future legal proceedings) are made clear to the person so that he/she is able to give an informed consent otherwise there is a risk that the courts may overturn the caution (*R (On the Application of Stratton* v *Chief Constable of Thames Val*ley [2013] EWHC 1561 (Admin)). The necessity for an informed consent to be given may require consideration to be given regarding disclosure. While there is no general obligation on the police to disclose material prior to charge, there may be a need to make some disclosure to a suspect's legal representative in order that he/she can advise on whether a caution should be accepted (*DPP* v *Ara* [2001] EWHC Admin 493). In *Ara*, the suspect had been interviewed without a legal representative being present but the officers refused to disclose the terms of the interview.

Admitting the Offence

The admission of guilt does not need to be made within a formal interview under PACE84. However, the method for obtaining and recording the admission must be PACE84-compliant. In *R* v *Chief Constable of Lancashire Constabulary, ex parte Atkinson* (1998) 162 JP 275, the court considered the level of evidence required before a caution can be considered. There the court said that, provided it was clear that there had been an admission of guilt, it was not necessary, for the purposes of administering a caution, to show that the admission had been obtained in circumstances which satisfied the *Codes of Practice*. However, police officers would be well advised to take precautions that would satisfy Code C.

Decision-making

Before making a case disposal decision it is essential that the matter has been fully investigated in order to reach an informed decision. In *Omar* v *Chief Constable of Bedfordshire Constabulary* [2002] EWHC 3060 (Admin), the Divisional Court quashed a caution that had been administered in order to allow a prosecution to be pursued. The court held that a number of reasonable lines of inquiry had not been made; for instance, the police had failed to take a statement from the victim's friend or obtain CCTV footage that was available or fully investigate the victim's injuries. Further, the length of time in custody (17 hours) should *not* have been a relevant consideration and also the suspect's admission was ambiguous. Therefore, it was in the public interest that a decision to caution rather than to charge should not prevent the subsequent pursuit of the prosecution of the offender.

2.6.20.2 Youth and Adult Conditional Cautions

A conditional caution allows an authorised person (usually a police officer) or a relevant prosecutor (usually the CPS) to decide to give a caution with one or more conditions attached. When an offender is given a conditional caution for an offence, criminal proceedings for that offence are halted while the offender is given an opportunity to comply with the conditions. Where the conditions are complied with, the prosecution is not normally commenced. However, where there is no reasonable excuse for non-compliance, criminal proceedings may be commenced for the original offence and the conditional caution will cease to have effect. A conditional caution can be given for one or more offences.

Like youth cautions and simple cautions, the Ministry of Justice Guidance regarding the decision-making processes and administration of youth conditional cautions and adult conditional cautions is lengthy and a reproduction of such detail is beyond the scope of this Manual; however, a brief summary of the youth conditional caution and adult conditional caution framework is presented below:

	Youth Conditional Caution	Adult Conditional Caution
Relevant age?	Person aged 10 to 17	Person aged 18 or over
Administered when?	the offender admits the offence + there is sufficient evidence to charge the offender with the offence + public interest may be met with a caution with conditions	
Who decides if a caution is suitable?	If the offence is summary only or triable either way, the police. If the offence is indicatable only, the case should be referred to the CPS for a decision	
Who delivers the caution?	An officer of the rank of sergeant or higher or a suitably qualified police officer or any other person specifically authorised to do so by the DPP	A police officer not below the rank of sergeant or any person specifically authorised to do so by the DPP
Where is the caution delivered?	In a police station, court building, YOT premises, the offices of any prosecutor, or any other suitable location consistent with achieving the appropriate impact on the young person	May be administered in a police station, court building or other suitable location
Unsuitable location for delivery?	In the street or the individual's home	

KEYNOTE

The youth or adult *must consent* to be given a conditional caution.

The conditions that can be attached to a conditional caution must have one or more of the following objectives:

- rehabilitation—conditions which help to modify the behaviour of the offender (e.g. counselling or therapy such as attending an anger management course, or it could involve treatment for drug or alcohol addiction) that serve to reduce the likelihood of re-offending or help to reintegrate the offender into society;
- reparation—conditions which serve to repair the damage done either directly or indirectly by the offender or it could be to carry out unpaid work within the community;

- punishment—financial penalty conditions which punish the offender for their unlawful conduct or involve financial reparation to the victim.

A specific power allowing a police officer to arrest and detain offenders is provided by s. 24A(1) of the Criminal Justice Act 2003. The power arises when a constable has reasonable grounds for believing that a young person/adult has failed without reasonable excuse to comply with any conditions attached to a youth/adult conditional caution but should only be exercised where considered necessary. In determining when arrest might be necessary, regard should be had to the criteria in s. 24(4) and (5) PACE84. Once arrested, detention may be authorised where it is necessary to investigate reasons for any non-compliance or to seek a charging decision from a prosecutor and formally charge a young person/ adult offender.

2.6.21

Code C—17 Testing Persons for the Presence of Specified Class A Drugs

(A) Action

17.1 This section of Code C applies only in selected police stations in police areas where the provisions for drug testing under section 63B of PACE (as amended by section 5 of the Criminal Justice Act 2003 and section 7 of the Drugs Act 2005) are in force and in respect of which the Secretary of State has given a notification to the relevant chief officer of police that arrangements for the taking of samples have been made. Such a notification will cover either a police area as a whole or particular stations within a police area. The notification indicates whether the testing applies to those arrested or charged or under the age of 18 as the case may be and testing can only take place in respect of the persons so indicated in the notification. Testing cannot be carried out unless the relevant notification has been given and has not been withdrawn.

KEYNOTE

The power to take samples is subject to notification by the Secretary of State that appropriate arrangements for the taking of samples have been made for the police area as a whole or for the particular police station concerned for whichever of the following is specified in the notification:

(a) persons in respect of whom the arrest condition is met;
(b) persons in respect of whom the charge condition is met;
(c) persons who have not attained the age of 18.

17.2 A sample of urine or a non-intimate sample may be taken from a person in police detention for the purpose of ascertaining whether they have any specified Class A drug in their body only where they have been brought before the custody officer and:

(a) either the arrest condition, see *paragraph 17.3*, or the charge condition, see *paragraph 17.4* is met;
(b) the age condition see *paragraph 17.5*, is met;
(c) the notification condition is met in relation to the arrest condition, the charge condition, or the age condition, as the case may be. (Testing on charge and/or arrest must be specifically provided for in the notification for the power to apply. In addition, the fact that testing of under 18s is authorised must be expressly provided for in the notification before the power to test such persons applies.). See *paragraph 17.1*; and

(d) a police officer has requested the person concerned to give the sample (the request condition).

17.3 The arrest condition is met where the detainee:

(a) has been arrested for a trigger offence, but not charged with that offence; or

(b) has been arrested for any other offence but not charged with that offence and a police officer of inspector rank or above, who has reasonable grounds for suspecting that their misuse of any specified Class A drug caused or contributed to the offence, has authorised the sample to be taken.

KEYNOTE

The trigger offences referred to in the section are:

- From the Theft Act 1968, theft, robbery, burglary, aggravated burglary, taking a conveyance without consent, aggravated vehicle-taking, handling stolen good and going equipped.
- From the Misuse of Drugs Act 1971, restriction on production and supply of controlled drugs, possession of a controlled drug and possession of a controlled drug with intent to supply (note that these offences must be committed in respect of a specified Class A drug).
- From the Fraud Act 2005, fraud, possession, etc. of articles for use in frauds and making or supplying articles for use in frauds.
- An offence under s. 1(1) of the Criminal Attempts Act 1981 if committed in respect of an offence of theft, robbery, burglary, handling stolen goods or fraud.
- From the Vagrancy Act 1824, begging or persistent begging.

17.4 The charge condition is met where the detainee:

(a) has been charged with a trigger offence, or

(b) has been charged with any other offence and a police officer of inspector rank or above, who has reasonable grounds for suspecting that the detainee's misuse of any specified Class A drug caused or contributed to the offence, has authorised the sample to be taken.

17.5 The age condition is met where:

(a) in the case of a detainee who has been arrested but not charged as in *paragraph 17.3*, they are aged 18 or over;

(b) in the case of a detainee who has been charged as in *paragraph 17.4*, they are aged 14 or over.

17.6 Before requesting a sample from the person concerned, an officer must:

(a) inform them that the purpose of taking the sample is for drug testing under PACE. This is to ascertain whether they have a specified Class A drug present in their body;

(b) warn them that if, when so requested, they fail without good cause to provide a sample they may be liable to prosecution;

(c) where the taking of the sample has been authorised by an inspector or above in accordance with *paragraph 17.3(b)* or *17.4(b)* above, inform them that the authorisation has been given and the grounds for giving it;

(d) remind them of the following rights, which may be exercised at any stage during the period in custody:

(i) the right to have someone informed of their arrest [see section 5];

(ii) the right to consult privately with a solicitor and that free independent legal advice is available [see section 6]; and

(iii) the right to consult these Codes of Practice [see section 3].

KEYNOTE

When warning a person who is asked to provide a urine or non-intimate sample in accordance with para. 17.6(b), the following form of words may be used:

> You do not have to provide a sample, but I must warn you that if you fail or refuse without good cause to do so, you will commit an offence for which you may be imprisoned, or fined, or both.

Where the Welsh language is appropriate, the following form of words may be used:

> Does dim rhaid i chi roi sampl, ond mae'n rhaid i mi eich rhybuddio y byddwch chi'n cyflawni trosedd os byddwch chi'n methu neu yn gwrthod gwneud hynny heb reswm da, ac y gellir, oherwydd hynny, eich carcharu, eich dirwyo, neu'r ddau.

17.7 In the case of a person who has not attained the age specified in section 63B(5A) of PACE—

(a) the making of the request for a sample under *paragraph 17.2(d)* above;

(b) the giving of the warning and the information under *paragraph 17.6* above; and

(c) the taking of the sample,

may not take place except in the presence of an appropriate adult.

KEYNOTE

For the purposes of needing the presence of an appropriate adult for Code C, para. 17.7, an appropriate adult means the person's:

(a) parent or guardian or, if they are in the care of a local authority or voluntary organisation, a person representing that authority or organisation; or

(b) a social worker of a local authority; or

(c) if no person falling within (a) or (b) above is available, any responsible person aged 18 or over who is not:

- employed by the police;
- under the direction or control of the chief officer of police force;
- or a person who provides services under contractual arrangements (but without being employed by the chief officer of a police force), to assist that force in relation to the discharge of its chief officer's functions;

whether or not they are on duty at the time.

17.8 Authorisation by an officer of the rank of inspector or above within *paragraph 17.3(b)* or *17.4(b)* may be given orally or in writing but, if it is given orally, it must be confirmed in writing as soon as practicable.

17.9 If a sample is taken from a detainee who has been arrested for an offence but not charged with that offence as in *paragraph 17.3*, no further sample may be taken during the same continuous period of detention. If during that same period the charge condition is also met in respect of that detainee, the sample which has been taken shall be treated as being taken by virtue of the charge condition, see *paragraph 17.4*, being met.

17.10 A detainee from whom a sample may be taken may be detained for up to six hours from the time of charge if the custody officer reasonably believes the detention is necessary to enable a sample to be taken. Where the arrest condition is met, a detainee whom the custody officer has decided to release on bail without charge may continue to be detained, but not beyond 24 hours from the relevant time (as defined in section 41(2) of PACE), to enable a sample to be taken.

17.11 A detainee in respect of whom the arrest condition is met, but not the charge condition, see *paragraphs 17.3* and *17.4*, and whose release would be required before a sample can be taken had they not continued to be detained as a result of being arrested for a further offence which does not satisfy the arrest condition, may have a sample taken at any time within 24 hours after the arrest for the offence that satisfies the arrest condition.

KEYNOTE

A sample has to be sufficient and suitable. A sufficient sample is sufficient in quantity and quality to enable drug-testing analysis to take place. A suitable sample is one which by its nature is suitable for a particular form of drug analysis.

Samples, and the information derived from them, may not subsequently be used in the investigation of any offence or in evidence against the persons from whom they were taken.

(B) Documentation

17.12 The following must be recorded in the custody record:

(a) if a sample is taken following authorisation by an officer of the rank of inspector or above, the authorisation and the grounds for suspicion;

(b) the giving of a warning of the consequences of failure to provide a sample;

(c) the time at which the sample was given; and

(d) the time of charge or, where the arrest condition is being relied upon, the time of arrest and, where applicable, the fact that a sample taken after arrest but before charge is to be treated as being taken by virtue of the charge condition, where that is met in the same period of continuous detention. See *paragraph 17.9*.

(C) General

17.13 A sample may only be taken by a prescribed person.

KEYNOTE

Regulation 2 of the Police and Criminal Evidence Act 1984 (Drug Testing of Persons in Police Detention) (Prescribed Persons) Regulations 2001 sets out who are prescribed persons for the purposes of s. 63B PACE84. They are:

(a) a police officer;

(b) a person employed by a local policing body or chief officer of police whose contractual duties include taking samples for the purpose of testing for the presence of specified Class A drugs; or

(c) a person employed by a contractor engaged by a local policing body or chief officer of police whose duties include taking samples for the purpose of testing for the presence of specified Class A drugs.

A 'contractor' (referred to in (c) above) means any person or body obliged, under any of the terms of a contract with a local policing body or chief officer of police, to provide, when required, the service of taking samples for the purpose of testing for the presence of specified Class A drugs.

17.14 Force may not be used to take any sample for the purpose of drug testing.

17.15 The terms 'Class A drug' and 'misuse' have the same meanings as in the Misuse of Drugs Act 1971. 'Specified' (in relation to a Class A drug) and 'trigger offence' have the same meanings as in Part III of the Criminal Justice and Court Services Act 2000.

17.16 Any sample taken:

(a) may not be used for any purpose other than to ascertain whether the person concerned has a specified Class A drug present in his body; and

(b) can be disposed of as clinical waste unless it is to be sent for further analysis in cases where the test result is disputed at the point when the result is known, including on the basis that medication has been taken, or for quality assurance purposes.

(D) Assessment of misuse of drugs

17.17 Under the provisions of Part 3 of the Drugs Act 2005, where a detainee has tested positive for a specified Class A drug under section 63B of PACE a police officer may, at any time before the person's release from the police station, impose a requirement on the detainee to attend an initial assessment of their drug misuse by a suitably qualified person and to remain for its duration. Where such a requirement is imposed, the officer must, at the same time, impose a second requirement on the detainee to attend and remain for a follow-up assessment. The officer must inform the detainee that the second requirement will cease to have effect if, at the initial assessment they are informed that a follow-up assessment is not necessary These requirements may only be imposed on a person if:

(a) they have reached the age of 18

(b) notification has been given by the Secretary of State to the relevant chief officer of police that arrangements for conducting initial and follow-up assessments have been made for those from whom samples for testing have been taken at the police station where the detainee is in custody.

17.18 When imposing a requirement to attend an initial assessment and a follow-up assessment the police officer must:

(a) inform the person of the time and place at which the initial assessment is to take place;

(b) explain that this information will be confirmed in writing; and

(c) warn the person that they may be liable to prosecution if they fail without good cause to attend the initial assessment and remain for its duration and if they fail to attend the follow-up assessment and remain for its duration (if so required).

17.19 Where a police officer has imposed a requirement to attend an initial assessment and a follow-up assessment in accordance with *paragraph 17.17*, he must, before the person is released from detention, give the person notice in writing which:

(a) confirms their requirement to attend and remain for the duration of the assessments; and

(b) confirms the information and repeats the warning referred to in *paragraph 17.18*.

17.20 The following must be recorded in the custody record:

(a) that the requirement to attend an initial assessment and a follow-up assessment has been imposed; and

(b) the information, explanation, warning and notice given in accordance with *paragraphs 17.17* and *17.19*.

17.21 Where a notice is given in accordance with *paragraph 17.19*, a police officer can give the person a further notice in writing which informs the person of any change to the time or place at which the initial assessment is to take place and which repeats the warning referred to in *paragraph 17.18(c)*.

17.22 Part 3 of the Drugs Act 2005 also requires police officers to have regard to any guidance issued by the Secretary of State in respect of the assessment provisions.

2.6.22

Code C—Annex A: Intimate and Strip Searches

A Intimate Search

1. An intimate search consists of the physical examination of a person's body orifices other than the mouth. The intrusive nature of such searches means the actual and potential risks associated with intimate searches must never be underestimated.

KEYNOTE

Intimate searches are legislated for by s. 55 PACE84. An intimate search can only be authorised in relation to a person who has been arrested and is in police detention (s. 55(1)) (**see para 2.6.5.2**).

In *Owens* v *CC of Merseyside* [2021] EWHC 3119 (QB), whilst in custody the detainee having been 'asked' to remove his trousers and underwear was then 'asked to separate his penis and testicles, to pull his foreskin back and then to turn around and lean over, separating his bottom cheeks'. This was to check whether Class A drugs had been secreted in these areas. The question for the court was whether this was a strip search or intimate search. The court found that the definition of 'intimate search' ('the physical examination of a person's body orifices other than the mouth') requires an act of physical intrusion into a body orifice. In this case, the only 'examination', taking place inside the body orifice, was 'visual' and therefore was not an intimate search. What matters is the exploration inside the body orifice: where that exploration is physically penetrative, it is 'physical intrusion into the body orifice' and therefore 'some physical examination'.

(a) Action

2. Body orifices other than the mouth may be searched only:
   - (a) if authorised by an officer of inspector rank or above who has reasonable grounds for believing that the person may have concealed on themselves:
     - (i) anything which they could and might use to cause physical injury to themselves or others at the station; or
     - (ii) a Class A drug which they intended to supply to another or to export;
     - (iii) and the officer has reasonable grounds for believing that an intimate search is the only means of removing those items; and
   - (b) if the search is under *paragraph 2(a)(ii)* (a drug offence search), the detainee's appropriate consent has been given in writing.

KEYNOTE

Before authorising any intimate search, the authorising officer must make every reasonable effort to persuade the detainee to hand the article over without a search. If the detainee agrees, a registered medical practitioner or registered nurse should whenever possible be asked to assess the risks involved and, if necessary, attend to assist the detainee.

If the detainee does not agree to hand the article over without a search, the authorising officer must carefully review all the relevant factors before authorising an intimate search. In particular, the officer must consider whether the grounds for believing an article may be concealed are reasonable.

If authority is given for a search under para. 2(a)(i), a registered medical practitioner or registered nurse shall be consulted whenever possible. The presumption should be that the search will be conducted by the registered medical practitioner or registered nurse and the authorising officer must make every reasonable effort to persuade the detainee to allow the medical practitioner or nurse to conduct the search.

An officer may give an authorisation orally or in writing but, if he/she gives it orally, he/she shall confirm it in writing as soon as practicable (s. 55(3)).

2A. Before the search begins, a police officer or designated detention officer, must tell the detainee:—
   - (a) that the authority to carry out the search has been given;
   - (b) the grounds for giving the authorisation and for believing that the article cannot be removed without an intimate search.

2B. Before a detainee is asked to give appropriate consent to a search under *paragraph 2(a)(ii)* (a drug offence search) they must be warned that if they refuse without good cause their refusal may harm their case if it comes to trial. This warning may be given by a police officer or member of police staff. In the case of juveniles, or vulnerable suspects, the seeking and giving of consent must take place in the presence of the appropriate adult. A juvenile's consent is only valid if their parent's or guardian's consent is also obtained unless the juvenile is under 14, when their parent's or guardian's consent is sufficient in its own right. A detainee who is not legally represented must be reminded of their entitlement to have free legal advice, see Code C, *paragraph 6.5*, and the reminder noted in the custody record.

KEYNOTE

In warning a detainee who is asked to consent to an intimate drug offence search, as in para. 2B, the following form of words may be used:

> You do not have to allow yourself to be searched, but I must warn you that if you refuse without good cause, your refusal may harm your case if it comes to trial.

Where the use of the Welsh language is appropriate, the following form of words may be used:

> Nid oes rhaid i chi roi caniatâd i gael eich archwilio, ond mae'n rhaid i mi eich rhybuddio os gwrthodwch heb reswm da, y gallai eich penderfyniad i wrthod wneud niwed i'ch achos pe bai'n dod gerbron llys.

3. An intimate search may only be carried out by a registered medical practitioner or registered nurse, unless an officer of at least inspector rank considers this is not practicable and the search is to take place under *paragraph 2(a)(i)*, in which case a police officer may carry out the search.

KEYNOTE

A constable should only be authorised to carry out a search as a last resort and when all other approaches have failed. In these circumstances, the authorising officer must be satisfied the detainee might use the article for one or more of the purposes in para. 2(a)(i) and the physical injury likely to be caused is sufficiently severe to justify authorising a constable to carry out the search.

If an officer has any doubts whether to authorise an intimate search by a constable, the officer should seek advice from an officer of superintendent rank or above.

3A. Any proposal for a search under *paragraph 2(a)(i)* to be carried out by someone other than a registered medical practitioner or registered nurse must only be considered as a last resort and when the authorising officer is satisfied the risks associated with allowing the item to remain with the detainee outweigh the risks associated with removing it.

4. An intimate search under:
   - *paragraph 2(a)(i)* may take place only at a hospital, surgery, other medical premises or police station;
   - *paragraph 2(a)(ii)* may take place only at a hospital, surgery or other medical premises and must be carried out by a registered medical practitioner or a registered nurse.
5. An intimate search at a police station of a juvenile or vulnerable person may take place only in the presence of an appropriate adult of the same sex (see *Annex L*), unless the detainee specifically requests a particular adult of the opposite sex who is readily available. In the case of a juvenile, the search may take place in the absence of the appropriate adult only if the juvenile signifies in the presence of the appropriate adult they do not want the adult present during the search and the adult agrees. A record shall be made of the juvenile's decision and signed by the appropriate adult.
6. When an intimate search under *paragraph 2(a)(i)* is carried out by a police officer, the officer must be of the same sex as the detainee (see *Annex L*). A minimum of two people, other than

the detainee, must be present during the search. Subject to *paragraph 5*, no person of the opposite sex who is not a medical practitioner or nurse shall be present, nor shall anyone whose presence is unnecessary. The search shall be conducted with proper regard to the dignity, sensitivity and vulnerability of the detainee including in particular, their health, hygiene and welfare needs to which *paragraphs 9.3A* and *9.3B* apply.

(b) Documentation

7. In the case of an intimate search, the following shall be recorded as soon as practicable in the detainee's custody record:
   (a) for searches under paragraphs 2(a)(i) and (ii);
   - the authorisation to carry out the search;
   - the grounds for giving the authorisation;
   - the grounds for believing the article could not be removed without an intimate search;
   - which parts of the detainee's body were searched;
   - who carried out the search;
   - who was present;
   - the result.

   (b) for searches under paragraph 2(a)(ii):
   - the giving of the warning required by *paragraph 2B*;
   - the fact that the appropriate consent was given or (as the case may be) refused, and if refused, the reason given for the refusal (if any).
8. If an intimate search is carried out by a police officer, the reason why it was impracticable for a registered medical practitioner or registered nurse to conduct it must be recorded.

B Strip Search

9. A strip search is a search involving the removal of more than outer clothing. In this Code, outer clothing includes shoes and socks.

KEYNOTE

A strip search is carried out using the power to search a detained person under s. 54 PACE84 (see para. 2.6.9) and is authorised by the custody officer.

(a) Action

10. A strip search may take place only if it is considered necessary to remove an article which a detainee would not be allowed to keep and the officer reasonably considers the detainee might have concealed such an article. Strip searches shall not be routinely carried out if there is no reason to consider that articles are concealed.

The conduct of strip searches

11. When strip searches are conducted:
    (a) a police officer carrying out a strip search must be the same sex as the detainee (see *Annex L*);
    (b) the search shall take place in an area where the detainee cannot be seen by anyone who does not need to be present, nor by a member of the opposite sex (see *Annex L*) except an appropriate adult who has been specifically requested by the detainee;

KEYNOTE

The Codes do not preclude officers of the opposite sex being indirectly involved in the strip search process. In the case of *PD (by her mother and litigation friend ZD)* v *Chief Constable of Merseyside Police* [2015] EWCA Civ 114, a 14-year-old, female detainee was flagged as a suicide risk by the custody officer; as a result of this, she was ordered to have her clothing removed, as part of a safety procedure to reduce risk factors. Two female officers, and two male officers, took the claimant into a private room. The court found that para. 11(b) of Annex A allows a male officer to be involved in the management of the detained person. The essential requirement was that the removal should take place in an area where no one who was not immediately involved, and no male officer, could observe the detainee. In this case, the two male officers left the cell and stayed in the corridor outside while the 14-year-old was undressed. The cell door was left ajar for security reasons but a safety blanket was used to protect the detainee's dignity.

(c) except in cases of urgency, where there is risk of serious harm to the detainee or to others, whenever a strip search involves exposure of intimate body parts, there must be at least two people present other than the detainee, and if the search is of a juvenile or vulnerable person, one of the people must be the appropriate adult. Except in urgent cases as above, a search of a juvenile may take place in the absence of the appropriate adult only if the juvenile signifies in the presence of the appropriate adult that they do not want the appropriate adult to be present during the search and the appropriate adult agrees. A record shall be made of the juvenile's decision and signed by the appropriate adult. The presence of more than two people, other than an appropriate adult, shall be permitted only in the most exceptional circumstances;

(d) the search shall be conducted with proper regard to the dignity, sensitivity and vulnerability of the detainee in these circumstances, including in particular, their health, hygiene and welfare needs to which *paragraphs 9.3A* and *9.3B* apply. Every reasonable effort shall be made to secure the detainee's co-operation, maintain their dignity and minimise embarrassment. Detainees who are searched shall not normally be required to remove all their clothes at the same time, e.g. a person should be allowed to remove clothing above the waist and redress before removing further clothing;

(e) if necessary to assist the search, the detainee may be required to hold their arms in the air or to stand with their legs apart and bend forward so a visual examination may be made of the genital and anal areas provided no physical contact is made with any body orifice;

(f) if articles are found, the detainee shall be asked to hand them over. If articles are found within any body orifice other than the mouth, and the detainee refuses to hand them over, their removal would constitute an intimate search, which must be carried out as in *Part A*;

(g) a strip search shall be conducted as quickly as possible, and the detainee allowed to dress as soon as the procedure is complete.

KEYNOTE

Annex A, para. 11 applies to all the powers given to custody officers under s. 54 PACE84, including the power to remove and seize clothing under s. 54(4). In *Davies* v *Chief Constable of Merseyside* [2015] EWCA Civ 114 the court held that Annex A, para. 11 applied to any strip search, not just those strip searches carried out in compliance with para. 10. For example it would apply where the custody officer determines that a detained person is a suicide risk and orders the removal of their clothing under s. 54 so they can be dressed in a safety gown.

(b) Documentation

12. A record shall be made on the custody record of a strip search including the reason it was considered necessary, those present and any result.

2.6.23

Code C—Annex B: Delay in Notifying Arrest or Allowing Access to Legal Advice

A Persons detained under PACE

1. The exercise of the rights in *Section 5* or *Section 6*, or both, may be delayed if the person is in police detention, as in PACE, section 118(2), in connection with an indictable offence, has not yet been charged with an offence and an officer of superintendent rank or above, or inspector rank or above only for the rights in *Section 5*, has reasonable grounds for believing their exercise will:
   (i) lead to:
      - interference with, or harm to, evidence connected with an indictable offence; or
      - interference with, or physical harm to, other people; or

   (ii) lead to alerting other people suspected of having committed an indictable offence but not yet arrested for it; or

   (iii) hinder the recovery of property obtained in consequence of the commission of such an offence.
2. These rights may also be delayed if the officer has reasonable grounds to believe that:
   (i) the person detained for an indictable offence has benefited from their criminal conduct (decided in accordance with Part 2 of the Proceeds of Crime Act 2002); and

   (ii) the recovery of the value of the property constituting that benefit will be hindered by the exercise of either right.

KEYNOTE

When considering the delay of access to a solicitor the authorising officer must bear in mind that access to a solicitor is 'a fundamental right of a citizen' (*R* v *Samuel* [1988] QB 615). The authorising officer must actually believe that by allowing access to the solicitor he/she will intentionally or inadvertently alert other suspects.

3. Authority to delay a detainee's right to consult privately with a solicitor may be given only if the authorising officer has reasonable grounds to believe the solicitor the detainee wants to consult will, inadvertently or otherwise, pass on a message from the detainee or act in some other way which will have any of the consequences specified under *paragraphs 1 or 2*. In these circumstances, the detainee must be allowed to choose another solicitor.

KEYNOTE

Occasions where delay will be authorised in such circumstances will be rare and only when it can be shown that the suspect is capable of misleading that particular solicitor and there is more than a substantial risk that the suspect will succeed in causing information to be conveyed which will lead to one or more of the specified consequences. In deciding whether such an interview will be admissible, the court will consider how reliable it is and will consider how the refusal to allow that particular detained person access to a solicitor affected his/her decision to make a confession. One such case where the confession was excluded is *R* v *Sanusi* [1992] Crim LR 43, where a person from another country was denied access to a solicitor and the court held that his right to advice was particularly significant due to his lack of familiarity with police procedures.

4. If the detainee wishes to see a solicitor, access to that solicitor may not be delayed on the grounds they might advise the detainee not to answer questions or the solicitor was initially asked to attend the police station by someone else. In the latter case, the detainee must be told the solicitor has come to the police station at another person's request, and must be asked to sign the custody record to signify whether they want to see the solicitor.
5. The fact the grounds for delaying notification of arrest may be satisfied does not automatically mean the grounds for delaying access to legal advice will also be satisfied.
6. These rights may be delayed only for as long as grounds exist and in no case beyond 36 hours after the relevant time as in PACE, section 41. If the grounds cease to apply within this time, the detainee must, as soon as practicable, be asked if they want to exercise either right, the custody record must be noted accordingly, and action taken in accordance with the relevant section of the Code.
7. A detained person must be permitted to consult a solicitor for a reasonable time before any court hearing.

B *Not used*

C Documentation

13. The grounds for action under this Annex shall be recorded and the detainee informed of them as soon as practicable.
14. Any reply given by a detainee under *paragraphs 6* or *11* must be recorded and the detainee asked to endorse the record in relation to whether they want to receive legal advice at this point.

D Cautions and special warnings

15. When a suspect detained at a police station is interviewed during any period for which access to legal advice has been delayed under this Annex, the court or jury may not draw adverse inferences from their silence.

KEYNOTE

Even if Annex B applies in the case of a juvenile, or a vulnerable person, action to inform the appropriate adult and the person responsible for a juvenile's welfare, if that is a different person, must nevertheless be taken as in paras 3.13 and 3.15. Similarly, for detained persons who are citizens of independent Commonwealth countries or foreign nationals the exercise of the rights in Code C, s. 7 may not be interfered with.

Code C—Annex C: Restriction on Drawing Adverse Inferences from Silence and Terms of the Caution when the Restriction Applies [see chapter 2.8]

Code C—Annex D: Written Statements Under Caution [see chapter 2.8]

2.6.24 Code C—Annex E: Summary of Provisions Relating to Vulnerable Persons

1. If at any time, an officer has reason to suspect that a person of any age may be vulnerable (see *paragraph 1.13(d)*), in the absence of clear evidence to dispel that suspicion that person shall be treated as such for the purposes of this Code and to establish whether any such reason may exist in relation to a person suspected of committing an offence (see *paragraph 10.1*), the custody officer. In the case of a detained person, or the officer investigating the offence in the case of a person who has not been arrested or detained, shall take, or cause to be taken, (see *paragraph 3.5*) the following action:

(a) reasonable enquiries shall be made to ascertain what information is available that is relevant to any of the factors described in *paragraph 1.13(d)* as indicating that the person may be vulnerable might apply;

(b) a record shall be made describing whether any of those factors appear to apply and provide any reason to suspect that the person may be vulnerable or (as the case may be) may not be vulnerable; and

(c) the record mentioned in sub-paragraph (b) shall be made available to be taken into account by police officers, police staff and any others who, in accordance with the provisions of this or any other Code, are entitled to communicate with the person in question. This would include any solicitor, appropriate adult and health care professional and is particularly relevant to communication by telephone or by means of a live link (see *paragraphs 12.9A* (interviews), *13.12* (interpretation), and *15.3C, 15.11A, 15.11B, 15.11C* and *15.11D* (reviews and extension of detention)).

KEYNOTE

For the purposes of inquiries as to whether a suspect may be vulnerable, examples of relevant information that may be available include:

- the behaviour of the adult or juvenile;
- the mental health and capacity of the adult or juvenile;
- what the adult or juvenile says about themselves;
- information from relatives and friends of the adult or juvenile;
- information from police officers and staff and from police records;
- information from health and social care (including liaison and diversion services) and other professionals who know, or have had previous contact with, the individual and may be able to contribute to assessing their need for help and support from an appropriate adult. This includes contacts and assessments arranged by the police or at the request of the individual or (as applicable) their appropriate adult or solicitor.

When a person is under the influence of drink and/or drugs, it is not intended that they are to be treated as vulnerable and requiring an appropriate adult for the purpose of Annex E, para. 1 unless other information indicates that any of the factors described in para. 1.13(d) may apply to that person. When the person has recovered from the effects of drink and/or drugs, they should be reassessed in accordance with Annex E, para. 1. See para. 15.4A for application to live link.

2. In the case of a person who is vulnerable, 'the appropriate adult' means:
   (i) a relative, guardian or other person responsible for their care or custody;
   (ii) someone experienced in dealing with vulnerable persons but who is not: ~ a police officer;
      ~ employed by the police;
      ~ under the direction or control of the chief officer of a police force;
      ~ a person who provides services under contractual arrangements (but without being employed by the chief officer of a police force), to assist that force in relation to the discharge of its chief officer's functions, whether or not they are on duty at the time.
   (iii) failing these, some other responsible adult aged 18 or over who is other than a person described in the bullet points in *sub-paragraph (ii)* above.

   See *paragraph 1.7(b)*.

2A The role of the appropriate adult is to safeguard the rights, entitlements and welfare of 'vulnerable persons' (see *paragraph 1)* to whom the provisions of this and any other Code of Practice apply. For this reason, the appropriate adult is expected, amongst other things, to:
- support, advise and assist them when, in accordance with this Code or any other Code of Practice, they are given or asked to provide information or participate in any procedure;
- observe whether the police are acting properly and fairly to respect their rights and entitlements, and inform an officer of the rank of inspector or above if they consider that they are not;

- assist them to communicate with the police whilst respecting their right to say nothing unless they want to as set out in the terms of the caution (see *paragraphs 10.5* and *10.6*); and
- help them understand their rights and ensure that those rights are protected and respected (see *paragraphs 3.15, 3.17, 6.5A* and *11.17*).

See *paragraph 1.7A*.

KEYNOTE

Although vulnerable persons are often capable of providing reliable evidence, they may, without knowing or wanting to do so, be particularly prone in certain circumstances to provide information that may be unreliable, misleading or self-incriminating. Special care should always be taken when questioning such a person, and the appropriate adult should be involved if there is any doubt about a person's mental state or capacity. Because of the risk of unreliable evidence, it is important to obtain corroboration of any facts admitted whenever possible.

Because of the risks referred to above, which the presence of the appropriate adult is intended to minimise, officers of superintendent rank or above should exercise their discretion to authorise the commencement of an interview in the appropriate adult's absence only in exceptional cases, if it is necessary to avert one or more of the specified risks in para. 11.1. See paras 11.1 and 11.18 to 11.20.

There is no requirement for an appropriate adult to be present if a person is detained under s. 136 of the Mental Health Act 1983 for assessment.

3. If the custody officer authorises the detention of a vulnerable person, the custody officer must as soon as practicable inform the appropriate adult of the grounds for detention and the person's whereabouts, and ask the adult to come to the police station to see them. If the appropriate adult:
   - is already at the station when information is given as in *paragraphs 3.1* to *3.5* the information must be given in their presence;
   - is not at the station when the provisions of *paragraph 3.1* to *3.5* are complied with these provisions must be complied with again in their presence once they arrive.

   See *paragraphs 3.15* to *3.17*.
4. If the appropriate adult, having been informed of the right to legal advice, considers legal advice should be taken, the provisions of *section 6* apply as if the vulnerable person had requested access to legal advice. See *paragraphs 3.19, 6.5A*.

KEYNOTE

The purpose of the provisions at paras 3.19 and 6.5A (access to legal advice) is to protect the rights of a vulnerable person who does not understand the significance of what is said to them. A vulnerable person should always be given an opportunity, when an appropriate adult is called to the police station, to consult privately with a solicitor in the absence of the appropriate adult if they want.

5. The custody officer must make sure a person receives appropriate clinical attention as soon as reasonably practicable if the person appears to be suffering from a mental disorder or in urgent cases immediately call the nearest appropriate healthcare professional or an ambulance. See Code C *paragraphs 3.16, 9.5* and *9.6* which apply when a person is detained under the Mental Health Act 1983, sections 135 and 136, as amended by the Policing and Crime Act 2017.
6. *Not used.*
7. If a vulnerable person is cautioned in the absence of the appropriate adult, the caution must be repeated in the appropriate adult's presence. See *paragraph 10.12*.

8. A vulnerable person must not be interviewed or asked to provide or sign a written statement in the absence of the appropriate adult unless the provisions of *paragraphs 11.1* or *11.18* to *11.20* apply. Questioning in these circumstances may not continue in the absence of the appropriate adult once sufficient information to avert the risk has been obtained. A record shall be made of the grounds for any decision to begin an interview in these circumstances. See *paragraphs 11.1, 11.15* and *11.18* to *11.20.*
9. If the appropriate adult is present at an interview, they shall be informed they are not expected to act simply as an observer and the purposes of their presence are to:
   - advise the interviewee;
   - observe whether or not the interview is being conducted properly and fairly;
   - facilitate communication with the interviewee.

   See *paragraph 11.17.*
10. If the detention of a vulnerable person is reviewed by a review officer or a superintendent, the appropriate adult must, if available at the time, be given an opportunity to make representations to the officer about the need for continuing detention. See *paragraph 15.3.*
11. If the custody officer charges a vulnerable person with an offence or takes such other action as is appropriate when there is sufficient evidence for a prosecution this must be carried out in the presence of the appropriate adult if they are at the police station. A copy of the written notice embodying any charge must also be given to the appropriate adult. See *paragraphs 16.1* to *16.4A.*
12. An intimate or strip search of a vulnerable person may take place only in the presence of the appropriate adult of the same sex, unless the detainee specifically requests the presence of a particular adult of the opposite sex. A strip search may take place in the absence of an appropriate adult only in cases of urgency when there is a risk of serious harm to the detainee or others. See *Annex A, paragraphs 5* and *11(c).*
13. Particular care must be taken when deciding whether to use any form of approved restraints on a mentally disordered or otherwise mentally vulnerable person in a locked cell. See *paragraph 8.2.*

Code C—Annex F: *Not used*

2.6.25

Code C—Annex G: Fitness to be Interviewed

1. This Annex contains general guidance to help police officers and healthcare professionals assess whether a detainee might be at risk in an interview.
2. A detainee may be at risk in a interview if it is considered that:
   (a) conducting the interview could significantly harm the detainee's physical or mental state;
   (b) anything the detainee says in the interview about their involvement or suspected involvement in the offence about which they are being interviewed **might** be considered unreliable in subsequent court proceedings because of their physical or mental state.
3. In assessing whether the detainee should be interviewed, the following must be considered:
   (a) how the detainee's physical or mental state might affect their ability to understand the nature and purpose of the interview, to comprehend what is being asked and to appreciate the significance of any answers given and make rational decisions about whether they want to say anything;
   (b) the extent to which the detainee's replies may be affected by their physical or mental condition rather than representing a rational and accurate explanation of their involvement in the offence;

(c) how the nature of the interview, which could include particularly probing questions, might affect the detainee.

4. It is essential healthcare professionals who are consulted consider the functional ability of the detainee rather than simply relying on a medical diagnosis, e.g. it is possible for a person with severe mental illness to be fit for interview.
5. Healthcare professionals should advise on the need for an appropriate adult to be present, whether reassessment of the person's fitness for interview may be necessary if the interview lasts beyond a specified time, and whether a further specialist opinion may be required.
6. When healthcare professionals identify risks they should be asked to quantify the risks. They should inform the custody officer:
   - whether the person's condition:
     - ~ is likely to improve;
     - ~ will require or be amenable to treatment; and
   - indicate how long it may take for such improvement to take effect.
7. The role of the healthcare professional is to consider the risks and advise the custody officer of the outcome of that consideration. The healthcare professional's determination and any advice or recommendations should be made in writing and form part of the custody record.
8. Once the healthcare professional has provided that information, it is a matter for the custody officer to decide whether or not to allow the interview to go ahead and if the interview is to proceed, to determine what safeguards are needed. Nothing prevents safeguards being provided in addition to those required under the Code. An example might be to have an appropriate healthcare professional present during the interview, in addition to an appropriate adult, in order constantly to monitor the person's condition and how it is being affected by the interview.

2.6.26 Code C—Annex H: Detained Person: Observation List

1. If any detainee fails to meet any of the following criteria, an appropriate healthcare professional or an ambulance must be called.
2. When assessing the level of rousability, consider:

   Rousability—can they be woken?
   - go into the cell
   - call their name
   - shake gently

   Response to questions—can they give appropriate answers to questions such as:
   - What's your name?
   - Where do you live?
   - Where do you think you are?

   Response to commands—can they respond appropriately to commands such as:
   - Open your eyes!
   - Lift one arm, now the other arm!
3. Remember to take into account the possibility or presence of other illnesses, injury, or mental condition; a person who is drowsy and smells of alcohol may also have the following:
   - Diabetes
   - Epilepsy
   - Head injury
   - Drug intoxication or overdose
   - Stroke

Code C—Annex I: *Not used*

Code C—Annex J: *Not used*

2.6.27

Code C—Annex K: X-rays and Ultrasound Scans

(a) Action

1. PACE, section 55A allows a person who has been arrested and is in police detention to have an X-ray taken of them or an ultrasound scan to be carried out on them (or both) if:
   (a) authorised by an officer of inspector rank or above who has reasonable grounds for believing that the detainee:
      (i) may have swallowed a Class A drug; and
      (ii) was in possession of that Class A drug with the intention of supplying it to another or to export; and
   (b) the detainee's appropriate consent has been given in writing.
2. Before an x-ray is taken or an ultrasound scan carried out, a police officer or designated detention officer must tell the detainee:—
   (a) that the authority has been given; and
   (b) the grounds for giving the authorisation.
3. Before a detainee is asked to give appropriate consent to an x-ray or an ultrasound scan, they must be warned that if they refuse without good cause their refusal may harm their case if it comes to trial, This warning may be given by a police officer or member of police staff. In the case of juveniles and vulnerable persons, the seeking and giving of consent must take place in the presence of the appropriate adult. A juvenile's consent is only valid if their parent's or guardian's consent is also obtained unless the juvenile is under 14, when their parent's or guardian's consent is sufficient in its own right. A detainee who is not legally represented must be reminded of their entitlement to have free legal advice, see Code C, *paragraph 6.5*, and the reminder noted in the custody record.

KEYNOTE

If authority is given for an x-ray to be taken or an ultrasound scan to be carried out (or both), consideration should be given to asking a registered medical practitioner or registered nurse to explain to the detainee what is involved and to allay any concerns that the detainee might have about the effect on him/her of taking an x-ray or carrying out an ultrasound scan. If appropriate consent is not given, evidence of the explanation may, if the case comes to trial, be relevant to determining whether the detainee had a good cause for refusing.

The following form of words may be used to warn a detainee who is asked to consent to an x-ray being taken or an ultrasound scan being carried out (or both):

> You do not have to allow an x-ray of you to be taken or an ultrasound scan to be carried out on you, but I must warn you that if you refuse without good cause, your refusal may harm your case if it comes to trial.

Where the use of the Welsh language is appropriate, the following form of words may be provided in Welsh:

> Does dim rhaid i chi ganiatáu cymryd sgan uwchsain neu belydr-x (neu'r ddau) arnoch, ond mae'n rhaid i mi eich rhybuddio os byddwch chi'n gwrthod gwneud hynny heb reswm da, fe allai hynny niweidio eich achos pe bai'n dod gerbron llys.

4. An x-ray may be taken, or an ultrasound scan may be carried out, only by a registered medical practitioner or registered nurse, and only at a hospital, surgery or other medical premises.

(b) Documentation

5. The following shall be recorded as soon as practicable in the detainee's custody record:
   (a) the authorisation to take the x-ray or carry out the ultrasound scan (or both);
   (b) the grounds for giving the authorisation;
   (c) the giving of the warning required by *paragraph 3*; and
   (d) the fact that the appropriate consent was given or (as the case may be) refused, and if refused, the reason given for the refusal (if any); and
   (e) if an x-ray is taken or an ultrasound scan carried out:
      - where it was taken or carried out;
      - who took it or carried it out;
      - who was present;
      - the result.
6. *Not used.*

2.6.28 Code C—Annex L: Establishing Gender of Persons for the Purpose of Searching and Certain Other Procedures

1. Certain provisions of this and other PACE Codes explicitly state that searches and other procedures may only be carried out by, or in the presence of, persons of the same sex as the person subject to the search or other procedure or require action to be taken or information to be given which depends on whether the detainee is treated as being male or female.

KEYNOTE

Provisions to which para. 1 applies include:

- in Code C: paras 3.20A, 4.1 and Annex A, paras 5, 6 and 11 (searches, strip and intimate searches of detainees under ss. 54 and 55 PACE84);
- in Code A: paras 2.7 and 3.6 and Note 4;
- in Code D: para. 5.5 and Note 5F (searches, examinations and photographing of detainees under s. 54A PACE84) and para. 6.9 (taking samples);
- in Code H: paras 3.21A, 4.1 and Annex A, paras 6, 7 and 12 (searches, strip and intimate searches under ss. 54 and 55 PACE84 of persons arrested under s. 41 of the Terrorism Act 2000) and para. 9.4B.

2. All searches and procedures must be carried out with courtesy, consideration and respect for the person concerned. Police officers should show particular sensitivity when dealing with transgender individuals (including transsexual persons) and transvestite persons.

KEYNOTE

While there is no agreed definition of transgender (or trans), it is generally used as an umbrella term to describe people whose gender identity (self-identification as being a woman, man, neither or both) differs from the sex they were registered as at birth. The term includes, but is not limited to, transsexual people. Transsexual means a person who is proposing to undergo, is undergoing or has undergone a process (or part of a process) for the purpose of gender reassignment which is a protected characteristic under the Equality Act 2010 by changing physiological or other attributes of their sex. This includes aspects of gender such as dress and title. It would apply to a woman making the transition to being a man and a man making the transition to being a woman, as well as to a person who has only just started out on the process of gender reassignment and to a person who has completed the process. Both would share the characteristic of gender reassignment with each having the characteristics of one sex, but with certain characteristics of the other sex. Transvestite means a person of one gender who dresses in the clothes of a person of the opposite gender. However, transvestites do not live permanently in the gender opposite to their birth sex.

It is important to check the force guidance and instructions for the deployment of transgender officers and staff under their direction and control to duties which involve carrying out, or being present at, any of the searches and procedures described in para. 1. Force guidance which must be provided by each force's chief officer must comply with the Equality Act 2010.

(a) Consideration

3. In law, the gender (and accordingly the sex) of an individual is their gender as registered at birth unless they have been issued with a Gender Recognition Certificate (GRC) under the Gender Recognition Act 2004 (GRA), in which case the person's gender is their acquired gender. This means that if the acquired gender is the male gender, the person's sex becomes that of a man and, if it is the female gender, the person's sex becomes that of a woman and they must be treated as their acquired gender.
4. When establishing whether the person concerned should be treated as being male or female for the purposes of these searches, procedures and requirements, the following approach which is designed to maintain his dignity, minimise embarrassment and secure the person's co-operation should be followed:
   (a) The person must not be asked whether they have a GRC (see paragraph 8);
   (b) If there is no doubt as to as to whether the person concerned should be treated as being male or female, they should be dealt with as being of that sex.
   (c) If at any time (including during the search or carrying out the procedure or requirement) there is doubt as to whether the person should be treated, or continue to be treated, as being male or female:
      (i) the person should be asked what gender they consider themselves to be. If they express a preference to be dealt with as a particular gender, they should be asked to indicate and confirm their preference by signing the custody record or, if a custody record has not been opened, the search record or the officer's notebook. Subject to (ii) below, the person should be treated according to their preference except with regard to the requirements to provide that person with information concerning menstrual products and their personal needs relating to health, hygiene and welfare described in *paragraph 3.20A* (if aged under 18) and *paragraphs 9.3A* and *9.3B* (if aged 18 or over). In these cases, a person whose confirmed preference is to be dealt with as being male should be asked in private whether they wish to speak in private with a member of the custody staff of a gender of their choosing about the provision of menstrual products and their personal needs, notwithstanding their confirmed preference;
      (ii) if there are grounds to doubt that the preference in (i) accurately reflects the person's predominant lifestyle, for example, if they ask to be treated as a woman but documents and other information make it clear that they live predominantly as a man, or vice versa, they should be treated according to what appears to be their predominant lifestyle and not their stated preference;
      (iii) If the person is unwilling to express a preference as in (i) above, efforts should be made to determine their predominant lifestyle and they should be treated as such. For example, if they appear to live predominantly as a woman, they should be treated as being female; except with regard to the requirements to provide that person with information concerning menstrual products and their personal needs relating to health, hygiene and welfare described in *paragraph 3.20A* (if aged under 18) and *paragraphs 9.3A* and *9.3B* (if aged 18 or over). In these cases, a person whose predominant lifestyle has been determined to be male should be asked in

private whether they wish to speak in private with a member of the custody staff of a gender of their choosing about the provision of menstrual products and their personal needs, notwithstanding their determined predominant lifestyle; or

(iv) if none of the above apply, the person should be dealt with according to what reasonably appears to have been their sex as registered at birth.

KEYNOTE

The reason for the exception at para. 4(c)(i) in relation to paras 3.20A, 9.3A and 9.3B is to modify the same sex/gender approach for searching to acknowledge the possible needs of transgender individuals in respect of menstrual products and other personal needs relating to health, hygiene and welfare and ensure that they are not overlooked.

5. Once a decision has been made about which gender an individual is to be treated as, each officer responsible for the search, procedure or requirement should where possible be advised before the search or procedure starts of any doubts as to the person's gender and the person informed that the doubts have been disclosed. This is important so as to maintain the dignity of the person and any officers concerned.

(b) Documentation

6. The person's gender as established under *paragraph 4(c)(i)* to *(iv)* above must be recorded in the person's custody record or, if a custody record has not been opened, on the search record or in the officer's notebook.
7. Where the person elects which gender they consider themselves to be under *paragraph 4(b)(i)* but, following *4(b)(ii)* is not treated in accordance with their preference, the reason must be recorded in the search record, in the officer's notebook or, if applicable, in the person's custody record.

(c) Disclosure of information

8. Section 22 of the GRA defines any information relating to a person's application for a GRC or to a successful applicant's gender before it became their acquired gender as 'protected information'. Nothing in this Annex is to be read as authorising or permitting any police officer or any police staff who has acquired such information when acting in their official capacity to disclose that information to any other person in contravention of the GRA. Disclosure includes making a record of 'protected information' which is read by others.

2.6.29 Code C—Annex M: Documents and Records to be Translated

1. For the purposes of Directive 2010/64/EU of the European Parliament and of the Council of 20 October 2010 and this Code, essential documents comprise records required to be made in accordance with this Code which are relevant to decisions to deprive a person of their liberty, to any charge and to any record considered necessary to enable a detainee to defend themselves in criminal proceedings and to safeguard the fairness of the proceedings. Passages of essential documents which are not relevant need not be translated.

KEYNOTE

It is not necessary to disclose information in any translation which is capable of undermining or otherwise adversely affecting any investigative processes, for example, by enabling the suspect to fabricate an innocent explanation or to conceal lies from the interviewer.

2. The table below lists the documents considered essential for the purposes of this Code and when (subject to paragraphs 3 to 7) written translations must be created and provided. See *paragraphs 13.12* to *13.14* and *Annex N* for application to live-link interpretation.

Table of essential documents:

	Essential documents for the purposes of this code	When translation to be created	When translation to be provided
(i)	The grounds for each of the following authorisations to keep the person in custody as they are described and referred to in the custody record: (a) Authorisation for detention before and after charge given by the custody officer and by the review officer, see Code C paragraphs 3.4 and 15.16(a). (b) Authorisation to extend detention without charge beyond 24 hours given by a superintendent, see Code C paragraph 15.16(b). (c) A warrant of further detention issued by a magistrates' court and any extension(s) of the warrant, see Code C paragraph 15.16(c). (d) An authority to detain in accordance with the directions in a warrant of arrest issued in connection with criminal proceedings including the court issuing the warrant.	As soon as practicable after each authorisation has been recorded in the custody record.	As soon as practicable after the translation has been created, whilst the person is detained or after they have been released.
(ii)	Written notice showing particulars of the offence charged required by Code C paragraph 16.3 or the offence for which the suspect has been told they may be prosecuted.	As soon as practicable after the person has been charged or reported.	
(iii)	Written interview records: Code C11.11, 13.3, 13.4 & Code E4.7 Written Statement under caution: Code C Annex D.	To be created contemporaneously by the interpreter for the person to check and sign.	As soon as practicable after the person has been charged or told they may be prosecuted.

3. The custody officer may authorise an oral translation or oral summary of documents (i) to (ii) in the table (but not (iii)) to be provided (through an interpreter) instead of a written translation. Such an oral translation or summary may only be provided if it would not prejudice the fairness of the proceedings by in any way adversely affecting or otherwise undermining or limiting the ability of the suspect in question to understand their position and to communicate effectively with police officers, interviewers, solicitors and appropriate adults with regard to their detention and the investigation of the offence in question and to defend themselves in the event of criminal proceedings. The quantity and complexity of the information in the document should always be considered and specific additional consideration given if the suspect is vulnerable or is a juvenile (see *Code C paragraph 1.5*). The reason for the decision must be recorded (see *paragraph 13.11(e)*).
4. Subject to paragraphs 5 to 7 below, a suspect may waive their right to a written translation of the essential documents described in the table but only if they do so voluntarily after receiving legal advice or having full knowledge of the consequences and give their unconditional and fully informed consent in writing (see *paragraph 9*).
5. The suspect may be asked if they wish to waive their right to a written translation and before giving their consent, they must be reminded of their right to legal advice and asked whether they wish to speak to a solicitor.
6. No police officer or police staff should do or say anything with the intention of persuading a suspect who is entitled to a written translation of an essential document to waive that right.

KEYNOTE

No police officer or police staff shall indicate to any suspect, except to answer a direct question, whether the period for which they are liable to be detained or if not detained, the time taken to complete the interview, might be reduced:

- if they do not ask for legal advice before deciding whether they wish to waive their right to a written translation of an essential document; or
- if they decide to waive their right to a written translation of an essential document.

There is no power under PACE84 to detain a person or to delay their release solely to create and provide a written translation of any essential document.

7. For the purpose of the waiver:
   (a) the consent of a vulnerable person is only valid if the information about the circumstances under which they can waive the right and the reminder about their right to legal advice mentioned in *paragraphs 3* to *5* and their consent is given in the presence of the appropriate adult.
   (b) the consent of a juvenile is only valid if their parent's or guardian's consent is also obtained unless the juvenile is under 14, when their parent's or guardian's consent is sufficient in its own right and the information and reminder mentioned in *sub-paragraph (a)* above and their consent is also given in the presence of the appropriate adult (who may or may not be a parent or guardian).
8. The detainee, their solicitor or appropriate adult may make representations to the custody officer that a document which is not included in the table is essential and that a translation should be provided. The request may be refused if the officer is satisfied that the translation requested is not essential for the purposes described in *paragraph 1* above.
9. If the custody officer has any doubts about
   - providing an oral translation or summary of an essential document instead of a written translation (see paragraph 3);
   - whether the suspect fully understands the consequences of waiving their right to a written translation of an essential document (see *paragraph 4*), or
   - about refusing to provide a translation of a requested document (see *paragraph 7*),

   the officer should seek advice from an inspector or above.

Documentation

10. Action taken in accordance with this Annex shall be recorded in the detainee's custody record or interview record as appropriate (see *Code C paragraph 13.11(e)*).

2.6.30

Code C—Annex N: Live-link Interpretation (para. 13.12)

Part 1: When the physical presence of the interpreter is not required.

1. EU Directive 2010/64 (see *paragraph 13.1*), Article 2(6) provides 'Where appropriate, communication technology such as videoconferencing, telephone or the Internet may be used, unless the physical presence of the interpreter is required in order to safeguard the fairness of the proceedings.' This Article permits, but does not require the use of a live-link, and the following provisions of this Annex determine whether the use of a live-link is appropriate in any particular case.
2. Decisions in accordance with this Annex that the physical presence of the interpreter is not required and to permit live-link interpretation, must be made on a case by case basis. Each decision must take account of the age, gender and vulnerability of the suspect, the nature and

circumstances of the offence and the investigation and the impact on the suspect according to the particular purpose(s) for which the suspect requires the assistance of an interpreter and the time(s) when that assistance is required. For this reason, the custody officer in the case of a detained suspect, or in the case of a suspect who has not been arrested, the interviewer (subject to *paragraph 13.1(b)*), must consider whether the ability of the particular suspect, to communicate confidently and effectively for the purpose in question (see *paragraph 3*) is likely to be adversely affected or otherwise undermined or limited if the interpreter is not physically present and live-link interpretation is used. Although a suspect for whom an appropriate adult is required may be more likely to be adversely affected as described, it is important to note that a person who does not require an appropriate adult may also be adversely impacted by the use of live-link interpretation.

KEYNOTE

For purposes other than an interview, audio-only live-link interpretation, for example by telephone (see Code C, para. 13.12(b)) may provide an appropriate option until an interpreter is physically present or audio-visual live-link interpretation becomes available. A particular example would be the initial action required when a detained suspect arrives at a police station to inform them of, and to explain, the reasons for their arrest and detention and their various rights and entitlements. Another example would be to inform the suspect by telephone, that an interpreter they will be able to see and hear is being arranged. In these circumstances, telephone live-link interpretation may help to allay the suspect's concerns and contribute to the completion of the risk assessment (see Code C, para. 3.6).

3. Examples of purposes referred to in *paragraph 2* include:
   (a) understanding and appreciating their position having regard to any information given to them, or sought from them, in accordance with this or any other Code of Practice which, in particular, include:
   - the caution (see *paragraphs C10.1* and *10.12*).
   - the special warning (see *paragraphs 10.10* to *10.12*).
   - information about the offence (see *paragraphs 10.3, 11.1A*).
   - the grounds and reasons for detention (see *paragraphs 13.10* and *13.10A*).
   - the translation of essential documents (see *paragraph 13.10B* and *Annex M*).
   - their rights and entitlements (see *paragraph 3.12 and C3.21(b)*).
   - intimate and non-intimate searches of detained persons at police stations.
   - provisions and procedures to which Code D (Identification) applies concerning, for example, eye-witness identification, taking fingerprints, samples and photographs.

   (b) understanding and seeking clarification from the interviewer of questions asked during an interview conducted and recorded in accordance with Code E or Code F and of anything else that is said by the interviewer and answering the questions.

   (c) consulting privately with their solicitor and (if applicable) the appropriate adult (see *paragraphs 3.18, 13.2A, 13.6* and *13.9*):
   (i) to help decide whether to answer questions put to them during interview; and
   (ii) about any other matter concerning their detention and treatment whilst in custody.

   (d) communicating with practitioners and others who have some formal responsibility for, or an interest in, the health and welfare of the suspect. Particular examples include appropriate healthcare professionals (see *section 9* of this Code), Independent Custody Visitors and drug arrest referral workers.
4. If the custody officer or the interviewer (subject to *paragraph 13.1(b)*) is satisfied that for a particular purpose as described in *paragraphs 2 and 3 above*, the live-link interpretation *would not* adversely affect or otherwise undermine or limit the suspect's ability to communicate confidently and effectively for *that* purpose, they must so inform the suspect, their solicitor and (if applicable) the appropriate adult. At the same time, the operation of live-link interpretation must be explained and demonstrated to them, they must be advised of the chief officer's

obligations concerning the security of live-link communications under *paragraph 13.13* and they must be asked if they wish to make representations that live-link interpretation should not be used or if they require more information about the operation of the arrangements. They must also be told that at any time live-link interpretation is in use, they may make representations to the custody officer or the interviewer that its operation should cease and that the physical presence of an interpreter should be arranged.

KEYNOTE

The explanation and demonstration of live-link interpretation to the suspect prior to its use is intended to help the suspect, solicitor and appropriate adult make an informed decision and to allay any concerns they may have.

When the authority of an inspector is required

5. If:
   (i) representations are made that live-link interpretation should not be used, or that at any time live-link interpretation is in use, its operation should cease and the physical presence of an interpreter arranged; and
   (ii) the custody officer or interviewer (subject to *paragraph 13.1(b)*) is unable to allay the concerns raised; then live-link interpretation may not be used, or (as the case may be) continue to be used, unless authorised in writing by an officer of the rank of inspector or above, in accordance with *paragraph 6*.
6. Authority may be given if the officer is satisfied that for the purpose(s) in question at the time an interpreter is required, live-link interpretation is necessary and justified. In making this decision, the officer must have regard to:
   (a) the circumstances of the suspect;
   (b) the nature and seriousness of the offence;
   (c) the requirements of the investigation, including its likely impact on both the suspect and any victim(s);
   (d) the representations made by the suspect, their solicitor and (if applicable) the appropriate adult that live-link interpretation should not be used (see *paragraph 5*)
   (e) the availability of a suitable interpreter to be *physically* present compared with the availability of a suitable interpreter for live-link interpretation; and
   (f) the risk if the interpreter is not *physically* present, evidence obtained using link interpretation might be excluded in subsequent criminal proceedings; and
   (g) the likely impact on the suspect and the investigation of any consequential delay to arrange for the interpreter to be *physically* present with the suspect.

KEYNOTE

Factors affecting availability of a suitable interpreter will include the location of the police station and the language and type of interpretation (oral or sign language) required.

7. For the purposes of Code E and live-link interpretation, there is no requirement to make a visual recording which shows the interpreter as viewed by the suspect and others present at the interview. The audio recording required by that Code is sufficient. However, the authorising officer, in consultation with the officer in charge of the investigation, may direct that the interview is conducted and recorded in accordance with Code F. This will require the visual record to show the live-link interpretation arrangements and the interpreter as seen and experienced by the suspect during the interview. This should be considered if it appears that the admissibility of interview evidence might be challenged because the interpreter was not

physically present or if the suspect, solicitor or appropriate adult make representations that Code F should be applied.

Documentation

8. A record must be made of the actions, decisions, authorisations and outcomes arising from the requirements of this Annex. This includes representations made in accordance with *paragraphs 4* and *7*.

Part 2: Modifications for live-link interpretation

9. The following modification shall apply for the purposes of live-link interpretation:
   (a) Code C paragraph 13.3:
   For the third sentence, *substitute*: 'A clear legible copy of the complete record shall be sent without delay via the live-link to the interviewer. The interviewer, after confirming with the suspect that the copy is legible and complete, shall allow the suspect to read the record, or have the record read to them by the interpreter and to sign the copy as correct or indicate the respects in which they consider it inaccurate. The interviewer is responsible for ensuring that that the signed copy and the original record made by the interpreter are retained with the case papers for use in evidence if required and must advise the interpreter of their obligation to keep the original record securely for that purpose.';
   (b) Code C paragraph 13.4:
   For sub-paragraph (b), *substitute*: 'A clear legible copy of the complete statement shall be sent without delay via the live-link to the interviewer. The interviewer, after confirming with the suspect that the copy is legible and complete, shall invite the suspect to sign it. The interviewer is responsible for ensuring that that the signed copy and the original record made by the interpreter are retained with the case papers for use in evidence if required and must advise the interpreter of their obligation to keep the original record securely for that purpose.';
   (c) Code C paragraph 13.7:
   After the first sentence, *insert*: 'A clear legible copy of the certified record must be sent without delay via the live-link to the interviewer. The interviewer is responsible for ensuring that the original certified record and the copy are retained with the case papers for use as evidence if required and must advise the interpreter of their obligation to keep the original record securely for that purpose.'
   (d) Code C paragraph 11.2, Code E paragraphs 3.4 and 4.3 and Code F paragraph 2.5.-interviews
   At the beginning of each paragraph, *insert*: 'Before the interview commences, the operation of live-link interpretation shall be explained and demonstrated to the suspect, their solicitor and appropriate adult, unless it has been previously explained and demonstrated (see Code C Annex N *paragraph 4*).'
   (e) Code E, paragraph 3.20 (signing master recording label)
   After the *third sentence*, insert, 'If live-link interpretation has been used, the interviewer should ask the interpreter to observe the removal and sealing of the master recording and to confirm in writing that they have seen it sealed and signed by the interviewer. A clear legible copy of the confirmation signed by the interpreter must be sent via the live-link to the interviewer. The interviewer is responsible for ensuring that the original confirmation and the copy are retained with the case papers for use in evidence if required and must advise the interpreter of their obligation to keep the original confirmation securely for that purpose.'
   Note: By virtue of *paragraphs 2.1* and *2.3 of Code F*, this applies when a visually recording to which Code F applies is made.

2.7 Identification

PACE Code of Practice for the Identification of Persons by Police Officers (Code D)

A thick grey line down the margin denotes text that is an extract of the PACE Code itself (i.e. the actual wording of the legislation). This material is examinable for both Sergeants and Inspectors.

2.7.1 Introduction

A critical issue in the investigation and prosecution of offences is the identification of the offender. Many different methods of identification exist but the main feature which must be considered in relation to each is its *reliability*.

The visual identification of suspects by witnesses is one of the most common forms of identification; it is also one of the most unreliable. Even under research conditions, the recall of eye witnesses is inconsistent; where the witness sees or experiences the spontaneous commission of a crime, that reliability is reduced even further.

It was for these reasons that the *Turnbull* guidelines were set out, together with the provisions of Code D. In response to widespread concern over the problems posed by cases of mistaken identification, the Court of Appeal in *Turnbull* [1977] QB 224 laid down important guidelines for judges in trials that involve disputed identification evidence. The guidelines provide that where the case against an accused depends wholly or substantially on the correctness of one or more identifications of the accused—which the defence alleges to be mistaken—the judge should warn the jury of the special need for caution before convicting the accused in reliance on the correctness of the identification(s). The judge should tell the jury that:

- caution is required to avoid the risk of injustice;
- a witness who is honest may be wrong even if they are convinced they are right;
- a witness who is convincing may still be wrong;
- more than one witness may be wrong;
- a witness who recognises the defendant, even when the witness knows the defendant very well, may be wrong.

The judge should direct the jury to examine the circumstances in which the identification by each witness can be made. Some of these circumstances may include:

- the length of time the accused was observed by the witness;
- the distance the witness was from the accused;
- the state of the light;
- the length of time elapsed between the original observation and the subsequent identification to the police.

This also applies to recognition cases. It is commonly accepted that recognition is more reliable than identification of a stranger; however, even when the witness appears to recognise someone he/she knows, the jury should be reminded that mistakes in recognition of close relatives and friends are sometimes made. If there is no identification evidence, the *Turnbull* guidelines will not apply. Identification evidence relates to identifying the person and not necessarily the actions of that person, for instance evidence that a person was present at a scene is identification, evidence that the person identified stabbed someone is not identification evidence and does not need a *Turnbull* warning (*R* v *Nawaz* [2020] EWCA Crim 893). It should be remembered that a witness who does not identify the suspect may still be able to provide other valuable evidence to the case, for instance a description of the person who committed the offence, or a description of what he/she was wearing. Again it is not uncommon for witnesses to qualify their identification of the suspect by indicating that they 'cannot be quite certain'. While a defendant cannot be convicted on such a qualified identification alone, it may be admissible to support the case where other evidence is also available (*R* v *George* [2002] EWCA Crim 1923).

A lot will depend on the individual circumstances of each case, but it is essential that these issues are covered in any interview or other evidence-gathering process.

'Dock identifications', where the witness's first identification of the accused involves pointing out the person in the dock, are often dramatised by filmmakers but, in practice, are generally disallowed as being unreliable and unfair.

The Police and Criminal Evidence Act 1984 Code of Practice, Code D provides guidance for the identification of persons by police officers. This chapter sets out the actual Codes of Practice with keynotes which incorporate the notes of guidance to the Code.

Generally, the methods of identification covered by Code D can be divided into two:

- occasions where the identity of the suspect is known; and
- occasions where the identity of the suspect is not known.

Where the identity of the suspect is known this can be further divided into those cases where the suspect is available and those where he/she is not available.

Although a breach of Code D (or any of the other Codes of Practice) will not automatically result in the evidence being excluded (*R* v *Khan* (1999) 19 July, CA, unreported), the judge or magistrate(s) will consider the effects of any breach on the fairness of any subsequent proceedings. The Codes are intended to provide protection to suspects and, if it is felt that the breach of Code D has resulted in unfairness or other prejudicial effect on the defendant, the court may exclude the related evidence under s. 78 of the Police and Criminal Evidence Act 1984 (**see chapter 2.4**).

New Codes were introduced in 2017, eye-witness and witness identification procedures are updated to take account of changes and developments in case law and police practice and to address operational concerns raised by the police. In respect of the video identification procedure, these support and extend the identification officer's discretion concerning the selection and use of 'historic' images, the presence of solicitors at witness viewings and to direct other police officers and police staff to implement any arrangements for any identification procedures. The role and responsibility of the investigating officer is clarified in relation to viewing of CCTV and similar images by someone who is not an eye-witness. The revisions to the 2017 Code also reflect amendments to the Police and Criminal Evidence Act 1984 concerning the retention of fingerprints, footwear impressions and DNA profiles and samples, made by the Anti-social Behaviour, Crime and Policing Act 2014.

The Police Reform Act 2002 has introduced designated support staff who have some of the powers that police officers have (**see chapter 2.6**).

2.7.2 PACE Code of Practice for the Identification of Persons by Police Officers (Code D)

This code has effect in relation to any identification procedure carried out after midnight on 23 February 2017.

1 Introduction

1.1 This Code of Practice concerns the principal methods used by police to identify people in connection with the investigation of offences and the keeping of accurate and reliable criminal records. The powers and procedures in this code must be used fairly, responsibly, with respect for the people to whom they apply and without unlawful discrimination. Under the Equality Act 2010, section 149 (Public sector Equality Duty), police forces must, in carrying out their functions, have due regard to the need to eliminate unlawful discrimination, harassment, victimisation and any other conduct which is prohibited by that Act, to advance equality of opportunity between people who share a relevant protected characteristic and people who do not share it, and to foster good relations between those persons. The Equality Act also makes it unlawful for police officers to discriminate against, harass or victimise any person on the grounds of the 'protected characteristics' of age, disability, gender reassignment, race, religion or belief, sex and sexual orientation, marriage and civil partnership, pregnancy and maternity when using their powers.

1.2 In this Code, identification by an eye-witness arises when a witness who has seen the offender committing the crime and is given an opportunity to identify a person suspected of involvement in the offence in a video identification, identification parade or similar procedure. These eye-witness identification procedures which are in Part A of section 3 below, are designed to:

- test the eye-witness' ability to identify the suspect as the person they saw on a previous occasion
- provide safeguards against mistaken identification.

While this Code concentrates on visual identification procedures, it does not prevent the police making use of aural identification procedures such as a 'voice identification parade', where they judge that appropriate.

1.2A In this Code, separate provisions in Part B of section 3 below, apply when any person, including a police officer, is asked if they recognise anyone they see in an image as being someone who is known to them and to test their claim that they recognise that person. These separate provisions are not subject to the eye-witnesses identification procedures described in *paragraph 1.2.*

1.2B Part C applies when a film, photograph or image relating to the offence or any description of the suspect is broadcast or published in any national or local media or on any social networking site or on any local or national police communication systems.

1.3 Identification by fingerprints applies when a person's fingerprints are taken to:

- compare with fingerprints found at the scene of a crime
- check and prove convictions
- help to ascertain a person's identity.

1.3A Identification using footwear impressions applies when a person's footwear impressions are taken to compare with impressions found at the scene of a crime.

1.4 Identification by body samples and impressions includes taking samples such as a cheek swab, hair or blood to generate a DNA profile for comparison with material obtained from the scene of a crime, or a victim.

1.5 Taking photographs of arrested people applies to recording and checking identity and locating and tracing persons who:

- are wanted for offences
- fail to answer their bail.

1.6 Another method of identification involves searching and examining detained suspects to find, e.g., marks such as tattoos or scars which may help establish their identity or whether they have been involved in committing an offence.

1.7 The provisions of the Police and Criminal Evidence Act 1984 (PACE) and this Code are designed to make sure fingerprints, samples, impressions and photographs are taken, used and retained, and identification procedures carried out, only when justified and necessary for preventing, detecting or investigating crime. If these provisions are not observed, the application of the relevant procedures in particular cases may be open to question.

1.8 The provisions of this Code do not authorise, or otherwise permit, fingerprints or samples to be taken from a person detained solely for the purposes of assessment under section 136 of the Mental Health Act 1983.

2.7.2.1 **KEYNOTE**

In para. 1.1, under the Equality Act 2010, s. 149, the 'relevant protected characteristics' are: age, disability, gender reassignment, pregnancy and maternity, race, religion/belief, sex and sexual orientation. For further detailed guidance and advice on the Equality Act, see <https://www.gov.uk/guidance/equality-act-2010-guidance>. For advice on the use of voice identification parades, see Home Office Circular 57/2003.

2.7.3 Code D—2 General

2.1 This Code must be readily available at all police stations for consultation by:

- police officers and police staff
- detained persons
- members of the public

2.2 The provisions of this Code:

- include the *Annexes*
- do not include the *Notes for guidance.*

2.3 Code C, *paragraph 1.4* and the *Notes for guidance* applicable to those provisions apply to this Code with regard to a suspected person who may be mentally disordered or otherwise mentally vulnerable.

2.4 Code C, *paragraphs 1.5* and *1.5A* and the *Notes for guidance* applicable to those provisions apply to this Code with regard to a suspected person who appears to be under the age of 18.

2.5 Code C, *paragraph 1.6* applies to this Code with regard to a suspected person who appears to be blind, seriously visually impaired, deaf, unable to read or speak or has difficulty communicating orally because of a speech impediment.

2.6 In this Code:

- 'appropriate adult' means the same as in Code C, *paragraph 1.7*
- 'solicitor' means the same as in Code C, *paragraph 6.12* and the *Notes for guidance* applicable to those provisions apply to this Code.
- where a search or other procedure under this Code may only be carried out or observed by a person of the same sex as the person to whom the search or procedure applies, the gender of the detainee and other persons present should be established and recorded in line with Annex L of Code C.

2.7 References to a custody officer include any police officer who, for the time being, is performing the functions of a custody officer, see *paragraph 1.9* of Code C.

2.8 When a record of any action requiring the authority of an officer of a specified rank is made under this Code, subject to *paragraph 2.18*, the officer's name and rank must be recorded.

2.9 When this Code requires the prior authority or agreement of an officer of at least inspector or superintendent rank, that authority may be given by a sergeant or chief inspector who has been authorised to perform the functions of the higher rank under PACE, section 107.

2.10 Subject to *paragraph 2.18*, all records must be timed and signed by the maker.

2.11 Records must be made in the custody record, unless otherwise specified. In any provision of this Code which allows or requires police officers or police staff to make a record in their report book, the reference to 'report book' shall include any official report book or electronic recording device issued to them that enables the record in question to be made and dealt with in accordance with that provision. References in this Code to written records, forms and signatures include electronic records and forms and electronic confirmation that identifies the person completing the record or form.

Chief officers must be satisfied as to the integrity and security of the devices, records and forms to which this *paragraph* applies and that use of those devices, records and forms satisfies relevant data protection legislation.

(taken from *Code C paragraph 1.17*).

2.12 If any procedure in this Code requires a person's consent, the consent of a:

- mentally disordered or otherwise mentally vulnerable person is only valid if given in the presence of the appropriate adult
- juvenile is only valid if their parent's or guardian's consent is also obtained unless the juvenile is under 14, when their parent's or guardian's consent is sufficient in its own right. If the only obstacle to an identification procedure in *section 3* is that a juvenile's parent or guardian refuses consent or reasonable efforts to obtain it have failed, the identification officer may apply the provisions of *paragraph 3.21* (suspect known but not available).

2.13 If a person is blind, seriously visually impaired or unable to read, the custody officer or identification officer shall make sure their solicitor, relative, appropriate adult or some other person likely to take an interest in them and not involved in the investigation is available to help check any documentation. When this Code requires written consent or signing, the person assisting may be asked to sign instead, if the detainee prefers. This paragraph does not require an appropriate adult to be called solely to assist in checking and signing documentation for a person who is not a juvenile, or mentally disordered or otherwise mentally vulnerable (see Code C *paragraph 3.15*).

2.14 If any procedure in this Code requires information to be given to or sought from a suspect, it must be given or sought in the appropriate adult's presence if the suspect is mentally disordered, otherwise mentally vulnerable or a juvenile. If the appropriate adult is not present when the information is first given or sought, the procedure must be repeated in the presence of the appropriate adult when they arrive. If the suspect appears deaf or there is doubt about their hearing or speaking ability or ability to understand English, the custody officer or identification officer must ensure that the necessary arrangements in accordance with Code C are made for an interpreter to assist the suspect.

2.15 Any procedure in this Code involving the participation of a suspect who is mentally disordered, otherwise mentally vulnerable or a juvenile must take place in the presence of the appropriate adult. See Code C *paragraph 1.4*.

2.15A Any procedure in this Code involving the participation of a witness who is or appears to be mentally disordered, otherwise mentally vulnerable or a juvenile should take place in the presence of a pre-trial support person unless the witness states that they do not want a support person to be present. A support person must not be allowed to prompt any identification of a suspect by a witness.

2.16 References to:

- 'taking a photograph', include the use of any process to produce a single, still or moving, visual image
- 'photographing a person', should be construed accordingly
- 'photographs', 'films', 'negatives' and 'copies' include relevant visual images recorded, stored, or reproduced through any medium
- 'destruction' includes the deletion of computer data relating to such images or making access to that data impossible

2.17 This Code does not affect or apply to, the powers and procedures:

(i) for requiring and taking samples of breath, blood and urine in relation to driving offences, etc., when under the influence of drink, drugs or excess alcohol under the:

- Road Traffic Act 1988, sections 4 to 11
- Road Traffic Offenders Act 1988, sections 15 and 16
- Transport and Works Act 1992, sections 26 to 38;

(ii) under the Immigration Act 1971, Schedule 2, paragraph 18, for taking photographs, measuring and identifying and taking biometric information (not including DNA) from persons detained or liable to be detained under that Act, Schedule 2, paragraph 16 (Administrative Provisions as to Control on Entry etc.); or for taking fingerprints in accordance with the Immigration and Asylum Act 1999, sections 141 and 142(4), or other methods for collecting information about a person's external physical characteristics provided for by regulations made under that Act, section 144;

(iii) under the Terrorism Act 2000, Schedule 8, for taking photographs, fingerprints, skin impressions, body samples or impressions from people:

- arrested under that Act, section 41,
- detained for the purposes of examination under that Act, Schedule 7, and to whom the Code of Practice issued under that Act, Schedule 14, paragraph 6, applies ('the terrorism provisions')

(iv) for taking photographs, fingerprints, skin impressions, body samples or impressions from people who have been:

- arrested on warrants issued in Scotland, by officers exercising powers mentioned in Part X of the Criminal Justice and Public Order Act 1994;
- arrested or detained without warrant by officers from a police force in Scotland exercising their powers of arrest or detention mentioned in Part X of the Criminal Justice and Public Order Act 1994.

Note: In these cases, police powers and duties and the person's rights and entitlements whilst at a police station in England and Wales are the same as if the person had been arrested in Scotland by a Scottish police officer.

2.18 Nothing in this Code requires the identity of officers or police staff to be recorded or disclosed:

(a) in the case of enquiries linked to the investigation of terrorism;

(b) if the officers or police staff reasonably believe recording or disclosing their names might put them in danger.

In these cases, they shall use their warrant or other identification numbers and the name of their police station.

2.19 In this Code:

(a) 'designated person' means a person other than a police officer, who has specified powers and duties conferred or imposed on them by designation under section 38 or 39 of the Police Reform Act 2002;

(b) any reference to a police officer includes a designated person acting in the exercise or performance of the powers and duties conferred or imposed on them by their designation.

2.20 If a power conferred on a designated person:

(a) allows reasonable force to be used when exercised by a police officer, a designated person exercising that power has the same entitlement to use force;

(b) includes power to use force to enter any premises, that power is not exercisable by that designated person except:

(i) in the company, and under the supervision, of a police officer; or

(ii) for the purpose of:

- saving life or limb; or
- preventing serious damage to property.

2.21 In the case of a detained person, nothing in this Code prevents the custody officer, or other police officer or designated person given custody of the detainee by the custody officer for the purposes of the investigation of an offence for which the person is detained, from allowing another person (see *(a)* and *(b)* below) to carry out individual procedures or tasks at the police station if the law allows. However, the officer or designated person given custody remains responsible for making sure the procedures and tasks are carried out correctly in accordance with the Codes of Practice. The other person who is allowed to carry out the procedures or tasks must be *someone who at that time* is:

(a) under the direction and control of the chief officer of the force responsible for the police station in question; or

(b) providing services under contractual arrangements (but without being employed by the chief officer the police force), to assist a police force in relation to the discharge of its chief officer's functions.

2.22 Designated persons and others mentioned in *sub-paragraphs (a)* and *(b)* of *paragraph 2.21* must have regard to any relevant provisions of the Codes of Practice.

2.7.3.1 **KEYNOTE**

People who are seriously visually impaired or unable to read may be unwilling to sign police documents. The alternative, i.e. the representative signing on his/her behalf, seeks to protect the interests of both police and suspects.

For the purposes of any procedures within this Code which require an appropriate adult's consent, where a juvenile is in the care of a local authority or voluntary organisation the consent may be given by that authority or organisation. Where a parent, guardian or representative of a local authority or voluntary organisation is not acting as the appropriate adult under para. 2.14 or 2.15 he/she does not have to be present to give consent. However, it is important that a parent or guardian not present is fully informed before being asked to consent. He/she must be given the same information about the procedure and the juvenile's suspected involvement in the offence as the juvenile and appropriate adult. The parent or guardian must also be allowed to speak to the juvenile and the appropriate adult if he/she wishes. Provided the consent is fully informed and is not withdrawn, it may be obtained at any time before the procedure takes place.

The Youth Justice and Criminal Evidence Act 1999 guidance 'Achieving Best Evidence in Criminal Proceedings: Guidance on interviewing victims and witnesses, and guidance on using special measures' indicates that a pre-trial support person should accompany a vulnerable witness during any identification procedure. It states that this support person should not be (or not be likely to be) a witness in the investigation.

The purpose of using warrant or identification numbers instead of names referred to in Code D, para. 2.18(b) is to protect those involved in serious organised crime investigations or arrest of particularly violent suspects when there is reliable information that those arrested or their associates may threaten or cause harm to those involved. In cases of doubt, an officer of inspector rank or above should be consulted.

2.7.4 Code D—3 Identification by Witnesses

2.7.4.1 **KEYNOTE**

Visual Identification

Section 3 of Code D is split into Parts A and B, thereby distinguishing eye-witness identification procedures such as video identification from procedures for obtaining recognition evidence by viewing CCTV or similar images.

2.7.4.2

3 Identification and recognition of suspects

Part (A) Identification of a suspect by an eye-witness

3.0 This part applies when an eye-witness has seen a person committing a crime or in any other circumstances which tend to prove or disprove the involvement of the person they saw in a crime, for example, close to the scene of the crime, immediately before or immediately after it was committed. It sets out the procedures to be used to test the ability of that eye-witness to identify a person suspected of involvement in the offence ('the suspect') as the person they saw on the previous occasion. This part does not apply to the procedure described in Part B which is used to test the ability of someone who is not an eye-witness, to recognise anyone whose image they see.

3.1 A record shall be made of the description of the suspect as first given by the eye-witness. This record must:

(a) be made and kept in a form which enables details of that description to be accurately produced from it, in a visible and legible form, which can be given to the suspect or the suspect's solicitor in accordance with this Code; and

(b) unless otherwise specified, be made before the eye-witness takes part in any identification procedures under *paragraphs 3.5 to 3.10, 3.21, 3.23* or Annex E (Showing Photographs to Eye-Witnesses).

A copy of the record shall where practicable, be given to the suspect or their solicitor before any procedures under *paragraphs 3.5* to *3.10, 3.21* or *3.23* are carried out.

3.1A References in this Part:

(a) to the identity of the suspect being 'known' mean that there is sufficient information known to the police to establish, in accordance with Code G (Arrest), that there are reasonable grounds to suspect a particular person of involvement in the offence;

(b) to the suspect being 'available' mean that the suspect is immediately available, or will be available within a reasonably short time, in order that they can be invited to take part in at least one of the eye-witness identification procedures under *paragraphs 3.5* to *3.10* and it is practicable to arrange an effective procedure under *paragraphs 3.5 to 3.10*; and

(c) to the eye-witness identification procedures under *paragraphs 3.5* to *3.10* mean:

- Video identification (*paragraphs 3.5* and *3.6*);
- Identification parade (*paragraphs 3.7* and *3.8*); and
- Group identification (*paragraphs 3.9* and *3.10*).

(a) Cases when the suspect's identity is not known

3.2 In cases when the suspect's identity is not known, an eye-witness may be taken to a particular neighbourhood or place to see whether they can identify the person they saw on a previous occasion. Although the number, age, sex, race, general description and style of clothing of other people present at the location and the way in which any identification is made cannot be controlled, the principles applicable to the formal procedures under *paragraphs 3.5* to *3.10* shall be followed as far as practicable. For example:

(a) where it is practicable to do so, a record should be made of the eye-witness' description of the person they saw on the previous occasion, as in *paragraph 3.1(a)*, before asking the eye-witness to make an identification;

(b) Care must be taken not provide the eye-witness with any information concerning the description of the suspect (if such information is available) and not to direct the eye-witness' attention to any individual unless, taking into account all the circumstances, this cannot be avoided. However, this does not prevent an eye-witness being asked to look carefully at the people around at the time or to look towards a group or in a particular direction, if this appears necessary to make sure that the witness does not overlook a possible suspect simply because the eye-witness is looking in the opposite direction and also to enable the eye-witness to make comparisons between any suspect and others who are in the area;

(c) where there is more than one eye-witness, every effort should be made to keep them separate and eye-witnesses should be taken to see whether they can identify a person independently;

(d) once there is sufficient information to establish, in accordance with *paragraph 3.1A(a)*, that the suspect is 'known', e.g. after the eye-witness makes an identification, the provisions set out from *paragraph 3.4* onwards shall apply for that and any other eye-witnesses in relation to that individual;

(e) the officer or police staff accompanying the eye-witness must record, in their report book, the action taken as soon as practicable and in as much detail, as possible. The record should include:

(i) the date, time and place of the relevant occasion when the eye-witness claims to have previously seen the person committing the offence in question or in any other circumstances which tend to prove or disprove the involvement of the person they saw in a crime (see *paragraph 3.0*); and

(ii) where any identification was made:

- how it was made and the conditions at the time (e.g., the distance the eye-witness was from the suspect, the weather and light);
- if the eye-witness's attention was drawn to the suspect; the reason for this; and
- anything said by the eye-witness or the suspect about the identification or the conduct of the procedure.

3.3 An eye-witness must not be shown photographs, computerised or artist's composite likenesses or similar likenesses or pictures (including 'E-fit' images) if in accordance with *paragraph 3.1A*, the identity of the suspect is known and they are available to take part in one of the procedures under *paragraphs 3.5* to *3.10*. If the suspect's identity is not known, the showing of any such images to an eye-witness to see if they can identify a person whose image they are shown as the person they saw on a previous occasion must be done in accordance with *Annex E*.

2.7.4.3 **KEYNOTE**

Identification at the Scene

The need for 'scene identifications' was recognised by Lord Lane CJ in *R* v *Oscar* [1991] Crim LR 778 and by the Court of Appeal in *R* v *Rogers* [1993] Crim LR 386.

In *Oscar*, the court held that there had been no requirement for an identity parade in that case and Lord Lane pointed out that, in any case, a later parade where the suspect was dressed differently would be of no value at all. In *Rogers*, the suspect was found near a crime scene and was confronted by a witness who positively identified him. The court held that the identification in that case was necessary for an arrest to be made, although the court considered that a later parade could have been carried out.

The admissibility and value of identification evidence obtained when carrying out the procedure under para. 3.2 (taking an eye-witness to see whether they can identify the person they saw on a previous occasion) may be compromised if before a person is identified, the eye-witness' attention is specifically drawn to that person; or if the suspect's identity becomes known before the procedure.

Careful consideration must be given before a decision to identify a suspect in this manner is used. If there is sufficient evidence to arrest the suspect without using a witness's identification, then it is likely that the courts will find that one of the three identification methods outlined at Code D, para. 3.4 should have been used and the evidence may be excluded. Confrontations between witnesses and suspects on the street can be useful at times, but where this takes place it defeats the formal identification process and needs to be carefully considered. The reason for this is that, even if the suspect is picked out on the identification parade by that witness, the defence will be able to argue that the identification was from the confrontation after the incident and not at the time of the commission of the offence. If there is more than one witness available and a decision is taken to use a witness to try to identify a suspect at the scene, other witnesses should be moved away, so as to reduce the possibility of a chance encounter with the suspect. Where possible, these witnesses should be kept apart until the identification parade and ideally should not discuss the matter between themselves.

An example where a street identification was appropriate is *R* v *El-Hinnachi* [1998] 2 Cr App R 226. Here an affray took place in the car park of a public house. A witness had seen the man earlier in the pub and she'd had an unobstructed view in good light before the attack. The witness described the attacker's clothing to the police and then identified a group of men who had been stopped by other officers a short distance away. The court accepted that due to the fast-moving incident, this correct approach should, however, be avoided where possible. The defendants were not known suspects when they were stopped by the police prior to the witness's identification. The court also accepted that it had not been practicable for a record to have been made of the witness's description, as required by Code D, para. 3.1, prior to the identification.

A not uncommon situation is where police officers chase a suspect who is arrested by other officers on the description circulated by the chasing officer, who then attends the scene to confirm the person's identity. The case of *R* v *Nunes* [2001] EWCA Crim 2283, covers this point and points out the dangers of this practice. The facts of the case were that a police officer saw a man inside a house and circulated a description on his radio. A person fitting the description was seen and arrested. The first officer arrived on the scene and identified the arrested person as the man he had earlier seen in the house. The Court of Appeal held that on the particular facts of this case the identification amounted to a breach of the Code. By the time of the identification, the man had been arrested for suspected involvement in the offence and, on his arrest, the identity of the suspect was known to the police. Therefore, by the time the witnessing officer arrived on the scene, the case involved 'disputed identification evidence' because the suspect had said that he had not done anything while the police had told him he matched the description of a suspected burglar. That said, the court did go on to hold that the judge had the discretion to allow the identification evidence to be adduced notwithstanding the breach of the Codes, but a full and careful direction regarding the breaches, together with a warning about the shortcomings in the procedure, would have been necessary.

Where a suspect is identified by witnesses, other evidence should still be sought to strengthen the case (or to prove the person's innocence) as identification evidence is often challenged at court. Such supporting evidence may include admissions by the suspect that links him/her to the identification evidence; e.g. that he/she owns the vehicle that was driven at the time of the offence (*R* v *Ward* [2001] Crim LR 316).

2.7.4.4

(b) Cases when the suspect is known and available

3.4 If the suspect's identity is known to the police (see *paragraph 3.1A(a)*) and they are available (see *paragraph 3.1A(b)*), the identification procedures that may be used are set out in *paragraphs 3.5* to *3.10* below as follows:

- video identification;
- identification parade; or
- group identification.

(i) Video identification

3.5 A 'video identification' is when the eye-witness is shown images of a known suspect, together with similar images of others who resemble the suspect. *Moving* images must be used unless the conditions in sub-paragraph (a) or (b) below apply:

(a) this sub-paragraph applies if:

(i) the identification officer, in consultation with the officer in charge of the investigation, is satisfied that because of aging, or other physical changes or differences, the appearance of the suspect has significantly changed since the previous occasion when the eye-witness claims to have seen the suspect (see *paragraph 3.0*);

(ii) an image (moving or still) is available which the identification officer and the officer in charge of the investigation reasonably believe shows the appearance of the suspect as it was at the time the suspect was seen by the eye-witness; and

(iii) having regard to the extent of change and the purpose of eye-witness identification procedures (see *paragraph 3.0*), the identification officer believes that that such an image should be shown to the eye-witness.

In such a case, the identification officer may arrange a video identification procedure using the image described in (ii). In accordance with the 'Notice to suspect' (see *paragraph 3.17(vi)*), the suspect must first be given an opportunity to provide their own image(s) for use in the procedure but it is for the identification officer and officer in charge of the investigation to decide whether, following (ii) and (iii), any image(s) provided by the suspect should be used.

A video identification using an image described above may, at the discretion of the identification officer be arranged in addition to, or as an alternative to, a video identification using moving images taken after the suspect has been given the information and notice described in *paragraphs 3.17* and *3.18*.

See *paragraph 3.21* in any case where the suspect deliberately takes steps to frustrate the eye-witness identification arrangements and procedures.

(b) this sub-paragraph applies if, in accordance with *paragraph 2A* of *Annex A* of this Code, the identification officer does not consider that replication of a physical feature or concealment of the location of the feature can be achieved using a moving image. In these cases, still images may be used.

3.6 Video identifications must be carried out in accordance with *Annex A*.

(ii) Identification parade

3.7 An 'identification parade' is when the eye-witness sees the suspect in a line of others who resemble the suspect.

3.8 Identification parades must be carried out in accordance with *Annex B*.

(iii) Group identification

3.9 A 'group identification' is when the eye-witness sees the suspect in an informal group of people.

3.10 Group identifications must be carried out in accordance with *Annex C*.

Arranging eye-witness identification procedures—duties of identification officer

3.11 Except as provided for in *paragraph 3.19*, the arrangements for, and conduct of, the eye-witness identification procedures in *paragraphs 3.5* to *3.10* and circumstances in which any such identification procedure must be held shall be the responsibility of an officer not below inspector rank who is not involved with the investigation ('the identification officer'). The identification officer may direct another officer or police staff, see *paragraph 2.21*, to make arrangements for, and to conduct, any of these identification procedures and except as provided for in *paragraph 7* of *Annex A*, any reference in this section to the identification officer includes the officer or police staff to whom the arrangements for, and/or conduct of, any of these procedure has been delegated. In delegating these arrangements and procedures, the identification officer must be able to supervise effectively and either intervene or be contacted for advice. Where any action referred to in this paragraph is taken by another officer or police staff at the direction of the identification officer, the outcome shall, as soon as practicable, be reported to the identification officer. For the purpose of these procedures, the identification officer retains overall responsibility for ensuring that the procedure complies with this Code and in addition, in the case of detained suspect, their care and treatment until returned to the custody officer. Except as permitted by this Code, no officer or any other person involved with the investigation of the case against the suspect may take any part in these procedures or act as the identification officer.

This paragraph does not prevent the identification officer from consulting the officer in charge of the investigation to determine which procedure to use. When an identification procedure is required, in the interest of fairness to suspects and eye-witnesses, it must be held as soon as practicable.

Circumstances in which an eye-witness identification procedure must be held

3.12 If, before any identification procedure set out in *paragraphs 3.5* to *3.10* has been held

(a) an eye-witness has identified a suspect or purported to have identified them; or

(b) there is an eye-witness available who expresses an ability to identify the suspect; or

(c) there is a reasonable chance of an eye-witness being able to identify the suspect, and the eye-witness in (a) to (c) has not been given an opportunity to identify the suspect in any of the procedures set out in *paragraphs 3.5* to *3.10*, then an identification procedure shall be held if the suspect disputes being the person the eye-witness claims to have seen on a previous occasion (see *paragraph 3.0*), unless:

(i) it is not practicable to hold any such procedure; or

(ii) any such procedure would serve no useful purpose in proving or disproving whether the suspect was involved in committing the offence, for example

- where the suspect admits being at the scene of the crime and gives an account of what took place and the eye-witness does not see anything which contradicts that; or
- when it is not disputed that the suspect is already known to the eye-witness who claims to have recognised them when seeing them commit the crime.

3.13 An eye-witness identification procedure may also be held if the officer in charge of the investigation, after consultation with the identification officer, considers it would be useful.

2.7.4.5 **KEYNOTE**

When Must an Identification Procedure be Held?

Identification procedures should be held for the benefit of the defence as well as the prosecution (*R* v *Wait* [1998] Crim LR 68). The key factor to consider when deciding whether to hold an identification parade is whether *a failure to hold a parade could be a matter of genuine potential prejudice to the suspect.* In *R* v *SBC (A Juvenile)* [2001] EWCA Crim 885, the defence was one of duress but the appeal was based on the failure of the police to hold identification parades. The Court of Appeal stated that this was not a case about identification, as none of the defendants denied their presence at the scene. What they denied was their criminal participation in the activities that took place. It followed, therefore, that Code D did not apply. Other examples would be where it is not in dispute that the suspect is already well known to the witness who claims to have seen the suspect commit the crime or where there is no reasonable possibility that a witness would be able to make an identification.

Any decision to proceed without an identification parade must be capable of justification later to the relevant court. The courts have taken different approaches to justification based on practical difficulties. In an early case, the submissions of the identification officer that it was impracticable to find enough people who sufficiently resembled the defendant were treated fairly dismissively by the trial judge (*R* v *Gaynor* [1988] Crim LR 242). In other cases, however, the courts have been more lenient, accepting that the timescales involved in arranging identification parades may render them 'impracticable' (see *R* v *Jamel* [1993] Crim LR 52, where the court refused an objection by the defence to a group identification). A group identification was used in Jamel because a parade using mixed-race volunteers would have taken too long to arrange. All reasonable steps must be taken to investigate the possibility of one identification option before moving on to an alternative, and an offer from a suspect's solicitor to find volunteers to stand on a parade is such a 'reasonable' step (*R* v *Britton & Richards* [1989] Crim LR 144).

There have been a number of Court of Appeal cases concerning the requirement to hold identification parades. It is suggested that these should be applied to the Code regardless of which form of identification procedure is used. The leading case is *R* v *Forbes* [2001] 1 AC 473, which was based on earlier versions of the Code of Practice. The House of Lords held that if the police are in possession of sufficient evidence to justify the arrest of a suspect, and that suspect's identification depends on eye-witness identification evidence, even in part, then if the identification is disputed, the Code requires that an identification parade should be held with the suspect's consent, unless one of the exceptions applies.

The House of Lords went on to say that this mandatory obligation to hold an identification procedure applies even if there has been a 'fully satisfactory', 'actual and complete' or 'unequivocal' identification of the suspect.

Despite the wording of Code D, it has been held that a suspect's right to have an identification [procedure] is not confined to cases where a dispute over identity has already arisen; that right also applies where such a dispute might reasonably be anticipated (*R* v *Rutherford and Palmer* (1994) 98 Cr App R 191). Similarly, a suspect's failure to request an identification [procedure] does not mean that the police may proceed without one (*R* v *Graham* [1994] Crim LR 212).

It is important to consider the distinction between identification of a suspect and the suspect's clothing or other features. In *D* v *DPP* (1998) *The Times*, 7 August, a witness had observed two youths for a continuous period of five to six minutes and then informed the police of what he had seen, describing the age of the youths and the clothes that they were wearing. The court held that there had not been an identification within the terms of the Codes of Practice because the witness had at no stage identified the defendant or the co-accused. He had described only their clothing and their approximate ages, and the police, acting on that information, had made the arrests. An identification parade could have served no useful purpose, since the clothing would have been changed and those persons used for the parade would have been the same approximate age. This point was further supported in *R* v *Haynes* [2004] EWCA Crim 390, where the Court of Appeal held that as a practical point the identification parade, whether or not the suspect was regarded as a known or unknown suspect, was of little value where the witness identified the suspect by clothing and not by recognition of the suspect's features. An identification parade would have provided little assistance.

The question for the court will be whether it is fair to admit the identification evidence. When looking at this issue the court will consider how reliable that identification evidence is.

In para. 3.5(a)(i), examples of physical changes or differences that the identification officer may wish to consider include hair style and colour, weight, facial hair, wearing or removal of spectacles and tinted contact lenses, facial injuries, tattoos and make-up.

2.7.4.6 Selecting an eye-witness identification procedure

3.14 If, because of *paragraph 3.12*, an identification procedure is to be held, the suspect shall initially be invited to take part in a video identification unless:

(a) a video identification is not practicable; or

(b) an identification parade is both practicable and more suitable than a video identification; or

(c) *paragraph 3.16* applies.

The identification officer and the officer in charge of the investigation shall consult each other to determine which option is to be offered. An identification parade may not be practicable because of factors relating to the witnesses, such as their number, state of health, availability and travelling requirements. A video identification would normally be more suitable if it could be arranged and completed sooner than an identification parade. Before an option is offered the suspect must also be reminded of their entitlement to have free legal advice, see Code C, *paragraph 6.5*.

3.15 A suspect who refuses the identification procedure in which the suspect is first invited to take part shall be asked to state their reason for refusing and may get advice from their solicitor and/or if present, their appropriate adult. The suspect, solicitor and/or appropriate adult shall be allowed to make representations about why another procedure should be used. A record should be made of the reasons for refusal and any representations made. After considering any reasons given, and representations made, the identification officer shall, if appropriate, arrange for the suspect to be invited to take part in an alternative which the officer considers suitable and practicable. If the officer decides it is not suitable and practicable to invite the suspect to take part in an alternative identification procedure, the reasons for that decision shall be recorded.

3.16 A suspect may initially be invited to take part in a group identification if the officer in charge of the investigation considers it is more suitable than a video identification or an identification parade and the identification officer considers it practicable to arrange.

Notice to suspect

3.17 Unless *paragraph 3.20* applies, before any eye-witness identification procedure set out in *paragraphs 3.5* to *3.10* is arranged, the following shall be explained to the suspect:

(i) the purpose of the procedure (see *paragraph 3.0*);

(ii) their entitlement to free legal advice; see Code C, *paragraph 6.5*;

(iii) the procedures for holding it, including their right, subject to *Annex A, paragraph 9*, to have a solicitor or friend present;

(iv) that they do not have to consent to or co-operate in the procedure;

(v) that if they do not consent to, and co-operate in, a procedure, their refusal may be given in evidence in any subsequent trial and police may proceed covertly without their consent or make other arrangements to test whether an eye-witness can identify them, see *paragraph 3.21*;

(vi) whether, for the purposes of a video identification procedure, images of them have previously been obtained either:

- in accordance with *paragraph 3.20*, and if so, that they may co-operate in providing further, suitable images to be used instead; or
- in accordance with *paragraph 3.5(a)*, and if so, that they may provide their own images for the identification officer to consider using.

(vii) if appropriate, the special arrangements for juveniles;

(viii) if appropriate, the special arrangements for mentally disordered or otherwise mentally vulnerable people;

(ix) that if they significantly alter their appearance between being offered an identification procedure and any attempt to hold an identification procedure, this may be given in evidence if the case comes to trial, and the identification officer may then consider other forms of identification, see *paragraph 3.21*;

(x) that a moving image or photograph may be taken of them when they attend for any identification procedure;

(xi) whether, before their identity became known, the eye-witness was shown photographs, a computerised or artist's composite likeness or similar likeness or image by the police,

(xii) that if they change their appearance before an identification parade, it may not be practicable to arrange one on the day or subsequently and, because of the appearance change, the identification officer may consider alternative methods of identification,

(xiii) that they or their solicitor will be provided with details of the description of the suspect as first given by any eye-witnesses who are to attend the procedure or confrontation, see *paragraph 3.1*.

3.18 This information must also be recorded in a written notice handed to the suspect. The suspect must be given a reasonable opportunity to read the notice, after which, they should be asked to sign a copy of the notice to indicate if they are willing to co-operate with the making of a video or take part in the identification parade or group identification. The signed copy shall be retained by the identification officer.

3.19 In the case of a detained suspect, the duties under *paragraphs 3.17* and *3.18* may be performed by the custody officer or by another officer or police staff not involved in the investigation as directed by the custody officer, if:

(a) it is proposed to release the suspect in order that an identification procedure can be arranged and carried out and an inspector is not available to act as the identification officer, see *paragraph 3.11*, before the suspect leaves the station; or

(b) it is proposed to keep the suspect in police detention whilst the procedure is arranged and carried out and waiting for an inspector to act as the identification officer, see *paragraph 3.11*, would cause unreasonable delay to the investigation.

The officer concerned shall inform the identification officer of the action taken and give them the signed copy of the notice.

3.20 If the identification officer and officer in charge of the investigation suspect, on reasonable grounds that if the suspect was given the information and notice as in *paragraphs 3.17* and *3.18*, they would then take steps to avoid being seen by a witness in any identification procedure, the identification officer may arrange for images of the suspect suitable for use in a video identification procedure to be obtained before giving the information and notice. If suspect's images are obtained in these circumstances, the suspect may, for the purposes of a video identification procedure, co-operate in providing new images which if suitable, would be used instead, see *paragraph 3.17(vi)*.

2.7.4.7

KEYNOTE

When an eye-witness attending an identification procedure has previously been shown photographs, or been shown or provided with computerised or artist's composite likenesses, or similar likenesses or pictures, it is the officer in charge of the investigation's responsibility to make the identification officer aware of this. The purpose of allowing the custody officer or other officer not involved in the investigation to undertake the role of the identification officer at Code D, paras 3.17 and 3.18 is to avoid or reduce delays in arranging identification procedures by enabling the required information and warning to be given at the earliest opportunity.

2.7.4.8

(c) Cases when the suspect is known but not available

3.21 When a known suspect is not available or has ceased to be available, see *paragraph 3.1A*, the identification officer may make arrangements for a video identification (see paragraph 3.5 and Annex A). If necessary, the identification officer may follow the video identification procedures using any suitable moving or still images and these may be obtained covertly if necessary. Alternatively, the identification officer may make arrangements for a group identification without the suspect's consent (see Annex C *paragraph 34*). These provisions may also be applied to juveniles where the consent of their parent or guardian is either refused or reasonable efforts to obtain that consent have failed (see *paragraph 2.12*).

3.22 Any covert activity should be strictly limited to that necessary to test the ability of the eye-witness to identify the suspect as the person they saw on the relevant previous occasion.

3.23 The identification officer may arrange for the suspect to be confronted by the eye-witness if none of the options referred to in *paragraphs 3.5* to *3.10* or *3.21* are practicable. A 'confrontation' is when the suspect is directly confronted by the eye-witness. A confrontation does not require the suspect's consent. Confrontations must be carried out in accordance with Annex D.

3.24 Requirements for information to be given to, or sought from, a suspect or for the suspect to be given an opportunity to view images before they are shown to an eye-witness, do not apply if the suspect's lack of co-operation prevents the necessary action.

2.7.4.9

KEYNOTE

Which Identification Procedure should be Used?

Code D, para. 3.21 also apples where a suspect refuses or fails to take part in a video identification, an identification parade or a group identification, or refuses or fails to take part in the only practicable options from that list. It enables any suitable images of the suspect, moving or still, which are available or can be obtained, to be used in an identification procedure. Examples include images from custody and other CCTV systems and from visually recorded interview records.

It is only if none of the other options are practicable that the identification officer may arrange for the suspect to be confronted by the witness. A confrontation does not require the suspect's consent. In *R* v *McCulloch, Smith & Wheeler* (1999) 6 May, unreported, the Court of Appeal made it clear that confrontations between suspects and witnesses should only be carried out if no other identification procedure is practicable.

2.7.4.10

(d) Documentation

3.25 A record shall be made of the video identification, identification parade, group identification or confrontation on forms provided for the purpose.

3.26 If the identification officer considers it is not practicable to hold a video identification or identification parade requested by the suspect, the reasons shall be recorded and explained to the suspect.

3.27 A record shall be made of a person's failure or refusal to co-operate in a video identification, identification parade or group identification and, if applicable, of the grounds for obtaining images in accordance with *paragraph 3.20*.

(e) Not used

3.28 *Not used.*

3.29 *Not used.*

(f) Destruction and retention of photographs taken or used in eye-witness identification procedures

3.30 PACE, section 64A, see *paragraph 5.12*, provides powers to take photographs of suspects and allows these photographs to be used or disclosed only for purposes related to the prevention or detection of crime, the investigation of offences or the conduct of prosecutions by, or on behalf of, police or other law enforcement and prosecuting authorities inside and outside the United Kingdom or the enforcement of a sentence. After being so used or disclosed, they may be retained but can only be used or disclosed for the same purposes.

3.31 Subject to *paragraph 3.33*, the photographs (and all negatives and copies), of suspects *not* taken in accordance with the provisions in paragraph 5.12 which are taken for the purposes of, or in connection with, the identification procedures in *paragraphs 3.5* to *3.10, 3.21 or 3.23* must be destroyed unless the suspect:

(a) is charged with, or informed they may be prosecuted for, a recordable offence;

(b) is prosecuted for a recordable offence;

(c) is cautioned for a recordable offence or given a warning or reprimand in accordance with the Crime and Disorder Act 1998 for a recordable offence; or

(d) gives informed consent, in writing, for the photograph or images to be retained for purposes described in *paragraph 3.30*.

3.32 When *paragraph 3.31* requires the destruction of any photograph, the person must be given an opportunity to witness the destruction or to have a certificate confirming the destruction if they request one within five days of being informed that the destruction is required.

3.33 Nothing in *paragraph 3.31* affects any separate requirement under the Criminal Procedure and Investigations Act 1996 to retain material in connection with criminal investigations.

2.7.4.11

Part (B) Recognition by *controlled* showing of films, photographs and images

3.34 This Part of this section applies when, for the purposes of obtaining evidence of recognition, arrangements are made for a person, including a police officer, who is not an eye-witness

(a) to view a film, photograph or any other visual medium; and
(b) on the occasion of the viewing, to be asked whether they recognise anyone whose image is shown in the material as someone who is known to them.

The arrangements for such viewings may be made by the officer in charge of the relevant investigation. Although there is no requirement for the identification officer to make the arrangements or to be consulted about the arrangements, nothing prevents this.

3.35 To provide safeguards against mistaken recognition and to avoid any possibility of collusion, on the occasion of the viewing, the arrangements should ensure:

(a) that the films, photographs and other images are shown on an individual basis;
(b) that any person who views the material;
  (i) is unable to communicate with any other individual to whom the material has been, or is to be, shown;
  (ii) is not reminded of any photograph or description of any individual whose image is shown or given any other indication as to the identity of any such individual;
  (iii) is not be told whether a previous witness has recognised any one;
(c) that immediately before a person views the material, they are told that:
  (i) an individual who is known to them may, or may not, appear in the material they are shown and that if they do not recognise anyone, they should say so;
  (ii) at any point, they may ask to see a particular part of the material frozen for them to study and there is no limit on how many times they can view the whole or any part or parts of the material; and
(d) that the person who views the material is not asked to make any decision as to whether they recognise anyone whose image they have seen as someone known to them until they have seen the whole of the material at least twice, unless the officer in charge of the viewing decides that because of the number of images the person has been invited to view, it would not be reasonable to ask them to view the whole of the material for a second time. A record of this decision must be included in the record that is made in accordance with *paragraph 3.36*.

3.36 A record of the circumstances and conditions under which the person is given an opportunity to recognise an individual must be made and the record must include:

(a) whether the person knew or was given information concerning the name or identity of any suspect;
(b) what the person has been told *before* the viewing about the offence, the person(s) depicted in the images or the offender and by whom;
(c) how and by whom the witness was asked to view the image or look at the individual;
(d) whether the viewing was alone or with others and if with others, the reason for it;
(e) the arrangements under which the person viewed the film or saw the individual and by whom those arrangements were made;
(f) subject to *paragraph 2.18*, the name and rank of the officer responsible for deciding that the viewing arrangements should be made in accordance with this Part;
(g) the date time and place images were viewed or further viewed or the individual was seen;
(h) the times between which the images were viewed or the individual was seen;
(i) how the viewing of images or sighting of the individual was controlled and by whom;
(j) whether the person was familiar with the location shown in any images or the place where they saw the individual and if so, why;
(k) whether or not, on this occasion, the person claims to recognise any image shown, or any individual seen, as being someone known to them, and if they do:
  (i) the reason;
  (ii) the words of recognition;
  (iii) any expressions of doubt; and
  (iv) what features of the image or the individual triggered the recognition.

3.37 The record required under *paragraph 3.36* may be made by the person who views the image or sees the individual and makes the recognition; and if applicable, by the officer or police staff in charge of showing the images to that person or in charge of the conditions under which that person sees the individual. The person must be asked to read and check the completed record and as applicable, confirm that it is correctly and accurately reflects the part they played in the viewing.

2.7.4.12

KEYNOTE

Photographs, Image and Sound Reproduction Generally

The use of photographic and computer-generated images (such as E-Fit) to identify suspects has increased considerably over the past few years. Although the courts will exercise considerable caution when admitting such evidence (*R* v *Blenkinsop* [1995] 1 Cr App R 7), these methods of identification are particularly useful. Expert evidence may be admitted to interpret images on film (see e.g. *R* v *Stockwell* (1993) 97 Cr App R 260) and police officers who are very familiar with a particular film clip (e.g. of crowd violence at a football match) may be allowed to assist the court in interpreting and explaining events shown within it (*R* v *Clare* [1995] 2 Cr App R 333).

In *Thomasson & Warmington* v *R* [2021] EWCA Crim 114, the court held that an E-Fit picture should be treated as hearsay evidence and for these purposes it is to be treated in the same way as a written record made by a police officer of a description provided by an eye-witness as to the appearance of someone the witness had seen. In this case, the identification would have involved a number of police officers viewing the E-Fit picture and comparing it to their memory of the appearance of various other people. The officers would, therefore, have been expressing their opinion as to the match between the *perception* of the artist who compiled the E-Fit picture as to the *perception* of the eye-witness as to the suspect. The court highlighted the difference between this case and the process approved in *Attorney-General's Reference (No. 2 of 2002)* [2002] EWCA Crim 2373, when an officer or other witness, not present at the scene, gives identification evidence from photographs or film footage, whether or not they knew the defendant. The critical difference is that there is no hearsay involved in this situation, because the identifying witness who was not present is not reliant on the perception of another human being, for instance the individual who created an E-Fit picture or recorded a written description. The individual or machine taking the photograph or compiling the film footage which captured the image had no part to play other than the mechanical one of recording the image.

2.7.4.13

KEYNOTE

Recognition Cases

Recognition cases, that is to say, those cases where the witness states that he/she knows the person who committed the offence as opposed to only being able to give a description, need to be carefully considered and Part B of section 3 of this Code adhered to. The eye-witness identification procedures in Part A should not be used to test whether a witness can recognise a person as someone he/she knows and would be able to give evidence of recognition along the lines of 'On (describe date, time, location) I saw an image of an individual who I recognised as XY'. In these cases, the procedures in Part B of section 3 of this Code shall apply. The admissibility and value of evidence of recognition obtained when carrying out the procedures in Part B may be compromised if before the person is recognised, the witness who has claimed to know him/her is given or is made, or becomes, aware of, information about the person which was not previously known to the witness personally but which he/she has purported to rely on to support his/her claim that the person is in fact known to him/her.

In *R* v *Ridley* (1999) *The Times*, 13 October, the Court of Appeal stated that there has never been a rule that an identification parade had to be held in all recognition cases and that it will be a question of fact in each case whether or not there is a need to do so. The view that an identification procedure is not required in these cases is supported by para. 3.12(ii).

The facts in *Ridley*, which it is suggested are not uncommon among patrolling officers, were that two police officers in a marked police vehicle noticed a car, which had been stolen earlier that day, drive past them. Both officers said that they recognised the defendant driving the car. The officers gave chase and gave evidence that the car was speeding and being driven dangerously. They decided that it was unsafe to continue pursuit, but arrested the suspect six days later. One of the officers claimed to have recognised the suspect because she had interviewed him for some 20 minutes five months previously and had seen him about town. She gave evidence that she had a view of the suspect in the car for about nine seconds. The other officer said that he recognised the suspect from a photograph but could not say when he had seen that photograph. He said that he had seen the suspect in the car for about two seconds. The court found that the female police officer's identification had been complete and there was no requirement for her to have further identified the suspect.

Ridley can be contrasted with *R* v *Conway* (1990) 91 Cr App R 143, where the witnesses' evidence was not as strong. There the witnesses stated that they recognised the accused simply because they knew him. The defence argument was that the witnesses did not actually know the accused and so could not have recognised him at the time of the offence. His conviction was quashed because of the prejudice caused by the absence of a parade. In *R* v *Davies* [2004] EWCA Crim 2521, a witness identified a masked attacker from his voice and eyes. The court in this case held that this identification evidence coupled with other circumstantial evidence was sufficient for a conviction.

A case can still amount to one of recognition, even where the witness does not know the name of the suspect but later obtained those details from a third party, for example where the witness and the suspect went to the same school and the witness became aware of the suspect's full names from other pupils at the school (*R* v *C*; *R* v *B* [2003] EWCA Crim 718).

In *R (On the Application of H)* v *DPP* [2003] EWHC 133 (Admin), the court accepted that it was reasonable for the police not to undertake an identification procedure. In the circumstances of the case, the police had every reason to believe that the claimant and the victim were well known to each other. The claimant had accepted that the victim knew her. There was no question of doubt as to the victim's ability to recognise the claimant and as such this was a case of pure recognition where it was futile to hold an identification parade.

Care must be taken in cases where it is believed that the case is one of recognition not requiring an identification procedure. In *R* v *Harris* [2003] EWCA Crim 174, the witness stated that he recognised the suspect as being someone he went to school with. The suspect gave a prepared statement in which he disputed the suggestion that he was well known to the witness. Here the court held that an identification procedure should have been undertaken, as the circumstances of the case did not fall within the general exception of the Code, i.e. that an identification procedure would serve no useful purpose in proving or disproving whether the suspect had been involved in committing the offence. It is suggested therefore that where a suspect disputes that a witness knows him/her, an identification procedure should be considered.

When a suspect is filmed committing an offence, it may be admissible to give evidence of identification by way of recognition from a witness not present at the scene. In *Attorney-General's Reference (No. 2 of 2002)* [2002] EWCA Crim 2373, the court reviewed the previous case law and concluded that there are at least four circumstances in which a jury could be invited to conclude that a defendant committed an offence on the basis of photographic evidence from the scene:

- where the photographic image was sufficiently clear the jury could compare it with the defendant sitting in the dock;
- where a witness knew the defendant sufficiently well to recognise him or her as the offender depicted in the photographic image;
- where a witness who did not know the defendant spent substantial time viewing and analysing photographic images from the scene, thereby acquiring special knowledge which the jury did not have, evidence of identification based on comparison between them and a reasonably contemporary photo of the defendant could be given so long as the image and photograph were available to the jury. Further, in *R* v *Savalia* [2011] EWCA Crim 1334 the court held that this did not just apply to facial features but could properly be extended to apply to identification of a defendant from closed-circuit television footage based on a combination of factors, including build and gait;

- a suitably qualified expert with facial mapping skills giving opinion evidence of identification based on a comparison between images from the scene and a reasonably contemporary photograph of the defendant could be given so long as the image and photograph were available to the jury.

In *R* v *Purlis* [2017] EWCA Crim 1134, a dashboard camera captured a robber departing the scene in the car. The court allowed a facial mapping expert to give evidence that by comparing images from the dashcam with photographs of the suspect he could identify features which taken together lent powerful support to the contention that the images were of the same man. This followed the case of *R* v *Atkins* [2010] 1 Cr App R 8, where the court held that it is important to approach the evidence of facial mapping with caution. That does not mean that you cannot rely on the expert evidence. Simply that it needs to be considered with care. The court went on to say that an expert who spends many years studying this kind of evidence can properly form an opinion as to the significance of what he/she has found.

CCTV

The case of *R* v *Lariba* [2015] EWCA Crim 478 involved police officers while off duty recognising a suspect for a local 'gang' murder from CCTV pictures that had been circulated on the internet by their own police force. The officers were local officers who regularly came into contact with gang members; although the suspect's face was partially covered the officers recognised him from his general demeanour, skin tone, hairline, eyebrows and clothing. At the time of the recognition the officers did not make any notes.

The Court of Appeal considered that the strength of the connection between the witnesses and the appellant was relevant to the issue whether a partial facial view of the suspect would be sufficient to permit recognition, noting that the witnesses were police officers who saw and spoke to Lariba on many occasions. The Court of Appeal stated that the more familiar in face, head, build and manner the person is to the witness the more likely it is that the witness can make a reliable identification of that person from a CCTV recording providing a similarly incomplete view of his face. In relation to formal identification procedures, the Court of Appeal stated that Code D, para. 3.28 permits viewing of images with a view to recognition by a witness or police officer and tracing a suspect. Code D applies to any occasion when, for the purpose of obtaining evidence of recognition, any person including a police officer views a photographic or other recording (para. 3.34). The context of paras 3.35 and 3.36 was said to demonstrate that the procedure can in practice only apply to arrangements made by the police for specific viewing. They cannot practicably apply to invitations to the public in general to view scenes of crime or other images of suspects via television or internet outlets with a request that recognition is reported to the investigation team.

It is important that where pictures or film are shown to specific police officers to try to identify suspects, this must be done in a controlled way. In *R* v *Smith (Dean) and others* [2008] EWCA Crim 1342, the court held that a police officer who was asked to view a CCTV recording to see if he could recognise any suspects involved in a robbery was not in the same shoes as a witness asked to identify someone he/she had seen committing a crime. However, safeguards that Code D was designed to put in place were equally important in cases where a police officer was asked to see whether he/she could recognise anyone in a CCTV recording. Whether or not Code D applied, there had to be in place some record that assisted in gauging the reliability of the assertion that the police officer recognised an individual. It was important that a police officer's initial reactions to viewing a CCTV recording were set out and available for scrutiny. Thus, if the police officer failed to recognise anyone on first viewing but did so subsequently, those circumstances ought to be noted. If a police officer failed to pick anybody else out, that also should be recorded, as should any words of doubt.

Furthermore, it was necessary that if recognition took place a record was made of what it was about the image that was said to have triggered the recognition. The case of *R* v *JD* [2012] EWCA Crim 2637 further highlights the need to keep records and comply with the Codes. As there was no record of how the police officer in this case viewed the CCTV, the court held that the defence could not test the officer's account that he watched the footage alone and no records had been made as to what features of the image triggered the recognition and other aspects of the recognition. It had been highly suggestive of the investigating constable to tell C that she believed D to feature in the CCTV footage rather than simply asking him to watch it and waiting to see if he recognised anybody.

Another case is *R* v *McCook* [2012] EWCA Crim 2817, where the court commented on some of the processes required by Code D, for example the witness's statement did not reveal the nature of the viewing equipment, the number of times the footage was played, how the viewing arrangements were made, what the witness had been told prior to the viewing and whether or not he/she was alone.

If a film which has been shown to a witness is later lost or unavailable, the witness may give evidence of what he/she saw on that film but the court will have to consider all the relevant circumstances in deciding whether to admit that evidence and what weight to attach to it (*Taylor* v *Chief Constable of Cheshire* [1986] 1 WLR 1479).

In cases where officers view many hours of CCTV which results in them identifying suspects from these viewings, it is important that they provide an objective means of testing the accuracy of their recognition identification. This may include any initial reactions to seeing the CCTV images if the officer fails to recognise anyone on the initial viewing but does so at a later date; where there is recognition, any factors relating to the image that caused that recognition to occur (*R* v *Yaryare, Hassan and Oman* [2020] EWCA Crim 1314). In this case, the trial judge emphasised that from a practical point of view it may be unrealistic to expect an officer to note all of his/her passing thoughts whilst watching CCTV footage time and again. Any conclusions in a case such as the present are likely to emerge incrementally, and the fine detail of an improving or changing recognition may be difficult to record in a log. However, that said, the officer should record, in accordance with the approach established in Code D, at the least, the 'Red Letter' events—the moments, for instance, when they first begin to note similarities with a particular individual, along with any significant features that occur to them during the process of viewing. They should also note any factors that tend to indicate the suspect does not match a particular individual who is being considered.

Social Media Identifications

Other types of identification are also coming before the courts which have been seen on social media platforms. In *R* v *Crampton* [2020] EWCA Crim 1334, the victim, when aged between 4 and 6, was left at home by her parents with a man called Mark who sexually assaulted her. The family did not report the matter to police out of concern that this might further traumatise the child. They took the view that it was best to forget about the incident. The victim did not, however, forget and eventually, in 2018 aged 25, she reported the matter to police naming the perpetrator as Mark Crampton, having identified him as the offender after she found a photograph of him on Facebook. The complainant accurately recollected that the man who had abused her had blonde curly hair and this was not something that was evident from the Facebook image. Crampton was interviewed and charged with sexual offences; no formal identification procedure was held. The judgment was that this was a breach of Code D and a formal identification procedure should be held. The court commented that:

> The danger of course with these identifications is that they do not take place under the controlled conditions of an identification procedure, which of course these days 99 times out of 100 is a VIPER procedure. But as the CPS makes clear on their website Facebook identifications are increasingly common and are admissible in evidence and frankly if the position was the other way, then it would be a very strange state of affairs because it is the natural reaction of anybody seeking to identify the suspect of having committed a crime against them or somebody else to look on Facebook in order to identify who they are. So, the courts will have to wrestle with Facebook identifications for a considerable time into the future.

R v *McCullough* [2011] EWCA Crim 1413 was a case where the victim of a robbery identified the suspect from a photograph on Facebook and then later identified the suspect on a video identification parade. The Court of Appeal found that the Facebook identification was far from ideal and it was capable of having a substantial effect on the weight of the witness's subsequent identification of the defendant in the formal identification procedure. The key here is that the formal identification procedure is still required.

In *R* v *Alexander and McGill* [2012] EWCA Crim 2768 the victim identified the suspects through their Facebook account pictures. The court observed that it was therefore incumbent upon investigators to take steps to obtain, in as much detail as possible, evidence in relation to the initial identification. In this case, before trial, requests were made by the defence for photographs of the other Facebook pages that had been considered by victim and his sister so that the defendants could consider how their identifications might have been made.

2.7.4.14

KEYNOTE

Voice Identification

The Codes do not preclude the police making use of aural identification procedures such as a 'voice identification parade', where they judge that appropriate.

Generally, a witness may give evidence identifying the defendant's voice (*R* v *Robb* (1991) 93 Cr App R 161), while expert testimony may be admitted in relation to tape recordings of a voice which is alleged to belong to the defendant. In the latter case, the jury should be allowed to hear the recording(s) so that they can draw their own conclusions (*R* v *Bentum* (1989) 153 JP 538).

In *R* v *Flynn; R* v *St John* [2008] EWCA Crim 970, the Court of Appeal held that where the voice identification is from a recording a prerequisite for making a speaker identification was that there should be a sample of an adequate size from the disputed recording that could confidently be attributed to a single speaker. The court observed that identification of a suspect by voice recognition is more difficult than visual identification; identification by voice recognition is likely to be more reliable when carried out by experts rather than lay listener identification. An expert is able to draw up an overall profile of the individual's speech patterns. The lay listener's response is 'fundamentally opaque'.

The ability of a lay listener to correctly identify voices was subject to a number of variables, including the quality of the recording (if any) of the disputed voice or voices, the gap in time between the listener hearing the known voice and his/her attempt to recognise the voice, the ability of the individual lay witness listener to identify voices in general and the nature and duration of the speech which is sought to be identified. The greater the familiarity of the listener with a known voice, the better his/her chance of accurately identifying the disputed voice.

The court recognised that expert evidence showed that lay listeners with considerable familiarity with a voice and listening to a clear recording could still make mistakes. It is therefore suggested that other supporting evidence will be needed for a conviction to succeed.

Home Office Circular 57/2003, *Advice on the Use of Voice Identification Parades*, provides guidance on the use of voice identification parades.

2.7.4.15

KEYNOTE

Identification of Disqualified Drivers

Another common identification problem is that of disqualified drivers and being able to satisfy the court that the person charged with disqualified driving is the same person who was disqualified by the court. This is because s. 73 of the Police and Criminal Evidence Act 1984 requires proof that the person named in a certificate of conviction as having been convicted is the person whose conviction is to be proved. There has been some guidance from the courts as to how this can be achieved. In *R* v *Derwentside Justices, ex parte Heaviside* [1996] RTR 384, the court stated that this could be done by:

- fingerprints under s. 39 of the Criminal Justice Act 1948;
- the evidence of a person who was present in court when the disqualification order was made;
- admission of the defendant (preferably in interview) (*DPP* v *Mooney* (1997) RTR 434);
- requiring the suspect's solicitor who was present when he/she was disqualified on the earlier occasion to give evidence (such a summons is a last resort when there was no other means of identifying whether an individual had been disqualified from driving) (*R (On the Application of Howe) and Law Society (Interested Party)* v *South Durham Magistrates' Court and CPS (Interested Party)* [2004] EWHC 362 (Admin)).

The methods outlined in *Heaviside* are not exhaustive, but just suggested methods (*DPP* v *Mansfield* [1997] RTR 96).

2.7.4.16

Part (C) Recognition by *uncontrolled* viewing of films, photographs and images

3.38 This Part applies when, for the purpose of identifying and tracing suspects, films and photographs of incidents or other images are:

(a) shown to the public (which may include police officers and police staff as well as members of the public) through the national or local media or any social media networking site; or

(b) circulated through local or national police communication systems for viewing by police officers and police staff; and the viewing is not formally controlled and supervised as set out in Part B.

3.39 A copy of the relevant material released to the national or local media for showing as described in sub-paragraph 3.38(a), shall be kept. The suspect or their solicitor shall be allowed to view such material before any eye-witness identification procedure under *paragraphs 3.5* to *3.10, 3.21* or *3.23* of Part A are carried out, provided it is practicable and would not unreasonably delay the investigation. This paragraph does not affect any separate requirement under the Criminal Procedure and Investigations Act 1996 to retain material in connection with criminal investigations that might apply to *sub-paragraphs 3.38(a)* and *(b)*.

3.40 Each eye-witness involved in any eye-witness identification procedure under *paragraphs 3.5* to *3.10, 3.21* or *3.23* shall be asked, *after they have taken part*, whether they have seen any film, photograph or image relating to the offence or any description of the suspect which has been broadcast or published as described in *paragraph 3.38(a)* and their reply recorded. If they have, they should be asked to give details of the circumstances and subject to the eye-witness's recollection, the record described in *paragraph 3.41* should be completed.

3.41 As soon as practicable after an individual (member of the public, police officer or police staff) indicates in response to a viewing that they may have information relating to the identity and whereabouts of anyone they have seen in that viewing, arrangements should be made to ensure that they are asked to give details of the circumstances and, subject to the individual's recollection, a record of the circumstances and conditions under which the viewing took place is made. This record shall be made in accordance with the provisions of *paragraph 3.36* insofar as they can be applied to the viewing in question.

2.7.4.17

KEYNOTE

It is important that the record referred to in paras 3.36 and 3.41 is made as soon as practicable after the viewing and whilst it is fresh in the mind of the individual who makes the recognition.

2.7.5

Code D—4 Identification by Fingerprints and Footwear Impressions

(A) Taking fingerprints in connection with a criminal investigation

(a) General

4.1 References to 'fingerprints' means any record, produced by any method, of the skin pattern and other physical characteristics or features of a person's:

(i) fingers; or

(ii) palms.

(b) Action

4.2 A person's fingerprints may be taken in connection with the investigation of an offence only with their consent or if *paragraph 4.3* applies. If the person is at a police station consent must be in writing.

4.3 PACE, section 61, provides powers to take fingerprints without consent from any person aged ten or over as follows:

(a) under *section 61(3)*, from a person detained at a police station in consequence of being arrested for a recordable offence, if they have not had their fingerprints taken in the course of the investigation of the offence unless those previously taken fingerprints are not a complete set or some or all of those fingerprints are not of sufficient quality to allow satisfactory analysis, comparison or matching;

(b) under *section 61(4)*, from a person detained at a police station who has been charged with a recordable offence, or informed they will be reported for such an offence if they have not had their fingerprints taken in the course of the investigation of the offence unless those previously taken fingerprints are not a complete set or some or all of those fingerprints are not of sufficient quality to allow satisfactory analysis, comparison or matching.

(c) under *section 61(4A)*, from a person who has been bailed to appear at a court or police station if the person:

(i) has answered to bail for a person whose fingerprints were taken previously and there are reasonable grounds for believing they are not the same person; or

(ii) who has answered to bail claims to be a different person from a person whose fingerprints were previously taken;

and in either case, the court or an officer of inspector rank or above, authorises the fingerprints to be taken at the court or police station (an inspector's authority may be given in writing or orally and confirmed in writing as soon as practicable);

(ca) under *section 61(5A)* from a person who has been arrested for a recordable offence and released if the person:

(i) is on bail and has not had their fingerprints taken in the course of the investigation of the offence, or;

(ii) has had their fingerprints taken in the course of the investigation of the offence, but they do not constitute a complete set or some, or all, of the fingerprints are not of sufficient quality to allow satisfactory analysis, comparison or matching;

(cb) under *section 61(5B)* from a person not detained at a police station who has been charged with a recordable offence or informed they will be reported for such an offence if:

(i) they have not had their fingerprints taken in the course of the investigation; or

(ii) their fingerprints have been taken in the course of the investigation of the offence but either:

- they do not constitute a complete set or some, or all, of the fingerprints are not of sufficient quality to allow satisfactory analysis, comparison or matching; or
- the investigation was discontinued but subsequently resumed and, before the resumption, their fingerprints were destroyed pursuant to section 63D(3).

(d) under *section 61(6)*, from a person who has been:

(i) convicted of a recordable offence; or

(ii) given a caution in respect of a recordable offence which, at the time of the caution, the person admitted;

if, since being convicted or cautioned:

- their fingerprints have not been taken; or
- their fingerprints which have been taken do not constitute a complete set or some, or all, of the fingerprints are not of sufficient quality to allow satisfactory analysis, comparison or matching;

and in either case, an officer of inspector rank or above, is satisfied that taking the fingerprints is necessary to assist in the prevention or detection of crime and authorises the taking;

(e) under *section 61(6A)* from a person a constable reasonably suspects is committing or attempting to commit, or has committed or attempted to commit, any offence if either:
   (i) the person's name is unknown to, and cannot be readily ascertained by, the constable; or
   (ii) the constable has reasonable grounds for doubting whether a name given by the person is their real name.

   Note: fingerprints taken under this power are not regarded as having been taken in the course of the investigation of an offence.

(f) under *section 61(6D)* from a person who has been convicted outside England and Wales of an offence which if committed in England and Wales would be a qualifying offence as defined by PACE, section 65A if:
   (i) the person's fingerprints have not been taken previously under this power or their fingerprints have been so taken on a previous occasion but they do not constitute a complete set or some, or all, of the fingerprints are not of sufficient quality to allow satisfactory analysis, comparison or matching; and
   (ii) a police officer of inspector rank or above is satisfied that taking fingerprints is necessary to assist in the prevention or detection of crime and authorises them to be taken.

4.4 PACE, section 63A(4) and Schedule 2A provide powers to:

(a) make a requirement (in accordance with Annex G) for a person to attend a police station to have their fingerprints taken in the exercise of one of the following powers (described in *paragraph 4.3* above) within certain periods as follows:
   (i) *section 61(5A)*—Persons arrested for a recordable offence and released, see *paragraph 4.3(ca)*: In the case of a person whose fingerprints were taken in the course of the investigation but those fingerprints do not constitute a complete set or some, or all, of the fingerprints are not of sufficient quality, the requirement may not be made more than six months from the day the investigating officer was informed that the fingerprints previously taken were incomplete or below standard. In the case of a person whose fingerprints were destroyed prior to the resumption of the investigation, the requirement may not be made more than six months from the day on which the investigation resumed.
   (ii) *section 61(5B)*—Persons not detained at a police station charged etc. with a recordable offence, see *paragraph 4.3(cb)*: The requirement may not be made more than six months from:
      - the day the person was charged or informed that they would be reported, if fingerprints have not been taken in the course of the investigation of the offence; or
      - the day the investigating officer was informed that the fingerprints previously taken were incomplete or below standard, if fingerprints have been taken in the course of the investigation but those fingerprints do not constitute a complete set or some, or all, of the fingerprints are not of sufficient quality; or
      - the day on which the investigation was resumed, in the case of a person whose fingerprints were destroyed prior to the resumption of the investigation.
   (iii) *section 61(6)*—Person convicted or cautioned for a recordable offence in England and Wales, see *paragraph 4.3(d)*: Where the offence for which the person was convicted or cautioned is a qualifying offence, there is no time limit for the exercise of this power. Where the conviction or caution is for a recordable offence which is not a qualifying offence, the requirement may not be made more than two years from:
      - in the case of a person who has not had their fingerprints taken since the conviction or caution, the day on which the person was convicted or cautioned, or, if later, the day on which Schedule 2A came into force (March 7, 2011); or

- in the case of a person whose fingerprints have been taken in the course of the investigation but those fingerprints do not constitute a complete set or some, or all, of the fingerprints are not of sufficient quality, the day on which an officer from the force investigating the offence was informed that the fingerprints previously taken were incomplete or below standard, or, if later, the day on which Schedule 2A came into force (March 7, 2011).

(iv) *section 61(6D)*—A person who has been convicted of a qualifying offence outside England and Wales, see *paragraph 4.3(g)*: There is no time limit for making the requirement.

Note: A person who has had their fingerprints taken under any of the powers in section 61 mentioned in *paragraph 4.3* on two occasions in relation to any offence may not be required under Schedule 2A to attend a police station for their fingerprints to be taken again under section 61 in relation to that offence, unless authorised by an officer of inspector rank or above. The fact of the authorisation and the reasons for giving it must be recorded as soon as practicable.

(b) arrest, without warrant, a person who fails to comply with the requirement.

4.5 A person's fingerprints may be taken, as above, electronically.

4.6 Reasonable force may be used, if necessary, to take a person's fingerprints without their consent under the powers as in *paragraphs 4.3* and *4.4*.

4.7 Before any fingerprints are taken:

(a) without consent under any power mentioned in *paragraphs 4.3* and *4.4* above, the person must be informed of:

(i) the reason their fingerprints are to be taken;

(ii) the power under which they are to be taken; and

(iii) the fact that the relevant authority has been given if any power mentioned in *paragraph 4.3(c), (d)* or *(f)* applies

(b) with or without consent at a police station or elsewhere, the person must be informed:

(i) that their fingerprints may be subject of a speculative search against other fingerprints, and

(ii) that their fingerprints may be retained in accordance with *Annex F, Part (a)* unless they were taken under the power mentioned in paragraph 4.3(e) when they must be destroyed after they have being checked.

(c) Documentation

4.8A A record must be made as soon as practicable after the fingerprints are taken, of:

- the matters in paragraph 4.7(a)(i) to (iii) and the fact that the person has been informed of those matters; and
- the fact that the person has been informed of the matters in paragraph 4.7(b)(i) and (ii).

The record must be made in the person's custody record if they are detained at a police station when the fingerprints are taken.

4.8 If force is used, a record shall be made of the circumstances and those present.

4.9 *Not used*

2.7.5.1

KEYNOTE

The power under s. 61(6A) of the 1984 Act described in para. 4.3(e) allows fingerprints of a suspect who has not been arrested to be taken in connection with any offence (whether recordable or not) using a mobile device and then checked on the street against the database containing the national fingerprint collection. Fingerprints taken under this power cannot be retained after they have been checked. The results may make an arrest for the suspected offence based on the name condition unnecessary (see Code G, para. 2.9(a)) and enable the offence to be disposed of without arrest, e.g. by summons/charging by post, penalty notice or words of advice. If arrest for a non-recordable offence is necessary for any other reasons, this power may also be exercised at the station. Before the power is exercised, the officer should:

- inform the person of the nature of the suspected offence and why he/she is suspected of committing it;
- give the person a reasonable opportunity to establish his/her real name before deciding that his/her name is unknown and cannot be readily ascertained or that there are reasonable grounds to doubt that a name that he/she has given is his/her real name;
- as applicable, inform the person of the reason why his/her name is not known and cannot be readily ascertained or of the grounds for doubting that a name he/she has given is his/her real name, including, for example, the reason why a particular document the person has produced to verify his/her real name is not sufficient.

Speculative Search

Paragraph 4.7(b) makes reference to a 'speculative search'. Fingerprints, footwear impressions or a DNA sample (and the information derived from it) taken from a person arrested on suspicion of being involved in a recordable offence, or charged with such an offence, or informed they will be reported for such an offence, may be the subject of a speculative search. This means that the fingerprints, footwear impressions or DNA sample may be checked against other fingerprints, footwear impressions and DNA records held by, or on behalf of, the police and other law enforcement authorities in, or outside, the United Kingdom, or held in connection with, or as a result of, an investigation of an offence inside or outside the United Kingdom. Fingerprints, footwear impressions and samples taken from a person suspected of committing a recordable offence but not arrested, charged or informed that he/she will be reported for it, may be subject to a speculative search only if the person consents in writing. The following is an example of a basic form of words:

> I consent to my fingerprints/DNA sample and information derived from it being retained and used only for purposes related to the prevention and detection of a crime, the investigation of an offence or the conduct of a prosecution either nationally or internationally.
>
> I understand that this sample may be checked against other fingerprint/DNA records held by or on behalf of relevant law enforcement authorities, either nationally or internationally.
>
> I understand that once I have given my consent for the sample to be retained and used I cannot withdraw this consent.

2.7.5.2

4.10 *Not used*

4.11 *Not used*

4.12 *Not used*

4.13 *Not used*

4.14 *Not used*

4.15 *Not used*

2.7.5.3

(C) Taking footwear impressions in connection with a criminal investigation

(a) Action

4.16 Impressions of a person's footwear may be taken in connection with the investigation of an offence only with their consent or if *paragraph 4.17* applies. If the person is at a police station consent must be in writing.

4.17 PACE, section 61A, provides power for a police officer to take footwear impressions without consent from any person over the age of ten years who is detained at a police station:

(a) in consequence of being arrested for a recordable offence; or if the detainee has been charged with a recordable offence, or informed they will be reported for such an offence; and

(b) the detainee has not had an impression of their footwear taken in the course of the investigation of the offence unless the previously taken impression is not complete or is not of sufficient quality to allow satisfactory analysis, comparison or matching (whether in the case in question or generally).

4.18 Reasonable force may be used, if necessary, to take a footwear impression from a detainee without consent under the power in *paragraph 4.17*.

4.19 Before any footwear impression is taken with, or without, consent as above, the person must be informed:

(a) of the reason the impression is to be taken;

(b) that the impression may be retained and may be subject of a speculative search against other impressions, unless destruction of the impression is required in accordance with *Annex F, Part B*.

(b) Documentation

4.20 A record must be made as soon as possible, of the reason for taking a person's footwear impressions without consent. If force is used, a record shall be made of the circumstances and those present.

4.21 A record shall be made when a person has been informed under the terms of *paragraph 4.19(b)*, of the possibility that their footwear impressions may be subject of a speculative search.

2.7.5.4

KEYNOTE

Recordable Offences

References to 'recordable offences' in this Code relate to those offences for which convictions, cautions, reprimands and warnings may be recorded in national police records. See the Police and Criminal Evidence Act 1984, s. 27(4). The recordable offences current at the time when this Code was prepared are any offences which carry a sentence of imprisonment on conviction (irrespective of the period, or the age of the offender or actual sentence passed) as well as the non-imprisonable offences under the Vagrancy Act 1824, ss. 3 and 4 (begging and persistent begging), the Street Offences Act 1959, s. 1 (loitering or soliciting for purposes of prostitution), the Road Traffic Act 1988, s. 25 (tampering with motor vehicles), the Criminal Justice and Public Order Act 1994, s. 167 (touting for hire car services) and others listed in the National Police Records (Recordable Offences) Regulations 2000 (SI 2000/1139), as amended.

Qualifying Offences

A qualifying offence is one of the offences specified in PACE, s. 65A. These include offences which involve the use or threat of violence or unlawful force against persons, sexual offences, offences against children and other offences, for example:

- murder, false imprisonment, kidnapping contrary to common law;
- manslaughter, conspiracy to murder, threats to kill, wounding with intent to cause grievous bodily harm (GBH), causing GBH and assault occasioning actual bodily harm contrary to the Offences Against the Person Act 1861;
- criminal possession or use of firearms contrary to ss. 16 to 18 of the Firearms Act 1968;
- robbery, burglary and aggravated burglary contrary to ss. 8, 9 or 10 of the Theft Act 1968 or an offence under s. 12A of that Act involving an accident which caused a person's death;
- criminal damage required to be charged as arson contrary to s. 1 of the Criminal Damage Act 1971;
- taking, possessing and showing indecent photographs of children contrary to s. 1 of the Protection of Children Act 1978;
- rape, sexual assault, child sex offences, exposure and other offences contrary to the Sexual Offences Act 2003.

It should be noted that this list is not exhaustive.

Whether fingerprint evidence is admissible as evidence tending to prove guilt, depends on:

- the experience and expertise of the witness: this requires at least three years' experience;

- the number of similar ridge characteristics (if there are fewer than eight ridge characteristics matching the fingerprints of the accused with those found by the police, it is unlikely that a judge would exercise his/her discretion to admit such evidence);
- whether there are dissimilar characteristics;
- the size of print relied on; and
- the quality and clarity of print relied on.

The jury should be warned that expert evidence is not conclusive in itself and that guilt has to be proved in the light of all evidence (*R* v *Buckley* [1999] EWCA Crim 1191).

2.7.5.5 **KEYNOTE**

Power to Require Persons to Attend a Police Station to Provide Samples

Code D, Annex G deals with the requirement for a person to attend a police station for fingerprints and samples.

2.7.5.6 **KEYNOTE**

Retention of Fingerprints

Code D, Annex F deals with the destruction and the speculative searches of fingerprints and samples and speculative searches of footwear impressions, see para. 2.7.13.

2.7.5.7 **KEYNOTE**

Criminal Record and Conviction Certificates

Under s. 118 of the Police Act 1997, in certain circumstances the Secretary of State issues certificates concerning an individual's previous convictions. In some cases, the Secretary of State will not do this until it has been possible to verify the person's identity, which can be done through the taking of his/her fingerprints. Where this is the case, the Secretary of State may require the police officer in charge of the specified police station, or any other police station the Secretary of State reasonably determines, to take the applicant's fingerprints at the specified station at such reasonable time as the officer may direct and notify the applicant.

If fingerprints are taken in these circumstances they must be destroyed as soon as is practicable after the identity of the applicant is established to the satisfaction of the Secretary of State. The destruction can be witnessed by the person giving the fingerprints if he/she requests and/or the person can ask for a certificate stating that the fingerprints have been destroyed. The certificate must be issued within three months of the request.

In the case of an individual under the age of 18 years the consent of the applicant's parent or guardian to the taking of the applicant's fingerprints is also required.

2.7.5.8 **KEYNOTE**

Other Body Prints

While the more established and convincing body marks are fingerprints it is possible for other body prints to be used as evidence to identify a suspect. In *R* v *Kempster* [2008] EWCA Crim 975, the police recovered an ear print from the fixed window pane to the side of the window that had been forced in order to gain entry to the property. In this case, the conviction was not successful, but it was recognised that an ear print comparison was capable of providing information that could identify a person who had left an ear print on a surface. This would only be achieved with certainty where the minutiae of the ear structure could be identified and matched.

The Judicial College publication *The Crown Court Compendium* states that ear print comparison suffers a disadvantage in common with facial mapping. While there is general agreement among experts that no two ears are the same, it is virtually impossible to obtain an ear impression which contains all relevant features of the ear. The crime scene impression is also likely to have been subject to variations in pressure and to at least minute movement, either of which will affect the reliability of the detail left. The scope for a significant number of reliable features for comparison is therefore limited and even if there is a match between them, there is no means of assessing the statistical probability that the crime scene impression was left by someone other than the defendant.

Fingerprints etc. and non-intimate samples may be taken from an arrested or detained person with the authority of an officer of a rank no lower than inspector.

2.7.6 Code D—5 Examinations to Establish Identity and the Taking of Photographs

(A) Detainees at police stations

(a) Searching or examination of detainees at police stations

5.1 PACE, section 54A(1), allows a detainee at a police station to be searched or examined or both, to establish:

(a) whether they have any marks, features or injuries that would tend to identify them as a person involved in the commission of an offence and to photograph any identifying marks, *see paragraph 5.5*; or

(b) their identity.

A person detained at a police station to be searched under a stop and search power, see Code A, is not a detainee for the purposes of these powers.

5.2 A search and/or examination to find marks under section 54A(1)(a) may be carried out without the detainee's consent, see *paragraph 2.12*, only if authorised by an officer of at least inspector rank when consent has been withheld or it is not practicable to obtain consent.

5.3 A search or examination to establish a suspect's identity under section 54A(1)(b) may be carried out without the detainee's consent, see *paragraph 2.12*, only if authorised by an officer of at least inspector rank when the detainee has refused to identify themselves or the authorising officer has reasonable grounds for suspecting the person is not who they claim to be.

5.4 Any marks that assist in establishing the detainee's identity, or their identification as a person involved in the commission of an offence, are identifying marks. Such marks may be photographed with the detainee's consent, see *paragraph 2.12*; or without their consent if it is withheld or it is not practicable to obtain it.

5.5 A detainee may only be searched, examined and photographed under section 54A, by a police officer of the same sex.

5.6 Any photographs of identifying marks, taken under section 54A, may be used or disclosed only for purposes related to the prevention or detection of crime, the investigation of offences or the conduct of prosecutions by, or on behalf of, police or other law enforcement and prosecuting authorities inside, and outside, the UK. After being so used or disclosed, the photograph may be retained but must not be used or disclosed except for these purposes.

5.7 The powers, as in *paragraph 5.1*, do not affect any separate requirement under the Criminal Procedure and Investigations Act 1996 to retain material in connection with criminal investigations.

5.8 Authority for the search and/or examination for the purposes of *paragraphs 5.2* and *5.3* may be given orally or in writing. If given orally, the authorising officer must confirm it in writing as soon as practicable. A separate authority is required for each purpose which applies.

5.9 If it is established a person is unwilling to co-operate sufficiently to enable a search and/or examination to take place or a suitable photograph to be taken, an officer may use reasonable force to:

(a) search and/or examine a detainee without their consent; and

(b) photograph any identifying marks without their consent.

5.10 The thoroughness and extent of any search or examination carried out in accordance with the powers in section 54A must be no more than the officer considers necessary to achieve the required purpose. Any search or examination which involves the removal of more than the person's outer clothing shall be conducted in accordance with Code C, Annex A, paragraph 11.

5.11 An intimate search may not be carried out under the powers in section 54A.

(b) Photographing detainees at police stations and other persons elsewhere than at a police station

5.12 Under PACE, section 64A, an officer may photograph:

(a) any person whilst they are detained at a police station; and

(b) any person who is elsewhere than at a police station and who has been:

(i) arrested by a constable for an offence;

(ii) taken into custody by a constable after being arrested for an offence by a person other than a constable;

(iii) made subject to a requirement to wait with a community support officer under paragraph 2(3) or (3B) of Schedule 4 to the Police Reform Act 2002;

(iiia) given a direction by a constable under section 27 of the Violent Crime Reduction Act 2006.

(iv) given a penalty notice by a constable in uniform under Chapter 1 of Part 1 of the Criminal Justice and Police Act 2001, a penalty notice by a constable under section 444A of the Education Act 1996, or a fixed penalty notice by a constable in uniform under section 54 of the Road Traffic Offenders Act 1988;

(v) given a notice in relation to a relevant fixed penalty offence (within the meaning of paragraph 1 of Schedule 4 to the Police Reform Act 2002) by a community support officer by virtue of a designation applying that paragraph to him;

(vi) given a notice in relation to a relevant fixed penalty offence (within the meaning of paragraph 1 of Schedule 5 to the Police Reform Act 2002) by an accredited person by virtue of accreditation specifying that that paragraph applies to him; or

(vii) given a direction to leave and not return to a specified location for up to 48 hours by a police constable (under section 27 of the Violent Crime Reduction Act 2006).

5.12A Photographs taken under PACE, section 64A:

(a) may be taken with the person's consent, or without their consent if consent is withheld or it is not practicable to obtain their consent, and

(b) may be used or disclosed only for purposes related to the prevention or detection of crime, the investigation of offences or the conduct of prosecutions by, or on behalf of, police or other law enforcement and prosecuting authorities inside and outside the United Kingdom or the enforcement of any sentence or order made by a court when dealing with an offence. After being so used or disclosed, they may be retained but can only be used or disclosed for the same purposes.

5.13 The officer proposing to take a detainee's photograph may, for this purpose, require the person to remove any item or substance worn on, or over, all, or any part of, their head or face. If they do not comply with such a requirement, the officer may remove the item or substance.

5.14 If it is established the detainee is unwilling to co-operate sufficiently to enable a suitable photograph to be taken and it is not reasonably practicable to take the photograph covertly, an officer may use reasonable force.

(a) to take their photograph without their consent; and

(b) for the purpose of taking the photograph, remove any item or substance worn on, or over, all, or any part of, the person's head or face which they have failed to remove when asked.

5.15 For the purposes of this Code, a photograph may be obtained without the person's consent by making a copy of an image of them taken at any time on a camera system installed anywhere in the police station.

(c) Information to be given

5.16 When a person is searched, examined or photographed under the provisions as in *paragraph 5.1* and *5.12*, or their photograph obtained as in *paragraph 5.15*, they must be informed of the:

(a) purpose of the search, examination or photograph;

(b) grounds on which the relevant authority, if applicable, has been given; and

(c) purposes for which the photograph may be used, disclosed or retained. This information must be given before the search or examination commences or the photograph is taken, except if the photograph is:

(i) to be taken covertly;

(ii) obtained as in *paragraph 5.15*, in which case the person must be informed as soon as practicable after the photograph is taken or obtained.

(d) Documentation

5.17 A record must be made when a detainee is searched, examined, or a photograph of the person, or any identifying marks found on them, are taken. The record must include the:

(a) identity, subject to *paragraph 2.18*, of the officer carrying out the search, examination or taking the photograph;

(b) purpose of the search, examination or photograph and the outcome;

(c) detainee's consent to the search, examination or photograph, or the reason the person was searched, examined or photographed without consent;

(d) giving of any authority as in *paragraphs 5.2* and *5.3*, the grounds for giving it and the authorising officer.

5.18 If force is used when searching, examining or taking a photograph in accordance with this section, a record shall be made of the circumstances and those present.

(B) Persons at police stations not detained

5.19 When there are reasonable grounds for suspecting the involvement of a person in a criminal offence, but that person is at a police station **voluntarily** and not detained, the provisions of *paragraphs 5.1* to *5.18* should apply, subject to the modifications in the following paragraphs.

5.20 References to the 'person being detained' and to the powers mentioned in *paragraph 5.1* which apply only to detainees at police stations shall be omitted.

5.21 Force may not be used to:

(a) search and/or examine the person to:

(i) discover whether they have any marks that would tend to identify them as a person involved in the commission of an offence; or

(ii) establish their identity,

(b) take photographs of any identifying marks, see *paragraph 5.4*; or

(c) take a photograph of the person.

5.22 Subject to *paragraph 5.24*, the photographs of persons or of their identifying marks which are not taken in accordance with the provisions mentioned in *paragraphs 5.1* or *5.12*, must be destroyed (together with any negatives and copies) unless the person:

(a) is charged with, or informed they may be prosecuted for, a recordable offence;

(b) is prosecuted for a recordable offence;

(c) is cautioned for a recordable offence or given a warning or reprimand in accordance with the Crime and Disorder Act 1998 for a recordable offence; or

(d) gives informed consent, in writing, for the photograph or image to be retained as in *paragraph 5.6*.

5.23 When *paragraph 5.22* requires the destruction of any photograph, the person must be given an opportunity to witness the destruction or to have a certificate confirming the destruction provided they so request the certificate within five days of being informed the destruction is required.

5.24 Nothing in *paragraph 5.22* affects any separate requirement under the Criminal Procedure and Investigations Act 1996 to retain material in connection with criminal investigations.

2.7.6.1 **KEYNOTE**

The Police, Crime, Sentencing and Courts Act 2022 amended s 64A PACE but PACE Code D has, at the time of printing, not yet been updated to reflect these amendments.

Where the current Code does not already allow for a person to be photographed then they may be photographed at a police station without the appropriate consent if that person has been:

(a) arrested for a recordable offence and released;

(b) charged with a recordable offence; or

(c) informed that they will be reported for such an offence;

(d) convicted of a recordable offence; or

(e) given a caution in respect of a recordable offence which, at the time of the caution, they have admitted;

(f) if under the law in force in a country or territory outside England and Wales, the person has been convicted of an offence under that law (whether before or after the coming into force of this subsection and whether or not they have been punished for it);

(g) if the act constituting the offence would constitute a qualifying offence if done in England and Wales (whether or not it constituted such an offence when the person was convicted;

and that, where applicable, the person has not been photographed in the course of the investigation of the offence by the police or that the person has not been photographed since being convicted or cautioned, or that the person has been so photographed but any photograph taken on such a previous occasion is unavailable or inadequate, and a constable considers that taking a further photograph is necessary to assist in the prevention or detection of crime.

In relation to (d) to (g), the power to take the photograph requires the authorisation of an officer of at least the rank of inspector.

The time limits for making a requirement vary depending on whether the matter is pre or post-conviction and also whether a photograph has been previously taken. The conditions under which fingerprints may be taken to assist in establishing a person's identity, are described in s. 4.

A photograph taken under s. 54A of the Police and Criminal Evidence Act 1984 may be used by, or disclosed to, any person for any purpose related to the prevention or detection of crime, the investigation of an offence or the conduct of a prosecution. The use of the photograph is for any conduct which constitutes a criminal offence (whether under UK law or in another country). Examples of purposes related to the prevention or detection of crime, the investigation of offences or the conduct of prosecutions include:

- checking the photograph against other photographs held in records or in connection with, or as a result of, an investigation of an offence to establish whether the person is liable to arrest for other offences;
- when the person is arrested at the same time as other people, or at a time when it is likely that other people will be arrested, using the photograph to help establish who was arrested, at what time and where;
- when the real identity of the person is not known and cannot be readily ascertained or there are reasonable grounds for doubting that a name and other personal details given by the person are his/her real

name and personal details. In these circumstances, using or disclosing the photograph to help to establish or verify the person's real identity or determine whether he/she is liable to arrest for some other offence, e.g. by checking it against other photographs held in records or in connection with, or as a result of, an investigation of an offence;

- when it appears that any identification procedure in s. 3 may need to be arranged for which the person's photograph would assist;
- when the person's release without charge may be required, and if the release is:
  - (i) on bail to appear at a police station, using the photograph to help verify the person's identity when he/she answers bail and if the person does not answer bail, to assist in arresting him/her; or
  - (ii) without bail, using the photograph to help verify the person's identity or assist in locating him/her for the purposes of serving him/her with a summons to appear at court in criminal proceedings;
- when the person has answered to bail at a police station and there are reasonable grounds for doubting that he/she is the person who was previously granted bail, using the photograph to help establish or verify his/her identity;
- when the person has been charged with, reported for, or convicted of, a recordable offence and his/her photograph is not already on record as a result of any of the circumstances set out in the bullet points above or his/her photograph is on record but his/her appearance has changed since it was taken and the person has not yet been released or brought before a court;
- when the person arrested on a warrant claims to be a different person from the person named on the warrant and a photograph would help to confirm or disprove this claim.

Looking at paras 5.2 and 5.4, examples of when it would not be practicable to obtain a detainee's consent for the examination of, or the taking of a photograph of, an identifying mark include:

- when the person is drunk or otherwise unfit to give consent;
- when there are reasonable grounds to suspect that if the person became aware that a search or examination was to take place or an identifying mark was to be photographed, he/she would take steps to prevent this happening, e.g. by violently resisting, covering or concealing the mark, etc., and it would not otherwise be possible to carry out the search or examination or to photograph any identifying mark;
- in the case of a juvenile, if the parent or guardian cannot be contacted in sufficient time to allow the search or examination to be carried out or the photograph to be taken.

Looking at para. 5.12A, examples of when it would not be practicable to obtain the person's consent to a photograph being taken include:

- when the person is drunk or otherwise unfit to give consent;
- when there are reasonable grounds to suspect that if the person became aware that a photograph suitable to be used or disclosed for the use and disclosure described in para. 5.6 was to be taken, he/she would take steps to prevent it being taken, e.g. by violently resisting, covering or distorting his/her face, etc., and it would not otherwise be possible to take a suitable photograph;
- when, in order to obtain a suitable photograph, it is necessary to take it covertly; and
- in the case of a juvenile, if the parent or guardian cannot be contacted in sufficient time to allow the photograph to be taken.

There is no power to arrest a person convicted of a recordable offence solely to take his/her photograph. The power to take photographs in this section applies only where the person is in custody as a result of the exercise of another power, e.g. arrest for fingerprinting under PACE, sch. 2A, para. 17

The use of reasonable force to take the photograph of a suspect elsewhere than at a police station must be carefully considered. In order to obtain a suspect's consent and co-operation to remove an item of religious headwear to take his/her photograph, a constable should consider whether in the circumstances of the situation the removal of the headwear and the taking of the photograph should be by an officer of the same sex as the person. It would be appropriate for these actions to be conducted out of public view.

2.7.7 ## Code D—6 Identification by Body Samples and Impressions

(A) General

6.1 References to:

(a) an 'intimate sample' mean a dental impression or sample of blood, semen or any other tissue fluid, urine, or pubic hair, or a swab taken from any part of a person's genitals or from a person's body orifice other than the mouth;

(b) a 'non-intimate sample' means:

(i) a sample of hair, other than pubic hair, which includes hair plucked with the root;

(ii) a sample taken from a nail or from under a nail;

(iii) a swab taken from any part of a person's body other than a part from which a swab taken would be an intimate sample;

(iv) saliva;

(v) a skin impression which means any record, other than a fingerprint, which is a record, in any form and produced by any method, of the skin pattern and other physical characteristics or features of the whole, or any part of, a person's foot or of any other part of their body.

2.7.7.1 **KEYNOTE**

Intimate and Non-intimate Samples—General

The analysis of intimate and non-intimate samples may provide essential evidence in showing or refuting a person's involvement in an offence. However, the courts have made it clear that DNA evidence alone will not be sufficient for a conviction and that there needs to be supporting evidence to link the suspect to the crime.

The purpose behind the taking of many samples is to enable the process of DNA profiling. Very basically, this involves an analysis of the sample taken from the suspect (the first sample), an analysis of samples taken from the crime scene or victim (the second sample) and then a comparison of the two. Both the process and the conclusions which might be drawn from the results are set out by Lord Taylor CJ in *R* v *Deen* (1994) *The Times*, 10 January.

The matching process involves creating 'bands' from each sample and then comparing the number of those bands which the two samples share. The more 'matches' that exist between the first and second samples, the less probability there is of that happening by pure chance. A 'good match' between the two samples does not of itself prove that the second sample came from the defendant. In using such samples to prove identification, the prosecution will give evidence of:

- the probability of such a match happening by chance; and
- the likelihood that the person responsible was in fact the defendant.

While DNA evidence is often portrayed in the media as conclusive evidence of guilt, the question for the courts remains 'How reliable is this piece of evidence in proving or disproving the person's involvement in the offence?'

In most cases there will be other evidence against the defendant which clearly increases the likelihood of his/her having committed the offence. Such evidence may include confessions, or may show that the suspect was near the crime scene at the time of the offence or that the suspect lived in the locality or had connections in the area.

It will be for the prosecution to produce other facts to the court which reduce the 'chance' of the DNA sample belonging to someone other than the defendant. This may require further inquiries linking the suspect to the area or circumstances of the crime or may come from questions put to the suspect during interview. In *R* v *Lashley* (2000) 25 February, unreported, the sole evidence against the defendant for a robbery was DNA evidence from a half-smoked cigarette found behind the counter of the post office. The DNA matched a sample obtained from the suspect and would have matched the profile of seven to 10 other males in the United Kingdom. The court held that the significance of DNA evidence depended critically upon what else was known about the suspect. Had there been evidence that the suspect was in the area, or normally lived there, or had connections there, at the material time, then the jury could have found that the case was compelling. This, the court said, would be because it may have been almost incredible that two out of seven men in the United Kingdom were in the vicinity at the relevant time.

In *R* v *Gabriel and Others* [2020] EWCA Crim 998, the three defendants were monozygotic triplets whose DNA was indistinguishable as between each other. The court held that the Crown's case was not and could not be founded solely on the DNA evidence. It was in its fundamentals founded on mobile phone and cell-site evidence, with the DNA evidence being advanced as capable of supporting the case on which it was based.

The courts are willing to allow the jury to consider partial or incomplete DNA profiles in some circumstances. In *R* v *Bates* [2006] EWCA Crim 1395, DNA evidence at the scene produced a partial profile that was interpreted as providing a 1 in 610,000 probability that Bates was the killer. The Court of Appeal held that there was no reason why partial-profile DNA evidence should not be admissible provided that the jury were made aware of its inherent limitations and were given a sufficient explanation to enable them to evaluate it.

If there is a decision to charge on partial DNA profile basis of such a match, the supporting evidence needs to be all the stronger. The amount of supporting evidence required will depend on the value of the DNA evidence in the context of the case. A scientist should be consulted where the value of the DNA evidence requires clarification.

While it is still the case that other evidence to support a DNA profile should be found, the case of *R* v *FNC* [2015] EWCA Crim 1732 held that where DNA is directly deposited in the course of the commission of a crime by the offender, a very high DNA match with the defendant is sufficient to raise a case for the defendant to answer. There was a clear distinction between DNA deposited on an article left at the scene and a case where there could be no doubt that the DNA was deposited in the course of the commission of the offence by the person who committed it. In this case, the allegation was that the semen on the back of the complainant's trousers was consistent with the defendant ejaculating on to the complainant's trousers as alleged.

R v *Tsekiri* [2017] EWCA Crim 40 was a case where the DNA of a suspect of a robbery was found on the external door handle of the car belonging to the victim. The suspect gave a no comment interview, the DNA therefore being the main evidence in the case. The court identified relevant matters when deciding if the DNA was sufficient evidence to convict on. These matters being:

- Is there any evidence of some other explanation for the presence of the defendant's DNA on the item other than involvement in the crime?
- Was the article apparently associated with the offence itself? The position could be different if the article was not necessarily so connected with the offence, e.g. if a DNA profile were to be found on a cigarette stub discarded at the scene of a street robbery.
- How readily movable is the article in question? A DNA profile on a small article of clothing or something such as a cigarette end at the scene of a crime might be of less probative force than the same profile on a vehicle.
- Is there evidence of some geographical association between the offence and the offender?
- In the case of a mixed profile, is the DNA profile which matches the defendant the major contributor to the overall DNA profile?
- Is it more or less likely that the DNA profile attributable to the defendant was deposited by primary or secondary transfer?

This is not an exhaustive list and each case will depend on its own facts.

These points may need to be considered when preparing questions for an interview with the suspect.

It is also important to ensure that there is no cross-contamination of DNA evidence between crime scenes, victims and suspects, as was seen in the infamous American case of OJ Simpson's murder trial. It will be important to ensure that any allegations that officers may have contaminated evidence through handling/being present at several crime scenes can be successfully challenged. It is suggested that the best evidence here will be through records of crime scene logs and, where suspects have been or are being held in custody, records of who visited the custody suite. It will also be important that suspects and victims are kept apart.

The integrity and continuity of DNA samples will be important evidence and likely to be challenged by the defence if not managed properly.

Speculative searches may be carried out of the National DNA Database and a suspect may now be charged on the basis of a match between a profile from DNA from the scene of the crime and a profile on the National DNA Database from an individual, so long as there is further supporting evidence (Home Office Circular 58/2004, *Charges on Basis of Speculative Search Match on the National DNA Database*).

It should also be noted that the databases can also now be used for the purpose of identifying a deceased person or a person from whom a body part came (Serious Organised Crime and Police Act 2005, s. 117(7) amending s. 64 of the 1984 Act).

An insufficient sample is one which is not sufficient either in quantity or quality to provide information for a particular form of analysis, such as DNA analysis. A sample may also be insufficient if enough information cannot be obtained from it by analysis because of loss, destruction, damage or contamination of the sample or as a result of an earlier, unsuccessful attempt at analysis. An unsuitable sample is one which, by its nature, is not suitable for a particular form of analysis.

2.7.7.2

(B) Action

(a) Intimate samples

6.2 PACE, section 62, provides that intimate samples may be taken under:

(a) section 62(1), from a person in police detention only:

(i) if a police officer of inspector rank or above has reasonable grounds to believe such an impression or sample will tend to confirm or disprove the suspect's involvement in a recordable offence, and gives authorisation for a sample to be taken; and

(ii) with the suspect's written consent;

(b) section 62(1A), from a person not in police detention but from whom two or more non-intimate samples have been taken in the course of an investigation of an offence and the samples, though suitable, have proved insufficient if:

(i) a police officer of inspector rank or above authorises it to be taken; and

(ii) the person concerned gives their written consent.

(c) section 62(2A), from a person convicted outside England and Wales of an offence which if committed in England and Wales would be qualifying offence as defined by PACE, section 65A from whom two or more non-intimate samples taken under section 63(3E) (see *paragraph 6.6(h)* have proved insufficient if:

(i) a police officer of inspector rank or above is satisfied that taking the sample is necessary to assist in the prevention or detection of crime and authorises it to be taken; and

(ii) the person concerned gives their written consent.

6.2A PACE, section 63A(4) and Schedule 2A provide powers to:

(a) make a requirement (in accordance with Annex G) for a person to attend a police station to have an intimate sample taken in the exercise of one of the following powers (see *paragraph 6.2*):

(i) *section 62(1A)*—Persons from whom two or more non-intimate samples have been taken and proved to be insufficient, see *paragraph 6.2(b)*: There is no time limit for making the requirement.

(ii) *section 62(2A)*—Persons convicted outside England and Wales from whom two or more non-intimate samples taken under section 63(3E) (see *paragraph 6.6(g)* have proved insufficient, see *paragraph 6.2(c)*: There is no time limit for making the requirement.

(b) arrest without warrant a person who fails to comply with the requirement

6.3 Before a suspect is asked to provide an intimate sample, they must be:

(a) informed:

(i) of the reason, including the nature of the suspected offence (except if taken under paragraph 6.2(c) from a person convicted outside England and Wales.

(ii) that authorisation has been given and the provisions under which given;

(iii) that a sample taken at a police station may be subject of a speculative search;

(b) warned that if they refuse without good cause their refusal may harm their case if it comes to trial. If the suspect is in police detention and not legally represented, they must also be reminded of their entitlement to have free legal advice, see Code C, *paragraph 6.5*, and the reminder noted in the custody record. If *paragraph 6.2(b)* applies and the person is attending a station voluntarily, their entitlement to free legal advice as in Code C, *paragraph 3.21* shall be explained to them.

6.4 Dental impressions may only be taken by a registered dentist. Other intimate samples, except for samples of urine, may only be taken by a registered medical practitioner or registered nurse or registered paramedic.

2.7.7.3

KEYNOTE

Intimate Samples

Taking a sample without the relevant authority may amount to inhuman or degrading treatment under Article 3 of the European Convention on Human Rights. It may also amount to a criminal offence of assault (see *Crime*, **chapter 1.9**) and give rise to liability at civil law.

For recordable offences and qualifying offences, **see para. 2.7.5.4, Keynote.**

Nothing in para. 6.2 prevents intimate samples being taken for elimination purposes with the consent of the person concerned, but the provisions of para. 2.12, relating to the role of the appropriate adult, should be applied. Paragraph 6.2(b) does not, however, apply where the non-intimate samples were previously taken under the Terrorism Act 2000, sch. 8, para. 10.

In warning a person who is asked to provide an intimate sample, the following form of words may be used:

> You do not have to provide this sample/allow this swab or impression to be taken, but I must warn you that if you refuse without good cause, your refusal may harm your case if it comes to trial.

2.7.7.4

(b) Non-intimate samples

6.5 A non-intimate sample may be taken from a detainee only with their written consent or if *paragraph 6.6* applies.

6.6 A non-intimate sample may be taken from a person without the appropriate consent in the following circumstances:

(a) under *section 63(2A)* from a person who is in police detention as a consequence of being arrested for a recordable offence and who has not had a non-intimate sample of the same type and from the same part of the body taken in the course of the investigation of the offence by the police or they have had such a sample taken but it proved insufficient.

(b) Under *section 63(3)* from a person who is being held in custody by the police on the authority of a court if an officer of at least the rank of inspector authorises it to be taken. An authorisation may be given:

(i) if the authorising officer has reasonable grounds for suspecting the person of involvement in a recordable offence and for believing that the sample will tend to confirm or disprove that involvement, and

(ii) in writing or orally and confirmed in writing, as soon as practicable; but an authorisation may not be given to take from the same part of the body a further non-intimate sample consisting of a skin impression unless the previously taken impression proved insufficient

(c) under *section 63(3ZA)* from a person who has been arrested for a recordable offence and released if:

  (i) [in the case of a person who is on bail,] they have not had a sample of the same type and from the same part of the body taken in the course of the investigation of the offence, or;

  (ii) [in any case,] the person has had such a sample taken in the course of the investigation of the offence, but either:

  - it was not suitable or proved insufficient; or
  - the investigation was discontinued but subsequently resumed and before the resumption, any DNA profile derived from the sample was destroyed and the sample itself was destroyed pursuant to section 63R(4), (5) or (12).

(d) under *section 63(3A)*, from a person (whether or not in police detention or held in custody by the police on the authority of a court) who has been charged with a recordable offence or informed they will be reported for such an offence if the person:

  (i) has not had a non-intimate sample taken from them in the course of the investigation of the offence; or

  (ii) has had a sample so taken, but it was not suitable or proved insufficient, or

  (iii) has had a sample taken in the course of the investigation of the offence and the sample has been destroyed and in proceedings relating to that offence there is a dispute as to whether a DNA profile relevant to the proceedings was derived from the destroyed sample.

(e) under *section 63(3B)*, from a person who has been:

  (i) convicted of a recordable offence; or

  (ii) given a caution in respect of a recordable offence which, at the time of the caution, the person admitted;

  if, since their conviction or caution a non-intimate sample has not been taken from them or a sample which has been taken since then was not suitable or proved insufficient and in either case, an officer of inspector rank or above, is satisfied that taking the fingerprints is necessary to assist in the prevention or detection of crime and authorises the taking;

(f) under *section 63(3C)* from a person to whom section 2 of the Criminal Evidence (Amendment) Act 1997 applies (persons detained following acquittal on grounds of insanity or finding of unfitness to plead).

(g) under *section 63(3E)* from a person who has been convicted outside England and Wales of an offence which if committed in England and Wales would be a qualifying offence as defined by PACE, section 65A if:

  (i) a non-intimate sample has not been taken previously under this power or unless a sample was so taken but was not suitable or proved insufficient; and

  (ii) a police officer of inspector rank or above is satisfied that taking a sample is necessary to assist in the prevention or detection of crime and authorises it to be taken.

6.6A PACE, *section 63A(4)* and *Schedule 2A* provide powers to:

(a) make a requirement (in accordance with Annex G) for a person to attend a police station to have a non-intimate sample taken in the exercise of one of the following powers (see *paragraph 6.6* above) within certain time limits as follows:

  (i) *section 63(3ZA)*—Persons arrested for a recordable offence and released, see paragraph 6.6(c): In the case of a person from whom a non-intimate sample was taken in the course of the investigation but that sample was not suitable or proved insufficient, the requirement may not be made more than six months from the day the investigating officer was informed that the sample previously taken was not suitable or proved insufficient. In the case of a person whose DNA profile and sample was destroyed prior to the resumption of the investigation, the requirement may not be made more than six months from the day on which the investigation resumed.

(ii) *section 63(3A)*—Persons charged etc. with a recordable offence, see paragraph 6.6(d): The requirement may not be made more than six months from:

- the day the person was charged or informed that they would be reported, if a sample has not been taken in the course of the investigation;
- the day the investigating officer was informed that the sample previously taken was not suitable or proved insufficient, if a sample has been taken in the course of the investigation but the sample was not suitable or proved insufficient; or
- the day on which the investigation was resumed, in the case of a person whose DNA profile and sample were destroyed prior to the resumption of the investigation.

(iii) *section 63(3B)*—Person convicted or cautioned for a recordable offence in England and Wales, see paragraph 6.6(e): Where the offence for which the person was convicted etc. is also a qualifying offence, there is no time limit for the exercise of this power. Where the conviction etc. was for a recordable offence that is not a qualifying offence, the requirement may not be made more than two years from:

- in the case of a person whose sample has not been taken since they were convicted or cautioned, the day the person was convicted or cautioned, or, if later. the day Schedule 2A came into force (March 7 2011); or
- in the case of a person whose sample has been taken but was not suitable or proved insufficient, the day an officer from the force investigating the offence was informed that the sample previously taken was not suitable or proved insufficient or, if later, the day Schedule 2A came into force (March 7 2011).

(iv) *section 63(3E)*—A person who has been convicted of qualifying offence outside England and Wales, see *paragraph 6.6(h)*: There is no time limit for making the requirement.

Note: A person who has had a non-intimate sample taken under any of the powers in section 63 mentioned in paragraph 6.6 on two occasions in relation to any offence may not be required under Schedule 2A to attend a police station for a sample to be taken again under section 63 in relation to that offence, unless authorised by an officer of inspector rank or above. The fact of the authorisation and the reasons for giving it must be recorded as soon as practicable.

(b) arrest, without warrant, a person who fails to comply with the requirement.

6.7 Reasonable force may be used, if necessary, to take a non-intimate sample from a person without their consent under the powers mentioned in *paragraph 6.6*.

6.8 Before any non-intimate sample is taken:

(a) without consent under any power mentioned in *paragraphs 6.6* and *6.6A*, the person must be informed of:

(i) the reason for taking the sample;

(ii) the power under which the sample is to be taken;

(iii) the fact that the relevant authority has been given if any power mentioned in *paragraph 6.6(b), (e)* or *(g)* applies, including the nature of the suspected offence (except if taken under *paragraph 6.6(e)* from a person convicted or cautioned, or under *paragraph 6.6(g)* if taken from a person convicted outside England and Wales;

(b) with or without consent at a police station or elsewhere, the person must be informed:

(i) that their sample or information derived from it may be subject of a speculative search against other samples and information derived from them and

(ii) that their sample and the information derived from it may be retained in accordance with Annex F, Part (a).

(c) Removal of clothing

6.9 When clothing needs to be removed in circumstances likely to cause embarrassment to the person, no person of the opposite sex who is not a registered medical practitioner or registered health care professional shall be present, (unless in the case of a juvenile, mentally disordered or mentally vulnerable person, that person specifically requests the presence of an appropriate adult of the opposite sex who is readily available) nor shall anyone whose presence is unnecessary. However, in the case of a juvenile, this is subject to the overriding proviso that such a removal of clothing may take place in the absence of the appropriate adult only if the juvenile signifies in their presence, that they prefer the adult's absence and they agree.

(c) Documentation

6.10 A record must be made as soon as practicable after the sample is taken of:

- The matters in *paragraph 6.8(a)(i)* to *(iii)* and the fact that the person has been informed of those matters; and
- The fact that the person has been informed of the matters in paragraph 6.8(b)(i) and (ii).

6.10A If force is used, a record shall be made of the circumstances and those present.

6.11 A record must be made of a warning given as required by *paragraph 6.3*.

6.12 *Not used.*

2.7.7.5

KEYNOTE

Taking a Non-intimate Sample

Where a non-intimate sample consisting of a skin impression is taken electronically from a person, it must be taken only in such manner, and using such devices, as the Secretary of State has approved for the purpose of the electronic taking of such an impression (s. 63(9A) of PACE). No such devices are currently approved.

When hair samples are taken for the purpose of DNA analysis (rather than for other purposes, such as making a visual match), the suspect should be permitted a reasonable choice as to what part of the body the hairs are taken from. When hairs are plucked, they should be plucked individually, unless the suspect prefers otherwise and no more should be plucked than the person taking them reasonably considers necessary for a sufficient sample.

Fingerprints, footwear impressions or a DNA sample (and the information derived from it) taken from a person arrested on suspicion of being involved in a recordable offence, or charged with such an offence, or informed they will be reported for such an offence, may be the subject of a speculative search. This means the fingerprints, footwear impressions or DNA sample may be checked against other fingerprints, footwear impressions and DNA records held by, or on behalf of, the police and other law enforcement authorities in, or outside, the United Kingdom, or held in connection with, or as a result of, an investigation of an offence inside or outside the United Kingdom. See Annex F regarding the retention and use of fingerprints and samples taken with consent for elimination purposes.

Urine and non-intimate samples and the information derived from testing detained persons for the presence of specified Class A drugs, may not be subsequently used in the investigation of any offence or in evidence against the persons from whom they were taken.

2.7.7.6

KEYNOTE

Power to Require Persons to Attend a Police Station to Provide Samples

Code D, Annex G deals with the requirement for a person to attend a police station for fingerprints and samples.

2.7.7.7

> **KEYNOTE**
>
> **Destruction of Samples**
>
> Code D, Annex F deals with the destruction and the speculative searches of fingerprints and samples and speculative searches of footwear impressions. It is important that the Annex is followed, particularly in relation to obtaining consent and explaining to volunteers what they are consenting to.

2.7.8

Code D—Annex A: Video Identification

(a) General

1. The arrangements for obtaining and ensuring the availability of a suitable set of images to be used in a video identification must be the responsibility of an identification officer (see *paragraph 3.11* of this Code) who has no direct involvement with the case.
2. The set of images must include the suspect and at least eight other people who, so far as possible, and subject to *paragraph 7*, resemble the suspect in age, general appearance and position in life. Only one suspect shall appear in any set unless there are two suspects of roughly similar appearance, in which case they may be shown together with at least twelve other people.

2A. If the suspect has an unusual physical feature, e.g., a facial scar, tattoo or distinctive hairstyle or hair colour which does not appear on the images of the other people that are available to be used, steps may be taken to:

(a) conceal the location of the feature on the images of the suspect and the other people; or

(b) replicate that feature on the images of the other people.

For these purposes, the feature may be concealed or replicated electronically or by any other method which it is practicable to use to ensure that the images of the suspect and other people resemble each other. The identification officer has discretion to choose whether to conceal or replicate the feature and the method to be used.

2B. If the identification officer decides that a feature should be concealed or replicated, the reason for the decision and whether the feature was concealed or replicated in the images shown to any eye-witness shall be recorded.

2C. If the eye-witness requests to view any image where an unusual physical feature has been concealed or replicated without the feature being concealed or replicated, the identification officer has discretion to allow the eye-witness to view such image(s) if they are available.

3. The images used to conduct a video identification shall, as far as possible, show the suspect and other people in the same positions or carrying out the same sequence of movements. They shall also show the suspect and other people under identical conditions unless the identification officer reasonably believes:
   (a) because of the suspect's failure or refusal to co-operate or other reasons, it is not practicable for the conditions to be identical; and
   (b) any difference in the conditions would not direct an eye-witness' attention to any individual image.
4. The reasons identical conditions are not practicable shall be recorded on forms provided for the purpose.
5. Provision must be made for each person shown to be identified by number.
6. If police officers are shown, any numerals or other identifying badges must be concealed. If a prison inmate is shown, either as a suspect or not, then either all, or none of, the people shown should be in prison clothing.
7. The suspect or their solicitor, friend, or appropriate adult must be given a reasonable opportunity to see the complete set of images before it is shown to any eye-witness. If the suspect has a reasonable objection to the set of images or any of the participants, the suspect shall

be asked to state the reasons for the objection. Steps shall, if practicable, be taken to remove the grounds for objection. If this is not practicable, the suspect and/or their representative shall be told why their objections cannot be met and the objection, the reason given for it and why it cannot be met shall be recorded on forms provided for the purpose. The requirement in *paragraph 2* that the images of the other people 'resemble' the suspect does not require the images to be identical or extremely similar.

8. Before the images are shown in accordance with *paragraph 7*, the suspect or their solicitor shall be provided with details of the first description of the suspect by any eye-witnesses who are to attend the video identification. When a broadcast or publication is made, as in *paragraph 3.38(a)*, the suspect or their solicitor must also be allowed to view any material released to the media by the police for the purpose of recognising or tracing the suspect, provided it is practicable and would not unreasonably delay the investigation.
9. No unauthorised people may be present when the video identification is conducted. The suspect's solicitor, if practicable, shall be given reasonable notification of the time and place the video identification is to be conducted. The suspect's solicitor may only be present at the video identification on request and with the prior agreement of the identification officer, if the officer is satisfied that the solicitor's presence will not deter or distract any eye-witness from viewing the images and making an identification. If the identification officer is not satisfied and does not agree to the request, the reason must be recorded. The solicitor must be informed of the decision and the reason for it. and that they may then make representations about why they should be allowed to be present. The representations may be made orally or in writing, in person or remotely by electronic communication and must be recorded. These representations must be considered by an officer of at least the rank of inspector who is not involved with the investigation and responsibility for this may not be delegated under *paragraph 3.11*. If, after considering the representations, the officer is satisfied that the solicitor's presence will deter or distract the eye-witness, the officer shall inform the solicitor of the decision and reason for it and ensure that any response by the solicitor is also recorded. If allowed to be present, the solicitor is not entitled to communicate in any way with an eye-witness during the procedure but this does not prevent the solicitor from communicating with the identification officer. The suspect may not be present when the images are shown to any eye-witness and is not entitled to be informed of the time and place the video identification procedure is to be conducted. The video identification procedure itself shall be recorded on video with sound. The recording must show all persons present within the sight or hearing of the eye-witness whilst the images are being viewed and must include what the eye-witness says and what is said to them by the identification officer and by any other person present at the video identification procedure. A supervised viewing of the recording of the video identification procedure by the suspect and/or their solicitor may be arranged on request, at the discretion of the investigating officer. Where the recording of the video identification procedure is to be shown to the suspect and/or their solicitor, the investigating officer may arrange for anything in the recording that might allow the eye-witness to be identified to be concealed if the investigating officer considers that this is justified. In accordance with *paragraph 2.18*, the investigating officer may also arrange for anything in that recording that might allow any police officers or police staff to be identified to be concealed.

(b) Conducting the video identification

10. The identification officer is responsible for making the appropriate arrangements to make sure, before they see the set of images, eye-witnesses are not able to communicate with each other about the case, see any of the images which are to be shown, see, or be reminded of, any photograph or description of the suspect or be given any other indication as to the suspect's identity, or overhear an eye-witness who has already seen the material. There must

be no discussion with the eye-witness about the composition of the set of images and they must not be told whether a previous eye-witness has made any identification.

11. Only one eye-witness may see the set of images at a time. Immediately before the images are shown, the eye-witness shall be told that the person they saw on a specified earlier occasion may, or may not, appear in the images they are shown and that if they cannot make an identification, they should say so. The eye-witness shall be advised that at any point, they may ask to see a particular part of the set of images or to have a particular image frozen for them to study. Furthermore, it should be pointed out to the eye-witness that there is no limit on how many times they can view the whole set of images or any part of them. However, they should be asked not to make any decision as to whether the person they saw is on the set of images until they have seen the whole set at least twice.
12. Once the eye-witness has seen the whole set of images at least twice and has indicated that they do not want to view the images, or any part of them, again, the eye-witness shall be asked to say whether the individual they saw in person on a specified earlier occasion has been shown and, if so, to identify them by number of the image. The eye-witness will then be shown that image to confirm the identification, see *paragraph 17.*
13. Care must be taken not to direct the eye-witness' attention to any one individual image or give any indication of the suspect's identity. Where an eye-witness has previously made an identification by photographs, or a computerised or artist's composite or similar likeness, they must not be reminded of such a photograph or composite likeness once a suspect is available for identification by other means in accordance with this Code. Nor must the eye-witness be reminded of any description of the suspect.

13A. If after the video identification procedure has ended, the eye-witness informs any police officer or police staff involved in the post-viewing arrangements that they wish to change their decision about their identification, or they have not made an identification when in fact they could have made one, an accurate record of the words used by the eye-witness and of the circumstances immediately after the procedure ended, shall be made. If the eye-witness has not had an opportunity to communicate with other people about the procedure, the identification officer has the discretion to allow the eye-witness a second opportunity to make an identification by repeating the video identification procedure using the same images but in different positions.

14. After the procedure, action required in accordance with *paragraph 3.40* applies.

(c) Image security and destruction

15. Arrangements shall be made for all relevant material containing sets of images used for specific identification procedures to be kept securely and their movements accounted for. In particular, no-one involved in the investigation shall be permitted to view the material prior to it being shown to any witness.
16. As appropriate, *paragraph 3.30* or *3.31* applies to the destruction or retention of relevant sets of images.

(d) Documentation

17. A record must be made of all those participating in, or seeing, the set of images whose names are known to the police.
18. A record of the conduct of the video identification must be made on forms provided for the purpose. This shall include anything said by the witness about any identifications or the conduct of the procedure and any reasons it was not practicable to comply with any of the provisions of this Code governing the conduct of video identifications. This record is in addition to any statement that is taken from any eye-witness after the procedure.

2.7.8.1 **KEYNOTE**

Annex A Video Identification

The purpose of the video identification is to test the eye-witness's ability to distinguish the suspect from others and it would not be a fair test if all the images shown were identical or extremely similar to each other. The identification officer is responsible for ensuring that the images shown are suitable for the purpose of this test. *R* v *Day* [2019] EWCA Crim 935 provides an example of this responsibility. In this case, the victim was attacked by a man whom she did not know as she was crossing an isolated footbridge between two villages. She described her attacker to police as being aged in his mid-40s, 5ft 10ins tall, of medium build, with a bald head and a scab above his right eye. She said that she would remember him again due to his scab and also due to the impact the incident had had upon her. A video identification procedure was held. The suspect was wearing spectacles when he attended the police station. Video clips of the suspect were of him both with and without spectacles, and had used the clip in which he was not wearing spectacles. The reason for this was that it would have been virtually impossible to find in the database images of a sufficient number of men wearing glasses who sufficiently resembled the appellant. Neither the suspect nor anyone else whose image was used in the procedure was bald, the images chosen were as close as possible a match to the appearance of the suspect. The defence appealed against the video identification. The court held that the Code of Practice in relation to video identification requires that the images chosen to be shown with the image of the suspect must, so far as possible, resemble the suspect in age, general appearance and position in life. The first responsibility of the identification officer is to assemble images which as closely as possible resemble the suspect. Provided this is done, it is then permissible for the identification officer to arrange for the imagery either to include or not to include some non-permanent feature of clothing or accessories in order as closely as possible to match the description of the offender. Given that the victim described her attacker as not wearing glasses, it was correct to use images which showed the appellant and others not wearing glasses.

The purpose of allowing the identity of the eye-witness to be concealed is to protect them in cases when there is information that suspects or their associates may threaten the witness or cause them harm or when the investigating officer considers that special measures may be required to protect their identity during the criminal process.

2.7.9 Code D—Annex B: Identification Parades

(a) General

1. A suspect must be given a reasonable opportunity to have a solicitor or friend present, and the suspect shall be asked to indicate on a second copy of the notice whether or not they wish to do so.
2. An identification parade may take place either in a normal room or one equipped with a screen permitting witnesses to see members of the identification parade without being seen. The procedures for the composition and conduct of the identification parade are the same in both cases, subject to *paragraph 8* (except that an identification parade involving a screen may take place only when the suspect's solicitor, friend or appropriate adult is present or the identification parade is recorded on video).
3. Before the identification parade takes place, the suspect or their solicitor shall be provided with details of the first description of the suspect by any witnesses who are attending the identification parade. When a broadcast or publication is made as in *paragraph 3.38(a)*, the suspect or their solicitor should also be allowed to view any material released to the media by the police for the purpose of identifying and tracing the suspect, provided it is practicable to do so and would not unreasonably delay the investigation.

(b) Identification parades involving prison inmates

4. If a prison inmate is required for identification, and there are no security problems about the person leaving the establishment, they may be asked to participate in an identification parade or video identification.
5. An identification parade may be held in a Prison Department establishment but shall be conducted, as far as practicable under normal identification parade rules. Members of the public shall make up the identification parade unless there are serious security, or control, objections to their admission to the establishment. In such cases, or if a group or video identification is arranged within the establishment, other inmates may participate. If an inmate is the suspect, they are not required to wear prison clothing for the identification parade unless the other people taking part are other inmates in similar clothing, or are members of the public who are prepared to wear prison clothing for the occasion.

(c) Conduct of the identification parade

6. Immediately before the identification parade, the suspect must be reminded of the procedures governing its conduct and cautioned in the terms of Code C, paragraphs 10.5 or 10.6, as appropriate.
7. All unauthorised people must be excluded from the place where the identification parade is held.
8. Once the identification parade has been formed, everything afterwards, in respect of it, shall take place in the presence and hearing of the suspect and any interpreter, solicitor, friend or appropriate adult who is present (unless the identification parade involves a screen, in which case everything said to, or by, any witness at the place where the identification parade is held, must be said in the hearing and presence of the suspect's solicitor, friend or appropriate adult or be recorded on video).
9. The identification parade shall consist of at least eight people (in addition to the suspect) who, so far as possible, resemble the suspect in age, height, general appearance and position in life. Only one suspect shall be included in an identification parade unless there are two suspects of roughly similar appearance, in which case they may be paraded together with at least twelve other people. In no circumstances shall more than two suspects be included in one identification parade and where there are separate identification parades, they shall be made up of different people.
10. If the suspect has an unusual physical feature, e.g., a facial scar, tattoo or distinctive hairstyle or hair colour which cannot be replicated on other members of the identification parade, steps may be taken to conceal the location of that feature on the suspect and the other members of the identification parade if the suspect and their solicitor, or appropriate adult, agree. For example, by use of a plaster or a hat, so that all members of the identification parade resemble each other in general appearance.
11. When all members of a similar group are possible suspects, separate identification parades shall be held for each unless there are two suspects of similar appearance when they may appear on the same identification parade with at least twelve other members of the group who are not suspects. When police officers in uniform form an identification parade any numerals or other identifying badges shall be concealed.
12. When the suspect is brought to the place where the identification parade is to be held, they shall be asked if they have any objection to the arrangements for the identification parade or to any of the other participants in it and to state the reasons for the objection. The suspect may obtain advice from their solicitor or friend, if present, before the identification parade proceeds. If the suspect has a reasonable objection to the arrangements or any of the participants, steps shall, if practicable, be taken to remove the grounds for objection. When it is not practicable to do so, the suspect shall be told why their objections cannot be

met and the objection, the reason given for it and why it cannot be met, shall be recorded on forms provided for the purpose.

13. The suspect may select their own position in the line, but may not otherwise interfere with the order of the people forming the line. When there is more than one witness, the suspect must be told, after each witness has left the room, that they can, if they wish, change position in the line. Each position in the line must be clearly numbered, whether by means of a number laid on the floor in front of each identification parade member or by other means.

14. Appropriate arrangements must be made to make sure, before witnesses attend the identification parade, they are not able to:
   (i) communicate with each other about the case or overhear a witness who has already seen the identification parade;
   (ii) see any member of the identification parade;
   (iii) see, or be reminded of, any photograph or description of the suspect or be given any other indication as to the suspect's identity; or
   (iv) see the suspect before or after the identification parade.

15. The person conducting a witness to an identification parade must not discuss with them the composition of the identification parade and, in particular, must not disclose whether a previous witness has made any identification.

16. Witnesses shall be brought in one at a time. Immediately before the witness inspects the identification parade, they shall be told the person they saw on a specified earlier occasion may, or may not, be present and if they cannot make an identification, they should say so. The witness must also be told they should not make any decision about whether the person they saw is on the identification parade until they have looked at each member at least twice.

17. When the officer or police staff (see *paragraph 3.11*) conducting the identification procedure is satisfied the witness has properly looked at each member of the identification parade, they shall ask the witness whether the person they saw on a specified earlier occasion is on the identification parade and, if so, to indicate the number of the person concerned, see *paragraph 28*.

18. If the witness wishes to hear any identification parade member speak, adopt any specified posture or move, they shall first be asked whether they can identify any person(s) on the identification parade on the basis of appearance only. When the request is to hear members of the identification parade speak, the witness shall be reminded that the participants in the identification parade have been chosen on the basis of physical appearance only. Members of the identification parade may then be asked to comply with the witness' request to hear them speak, see them move or adopt any specified posture.

19. If the witness requests that the person they have indicated remove anything used for the purposes of *paragraph 10* to conceal the location of an unusual physical feature, that person may be asked to remove it.

20. If the witness makes an identification after the identification parade has ended, the suspect and, if present, their solicitor, interpreter or friend shall be informed. When this occurs, consideration should be given to allowing the witness a second opportunity to identify the suspect.

21. After the procedure, action required in accordance with *paragraph 3.40* applies.

22. When the last witness has left, the suspect shall be asked whether they wish to make any comments on the conduct of the identification parade.

(d) Documentation

23. A video recording must normally be taken of the identification parade. If that is impracticable, a colour photograph must be taken. A copy of the video recording or photograph shall be supplied, on request, to the suspect or their solicitor within a reasonable time.

24. As appropriate, *paragraph 3.30* or *3.31*, should apply to any photograph or video taken as in *paragraph 23*.
25. If any person is asked to leave an identification parade because they are interfering with its conduct, the circumstances shall be recorded.
26. A record must be made of all those present at an identification parade whose names are known to the police.
27. If prison inmates make up an identification parade, the circumstances must be recorded.
28. A record of the conduct of any identification parade must be made on forms provided for the purpose. This shall include anything said by the witness or the suspect about any identifications or the conduct of the procedure, and any reasons it was not practicable to comply with any of this Code's provisions.

2.7.9.1 **KEYNOTE**

Conduct of Identification Parades

Identification evidence can be crucial to the success of a prosecution. There are clear guidelines that must be followed. Where such guidelines are not followed it is likely that the defence will argue strongly to have the identification evidence excluded. In *R* v *Jones* (1999) *The Times*, 21 April, identification evidence was excluded as the officers told the suspect that if he did not comply with the procedure, force would be used against him.

Annexes A to F of Code D set out in detail the procedures and requirements which must be followed in conducting identification procedures.

Although the courts are aware of the many practical difficulties involved in organising and running identification procedures (see e.g. *R* v *Jamel* [1993] Crim LR 52), any flaws in the procedure will be considered in the light of their potential impact on the defendant's trial. Serious or deliberate breaches (such as the showing of photographs to witnesses before the parade), will invariably lead to any evidence so gained being excluded (*R* v *Finley* [1993] Crim LR 50). The key question for the court will be whether the breach of the Codes is likely to have made the identification less reliable. Things may not always go according to plan, for instance in *Abdullah, Pululu* v *R* [2019] EWCA Crim 1137, two victims were attacked and robbed by a group of men. One of the victims attended an identification procedure and, although he was aware that only one suspect was on the procedure, he in fact picked out two men. Even though the victim had been told he could only pick out one person, he picked out two because they looked like each other. Whilst this is not ideal, the Court of Appeal held that the victim's video identification evidence was correctly admitted as potentially probative and its weaknesses were properly identified in the Turnbull direction.

Breaches which appear to impact on the safeguards imposed by Annexes A–F to separate the functions of investigation and identification (e.g. where the investigating officer becomes involved with the running of the parade in a way which allows him/her to talk to the witnesses (*R* v *Gall* (1990) 90 Cr App R 64)) will also be treated seriously by the court.

The case of *R* v *Marrin* [2002] EWCA Crim 251, provides some guidance as to methods that could be used to get a suitable pool of participants for an identification parade. The court held that there was nothing inherently unfair or objectionable in some colouring or dye being used on the facial stubble of some volunteers to make them look more like the suspect. However, care needed to be taken with such measures because the procedure would be undermined if it was obvious to the witness that make-up had been used. Another point raised was that it may sometimes be appropriate for those on parade to wear hats, but if possible the wearing of hats should be avoided if hats had not been worn during the offence because this would make it more difficult for a witness to make an identification. However, there could be circumstances where the wearing of hats could help to achieve a resemblance and might be desirable to minimise differences. Finally, an identification of a suspect was not invalidated by the witness's request for the removal of a hat. There was nothing unfair in that taking place and there was no breach of any Code either.

It is important to follow the guidance in the Codes regardless of what agreement is obtained from the suspect or his/her solicitor. In *R* v *Hutton* [1999] Crim LR 74, at the suggestion of the suspect's solicitor, all the participants in the identification parade wore back-to-front baseball caps and had the lower part of their faces obscured by material. That identification was the only evidence against the defendant on that count. The court excluded the evidence and did not accept the fact that the decision had been agreed by the defence.

It will be essential that any photographs, photofits or other such material is stored securely in a manner that restricts access so as to be able to demonstrate to the court that the material cannot have been viewed by any of the witnesses and that copies have not been made that have not been accounted for. Where a witness attending an identification procedure has previously been shown photographs, or been shown or provided with computerised or artist's composite likenesses, or similar likenesses or pictures, it is the officer in charge of the investigation's responsibility to make the identification officer aware of this.

2.7.10

Code D—Annex C: Group Identification

(a) General

1. The purpose of this Annex is to make sure, as far as possible, group identifications follow the principles and procedures for identification parades so the conditions are fair to the suspect in the way they test the witness' ability to make an identification.
2. Group identifications may take place either with the suspect's consent and co-operation or covertly without their consent.
3. The location of the group identification is a matter for the identification officer, although the officer may take into account any representations made by the suspect, appropriate adult, their solicitor or friend.
4. The place where the group identification is held should be one where other people are either passing by or waiting around informally, in groups such that the suspect is able to join them and be capable of being seen by the witness at the same time as others in the group. For example people leaving an escalator, pedestrians walking through a shopping centre, passengers on railway and bus stations, waiting in queues or groups or where people are standing or sitting in groups in other public places.
5. If the group identification is to be held covertly, the choice of locations will be limited by the places where the suspect can be found and the number of other people present at that time. In these cases, suitable locations might be along regular routes travelled by the suspect, including buses or trains or public places frequented by the suspect.
6. Although the number, age, sex, race and general description and style of clothing of other people present at the location cannot be controlled by the identification officer, in selecting the location the officer must consider the general appearance and numbers of people likely to be present. In particular, the officer must reasonably expect that over the period the witness observes the group, they will be able to see, from time to time, a number of others whose appearance is broadly similar to that of the suspect.
7. A group identification need not be held if the identification officer believes, because of the unusual appearance of the suspect, none of the locations it would be practicable to use, satisfy the requirements of *paragraph 6* necessary to make the identification fair.
8. Immediately after a group identification procedure has taken place (with or without the suspect's consent), a colour photograph or video should be taken of the general scene, if practicable, to give a general impression of the scene and the number of people present. Alternatively, if it is practicable, the group identification may be video recorded.
9. If it is not practicable to take the photograph or video in accordance with *paragraph 8*, a photograph or film of the scene should be taken later at a time determined by the identification officer if the officer considers it practicable to do so.
10. An identification carried out in accordance with this Code remains a group identification even though, at the time of being seen by the witness, the suspect was on their own rather than in a group.

11. Before the group identification takes place, the suspect or their solicitor shall be provided with details of the first description of the suspect by any witnesses who are to attend the identification. When a broadcast or publication is made, as *in paragraph 3.38(a)*, the suspect or their solicitor should also be allowed to view any material released by the police to the media for the purposes of identifying and tracing the suspect, provided that it is practicable and would not unreasonably delay the investigation.
12. After the procedure, action required in accordance with *paragraph 3.40* applies.

(b) Identification with the consent of the suspect

13. A suspect must be given a reasonable opportunity to have a solicitor or friend present. They shall be asked to indicate on a second copy of the notice whether or not they wish to do so.
14. The witness, the person carrying out the procedure and the suspect's solicitor, appropriate adult, friend or any interpreter for the witness, may be concealed from the sight of the individuals in the group they are observing, if the person carrying out the procedure considers this assists the conduct of the identification.
15. The person conducting a witness to a group identification must not discuss with them the forthcoming group identification and, in particular, must not disclose whether a previous witness has made any identification.
16. Anything said to, or by, the witness during the procedure about the identification should be said in the presence and hearing of those present at the procedure.
17. Appropriate arrangements must be made to make sure, before witnesses attend the group identification, they are not able to:
    (i) communicate with each other about the case or overhear a witness who has already been given an opportunity to see the suspect in the group;
    (ii) see the suspect; or
    (iii) see, or be reminded of, any photographs or description of the suspect or be given any other indication of the suspect's identity.
18. Witnesses shall be brought one at a time to the place where they are to observe the group. Immediately before the witness is asked to look at the group, the person conducting the procedure shall tell them that the person they saw on a specified earlier occasion may, or may not, be in the group and that if they cannot make an identification, they should say so. The witness shall be asked to observe the group in which the suspect is to appear. The way in which the witness should do this will depend on whether the group is moving or stationary.

Moving group

19. When the group in which the suspect is to appear is moving, e.g. leaving an escalator, the provisions of *paragraphs 20* to *24* should be followed.
20. If two or more suspects consent to a group identification, each should be the subject of separate identification procedures. These may be conducted consecutively on the same occasion.
21. The person conducting the procedure shall tell the witness to observe the group and ask them to point out any person they think they saw on the specified earlier occasion.
22. Once the witness has been informed as in *paragraph 21* the suspect should be allowed to take whatever position in the group they wish.
23. When the witness points out a person as in *paragraph 21* they shall, if practicable, be asked to take a closer look at the person to confirm the identification. If this is not practicable, or they cannot confirm the identification, they shall be asked how sure they are that the person they have indicated is the relevant person.
24. The witness should continue to observe the group for the period which the person conducting the procedure reasonably believes is necessary in the circumstances for them to be able to make comparisons between the suspect and other individuals of broadly similar appearance to the suspect as in *paragraph 6*.

Stationary groups

25. When the group in which the suspect is to appear is stationary, e.g. people waiting in a queue, the provisions of *paragraphs 26* to *29* should be followed.
26. If two or more suspects consent to a group identification, each should be subject to separate identification procedures unless they are of broadly similar appearance when they may appear in the same group. When separate group identifications are held, the groups must be made up of different people.
27. The suspect may take whatever position in the group they wish. If there is more than one witness, the suspect must be told, out of the sight and hearing of any witness, that they can, if they wish, change their position in the group.
28. The witness shall be asked to pass along, or amongst, the group and to look at each person in the group at least twice, taking as much care and time as possible according to the circumstances, before making an identification. Once the witness has done this, they shall be asked whether the person they saw on the specified earlier occasion is in the group and to indicate any such person by whatever means the person conducting the procedure considers appropriate in the circumstances. If this is not practicable, the witness shall be asked to point out any person they think they saw on the earlier occasion.
29. When the witness makes an indication as in *paragraph 28*, arrangements shall be made, if practicable, for the witness to take a closer look at the person to confirm the identification. If this is not practicable, or the witness is unable to confirm the identification, they shall be asked how sure they are that the person they have indicated is the relevant person.

All cases

30. If the suspect unreasonably delays joining the group, or having joined the group, deliberately conceals themselves from the sight of the witness, this may be treated as a refusal to co-operate in a group identification.
31. If the witness identifies a person other than the suspect, that person should be informed what has happened and asked if they are prepared to give their name and address. There is no obligation upon any member of the public to give these details. There shall be no duty to record any details of any other member of the public present in the group or at the place where the procedure is conducted.
32. When the group identification has been completed, the suspect shall be asked whether they wish to make any comments on the conduct of the procedure.
33. If the suspect has not been previously informed, they shall be told of any identifications made by the witnesses.

(c) Group Identification without the suspect's consent

34. Group identifications held covertly without the suspect's consent should, as far as practicable, follow the rules for conduct of group identification by consent.
35. A suspect has no right to have a solicitor, appropriate adult or friend present as the identification will take place without the knowledge of the suspect.
36. Any number of suspects may be identified at the same time.

(d) Identifications in police stations

37. Group identifications should only take place in police stations for reasons of safety, security or because it is not practicable to hold them elsewhere.
38. The group identification may take place either in a room equipped with a screen permitting witnesses to see members of the group without being seen, or anywhere else in the police station that the identification officer considers appropriate.

39. Any of the additional safeguards applicable to identification parades should be followed if the identification officer considers it is practicable to do so in the circumstances.

(e) Identifications involving prison inmates

40. A group identification involving a prison inmate may only be arranged in the prison or at a police station.
41. When a group identification takes place involving a prison inmate, whether in a prison or in a police station, the arrangements should follow those in *paragraphs 37* to *39*. If a group identification takes place within a prison, other inmates may participate. If an inmate is the suspect, they do not have to wear prison clothing for the group identification unless the other participants are wearing the same clothing.

(f) Documentation

42. When a photograph or video is taken as in *paragraph 8* or *9*, a copy of the photograph or video shall be supplied on request to the suspect or their solicitor within a reasonable time.
43. *Paragraph 3.30* or *3.31*, as appropriate, shall apply when the photograph or film taken in accordance with *paragraph 8* or *9* includes the suspect.
44. A record of the conduct of any group identification must be made on forms provided for the purpose. This shall include anything said by the witness or suspect about any identifications or the conduct of the procedure and any reasons why it was not practicable to comply with any of the provisions of this Code governing the conduct of group identifications.

2.7.11 Code D—Annex D: Confrontation by an Eye-witness

1. Before the confrontation takes place, the eye-witness must be told that the person they saw on a specified earlier occasion may, or may not, be the person they are to confront and that if they are not that person, then the witness should say so.
2. Before the confrontation takes place the suspect or their solicitor shall be provided with details of the first description of the suspect given by any eye-witness who is to attend. When a broadcast or publication is made, as in *paragraph 3.38(a)*, the suspect or their solicitor should also be allowed to view any material released to the media for the purposes of recognising or tracing the suspect, provided it is practicable to do so and would not unreasonably delay the investigation.
3. Force may not be used to make the suspect's face visible to the eye-witness.
4. Confrontation must take place in the presence of the suspect's solicitor, interpreter or friend unless this would cause unreasonable delay.
5. The suspect shall be confronted independently by each eye-witness, who shall be asked 'Is this the person?'. If the eye-witness identifies the person but is unable to confirm the identification, they shall be asked how sure they are that the person is the one they saw on the earlier occasion.
6. The confrontation should normally take place in the police station, either in a normal room or one equipped with a screen permitting the eye-witness to see the suspect without being seen. In both cases, the procedures are the same except that a room equipped with a screen may be used only when the suspect's solicitor, friend or appropriate adult is present or the confrontation is recorded on video.
7. After the procedure, action required in accordance with *paragraph 3.40* applies.

2.7.12 **Code D—Annex E: Showing Photographs to Eye-witnesses**

(a) Action

1. An officer of sergeant rank or above shall be responsible for supervising and directing the showing of photographs. The actual showing may be done by another officer or police staff, see *paragraph 3.11*.
2. The supervising officer must confirm the first description of the suspect given by the eye-witness has been recorded before they are shown the photographs. If the supervising officer is unable to confirm the description has been recorded they shall postpone showing the photographs.
3. Only one eye-witness shall be shown photographs at any one time. Each witness shall be given as much privacy as practicable and shall not be allowed to communicate with any other eye-witness in the case.
4. The eye-witness shall be shown not less than twelve photographs at a time, which shall, as far as possible, all be of a similar type.
5. When the eye-witness is shown the photographs, they shall be told the photograph of the person they saw on a specified earlier occasion may, or may not, be amongst them and if they cannot make an identification, they should say so. The eye-witness shall also be told they should not make a decision until they have viewed at least twelve photographs. The eye-witness shall not be prompted or guided in any way but shall be left to make any selection without help.
6. If an eye-witness makes an identification from photographs, unless the person identified is otherwise eliminated from enquiries or is not available, other eye-witnesses shall not be shown photographs. But both they, and the eye-witness who has made the identification, shall be asked to attend a video identification, an identification parade or group identification unless there is no dispute about the suspect's identification.
7. If the eye-witness makes a selection but is unable to confirm the identification, the person showing the photographs shall ask them how sure they are that the photograph they have indicated is the person they saw on the specified earlier occasion.
8. When the use of a computerised or artist's composite or similar likeness has led to there being a known suspect who can be asked to participate in a video identification, appear on an identification parade or participate in a group identification, that likeness shall not be shown to other potential eye-witnesses.
9. When an eye-witness attending a video identification, an identification parade or group identification has previously been shown photographs or computerised or artist's composite or similar likeness (and it is the responsibility of the officer in charge of the investigation to make the identification officer aware that this is the case), the suspect and their solicitor must be informed of this fact before the identification procedure takes place.
10. None of the photographs shown shall be destroyed, whether or not an identification is made, since they may be required for production in court. The photographs shall be numbered and a separate photograph taken of the frame or part of the album from which the eye-witness made an identification as an aid to reconstituting it.

(b) Documentation

11. Whether or not an identification is made, a record shall be kept of the showing of photographs on forms provided for the purpose. This shall include anything said by the eye-witness about any identification or the conduct of the procedure, any reasons it was not practicable to comply with any of the provisions of this Code governing the showing of photographs and the name and rank of the supervising officer.
12. The supervising officer shall inspect and sign the record as soon as practicable.

2.7.12.1

KEYNOTE

Identification Where There Is No Suspect

Where the police have no suspect, Code D provides for witnesses (including police officers) to be shown photographs. If photographs are to be shown, the procedure set out at Annex E must be followed. When it is proposed to show photographs to a witness in accordance with Annex E, it is the responsibility of the officer in charge of the investigation to confirm to the officer responsible for supervising and directing the showing, that the first description of the suspect given by that witness has been recorded. If this description has not been recorded, the procedure under Annex E must be postponed. Except for the provisions of Annex E, para. 1, a police officer who is a witness for the purposes of this part of the Code is subject to the same principles and procedures as a civilian witness.

Using photographs from police criminal records can affect the judgment of a jury and nothing should be done to draw their attention to the fact that the defendant's photograph was already held by the police (*R* v *Lamb* (1980) 71 Cr App R 198). This rule does not apply if the jury are already aware of the defendant's previous convictions (*R* v *Allen* [1996] Crim LR 426).

2.7.13 Code D—Annex F: Fingerprints, Samples and Footwear Impressions—Destruction and Speculative Searches

Part A: Fingerprints and samples

Paragraphs 1 to 12 summarise and update information which is available at: https://www.gov.uk/government/publications/protection-of-freedoms-act-2012-dna-and-fingerprintprovisions/protection-of-freedoms-act-2012-how-dna-and-fingerprint-evidence-is-protected-in-law

DNA samples

1. A DNA sample is an individual's biological material, containing all of their genetic information. The Act requires all DNA samples to be destroyed within 6 months of being taken. This allows sufficient time for the sample to be analysed and a DNA profile to be produced for use on the database.
2. The only exception to this is if the sample is or may be required for disclosure as evidence, in which case it may be retained for as long as this need exists under the Criminal Procedure and Investigations Act 1996.

DNA profiles and fingerprints

3. A DNA profile consists of a string of 16 pairs of numbers and 2 letters (XX for women, XY for men) to indicate gender. This number string is stored on the National DNA Database (NDNAD). It allows the person to be identified if they leave their DNA at a crime scene.
4. Fingerprints are usually scanned electronically from the individual in custody and the images stored on IDENT1, the national fingerprint database.

Retention Periods: Fingerprints and DNA profiles

5. The retention period depends on the outcome of the investigation of the recordable offence in connection with which the fingerprints and DNA samples was taken, the age of the person at the time the offence was committed and whether the recordable offence is a qualifying offence and whether it is an excluded offence (See Table Notes (a) to (c)), as follows:

Table—Retention periods

(a) Convictions

Age when offence committed	*Outcome*	*Retention Period*
Any age	Convicted or given a caution or youth caution for a recordable offence which is also a qualifying offence.	INDEFINITE
18 or over	Convicted or given a caution for a recordable offence which is NOT a qualifying offence.	INDEFINITE
Under 18	Convicted or given a youth caution for a recordable offence which is NOT a qualifying offence.	1st conviction or youth caution—5 years plus length of any prison sentence. Indefinite if prison sentence 5 years or more 2nd conviction or youth caution: Indefinite

(b) Non-Convictions

Age when offence committed	*Outcome*	*Retention Period*
Any age	Charged but not convicted of a recordable qualifying offence.	3 years plus a 2 year extension if granted by a District Judge (or indefinite if the individual has a previous conviction for a recordable offence which is not excluded)
Any age	Arrested for, but not charged with, a recordable qualifying offence	3 years if granted by the Biometrics Commissioner plus a 2 year extension if granted by a District Judge (or indefinite if the individual has a previous conviction for a recordable offence which is not excluded)
Any age	Arrested for or charged with a recordable offence which is not a qualifying offence.	Indefinite if the person has a previous conviction for a recordable offence which is not excluded otherwise NO RETENTION
18 or over	Given Penalty Notice for Disorder for recordable offence	2 years

Table Notes:

(a) A 'recordable' offence is one for which the police are required to keep a record. Generally speaking, these are imprisonable offences; however, it also includes a number of non-imprisonable offences such as begging and taxi touting. The police are not able to take or retain the DNA or fingerprints of an individual who is arrested for an offence which is not recordable.

(b) A 'qualifying' offence is one listed under section 65A of the Police and Criminal Evidence Act 1984 (the list comprises sexual, violent, terrorism and burglary offences).

(c) An 'excluded' offence is a recordable offence which is not a qualifying offence, was committed when the individual was under 18, for which they received a sentence of fewer than 5 years' imprisonment and is the only recordable offence for which the person has been convicted

Speculative searches

6. Where the retention framework above requires the deletion of a person's DNA profile and fingerprints, the Act first allows a *speculative search* of their DNA and fingerprints against DNA and fingerprints obtained from crime scenes which are stored on NDNAD and IDENT1. Once the speculative search has been completed, the profile and fingerprints are deleted unless there is a match, in which case they will be retained for the duration of any investigation and thereafter in accordance with the retention framework (e.g. if that investigation led to a conviction for a qualifying offence, they would be retained indefinitely).

Extensions of retention period

7. For qualifying offences, PACE allows chief constables to apply for extensions to the given retention periods for DNA profiles and fingerprints if considered necessary for prevention or detection of crime.
8. Section 20 of the Protection of Freedoms Act 2012 established the independent office of Commissioner for the Retention and Use of Biometric Material (the 'Biometrics Commissioner'). For details, see https://www.gov.uk/government/organisations/biometricscommissioner.
9. Where an individual is arrested for, but not charged with, a qualifying offence, their DNA profile and fingerprint record will normally be deleted. However, the police can apply to the Biometrics Commissioner for permission to retain their DNA profile and fingerprint record for a period of 3 years. The application must be made within 28 days of the decision not to proceed with a prosecution.
10. If the police make such an application, the Biometrics Commissioner would first give both them and the arrested individual an opportunity to make written representations and then, taking into account factors including the age and vulnerability of the victim(s) of the alleged offences, and their relationship to the suspect, make a decision on whether or not retention is appropriate.
11. If after considering the application, the Biometrics Commissioner decides that retention is not appropriate, the DNA profile and fingerprint record in question must be destroyed.
12. If the Biometrics Commissioner agrees to allow retention, the police will be able to retain that individual's DNA profile and fingerprint record for a period of 3 years from the date the samples were taken. At the end of that period, the police will be able to apply to a District Judge (Magistrates' Courts) for a single 2 year extension to the retention period. If the application is rejected, the force must then destroy the DNA profile and fingerprint record.

Part B: Footwear impressions

13. Footwear impressions taken in accordance with section 61A of PACE (see *paragraphs 4.16* to *4.21*) may be retained for as long as is necessary for purposes related to the prevention or detection of crime, the investigation of an offence or the conduct of a prosecution.

Part C: Fingerprints, samples and footwear impressions taken in connection with a criminal investigation from a person not suspected of committing the offence under investigation for elimination purposes.

14. When fingerprints, footwear impressions or DNA samples are taken from a person in connection with an investigation and the person is *not suspected of having committed the offence*, they must be destroyed as soon as they have fulfilled the purpose for which they were taken unless:
    (a) they were taken for the purposes of an investigation of an offence for which a person has been convicted; and
    (b) fingerprints, footwear impressions or samples were also taken from the convicted person for the purposes of that investigation.

    However, subject to *paragraph 14*, the fingerprints, footwear impressions and samples, and the information derived from samples, may not be used in the investigation of any offence or in evidence against the person who is, or would be, entitled to the destruction of the fingerprints, footwear impressions and samples.
15. The requirement to destroy fingerprints, footwear impressions and DNA samples, and information derived from samples and restrictions on their retention and use in *paragraph 14* do not apply if the person gives their written consent for their fingerprints, footwear impressions

or sample to be retained and used after they have fulfilled the purpose for which they were taken. This consent can be withdrawn at any time.

16. When a person's fingerprints, footwear impressions or sample are to be destroyed:
    (a) any copies of the fingerprints and footwear impressions must also be destroyed; and
    (b) neither the fingerprints, footwear impressions, the sample, or any information derived from the sample, may be used in the investigation of any offence or in evidence against the person who is, or would be, entitled to its destruction.

2.7.13.1 **KEYNOTE**

Fingerprints, footwear impressions and samples given voluntarily for the purposes of elimination play an important part in many police investigations. It is, therefore, important to make sure innocent volunteers are not deterred from participating and their consent to their fingerprints, footwear impressions and DNA being used for the purposes of a specific investigation is fully informed and voluntary. If the police or volunteer seek to have the fingerprints, footwear impressions or samples retained for use after the specific investigation ends, it is important the volunteer's consent to this is also fully informed and voluntary. The volunteer must be told that they may withdraw their consent at any time.

The consent must be obtained in writing using current nationally agreed forms provided for police use according to the purpose for which the consent is given. This purpose may be either:

- DNA/fingerprints/footwear impressions—to be used only for the purposes of a specific investigation; or
- DNA/fingerprints/footwear impressions—to be used in the specific investigation and retained by the police for future use.

To minimise the risk of confusion:

- if a police officer or member of police staff has any doubt about:
  - ◇ how the consent forms should be completed and signed, or
  - ◇ whether a consent form they propose to use and refer to is fully compliant with the current nationally agreed form,

  the relevant national police helpdesk (for DNA or fingerprints) should be contacted.
- in each case, the meaning of consent should be explained orally and care taken to ensure the oral explanation accurately reflects the contents of the written form the person is to be asked to sign.

The provisions for the retention of fingerprints, footwear impressions and samples in para. 15 allow for all fingerprints, footwear impressions and samples in a case to be available for any subsequent miscarriage of justice investigation.

2.7.14 Code D—Annex G: Requirement for a Person to Attend a Police Station for Fingerprints and Samples

1. A requirement under Schedule 2A for a person to attend a police station to have fingerprints or samples taken:
    (a) must give the person a period of at least seven days within which to attend the police station; and
    (b) may direct them to attend at a specified time of day or between specified times of day.
2. When specifying the period and times of attendance, the officer making the requirements must consider whether the fingerprints or samples could reasonably be taken at a time when the person is required to attend the police station for any other reason.
3. An officer of the rank of inspector or above may authorise a period shorter than 7 days if there is an urgent need for person's fingerprints or sample for the purposes of the investigation of an offence. The fact of the authorisation and the reasons for giving it must be recorded as soon as practicable.

4. The constable making a requirement and the person to whom it applies may agree to vary it so as to specify any period within which, or date or time at which, the person is to attend. However, variation shall not have effect for the purposes of enforcement, unless it is confirmed by the constable in writing.

2.7.14.1 **KEYNOTE**

The Police, Crime, Sentencing and Courts Act 2022 amended sch. 2A to PACE; however, PACE Code D has not yet been updated to reflect this amendment at the time of printing. This amendment means that sch. 2A to PACE applies to a requirement for a person to attend a police station for fingerprints, samples and also photographs. The requirement must direct the person to attend the police station on a specified date, and may either direct the person to attend the police station at a specified time or between specified times on that date. Under this amendment, Code D, Annex G, paras 3 and 4 are no longer relevant.

To justify the arrest without warrant of a person who fails to comply with a requirement (see paras 4.4(b) and 6.7(b) above), the officer making the requirement, or confirming a variation, should be prepared to explain how, when and where the requirement was made or the variation was confirmed and what steps were taken to ensure the person understood what to do and the consequences of not complying with the requirement.

Following the correct procedure for requesting samples is crucial. In *R (On the Application of R)* v *A Chief Constable* [2013] EWHC 2864 (Admin), R had been convicted of unlawful act manslaughter in 1984. Twenty years after a kidnap conviction in 1993, R was asked to provide a non-intimate sample to be placed on the police national DNA database. R refused to provide a sample and was handed a letter informing him that he had seven days to attend the police station to provide the sample, and if he failed to do so he would be arrested and a sample would be forcibly taken from him pursuant to the Police and Criminal Evidence Act 1984, s. 63(3B)(a). When the letter was served authority had not been given by an inspector. The court held that a requirement to attend a police station to provide a non-intimate sample under the 1984 Act could not be made to a person who did not consent to providing a sample unless an officer of the rank of inspector or above had first given authorisation for the taking of the sample under s. 63(3B)(b). The letter handed to R constituted a demand that he attend a police station to provide a sample within seven days. That demand was unlawful because it was made without prior authorisation by an inspector or an officer of higher rank.

The second point in this case related to the authority that was eventually given by the inspector and the historic nature of the conviction; the court held that the inspector was fully justified in concluding that the public interest in the detection of crime outweighed the limited interference with R's private life. The absence of specific grounds for suspicion of R did not render the requirement to provide a sample disproportionate. The conclusion that R might have committed other offences during the period of his admitted offending and after 1995 was justified. While there was a theoretical deterrent effect in the knowledge by R that police were in possession of his DNA profile, it was the objective of solving crime which provided the legitimate justification for the requirement in the instant case. The requirement that R attend the police station to give a sample was proportionate.

2.8 Interviews

PACE Code of Practice for the Detention, Treatment and Questioning of Persons by Police Officers (Code C)

PACE Code of Practice on Audio Recording Interviews with Suspects (Code E)

PACE Code of Practice on Visual Recording with Sound of Interviews with Suspects (Code F)

A thick grey line down the margin denotes text that is an extract of the PACE Code itself (i.e. the actual wording of the legislation). This material is examinable for both Sergeants and Inspectors.

2.8.1 Introduction

The PACE Codes of Practice C, E and F are intended to provide protection to people being interviewed by the police and lay down guidelines as to how interviews should be conducted. This chapter examines the treatment of suspects when they are interviewed. The chapter includes the relevant sections of Code C and all of Code E and F. The chapter sets out the actual Codes of Practice with keynotes, which incorporate the notes of guidance to the Code, relevant legislation and case law.

See chapter 2.6 regarding designated officers carrying out some functions of police officers.

Code C was amended on 23 February 2017. Code H applies to persons detained for the purposes of a terrorist investigation; references to terrorism matters, where appropriate, are included in the keynotes to this chapter.

2.8.2 PACE Code of Practice for the Detention, Treatment and Questioning of Persons by Police Officers (Code C)

10 Cautions

(a) When a caution must be given

10.1 A person whom there are grounds to suspect of an offence, must be cautioned before any questions about an offence, or further questions if the answers provide the grounds for suspicion, are put to them if either the suspect's answers or silence, (i.e. failure or refusal to answer or answer satisfactorily) may be given in evidence to a court in a prosecution. A person need not be cautioned if questions are for other necessary purposes, e.g.:

(a) solely to establish their identity or ownership of any vehicle;

(b) to obtain information in accordance with any relevant statutory requirement, see *paragraph 10.9*;

(c) in furtherance of the proper and effective conduct of a search, e.g. to determine the need to search in the exercise of powers of stop and search or to seek co-operation while carrying out a search; or

(d) to seek verification of a written record as in *paragraph 11.13*.

(e) *Not used*.

10.2 Whenever a person not under arrest is initially cautioned, or reminded that they are under caution, that person must at the same time be told they are not under arrest and must be informed of the provisions of *paragraph 3.21* which explain that they need to agree to be interviewed, how they may obtain legal advice according to whether they are at a police station or elsewhere and the other rights and entitlements that apply to a voluntary interview.

10.3 A person who is arrested, or further arrested, must be informed at the time if practicable or, if not, as soon as it becomes practicable thereafter, that they are under arrest and of the grounds and reasons for their arrest, see *paragraph 3.4* and *Code G, paragraphs 2.2 and 4.3*.

10.4 As required by *Code G, section 3*, a person who is arrested, or further arrested, must also be cautioned unless:

(a) it is impracticable to do so by reason of their condition or behaviour at the time;

(b) they have already been cautioned immediately prior to arrest as in *paragraph 10.1*.

2.8.2.1 **KEYNOTE**

In considering whether there are grounds to suspect a person of committing an offence there must be some reasonable, objective grounds for the suspicion, based on known facts or information which are/is relevant to the likelihood that the offence has been committed and that the person to be questioned committed it.

An arrested person must be given sufficient information to enable him/her to understand that he/she has been deprived of his/her liberty and the reason for the arrest, e.g. when a person is arrested on suspicion of committing an offence he/she must be informed of the suspected offence's nature, and when and where it was committed. The suspect must also be informed of the reason or reasons why the arrest is considered necessary. Vague or technical language should be avoided. If it appears that a person does not understand the caution, the person giving it should explain it in his/her own words.

Ibrahim v *United Kingdom* (Application nos 50541/08, 50571/08, 50573/08 and 40351/09) was a case in the European Court of Human Rights against the United Kingdom. The applicants alleged a violation of Article 6 in that they had been interviewed by the police without access to a lawyer and that statements made in those interviews had been used at their trials. The case stemmed from the investigation of the four bombs that were detonated on the London transport system in July 2005 but failed to explode. The perpetrators fled the scene. One person who was not suspected of having detonated a bomb was initially interviewed by the police as a witness. He started to incriminate himself by explaining his encounter with a suspected bomber shortly after the attacks and the assistance he had provided to that suspect. According to the applicable Code of Practice, he should have been cautioned and offered legal advice at that point. However, after taking instructions from a senior officer, the police continued to question him as a witness and took a written statement from him. The court held that there had been no compelling reasons for restricting his access to legal advice and for failing to inform him of his right to remain silent. It was significant that there was no basis in domestic law for the police to choose not to caution him at the point at which he had started to incriminate himself. Indeed, the Court stated that the decision had been contrary to the applicable Code of Practice. As a result, the applicant had been misled as to his procedural rights.

2.8.2.2

(b) Terms of the cautions

10.5 The caution which must be given on:

(a arrest; or

(b) all other occasions before a person is charged or informed they may be prosecuted; see *section 16*,

should, unless the restriction on drawing adverse inferences from silence applies, see *Annex C*, be in the following terms:

'You do not have to say anything. But it may harm your defence if you do not mention when questioned something which you later rely on in Court. Anything you do say may be given in evidence.'

Where the use of the Welsh Language is appropriate, a constable may provide the caution directly in Welsh in the following terms:

'Does dim rhaid i chi ddweud dim byd. Ond gall niweidio eich amddiffyniad os na fyddwch chi'n sôn, wrth gael eich holi, am rywbeth y byddwch chi'n dibynnu arno nes ymlaen yn y Llys. Gall unrhyw beth yr ydych yn ei ddweud gael ei roi fel tystiolaeth.'

10.6 *Annex C, paragraph 2* sets out the alternative terms of the caution to be used when the restriction on drawing adverse inferences from silence applies.

10.7 Minor deviations from the words of any caution given in accordance with this Code do not constitute a breach of this Code, provided the sense of the relevant caution is preserved.

10.8 After any break in questioning under caution, the person being questioned must be made aware they remain under caution. If there is any doubt the relevant caution should be given again in full when the interview resumes.

10.9 When, despite being cautioned, a person fails to co-operate or to answer particular questions which may affect their immediate treatment, the person should be informed of any relevant consequences and that those consequences are not affected by the caution. Examples are when a person's refusal to provide:

- their name and address when charged may make them liable to detention;
- particulars and information in accordance with a statutory requirement, e.g. under the Road Traffic Act 1988, may amount to an offence or may make the person liable to a further arrest.

2.8.2.3

KEYNOTE

As well as considering whether to administer the caution again after a break in questioning or at the beginning of a subsequent interview, the interviewing officer should summarise the reason for the break and confirm this with the suspect. This may help to show to the court that nothing occurred during an interview break or between interviews which influenced the suspect's recorded evidence.

Nothing in this Code requires a caution to be given or repeated when informing a person not under arrest that he/she may be prosecuted for an offence. However, a court will not be able to draw any inferences under the Criminal Justice and Public Order Act 1994, s. 34, if the person was not cautioned.

The giving of a warning or the service of the Notice of Intended Prosecution required by the Road Traffic Offenders Act 1988, s. 1 does not amount to informing a detainee that he/she may be prosecuted for an offence and so does not preclude further questioning in relation to that offence.

Section 34 of the Criminal Justice and Public Order Act 1994

Section 34 of the Criminal Justice and Public Order Act 1994 provides that inferences can be drawn if, when questioned by the police under caution, charged or officially informed that he/she may be prosecuted, the accused fails to mention a fact on which he/she later relies in his/her defence, and which he/she could reasonably have been expected to mention at the time.

Section 34 states:

(1) Where, in any proceedings against a person for an offence, evidence is given that the accused—

(a) at any time before he was charged with the offence, on being questioned under caution by a constable trying to discover whether or by whom the offence had been committed, failed to mention any fact relied on in his defence in those proceedings; or

(b) on being charged with the offence or officially informed that he might be prosecuted for it, failed to mention any such fact, or

(c) at any time after being charged with the offence, on being questioned under section 22 of the Counter-Terrorism Act 2008 (post-charge questioning), failed to mention any such fact,

being a fact which in the circumstances existing at the time the accused could reasonably have been expected to mention when so questioned, charged or informed, as the case may be, subsection (2) below applies.

(2) Where this subsection applies—

(a) ...

(b) a judge, in deciding whether to grant an application made by the accused under paragraph 2 of Schedule 3 to the Crime and Disorder Act 1998;

(c) the court, in determining whether there is a case to answer; and

(d) the court or jury, in determining whether the accused is guilty of the offence charged,

may draw such inferences from the failure as appear proper.

(2A) Where the accused was at an authorised place of detention at the time of the failure, subsections (1) and (2) above do not apply if he had not been allowed an opportunity to consult a solicitor prior to being questioned, charged or informed as mentioned in subsection (1) above.

(3) Subject to any directions by the court, evidence tending to establish the failure may be given before or after evidence tending to establish the fact which the accused is alleged to have failed to mention.

(4) This section applies in relation to questioning by persons (other than constables) charged with the duty of investigating offences or charging offenders as it applies in relation to questioning by constables; and in subsection (1) above 'officially informed' means informed by a constable or any such person.

(5) This section does not—

(a) prejudice the admissibility in evidence of the silence or other reaction of the accused in the face of anything said in his presence relating to the conduct in respect of which he is charged, in so far as evidence thereof would be admissible apart from this section; or

(b) preclude the drawing of any inference from any such silence or other reaction of the accused which could properly be drawn apart from this section.

Section 34 deals with the 'failure to mention any fact' and the word 'fact' is given its normal dictionary definition of 'something that is actually the case' (*R* v *Milford* [2001] Crim LR 330). Where an accused alleges that he/she did mention the relevant fact when being questioned, it is for the prosecution to prove the contrary before any adverse inference can be drawn. The court have said that the object of s. 34 is to deter late fabrication and to encourage early disclosure of genuine defences (*Brizzalari* [2004] EWCA Crim 310). The 'fact' later relied on by the defendant does not have to be made up (*R* v *Noor* [2021] EWCA Crim 1767).

There have been numerous domestic and European case decisions about failure to advance facts following legal advice to remain silent, and more recent cases have attempted to unravel the difficulties experienced in this area. These cases have accepted that a genuine reliance by a defendant on his/her solicitor's advice to remain silent is not in itself enough to preclude adverse comment. The real question to be answered is whether the defendant remained silent, not because of legal advice, but because there was no satisfactory explanation to give (*R* v *Beckles* [2004] EWCA Crim 2766, *R* v *Bresa* [2005] EWCA Crim 1414 and *R* v *Loizou* [2006] EWCA Crim 1719). In *R* v *Ahmed, Mohamed, Bahdon, R and G* [2019] EWCA Crim 1085, the victim was robbed by a group of youths and then assaulted with an iron bar. R was seen on CCTV footage holding something and it was the prosecution case that it was a metal pole. R gave a no comment interview; however, at trial he said he was carrying a piece of bendable plastic tubing (as opposed to an iron bar) and he explained why he was carrying it. R stated that he did not mention those things in interview because he was aged 16 and was acting on his solicitor's advice to say no comment during the interview. On appeal, the court held that the judge was right to direct the jury that they could draw a s. 34 adverse inference if they concluded that, in the context of him being just 16 and having been advised to make no comment at an early stage of the investigation when there had not been lengthy consideration of it, he could reasonably have been expected to have mentioned those matters at the interview, and the only sensible reason that he did not do so was that he had not yet thought of them or did not think that they would withstand scrutiny.

In assessing whether to draw an inference from a failure to mention facts later relied on as part of the defence, the court may look at the validity of the waiver to legal advice. In *R* v *Saunders* [2012] EWCA Crim 1380, the suspect declined the offer of legal representation, and in interview she either made no comment or denied the allegations put to her. At trial she blamed her cousin who she said had been staying at her flat at the time. The prosecution sought to rely on her interview to show that she had made no mention of her cousin at that stage. In accepting the prosecution's submission, the court considered the extent of her knowledge and the extent to which her decision caused her disadvantage. As to the first factor, the defendant had particular experience and understanding of the interview procedure having experienced it before and was well fitted to decide whether she wanted legal advice. She was neither unintelligent nor vulnerable and could be expected to be well aware of the benefit of legal advice.

In relation to s. 34, the accused cannot be convicted solely on an inference drawn from silence. The European Court of Human Rights, although accepting that there are cases which clearly call for an accused to provide an explanation, stated that the court is required to apply 'particular caution' before invoking the accused's silence against him (*Condron* v *United Kingdom* (2001) 31 EHRR 1). In *R* v *Condron* [1997] 1 WLR 827, the court held that the jury must be satisfied that the prosecution has established a case to answer before drawing any inferences from silence. In *R* v *Miah* [2009] EWCA Crim 2368, Hughes LJ said: 'Section 34 bites not on silence in interview but upon the late advancing of a case which could have been made earlier. What it does is to permit the jury to ask why, if there is an explanation for the evidence, or a defence to the accusation, the defendant did not advance it when he could have done, providing only that it was reasonable to expect him to have done so then.'

In *R* v *Argent* [1997] 2 Cr App R 27, the court stated that personal factors which might be relevant to an assessment of what an individual could reasonably have been expected to mention were age, experience, mental capacity, state of health, sobriety, tiredness, personality, knowledge and legal advice.

In *R* v *Flynn* [2001] EWCA Crim 1633, the court held that the police are entitled to conduct a second interview with a suspect, having obtained evidence from their witnesses which was not available in the first interview, and adverse inference could be drawn from the suspect's silence.

Where an accused, following legal advice, fails to answer questions during interview but presents a prepared statement, no adverse inference can be drawn where the accused's defence does not rely on any facts not mentioned in the interview (*R* v *Knight* [2003] EWCA Crim 1977). However, this would not be the case when evidence of facts relied on during the trial was not contained within the pre-prepared statement (*R* v *Turner* [2003] EWCA Crim 3108). If the prepared statement is very bland compared with any detailed defence given at trial, a jury may be directed to consider why a more detailed statement was not provided earlier (*R* v *Cross* [2017] EWCA Crim 1036).

Section 34 differs from the other 'inference' sections in that the questioning need not occur at a police station and therefore the presence of a legal representative is not required. However, it appears clear that, should the prosecution seek to draw any inferences of an accused's silence where such questioning has occurred, the questions would need to be asked of the suspect again once he/she had access to legal advice.

A requirement to caution the person is contained in s. 34(1)(a) in order to make clear the risks connected with a failure to mention facts which later form part of the defence.

Section 22(9) of the Counter-Terrorism Act 2008 adds s. 34(1)(c) to the Criminal Justice and Public Order Act 1994, which extends inferences from silence to post-charge questioning which has been authorised by a judge of the Crown Court if the offence is a terrorism offence or it appears to the judge that the offence has a terrorist connection. The post-charge questioning provisions of the 2008 Act require the issue of a mandatory Code for the video recording with sound of such questioning (**see appendix 2.1** of this manual).

2.8.2.4

(c) Special warnings under the Criminal Justice and Public Order Act 1994, sections 36 and 37

10.10 When a suspect interviewed at a police station or authorised place of detention after arrest fails or refuses to answer certain questions, or to answer satisfactorily, after due warning, a court or jury may draw such inferences as appear proper under the Criminal Justice and Public Order Act 1994, sections 36 and 37. Such inferences may only be drawn when:

(a) the restriction on drawing adverse inferences from silence, see *Annex C*, does not apply; and

(b) the suspect is arrested by a constable and fails or refuses to account for any objects, marks or substances, or marks on such objects found:

- on their person;
- in or on their clothing or footwear;
- otherwise in their possession; or
- in the place they were arrested;

(c) the arrested suspect was found by a constable at a place at or about the time the offence for which that officer has arrested them is alleged to have been committed, and the suspect fails or refuses to account for their presence there.

When the restriction on drawing adverse inferences from silence applies, the suspect may still be asked to account for any of the matters in (*b*) or (*c*) but the special warning described in *paragraph 10.11* will not apply and must not be given.

10.11 For an inference to be drawn when a suspect fails or refuses to answer a question about one of these matters or to answer it satisfactorily, the suspect must first be told in ordinary language:

(a) what offence is being investigated;

(b) what fact they are being asked to account for;

(c) this fact may be due to them taking part in the commission of the offence;

(d) a court may draw a proper inference if they fail or refuse to account for this fact; and

(e) a record is being made of the interview and it may be given in evidence if they are brought to trial.

(d) Juveniles and vulnerable persons

10.11A The information required in paragraph 10.11 must not be given to a suspect who is a juvenile or a vulnerable person unless the appropriate adult is present.

10.12 If a juvenile or a vulnerable person is cautioned in the absence of the appropriate adult, the caution must be repeated in the appropriate adult's presence.

10.12A *Not used.*

(e) Documentation

10.13 A record shall be made when a caution is given under this section, either in the interviewer's report book or in the interview record.

2.8.2.5

KEYNOTE

Sections 36 and 37 of the Criminal Justice and Public Order Act 1994

The Criminal Justice and Public Order Act 1994, ss. 36 and 37 apply only to suspects who have been arrested by a constable or an officer of Revenue and Customs and are given the relevant warning by the police or customs officer who made the arrest or who is investigating the offence. They do not apply to any interviews with suspects who have not been arrested. The suspect must also be at a police station or other authorised detention place.

Inferences from Silence: Failure to Account for Objects, Substances and Marks

Section 36 of the Criminal Justice and Public Order Act 1994 provides that inferences can be drawn from an accused's failure to give evidence or refusal to answer any question about any object, substance or mark which may be attributable to the accused in the commission of an offence.

Section 36 states:

(1) Where—

(a) a person is arrested by a constable, and there is—

(i) on his person; or

(ii) in or on his clothing or footwear; or

(iii) otherwise in his possession; or

(iv) in any place in which he is at the time of his arrest,

(b) any object, substance or mark, or there is any mark on any such object; and

(c) that or another constable investigating the case reasonably believes that the presence of the object, substance or mark may be attributable to the participation of the person arrested in the commission of an offence specified by the constable; and

(d) the constable informs the person arrested that he so believes, and requests him to account for the presence of the object, substance or mark; and

(e) the person fails or refuses to do so,

then if, in any proceedings against the person for the offence so specified, evidence of those matters is given, subsection (2) below applies.

(2) Where this subsection applies—

(a) a magistrates' court inquiring into the offence as examining justices; in deciding whether to grant an application for dismissal made by the accused under section 6 of the Magistrates' Courts Act 1980 (application for dismissal of charge in course of proceedings with a view to transfer for trial);

(b) a judge, in deciding whether to grant an application made by the accused under—

(i) section 6 of the Criminal Justice Act 1987 (application for dismissal of charge of serious fraud in respect of which notice of transfer has been given under section 4 of that Act); or

(ii) paragraph 5 of schedule 6 to the Criminal Justice Act 1991 (application for dismissal of charge of violent or sexual offence involving a child in respect of which notice of transfer has been given under section 53 of that Act);

(c) the court, in determining whether there is a case to answer; and

(d) the court or jury, in determining whether the accused is guilty of the offence charged,

may draw such inferences from the failure or refusal as appear proper.

(3) Subsections (1) and (2) above apply to the condition of clothing or footwear as they apply to a substance or mark thereon.

(4) Subsections (1) and (2) above do not apply unless the accused was told in ordinary language by the constable when making the request mentioned in subsection (1)(c) above what the effect of this section would be if he failed or refused to comply with the request.

(4A) Where the accused was at an authorised place of detention at the time of the failure or refusal, subsections (1) and (2) do not apply if he had not been allowed an opportunity to consult a solicitor prior to the request being made.

(5) This section applies in relation to officers of customs and excise as it applies in relation to constables.

(6) This section does not preclude the drawing of any inference from a failure or refusal of the accused to account for the presence of an object, substance or mark or from the condition of clothing or footwear which could properly be drawn apart from this section.

As with s. 37 below, an inference may only be drawn where four conditions are satisfied:

- the accused has been arrested;
- a constable reasonably believes that the object, substance or mark (or the presence of the accused (s. 37)) may be attributable to the accused's participation in a crime (s. 36 (an offence 'specified by the constable') or s. 37 (the offence for which he/she was arrested));
- the constable informs the accused of his/her belief and requests an explanation (by giving a special warning (see below));
- the constable tells the suspect (in ordinary language) the effect of a failure or refusal to comply with the request.

The request for information under both s. 36 and s. 37 is a form of questioning and should be undertaken during the interview at the police station. The request for such information prior to this would be an exception to the rule.

The interviewing officer is required to give the accused a 'special warning' for an inference to be drawn from a suspect's failure or refusal to answer a question about one of these matters or to answer it satisfactorily.

This 'special warning' is provided by PACE Code C, para. 10.11, which states that the interviewing officer must first tell the suspect *in ordinary language*:

- what offence is being investigated;
- what fact the suspect is being asked to account for;
- that the interviewing officer believes this fact may be due to the suspect's taking part in the commission of the offence in question;
- that a court may draw a proper inference if the suspect fails or refuses to account for the fact about which he/she is being questioned;
- that a record is being made of the interview and that it may be given in evidence at any subsequent trial.

Section 36 considers the circumstances of the suspect at the time of arrest; it is suggested therefore that in relation to items that are *otherwise in the possession of the suspect* under s. 36(1)(a) there must be some link to the suspect at the time of arrest and this would not for instance include items found sometime later at a search of the suspect's home address some distance away.

As with s. 34, in relation to s. 36 the accused cannot be convicted solely on an inference drawn from a failure or refusal (s. 38(3)).

Inferences from Silence: Failure to Account for Presence

Section 37 of the Criminal Justice and Public Order Act 1994 provides that inferences can be drawn from an accused's failure to give evidence or refusal to answer any question about his/her presence at a place or time when the offence for which he/she was arrested was committed.

Section 37 states:

(1) Where—

(a) a person arrested by a constable was found by him at a place at or about the time the offence for which he was arrested is alleged to have been committed; and

(b) that or another constable investigating the offence reasonably believes that the presence of the person at that place and at that time may be attributable to his participation in the commission of the offence; and

(c) the constable informs the person that he so believes, and requests him to account for that presence; and

(d) the person fails or refuses to do so,

then if, in any proceedings against the person for the offence, evidence of those matters is given, subsection (2) below applies.

(2) Where this subsection applies—

(a) a magistrates' court inquiring into the offence as examining justices; in deciding whether to grant an application for dismissal made by the accused under section 6 of the Magistrates' Courts Act 1980 (application for dismissal of charge in course of proceedings with a view to transfer for trial);

(b) a judge, in deciding whether to grant an application made by the accused under—

(i) section 6 of the Criminal Justice Act 1987 (application for dismissal of charge of serious fraud in respect of which notice of transfer has been given under section 4 of that Act); or

(ii) paragraph 5 of schedule 6 to the Criminal Justice Act 1991 (application for dismissal of charge of violent or sexual offence involving child in respect of which notice of transfer has been given under section 53 of that Act);

(c) the court, in determining whether there is a case to answer; and

(d) the court or jury, in determining whether the accused is guilty of the offence charged,

may draw such inferences from the failure or refusal as appear proper.

(3) Subsections (1) and (2) do not apply unless the accused was told in ordinary language by the constable when making the request mentioned in subsection (1)(c) above what the effect of this section would be if he failed or refused to comply with the request.

(3A) Where the accused was at an authorised place of detention at the time of the failure or refusal, subsections (1) and (2) do not apply if he had not been allowed an opportunity to consult a solicitor prior to the request being made.

(4) This section applies in relation to officers of customs and excise as it applies in relation to constables.

(5) This section does not preclude the drawing of any inference from a failure or refusal of the accused to account for his presence at a place which could properly be drawn apart from this section.

Section 37 appears somewhat restrictive in that it is only concerned with the suspect's location at the time of arrest and applies only when he/she was found at that location at or about the time of the offence. It would not apply where the suspect has been seen near the scene of a crime but is arrested elsewhere. In these circumstances, the provisions for mentioning relevant facts in s. 34 of the Act are likely to be appropriate.

PACE Code C also applies to s. 37 in relation to the 'special warning' required to be given by the interviewing officer.

Unlike s. 36, here the officer that sees the person at or near the scene of the alleged offence must be the arresting officer.

As with ss. 34 and 36, in relation to s. 37 the accused cannot be convicted solely on an inference drawn from a failure or refusal (s. 38(3)).

2.8.2.6 **KEYNOTE**

Inferences from Silence at Trial

Section 35 of the Criminal Justice and Public Order Act 1994 provides that inferences can be drawn from an accused's failure to give evidence or refusal to answer any question, without good cause, where the person has been sworn. Section 35 states:

(1) At the trial of any person for an offence, subsections (2) and (3) below apply unless—
   (a) the accused's guilt is not in issue; or
   (b) it appears to the court that the physical or mental condition of the accused makes it undesirable for him to give evidence;

   but subsection (2) below does not apply if, at the conclusion of the evidence for the prosecution, his legal representative informs the court that the accused will give evidence or, where he is unrepresented, the court ascertains from him that he will give evidence.

(2) Where this subsection applies, the court shall, at the conclusion of the evidence for the prosecution, satisfy itself (in the case of proceedings on indictment with a jury, in the presence of the jury) that the accused is aware that the stage has been reached at which evidence can be given for the defence and that he can, if he wishes, give evidence and that, if he chooses not to give evidence, or having been sworn, without good cause refuses to answer any question, it will be permissible for the court or jury to draw such inferences as appear proper from his failure to give evidence or his refusal, without good cause, to answer any question.

(3) Where this subsection applies, the court or jury, in determining whether the accused is guilty of the offence charged, may draw such inferences as appear proper from the failure of the accused to give evidence or his refusal, without good cause, to answer any question.

(4) This section does not render the accused compellable to give evidence on his own behalf, and he shall accordingly not be guilty of contempt of court by reason of a failure to do so.

(5) For the purposes of this section a person who, having been sworn, refuses to answer any question shall be taken to do so without good cause unless—
   (a) he is entitled to refuse to answer the question by virtue of any enactment, whenever passed or made, or on the ground of privilege; or
   (b) the court in the exercise of its general discretion excuses him from answering it.

(6) [Repealed]

In *R* v *Friend* [1997] 1 WLR 1433 (in considering s. 35(1)(b) of the Act), the accused was aged 15 with a mental age of nine and an IQ of 63. It was held that the accused's mental condition did not make it 'undesirable' for him to give evidence and it was right that inferences be drawn under s. 35(3).

As with s. 34, in relation to s. 35 the accused cannot be convicted solely on an inference drawn from a failure or refusal (s. 38(3)).

It must be made clear to the accused that when the prosecution case has finished he/she may give evidence if he/she so wishes. The court must inform the accused that if he/she fails to give evidence or, being sworn, refuses to answer any question without good cause, then the jury may infer such inferences that appear proper from such a failure to give evidence or a refusal to answer any question. In *R* v *Gough* [2001] EWCA Crim 2545, it was held that it is mandatory for the court to inform the accused of his/her right to give or not to give evidence even where the accused has absconded.

In *Murray* v *United Kingdom* (1996) 22 EHRR 29 it was held that it would be incompatible with the rights of an accused to base a conviction 'solely or mainly' on their silence, or on their refusal to answer questions or give evidence in person. The Court of Appeal also held that in cases involving directions under s. 34, the burden of proof remained on the Crown despite the fact that the accused chose to make no comment (*R* v *Gowland-Wynn* [2001] EWCA Crim 2715). In *Compton* [2002] EWCA Crim 2835, the court stated that the jury must be told that they can only hold against a defendant a failure to give an explanation if they are sure the defendant had no acceptable explanation to offer.

2.8.3 Code C—11 Interviews—General

(a) Action

11.1A An interview is the questioning of a person regarding their involvement or suspected involvement in a criminal offence or offences which, under paragraph 10.1, must be carried out under caution. Before a person is interviewed, they and, if they are represented, their solicitor must be given sufficient information to enable them to understand the nature of any such offence, and why they are suspected of committing it (see *paragraphs 3.4(a)* and *10.3*), in order to allow for the effective exercise of the rights of the defence. However, whilst the information must always be sufficient for the person to understand the nature of any offence, this does not require the disclosure of details at a time which might prejudice the criminal investigation. The decision about what needs to be disclosed for the purpose of this requirement therefore rests with the investigating officer who has sufficient knowledge of the case to make that decision. The officer who discloses the information shall make a record of the information disclosed and when it was disclosed. This record may be made in the interview record, in the officer's report book or other form provided for this purpose. Procedures under the Road Traffic Act 1988, section 7 or the Transport and Works Act 1992, section 31 do not constitute interviewing for the purpose of this Code.

11.1 Following a decision to arrest a suspect, they must not be interviewed about the relevant offence except at a police station or other authorised place of detention, unless the consequent delay would be likely to:

(a) lead to:
- interference with, or harm to, evidence connected with an offence;
- interference with, or physical harm to, other people; or
- serious loss of, or damage to, property;

(b) lead to alerting other people suspected of committing an offence but not yet arrested for it; or

(c) hinder the recovery of property obtained in consequence of the commission of an offence.

Interviewing in any of these circumstances shall cease once the relevant risk has been averted or the necessary questions have been put in order to attempt to avert that risk.

11.2 Immediately prior to the commencement or re-commencement of any interview at a police station or other authorised place of detention, the interviewer should remind the suspect of their entitlement to free legal advice and that the interview can be delayed for legal advice to be obtained, unless one of the exceptions in *paragraph 6.6* applies. It is the interviewer's responsibility to make sure all reminders are recorded in the interview record.

11.3 *Not used.*

11.4 At the beginning of an interview the interviewer, after cautioning the suspect, see *section 10*, shall put to them any significant statement or silence which occurred in the presence and hearing of a police officer or other police staff before the start of the interview and which have not been put to the suspect in the course of a previous interview. The interviewer shall ask the suspect whether they confirm or deny that earlier statement or silence and if they want to add anything.

11.4A A significant statement is one which appears capable of being used in evidence against the suspect, in particular a direct admission of guilt. A significant silence is a failure or refusal to answer a question or answer satisfactorily when under caution, which might, allowing for the restriction on drawing adverse inferences from silence, see *Annex C*, give rise to an inference under the Criminal Justice and Public Order Act 1994, Part III.

11.5 No interviewer may try to obtain answers or elicit a statement by the use of oppression. Except as in *paragraph 10.9*, no interviewer shall indicate, except to answer a direct question, what action will be taken by the police if the person being questioned answers questions, makes a statement or refuses to do either. If the person asks directly what action will be taken if they answer questions, make a statement or refuse to do either, the interviewer may inform them what action the police propose to take provided that action is itself proper and warranted.

11.6 The interview or further interview of a person about an offence with which that person has not been charged or for which they have not been informed they may be prosecuted, must cease when:

(a) the officer in charge of the investigation is satisfied all the questions they consider relevant to obtaining accurate and reliable information about the offence have been put to the suspect, this includes allowing the suspect an opportunity to give an innocent explanation and asking questions to test if the explanation is accurate and reliable, e.g. to clear up ambiguities or clarify what the suspect said;

(b) the officer in charge of the investigation has taken account of any other available evidence; and

(c) the officer in charge of the investigation, or in the case of a detained suspect, the custody officer, see *paragraph 16.1*, reasonably believes there is sufficient evidence to provide a realistic prospect of conviction for that offence.

This paragraph does not prevent officers in revenue cases or acting under the confiscation provisions of the Criminal Justice Act 1988 or the Drug Trafficking Act 1994 from inviting suspects to complete a formal question and answer record after the interview is concluded.

2.8.3.1 **KEYNOTE**

Code C, para. 11.1 deals with when an interview should be held. By itself this might suggest that an interview is not needed when there is other strong evidence. However, the Criminal Procedure and Investigations Act 1996 Code of Practice, para. 3.4 states: 'In conducting an investigation, the investigator should pursue all reasonable lines of enquiry, whether these point towards or away from the suspect. What is reasonable will depend on the particular circumstances.' Interviewers should keep this in mind when deciding what questions to ask in an interview. Although juveniles or vulnerable persons are often capable of providing reliable evidence, they may, without knowing or wishing to do so, be particularly prone in certain circumstances to providing information that may be unreliable, misleading or self incriminating. Special care should always be taken when questioning such a person, and the appropriate adult should be involved if there is any doubt about a person's age, mental state or capacity. Because of the risk of unreliable evidence it is also important to obtain corroboration of any facts admitted whenever possible. Because of the risks, which the presence of the appropriate adult is intended to minimise, officers of superintendent rank or above should exercise their discretion under para. 11.18(a) to authorise the commencement of an interview in the appropriate adult's absence only in exceptional cases, if it is necessary to avert one or more of the specified risks in para. 11.1.

Whether an interaction between a police officer and a member of the public is defined as an interview by the court can be crucial as to whether it will be admissible in evidence. It is therefore essential to understand the definition of an interview for the purposes of the Police and Criminal Evidence Act 1984 and when a caution must be given and which caution must be given.

If a person is asked questions for reasons *other than obtaining evidence about his/her involvement or suspected involvement in an offence*, this is not an interview (and a caution need not be given). This point is confirmed in the case of *R* v *McGuinness* [1999] Crim LR 318, where the court confirmed that it was only when a person was suspected of an offence that the caution must be administered before questioning. Consequently, in *R* v *Miller* [1998] Crim LR 209 the court held that asking a person the single question, 'Are these ecstasy tablets?' criminally implicated the person and therefore the conversation was an interview (i.e. it would not be necessary to ask such a question if there were no suspicion that the tablets were a controlled substance).

Guidance on when questions do not amount to an interview is given by Code C, para. 10.1. This is not an exhaustive list, and officers may have other valid reasons to speak to a person before it becomes an interview.

Before a person can be interviewed about his/her involvement in an offence, that person must be cautioned. So it might be said that an interview is any questioning of a person after such time as a caution has been or should have been administered. Where a person is arrested for an offence, he/she must also be cautioned, as any questioning will amount to an interview.

The requirement in para. 11.1A for a suspect to be given sufficient information about the offence applies prior to the interview and whether or not they are legally represented. What is sufficient will depend on the circumstances of the case, but it should normally include, as a minimum, a description of the facts relating to the suspected offence that are known to the officer, including the time and place in question. This aims to avoid suspects being confused or unclear about what they are supposed to have done and to help an innocent suspect to clear the matter up more quickly.

If a person has not been arrested then he/she can be interviewed almost anywhere (but an officer intending to interview a person on private property must consider whether he/she is trespassing). If the interview with a person not under arrest takes place in a police station, Code C, para. 3.21 must be followed. Juveniles should not be arrested at their place of education unless this is unavoidable. When a juvenile is arrested at his/her place of education, the principal or his/her nominee must be informed; this also applies to 17-year-olds.

Significant Statement/Silence

At the start of the interview the investigating officer should put to the suspect any significant statement or silence which occurred before his/her arrival at the police station.

Significant statements/silence described in paras 11.4 and 11.4A will always be relevant to the offence and must be recorded. When a suspect agrees to read records of interviews and other comments and sign them as correct, he/she should be asked to endorse the record with, for example, 'I agree that this is a correct record of what was said' and add his/her signature. If the suspect does not agree with the record, the interviewer should record the details of any disagreement and ask the suspect to read these details and sign them to the effect that they accurately reflect his/her disagreement. Any refusal to sign should be recorded. Even where, as required by para. 11.4, at the beginning of an interview the interviewer puts to the detainee any significant statement or silence which occurred in the presence and hearing of a police officer or other police staff, this does not prevent the interviewer from putting significant statements and silences to a suspect again at a later stage or a further interview as the interviewer may wish to go through any significant statement or silence again if during earlier interviews adverse inferences could not be drawn.

This aspect of the interview is very important in terms of establishing whether the facts are disputed. If they are not disputed at this stage, it is unlikely that they will be challenged at any later court hearing and, if challenged, the defence will have to explain why this was not done at the time of the interview.

The courts may view a failure to put the statement to the suspect in a sinister light. In *R* v *Allen* [2001] EWCA Crim 1607, the court was concerned that the police failed to put the admission to the suspect in interview, despite thorough questioning, which it felt clearly placed a question mark over the admission's reliability.

If the suspect remains silent in relation to a 'significant silence', that silence may give rise to an adverse inference being drawn under s. 34 of the Criminal Justice and Public Order Act 1994 if the person raises it in his/her defence at court (as this is a very important issue, it may be necessary to delay the interview until the arrest notes are completed or the officers witnessing the offence/arrest have been consulted to ensure that all matters are put to the suspect at this stage). Consideration should be given to putting questions to a suspect who makes no comment, or even where the legal representative has stated that the suspect will make no comment, as this may allow the court to draw inferences against a defence that the suspect raises at court (see para. 2.8.2.3).

Where live-link interpretation has been authorised, Code C, para. 11.2 should be read with the following inserted at the start of the paragraph:

> Before the interview commences, the operation of live-link interpretation shall be explained and demonstrated to the suspect, their solicitor and appropriate adult, unless it has been previously explained and demonstrated (see Code C Annex N paragraph 4).

The Policing and Crime Act 2017 has amended s. 39 of the 1984 Act to allow interviews to be conducted by live link. 'Live link' is defined by the Act as an arrangement by which the officer who is not at the police station is able to see and hear, and to be seen and heard by, the person in police detention, any legal representative of that person and the officer who has custody of that person at the police station if the custody officer, in accordance with any code of practice issued under this Act, transfers or permits the transfer of a person in police detention to an officer for the purpose of an interview that is to be conducted to any extent by means of a live link by another police officer who is investigating the offence but is not at the police station where the person in police detention is held at the time of the interview, then the officer who is not at the police station has the same duty to ensure that the person is treated in accordance with the provisions of the 1984 Act and the Codes of Practice.

2.8.3.2

(b) Interview records

11.7

(a) An accurate record must be made of each interview, whether or not the interview takes place at a police station.

(b) The record must state the place of interview, the time it begins and ends, any interview breaks and, subject to *paragraph 2.6A*, the names of all those present; and must be made on the forms provided for this purpose or in the interviewer's report book or in accordance with Codes of Practice E or F.

(c) Any written record must be made and completed during the interview, unless this would not be practicable or would interfere with the conduct of the interview, and must constitute either a verbatim record of what has been said or, failing this, an account of the interview which adequately and accurately summarises it.

11.8 If a written record is not made during the interview it must be made as soon as practicable after its completion.

11.9 Written interview records must be timed and signed by the maker.

11.10 If a written record is not completed during the interview the reason must be recorded in the interview record.

11.11 Unless it is impracticable, the person interviewed shall be given the opportunity to read the interview record and to sign it as correct or to indicate how they consider it inaccurate. If the person interviewed cannot read or refuses to read the record or sign it, the senior interviewer present shall read it to them and ask whether they would like to sign it as correct or make their mark or to indicate how they consider it inaccurate. The interviewer shall certify on the interview record itself what has occurred.

11.12 If the appropriate adult or the person's solicitor is present during the interview, they should also be given an opportunity to read and sign the interview record or any written statement taken down during the interview.

11.13 A record shall be made of any comments made by a suspect, including unsolicited comments, which are outside the context of an interview but which might be relevant to the offence. Any such record must be timed and signed by the maker. When practicable the suspect shall be given the opportunity to read that record and to sign it as correct or to indicate how they consider it inaccurate.

11.14 Any refusal by a person to sign an interview record when asked in accordance with this Code must itself be recorded.

(c) Juveniles and vulnerable persons

11.15 A juvenile or vulnerable person must not be interviewed regarding their involvement or suspected involvement in a criminal offence or offences, or asked to provide or sign a written statement under caution or record of interview, in the absence of the appropriate adult unless *paragraphs 11.1* or *11.18* to *11.20* apply.

11.16 Juveniles may only be interviewed at their place of education in exceptional circumstances and only when the principal or their nominee agrees. Every effort should be made to notify the parent(s) or other person responsible for the juvenile's welfare and the appropriate adult, if this is a different person, that the police want to interview the juvenile and reasonable time should be allowed to enable the appropriate adult to be present at the interview. If awaiting the appropriate adult would cause unreasonable delay, and unless the juvenile is suspected of an offence against the educational establishment, the principal or their nominee can act as the appropriate adult for the purposes of the interview.

11.17 If an appropriate adult is present at an interview, they shall be informed:

- that they are not expected to act simply as an observer; and
- that the purpose of their presence is to:
  - ~ advise the person being interviewed;
  - ~ observe whether the interview is being conducted properly and fairly; and
  - ~ facilitate communication with the person being interviewed. See *paragraph 1.7A*.

11.17A The appropriate adult may be required to leave the interview if their conduct is such that the interviewer is unable properly to put questions to the suspect. This will include situations where the appropriate adult's approach or conduct prevents or unreasonably obstructs proper questions being put to the suspect or the suspect's responses being recorded. If the interviewer considers an appropriate adult is acting in such a way, they will stop the interview and consult an officer not below superintendent rank, if one is readily available, and otherwise an officer not below inspector rank not connected with the investigation. After speaking to the appropriate adult, the officer consulted must remind the adult that their role under *paragraph 11.17* does not allow them to obstruct proper questioning and give the adult an opportunity to respond. The officer consulted will then decide if the interview should continue without the attendance of that appropriate adult. If they decide it should, another appropriate adult must be obtained before the interview continues, unless the provisions of *paragraph 11.18* below apply.

(d) Vulnerable suspects—urgent interviews at police stations

11.18 The following interviews may take place only if an officer of superintendent rank or above considers delaying the interview will lead to the consequences in *paragraph 11.1(a)* to *(c)*, and is satisfied the interview would not significantly harm the person's physical or mental state (see *Annex G*):

(a) an interview of a detained juvenile or person who is vulnerable without the appropriate adult being present;

(b) an interview of anyone detained other than in *(a)* who appears unable to:

- appreciate the significance of questions and their answers; or
- understand what is happening because of the effects of drink, drugs or any illness, ailment or condition;

(c) an interview, without an interpreter having been arranged, of a detained person whom the custody officer has determined requires an interpreter (see *paragraphs 3.5(c)(ii)* and *3.12*) which is carried out by an interviewer speaking the suspect's own language or (as the case may be) otherwise establishing effective communication which is sufficient to enable the necessary questions to be asked and answered in order to avert the consequences. See *paragraphs 13.2* and *13.5*.

11.19 These interviews may not continue once sufficient information has been obtained to avert the consequences in *paragraph 11.1(a)* to *(c)*.

11.20 A record shall be made of the grounds for any decision to interview a person under *paragraph 11.18*.

(e) Conduct and recording of Interviews at police stations—use of live link

11.21 When a suspect in police detention is interviewed using a live link by a police officer who is not at the police station where the detainee is held, the provisions of this section that govern the conduct and making a written record of that interview, shall be subject to *paragraph 12.9B* of this Code.

(f) Witnesses

11.22 The provisions of this Code and Codes E and F which govern the conduct and recording of interviews do not apply to interviews with, or taking statements from, witnesses.

2.8.3.3 **KEYNOTE**

Paragraph 17A makes provision for requiring the appropriate adult to leave the interview if their conduct is such that the interviewer is unable properly to put questions to the suspect. It must be noted that the appropriate adult may intervene if they consider it is necessary to help the suspect understand any question asked and to help the suspect to answer any question. Paragraph 11.17A only applies if the appropriate adult's approach or conduct prevents or unreasonably obstructs proper questions being put to the suspect or the suspect's response being recorded. Examples of unacceptable conduct include answering questions on a suspect's behalf or providing written replies for the suspect to quote. An officer who takes the decision to exclude an appropriate adult must be in a position to satisfy the court the decision was properly made. In order to do this, they may need to witness what is happening and give the suspect's solicitor (if they have one) who witnessed what happened, an opportunity to comment.

Paragraph 11.18(c) is worthy of note; this requires urgent interviews authorised by a superintendent under para. 11.18 which would have had an interpreter to be carried out by an interviewer who can speak the suspect's own language or in some other way establish effective communication to allow the questions to be asked and answered.

2.8.3.4 **KEYNOTE**

Statements from Suspects

Statements made by an accused under caution to the police, whether in writing or verbally are confidential in the sense that they may be used against the suspect in proceedings, not that they could be used for any purpose of the police. It is clearly implicit in the relationship between the police and the accused that the information, before being used in open court, is used only for the purposes for which it is provided and not for extraneous purposes, such as the media. However, the obligation of confidentiality (which is now included in the Police Standards of Professional Behaviour) in respect of such a statement will be brought to an end where the contents of the statement are already in the public domain (*Bunn v British Broadcasting Corporation* [1998] 3 All ER 552).

2.8.4 Code C—12 Interviews in Police Stations

(a) Action

When the interviewer and suspect are present in the same police station

12.1 If a police officer wants to interview or conduct enquiries which require the presence of a detainee, the custody officer is responsible for deciding whether to deliver the detainee into the officer's custody. An investigating officer who is given custody of a detainee takes over responsibility for the detainee's care and safe custody for the purposes of this Code until they return the detainee to the custody officer when they must report the manner in which they complied with the Code whilst having custody of the detainee.

12.2 Except as below, in any period of 24 hours a detainee must be allowed a continuous period of at least 8 hours for rest, free from questioning, travel or any interruption in connection with the investigation concerned. This period should normally be at night or other appropriate time which takes account of when the detainee last slept or rested. If a detainee is arrested at a police station after going there voluntarily, the period of 24 hours runs from the time of their arrest and not the time of arrival at the police station. The period may not be interrupted or delayed, except:

(a) when there are reasonable grounds for believing not delaying or interrupting the period would:
   (i) involve a risk of harm to people or serious loss of, or damage to, property;
   (ii) delay unnecessarily the person's release from custody; or
   (iii) otherwise prejudice the outcome of the investigation;
(b) at the request of the detainee, their appropriate adult or legal representative;
(c) when a delay or interruption is necessary in order to:
   (i) comply with the legal obligations and duties arising under section 15; or
   (ii) to take action required under *section 9* or in accordance with medical advice.

If the period is interrupted in accordance with *(a)*, a fresh period must be allowed. Interruptions under *(b)* and *(c)* do not require a fresh period to be allowed.

12.3 Before a detainee is interviewed, the custody officer, in consultation with the officer in charge of the investigation and appropriate healthcare professionals as necessary, shall assess whether the detainee is fit enough to be interviewed. This means determining and considering the risks to the detainee's physical and mental state if the interview took place and determining what safeguards are needed to allow the interview to take place. See *Annex G*. The custody officer shall not allow a detainee to be interviewed if the custody officer considers it would cause significant harm to the detainee's physical or mental state. Vulnerable suspects listed at *paragraph 11.18* shall be treated as always being at some risk during an interview and these persons may not be interviewed except in accordance with *paragraphs 11.18* to *11.20*.

12.4 As far as practicable interviews shall take place in interview rooms which are adequately heated, lit and ventilated.

12.5 A suspect whose detention without charge has been authorised under PACE because the detention is necessary for an interview to obtain evidence of the offence for which they have been arrested may choose not to answer questions but police do not require the suspect's consent or agreement to interview them for this purpose. If a suspect takes steps to prevent themselves being questioned or further questioned, e.g. by refusing to leave their cell to go to a suitable interview room or by trying to leave the interview room, they shall be advised their consent or agreement to interview is not required. The suspect shall be cautioned as in *section 10*, and informed if they fail or refuse to co-operate, the interview may take place in the cell and that their failure or refusal to co-operate may be given in evidence. The suspect shall then be invited to co-operate and go into the interview room. If they refuse and the custody officer considers, on reasonable grounds, that the interview should not be delayed, the custody officer has discretion to direct that the interview be conducted in a cell.

12.6 People being questioned or making statements shall not be required to stand.

12.7 Before the interview commences each interviewer shall, subject to *paragraph 2.6A*, identify themselves and any other persons present to the interviewee.

12.8 Breaks from interviewing should be made at recognised meal times or at other times that take account of when an interviewee last had a meal. Short refreshment breaks shall be provided at approximately two hour intervals, subject to the interviewer's discretion to delay a break if there are reasonable grounds for believing it would:

(i) involve a:
  - risk of harm to people;
  - serious loss of, or damage to, property;

(ii) unnecessarily delay the detainee's release; or

(iii) otherwise prejudice the outcome of the investigation.

12.9 If during the interview a complaint is made by or on behalf of the interviewee concerning the provisions of any of the Codes, or it comes to the interviewer's notice that the interviewee may have been treated improperly, the interviewer should:

(i) record the matter in the interview record; and

(ii) inform the custody officer, who is then responsible for dealing with it as in *section 9*.

Interviewer not present at the same station as the detainee—use of live link

12.9A Amendments to PACE, section 39, allow a person in police detention to be interviewed using a live link (see *paragraph 1.13(e)(i)*) by a police officer who is not at the police station where the detainee is held. Subject to *sub-paragraphs (a)* to *(f)* below, the custody officer is responsible for deciding on a case by case basis whether a detainee is fit to be interviewed (see *paragraph 12.3*) and should be delivered into the physical custody of an officer who is not involved in the investigation, for the purpose of enabling another officer who is investigating the offence for which the person is detained and who is not at the police station where the person is detained, to interview the detainee by means of a live link.

(a) The custody officer must be satisfied that the live link to be used provides for accurate and secure communication with the suspect. The provisions of *paragraph 13.13* shall apply to communications between the interviewing officer, the suspect and anyone else whose presence at the interview or, (as the case may be) whose access to any communications between the suspect and the interviewer, has been authorised by the custody officer or the interviewing officer.

(b) Each decision must take account of the age, gender and vulnerability of the suspect, the nature and circumstances of the offence and the investigation and the impact on the suspect of carrying out the interview by means of a live link. For this reason, the custody officer must consider whether the ability of the particular suspect, to communicate confidently and effectively for the purpose of the interview is likely to be adversely affected or otherwise undermined or limited if the interviewing officer is not physically present and a live-link is used. Although a suspect for whom an appropriate adult is required may be more likely to be adversely affected as described, it is important to note that a person who does not require an appropriate adult may also be adversely impacted if interviewed by means of a live link.

(c) If the custody officer is satisfied that interviewing the detainee by means of a live link *would not* adversely affect or otherwise undermine or limit the suspect's ability to communicate confidently and effectively for the purpose of the *interview*, the officer must so inform the suspect, their solicitor and (if applicable) the appropriate adult. At the same time, the operation of the live-link must be explained and demonstrated to them, they must be advised of the chief officer's obligations concerning the security of live-link communications under *paragraph 13.13* and they must be asked if they wish to make representations that the live-link should not be used or if they require more information about the operation of the arrangements. They must also be told that at any time live-link is in use, they may make representations to the custody officer or the interviewer that its operation should cease and that the physical presence of the interviewer should be arranged.

When the authority of an inspector is required

(d) If:

(i) representations are made that a live-link should not be used to carry out the interview, or that at any time it is in use, its operation should cease and the physical presence of the interviewer arranged; and

(ii) the custody officer in consultation with the interviewer is unable to allay the concerns raised;

then live-link may not be used, or (as the case may be) continue to be used, unless authorised in writing by an officer of the rank of inspector or above in accordance with *sub-paragraph (e)*.

(e) Authority may be given if the officer is satisfied that interviewing the detainee by means of a live link is necessary and justified. In making this decision, the officer must have regard to:

(i) the circumstances of the suspect;

(ii) the nature and seriousness of the offence;

(iii) the requirements of the investigation, including its likely impact on both the suspect and any victim(s);

(iv) the representations made by the suspect, their solicitor and (if applicable) the appropriate adult that a live-link should not be used (see *sub-paragraph (b)*);

(v) the impact on the investigation of making arrangements for the physical presence of the interviewer; and

(vi) the risk if the interpreter is not *physically* present, evidence obtained using link interpretation might be excluded in subsequent criminal proceedings; and

(vii) the likely impact on the suspect and the investigation of any consequential delay to arrange for the interpreter to be *physically* present with the suspect.

(f) The officer given custody of the detainee *and* the interviewer take over responsibility for the detainee's care, treatment and safe custody for the purposes of this Code until the detainee is returned to the custody officer. On that return, both must report the manner in which they complied with the Code during period in question.

12.9B When a suspect detained at a police station is interviewed using a live link in accordance with *paragraph 12.9A*, the officer given custody of the detainee at the police station and the interviewer who is not present at the police station, take over responsibility for ensuring compliance with the provisions of *sections 11* and *12* of this Code, or *Code E* (Audio recording) or *Code F* (Audio visual recording) that govern the conduct and recording of that interview. In these circumstances:

(a) *the interviewer who is not at the police station where the detainee is held* must direct the officer having physical custody of the suspect at the police station, to take the action required by those provisions and which the interviewer would be required to take if they were present at the police station.

(b) *the officer having physical custody of the suspect at the police station* must take the action required by those provisions and which would otherwise be required to be taken by the interviewer if they were present at the police station. This applies whether or not the officer has been so directed by the interviewer but in such a case, the officer must inform the interviewer of the action taken.

(c) *during the course of the interview*, the officers in (a) and (b) may consult each other as necessary to clarify any action to be taken and to avoid any misunderstanding. Such consultations must, if in the hearing of the suspect and any other person present with the suspect (for example, a solicitor, appropriate adult or interpreter) be recorded in the interview record.

(b) Documentation

12.10 A record must be made of the:

- time a detainee is not in the custody of the custody officer, and why reason
- for any refusal to deliver the detainee out of that custody.

12.11 A record shall be made of the following:

(a) the reasons it was not practicable to use an interview room;

(b) any action taken as in *paragraph 12.5*; and

(c) the actions, decisions, authorisations, representations and outcomes arising from the requirements of *paragraphs 12.9A* and *12.9B*.

The record shall be made on the custody record or in the interview record for action taken whilst an interview record is being kept, with a brief reference to this effect in the custody record.

12.12 Any decision to delay a break in an interview must be recorded, with reasons, in the interview record.

12.13 All written statements made at police stations under caution shall be written on forms provided for the purpose.

12.14 All written statements made under caution shall be taken in accordance with *Annex D*. Before a person makes a written statement under caution at a police station, they shall be reminded about the right to legal advice.

2.8.4.1

KEYNOTE

Meal breaks should normally last at least 45 minutes and shorter breaks after two hours should last at least 15 minutes. If the interviewer prolongs the interview to avoid the risk of harm to people, serious loss of, or damage to, property, to delay the detainee's release or otherwise prejudice the outcome of the investigation, a longer break should be provided. If there is a short interview, and another short interview is contemplated, the length of the break may be reduced if there are reasonable grounds to believe that this is necessary to avoid any of the consequences in para. 12.8(i)–(iii).

When deciding whether to hand over a detained person to the interviewing officer under para. 12.1 the custody officer should be mindful of whether there is sufficient relevant time remaining for the detained person to be interviewed (see Code C, para. 15).

Statements under caution, particularly of a detained person, are less common than interviews. If a person has been interviewed and it has been audio or visually recorded or an interview has been recorded contemporaneously in writing, statements under caution should normally be taken in these circumstances only at the person's express wish. See Code C, Annex C for restrictions on drawing inferences and Annex D for the variable declarations the person must include in his/her statements. A person may however be asked if they want to make such a statement.

2.8.4.2

KEYNOTE

Solicitors and Legal Advice

Code C, s. 6 provides guidance with regard to legal advice and access to solicitors during interview. Where a solicitor is available at the time the interview begins or while it is in progress, the solicitor must be allowed to be present while the person is interviewed (Code C, para. 6.8).

If the investigating officer considers that a solicitor is acting in such a way that he/she is unable properly to put questions to the suspect, he/she will stop the interview and consult an officer not below the rank of superintendent, if one is readily available, otherwise an officer not below the rank of inspector who is not connected with the investigation, to decide whether that solicitor should be excluded from the interview. The interview may also have to be stopped in order to allow another solicitor to be instructed (Code C, para. 6.10).

If a request for legal advice is made during an interview, the interviewing officer must stop the interview immediately and arrange for legal advice to be provided. If the suspect changes his/her mind again, the interview can continue provided Code C, para. 6.6 is complied with.

2.8.4.3 **KEYNOTE**

What Should Be Disclosed to the Solicitor Before Interview?

It is important not to confuse the duty of disclosure to a person once charged with the need to disclose evidence to suspects before interviewing them. After a person has been charged, and before trial, the rules of disclosure are clear (**see chapter 2.5**) and almost all material must be disclosed to the defence.

Prior to charge, Code C, para. 11.1A provides that some disclosure must be given before a person is interviewed in order to allow for the effective exercise of the rights of the defence. What is sufficient will depend on the circumstances of the case, but it should normally include, as a minimum, a description of the facts relating to the suspected offence that are known to the officer, including the time and place in question; additionally, the custody record must be provided. In respect of the provision of a copy of the 'first description' of a suspect, it should be noted that Code D (para. 3.1) states that a copy of the 'first description' shall, where practicable, be given to the suspect or his/her solicitor before any procedures under paras 3.5 to 3.10, 3.21 or 3.23 are carried out. In other words, the disclosure requirement is that a copy of the 'first description' shall, where practicable, be given to the suspect or his/her solicitor before a video identification, an identification parade, a group identification or confrontation takes place. Therefore, an officer disclosing information to a solicitor at the interview stage (which is taking place in advance of any identification procedures) need not provide the 'first description' of a suspect at that time.

Further, there is nothing within the Criminal Justice and Public Order Act 1994 that states that information must be disclosed before an inference from silence can be made. Indeed, in *R* v *Imran* [1997] Crim LR 754, the court held that it is totally wrong to submit that a defendant should be prevented from lying by being presented with the whole of the evidence against him/her prior to the interview.

In *R* v *Argent* [1997] Crim LR 346, the court dismissed the argument that an inference could not be drawn under s. 34 of the Criminal Justice and Public Order Act 1994 because there had not been full disclosure at the interview. However, the court did recognise that it may be a factor to take into account for the jury to decide whether the failure to answer questions was reasonable (**see para. 2.8.2.3** regarding s. 34 of the Criminal Justice and Public Order Act 1994).

In *Black* v *R* [2020] EWCA Crim 915, the court confirmed:

> that an inference should only be drawn under section 34 of the CJPOA 1994 if the prosecution case at the time of the interview is so strong as to justify an answer. ... [I]f nothing has been said or shown to the defendant at the police interview to call for an answer from the defendant, it would be wrong to draw an inference against the defendant for a failure to provide such an answer. It is also established that the strength or weakness of the prosecution case at interview may be a relevant circumstance for the jury to consider under section 34 of the CJPOA 1994.

In *R* v *Roble* [1997] Crim LR 449, the court suggested that an inference would not be drawn where a solicitor gave advice to remain silent where, for example, the interviewing officer had disclosed too little of the case for the solicitor usefully to advise his/her client, or where the nature of the offence, or the material in the hands of the police, was so complex or related to matters so long ago that no sensible immediate response was feasible.

It was not uncommon in the past for solicitors to advise on no comment interviews and this has been relied on by defendants to avoid adverse inferences being drawn from their silence. In *R* v *Morgan* [2001] EWCA Crim 445, the Court of Appeal stated that a court was entitled to assume that a solicitor would advise his/her client about the adverse inferences rule. In *R* v *Ali* [2001] EWCA Crim 683, the court stated that the question was not whether the advice to remain silent was good advice but whether it provided an adequate reason for failing to answer questions.

In *R* v *Hoare* [2004] EWCA Crim 784, the Court of Appeal held that the purpose of s. 34 was to qualify a defendant's right to silence, rather than to exclude a jury from drawing an adverse inference against a defendant merely because he/she had been advised by his/her solicitor to remain silent, whether or not he/

she genuinely or reasonably relied on that advice. Where a defendant had an explanation to give that was consistent with his/her innocence it was not 'reasonable', within the meaning of s. 34(1), for him/her to fail to give that explanation in interview even where he/she had been advised by his/her solicitor to remain silent. Legal advice by itself could not preclude the drawing of an adverse inference.

There is a balance to be struck between providing the solicitor with enough information to understand the nature of the case against his/her client and keeping back material which, if disclosed, may allow the suspect the opportunity to avoid implicating him/herself. For instance, in *R* v *Thirlwell* [2002] EWCA Crim 286, the Court of Appeal agreed that the solicitor had not been entitled to provisional medical evidence as to possible causes of death in a murder case.

Useful guidance is provided in the College of Policing Investigative Interviewing APP; this can be found at <https://www.app.college.police.uk/app-content/investigations/investigative-interviewing/#preinterview-briefings>.

2.8.4.4 **KEYNOTE**

'Live link' means an arrangement by means of which the interviewing officer who is not at the police station is able to see and hear, and to be seen and heard by, the detainee concerned, the detainee's solicitor, any appropriate adult present and the officer who has custody of that detainee. See paras 13.12 to 13.14 and Annex N for application to live-link interpretation. In considering whether the use of the live link is appropriate in a particular case, the custody officer, in consultation with the interviewer, should make an assessment of the detainee's ability to understand and take part in the interviewing process and make a record of the outcome. If the suspect has asked for legal advice, their solicitor should be involved in the assessment and in the case of a juvenile or vulnerable person, the appropriate adult should be involved.

The explanation and demonstration of live-link interpretation is intended to help the suspect, solicitor and appropriate adult make an informed decision and to allay any concerns they may have. Factors affecting the arrangements for the interviewer to be physically present will include the location of the police station where the interview would take place and the availability of an interviewer with sufficient knowledge of the investigation who can attend that station and carry out the interview.

2.8.5 Code C—Annex C: Restriction on Drawing Adverse Inferences from Silence and Terms of the Caution when the Restriction Applies

(a) The restriction on drawing adverse inferences from silence

1. The Criminal Justice and Public Order Act 1994, sections 34, 36 and 37 as amended by the Youth Justice and Criminal Evidence Act 1999, section 58 describe the conditions under which adverse inferences may be drawn from a person's failure or refusal to say anything about their involvement in the offence when interviewed, after being charged or informed they may be prosecuted. These provisions are subject to an overriding restriction on the ability of a court or jury to draw adverse inferences from a person's silence. This restriction applies:
   (a) to any detainee at a police station, who, before being interviewed, see *section 11* or being charged or informed they may be prosecuted, see *section 16*, has:
      (i) asked for legal advice, see *section 6, paragraph 6.1*;
      (ii) not been allowed an opportunity to consult a solicitor, including the duty solicitor, as in this Code; and
      (iii) not changed their mind about wanting legal advice, see *section 6, paragraph 6.6(d)*.
      Note the condition in (ii) will:
      - apply when a detainee who has asked for legal advice is interviewed before speaking to a solicitor as *in section 6, paragraph 6.6(a)* or *(b)*;
      - not apply if the detained person declines to ask for the duty solicitor, see *section 6, paragraphs 6.6(c)* and *(d)*.

(b) to any person charged with, or informed they may be prosecuted for, an offence who:

(i) has had brought to their notice a written statement made by another person or the content of an interview with another person which relates to that offence, see *section 16, paragraph 16.4*;

(ii) is interviewed about that offence, see *section 16, paragraph 16.5*; or

(iii) makes a written statement about that offence, see *Annex D, paragraphs 4* and *9*.

(b) Terms of the caution when the restriction applies

2. When a requirement to caution arises at a time when the restriction on drawing adverse inferences from silence applies, the caution shall be:

'You do not have to say anything, but anything you do say may be given in evidence.'

Where the use of the Welsh Language is appropriate, the caution may be used directly in Welsh in the following terms:

'Does dim rhaid i chi ddweud dim byd, ond gall unrhyw beth yr ydych chi'n ei ddweud gael ei roi fel tystiolaeth.'

3. Whenever the restriction either begins to apply or ceases to apply after a caution has already been given, the person shall be re-cautioned in the appropriate terms. The changed position on drawing inferences and that the previous caution no longer applies shall also be explained to the detainee in ordinary language.

2.8.5.1 **KEYNOTE**

The restriction on drawing inferences from silence does not apply to a person who has not been detained and who therefore cannot be prevented from seeking legal advice if he/she wants to (see Code C, paras 10.2 and 3.15).

The following is suggested as a framework to help explain changes in the position on drawing adverse inferences if the restriction on drawing adverse inferences from silence applies. Annex C, para. 2 sets out the alternative terms of the caution to be used when the restriction on drawing adverse inferences from silence applies. The situation is likely to occur during a detainee's detention where it will be necessary to administer both of these cautions at various times during his/her detention. As there is a significant difference between them in relation to the right to silence, it will be important to make it clear which caution applies to the detainee during any interview or charge procedure. Guidance as to what the detainee should be told is provided by Code C, Annex C, Note C2; this paragraph gives sample explanations that need to be explained to the detainee before the change in caution is given.

Full caution already given (in most cases given when arrested)	➔ Detainee's access to legal advice restricted as per Code C, Annex C, para. 1. Need to give alternative caution.	➔ Explain change in caution as set out at Code C, Annex C, Note C2(a)(i).	➔ Give caution as set out at Annex C, para. 2.
Full caution already given	➔ Detainee has been charged but is further interviewed (Code C, Annex C, para. 1). Need to give alternative caution.	➔ Explain change in caution as set out at Code C, Annex C, Note C2(a)(ii).	➔ Give caution as set out at Annex C, para. 2.
Caution as set out at Annex C, para. 2, given	➔ Detainee has now had access to a solicitor or changed his/her mind. Need to give alternative caution.	➔ Explain change in caution as set out at Code C, Annex C, Note C2(b).	➔ Give caution as set out at Code C, para. 10.5.

Where Code C, Annex C, para. 1 applies (i.e. the detainee has not been given access to a solicitor) and the detainee is charged with an offence or informed that he/she may be prosecuted, the caution at Annex C, para. 2 should be used; on all other occasions the caution at Code C, para. 16.2 should be used.

When the circumstances of the detained person change and restrictions on drawing adverse inferences now apply, the following form of words, where applicable, can be used:

> The caution you were previously given no longer applies. This is because after that caution:
> (i) you asked to speak to a solicitor but have not yet been allowed an opportunity to speak to a solicitor; or
> (ii) you have been charged with/informed you may be prosecuted.

See para. 1(b).

Followed by:

> This means that from now on, adverse inferences cannot be drawn at court and your defence will not be harmed just because you choose to say nothing. Please listen carefully to the caution I am about to give you because it will apply from now on. You will see that it does not say anything about your defence being harmed.

The following form of words should be used where the circumstances set out in Annex C, para. 1(a) that a restriction on drawing adverse inferences ceases to apply before or at the time the person is charged or informed that he/she may be prosecuted apply:

> The caution you were previously given no longer applies. This is because after that caution you have been allowed an opportunity to speak to a solicitor. Please listen carefully to the caution I am about to give you because it will apply from now on. It explains how your defence at court may be affected if you choose to say nothing.

2.8.6 Code C—Annex D: Written Statements under Caution

(a) Written by a person under caution

1. A person shall always be invited to write down what they want to say.
2. A person who has not been charged with, or informed they may be prosecuted for, any offence to which the statement they want to write relates, shall:
   (a) unless the statement is made at a time when the restriction on drawing adverse inferences from silence applies, see *Annex C*, be asked to write out and sign the following before writing what they want to say:

   'I make this statement of my own free will. I understand that I do not have to say anything but that it may harm my defence if I do not mention when questioned something which I later rely on in court. This statement may be given in evidence.';

   (b) if the statement is made at a time when the restriction on drawing adverse inferences from silence applies, be asked to write out and sign the following before writing what they want to say;

   'I make this statement of my own free will. I understand that I do not have to say anything. This statement may be given in evidence.'
3. When a person, on the occasion of being charged with or informed they may be prosecuted for any offence, asks to make a statement which relates to any such offence and wants to write it they shall:
   (a) unless the restriction on drawing adverse inferences from silence, see *Annex C*, applied when they were so charged or informed they may be prosecuted, be asked to write out and sign the following before writing what they want to say:

   'I make this statement of my own free will. I understand that I do not have to say anything but that it may harm my defence if I do not mention when questioned something which I later rely on in court. This statement may be given in evidence.';

(b) if the restriction on drawing adverse inferences from silence applied when they were so charged or informed they may be prosecuted, be asked to write out and sign the following before writing what they want to say:

'I make this statement of my own free will. I understand that I do not have to say anything. This statement may be given in evidence.'

4. When a person who has already been charged with or informed they may be prosecuted for any offence asks to make a statement which relates to any such offence and wants to write it, they shall be asked to write out and sign the following before writing what they want to say:

'I make this statement of my own free will. I understand that I do not have to say anything. This statement may be given in evidence.';

5. Any person writing their own statement shall be allowed to do so without any prompting except a police officer or other police staff may indicate to them which matters are material or question any ambiguity in the statement.

(b) Written by a police officer or other police staff

6. If a person says they would like someone to write the statement for them, a police officer, or other police staff shall write the statement.
7. If the person has not been charged with, or informed they may be prosecuted for, any offence to which the statement they want to make relates they shall, before starting, be asked to sign, or make their mark, to the following:
   (a) unless the statement is made at a time when the restriction on drawing adverse inferences from silence applies, see Annex C:

   'I, ..., wish to make a statement. I want someone to write down what I say. I understand that I do not have to say anything but that it may harm my defence if I do not mention when questioned something which I later rely on in court. This statement may be given in evidence.';

   (b) if the statement is made at a time when the restriction on drawing adverse inferences from silence applies:

   'I, ..., wish to make a statement. I want someone to write down what I say. I understand that I do not have to say anything. This statement may be given in evidence.'

8. If, on the occasion of being charged with or informed they may be prosecuted for any offence, the person asks to make a statement which relates to any such offence they shall before starting be asked to sign, or make their mark to, the following:
   (a) unless the restriction on drawing adverse inferences from silence applied, see *Annex C*, when they were so charged or informed they may be prosecuted:

   'I, ..., wish to make a statement. I want someone to write down what I say. I understand that I do not have to say anything but that it may harm my defence if I do not mention when questioned something which I later rely on in court. This statement may be given in evidence.';

   (b) if the restriction on drawing adverse inferences from silence applied when they were so charged or informed they may be prosecuted:

   'I, ..., wish to make a statement. I want someone to write down what I say. I understand that I do not have to say anything. This statement may be given in evidence.'

9. If, having already been charged with or informed they may be prosecuted for any offence, a person asks to make a statement which relates to any such offence they shall before starting, be asked to sign, or make their mark to:

'I, ..., wish to make a statement. I want someone to write down what I say. I understand that I do not have to say anything. This statement may be given in evidence.'

10. The person writing the statement must take down the exact words spoken by the person making it and must not edit or paraphrase it. Any questions that are necessary, e.g. to make it more intelligible, and the answers given must be recorded at the same time on the statement form.
11. When the writing of a statement is finished the person making it shall be asked to read it and to make any corrections, alterations or additions they want. When they have finished reading they shall be asked to write and sign or make their mark on the following certificate at the end of the statement:

'I have read the above statement, and I have been able to correct, alter or add anything I wish. This statement is true. I have made it of my own free will.'

12. If the person making the statement cannot read, or refuses to read it, or to write the above mentioned certificate at the end of it or to sign it, the person taking the statement shall read it to them and ask them if they would like to correct, alter or add anything and to put their signature or make their mark at the end. The person taking the statement shall certify on the statement itself what has occurred.

2.8.6.1 **KEYNOTE**

The sections of Code C above need to be read in conjunction with Code E where the interview of a suspect is to be audio recorded.

2.8.7 PACE Code of Practice on Audio Recording Interviews with Suspects (Code E)

This Code applies to interviews carried out after 00.00 on 31st July 2018, notwithstanding that the interview may have commenced before that time.

1 General

1.0 The procedures in this Code must be used fairly, responsibly, with respect for the people to whom they apply and without unlawful discrimination. Under the Equality Act 2010, section 149 (Public Sector Equality Duty), police forces must, in carrying out their functions, have due regard to the need to eliminate unlawful discrimination, harassment, victimisation and any other conduct which is prohibited by that Act, to advance equality of opportunity between people who share a relevant protected characteristic and people who do not share it, and to foster good relations between those persons. The Equality Act *also* makes it unlawful for police officers to discriminate against, harass or victimise any person on the grounds of the 'protected characteristics' of age, disability, gender reassignment, race, religion or belief, sex and sexual orientation, marriage and civil partnership, pregnancy and maternity, when using their powers.

1.1 This Code of Practice must be readily available for consultation by:
- police officers
- police staff
- detained persons
- members of the public.

1.2 The *Notes for Guidance* included are not provisions of this Code. They form guidance to police officers and others about its application and interpretation.

1.3 Nothing in this Code shall detract from the requirements of Code C, the Code of Practice for the detention, treatment and questioning of persons by police officers.

1.4 The interviews and other matters to which this Code applies are described in section 2. This Code does not apply to the conduct and recording in England and Wales, of:

- interviews of persons detained under section 41 of, or Schedule 7 to, the Terrorism Act 2000, and
- post-charge questioning of persons authorised under section 22 of the Counter Terrorism Act 2008.

These must be video recorded with sound in accordance with the provisions of the separate Code of Practice issued under *paragraph 3 of Schedule 8 to the Terrorism Act 2000* and under *section 25 of the Counter-Terrorism Act 2008*. If, during the course of an interview or questioning under this Code, it becomes apparent that the interview or questioning should be conducted under that separate Code, the interview should only continue in accordance with that Code.

Note: The provisions of this Code and Code F which govern the conduct and recording of interviews *do not apply* to interviews with, or taking statements from, witnesses.

1.5 In this Code:

- 'appropriate adult' has the same meaning as in Code C, *paragraph 1.7*.
- 'vulnerable person' has the same meaning as described in Code C *paragraph 1.13(d)*.
- 'solicitor' has the same meaning as in Code C, *paragraph 6.12*.
- 'interview' has the same meaning as in Code C, *paragraph 11.1A*.

1.5A The provisions of this Code which require interviews with suspects to be audio recorded and the provisions of Code F which permit simultaneous visual recording provide safeguards:

- for suspects against inaccurate recording of the words used in questioning them and of their demeanour during the interview; and;
- for police interviewers against unfounded allegations made by, or on behalf of, suspects about the conduct of the interview and what took place during the interview which might otherwise appear credible.

Recording of interviews must therefore be carried out openly to instil confidence in its reliability as an impartial and accurate record of the interview.

1.5B The provisions of Code C:

- *sections 10 and 11*, and the applicable *Notes for Guidance* apply to the conduct of interviews to which this Code applies.
- *paragraphs 11.7 to 11.14* apply only when a written record is needed.

1.5C Code C, *paragraphs 10.10, 10.11* and *Annex C* describe the restriction on drawing adverse inferences from an arrested suspect's failure or refusal to say anything about their involvement in the offence when interviewed or after being charged or informed they may be prosecuted, and how it affects the terms of the caution and determines if and by whom a special warning under sections 36 and 37 of the Criminal Justice and Public Order Act 1994 can be given.

1.6 In this Code:

(a) in relation to the place where an interview of a suspect to which this Code or (as the case may be) Code F, applies, is conducted and recorded:

(i) *'authorised'* in relation to the recording devices described in (ii) and (iii), means any such device that the chief officer has authorised interviewers under their direction and control to use to record the interview in question at the place in question, provided that the interviewer in question has been trained to set up and operate the device, in compliance with the manufacturer's instructions and subject to the operating procedures required by the chief officer;

(ii) *'removable recording media device'* means a recording device which, when set up and operated in accordance with the manufacturer's instructions and the operating procedures required by the chief officers, uses removable, physical recording media (such as magnetic tape, optical disc or solid state memory card) for the purpose of making a clear and accurate, audio recording or (as the case may be) audio-visual recording, of the interview in question which can then be played back and copied using that device or any other device. A sign or indicator on the device which is visible to the suspect must show when the device is recording;

(iii) *'secure digital recording network device'* means a recording device which, when set up and operated in accordance with the manufacturer's instructions and the operating procedures required by the chief officers, enables a clear and accurate original audio recording or (as the case may be) audio-visual recording, of the interview in question, to be made and stored using non-removable storage, as a digital file or a series of such files that can be securely transferred by a wired or wireless connection to a remote secure network file server system (which may have cloud based storage) which ensures that access to interview recordings for all purposes is strictly controlled and is restricted to those whose access, either generally or in specific cases, is necessary. Examples of access include playing back the whole or part of any original recording and making one or more copies of, the whole or part of that original recording. A sign or indicator on the device which is visible to the suspect must show when the device is recording.

(b) 'designated person' means a person other than a police officer, who has specified powers and duties conferred or imposed on them by designation under section 38 or 39 of the Police Reform Act 2002.

(c) any reference to a police officer includes a designated person acting in the exercise or performance of the powers and duties conferred or imposed on them by their designation.

1.7 Section 2 of this Code sets out the requirement that an authorised recording device, if available, must be used to record a suspect interview and when such a device cannot be used, it allows a 'relevant officer' (see *paragraph 2.3(c)*) to decide that the interview is to be recorded in writing in accordance with Code C. For detained suspects, the 'relevant officer' is the custody officer and for voluntary interviews, the officer is determined according to the type of offence (indictable or summary only) and where the interview takes place (police station or elsewhere). Provisions in sections 3 and 4 deal with the conduct and recording of interviews according to the type of authorised recording device used. Section 3 applies to *removable recording media devices* (see *paragraph 1.6(a)(i)*) and section 4 applies to *secure digital recording network devices* (see *paragraph 1.6(a)(ii)*). The Annex applies when a voluntary interview is conducted elsewhere than at a police station about one of the four offence types specified in the Annex. For such interviews, the relevant officer is the interviewer.

1.8 Nothing in this Code prevents the custody officer, or other officer given custody of the detainee, from allowing police staff who are not designated persons to carry out individual procedures or tasks at the police station if the law allows. However, the officer remains responsible for making sure the procedures and tasks are carried out correctly in accordance with this Code. Any such police staff must be:

(a) a person employed by a police force and under the control and direction of the chief officer of that force; or

(b) employed by a person with whom a police force has a contract for the provision of services relating to persons arrested or otherwise in custody.

1.9 Designated persons and other police staff must have regard to any relevant provisions of the Codes of Practice.

1.10 References to pocket book shall include any official report book or electronic recording device issued to police officers or police staff that enables a record required to be made by any provision of this Code (but which is not an audio record to which *paragraph 2.1* applies) to be made and dealt with in accordance with that provision. References in this Code to written records, forms and signatures include electronic records and forms and electronic confirmation that identifies the person making the record or completing the form.

Chief officers must be satisfied as to the integrity and security of the devices, records and forms to which this paragraph applies and that use of those devices, records and forms satisfies relevant data protection legislation.

1.11 References to a custody officer include those performing the functions of a custody officer as in *paragraph 1.9* of Code C.

1.12 *Not used.*

1.13 Nothing in this Code requires the identity of officers or police staff conducting interviews to be recorded or disclosed if the interviewer reasonably believes recording or disclosing their name might put them in danger. In these cases, the officers and staff should use warrant or other identification numbers and the name of their police station. Such instances and the reasons for them shall be recorded in the custody record or the interviewer's pocket book.

2.8.7.1 **KEYNOTE**

The Codes recognise the importance that detained persons are treated in accordance with the Equality Act 2010; section 149, the 'relevant protected characteristics' are: age, disability, gender reassignment, pregnancy and maternity, race, religion/belief, and sex and sexual orientation. For further detailed guidance and advice on the Equality Act, see: <https://www.gov.uk/guidance/equality-act-2010-guidance>.

It is important to ensure interviews are conducted at appropriate locations; an interviewer who is not sure, or has any doubt, about whether a place or location elsewhere than a police station is suitable for carrying out an interview of a juvenile or vulnerable person, using a particular recording device, should consult an officer of the rank of sergeant or above for advice. See Code C, paras 3.21 and 3.22.

Attention is drawn to the provisions set out in Code C about the matters to be considered when deciding whether a detained person is fit to be interviewed. Anyone who appears to be under 18, shall, in the absence of clear evidence that they are older and subject to Code C, para. 1.5A, be treated as a juvenile for the purposes of this Code.

The reason for the interviewer using his/her warrant number or other identification numbers and the name of his/her police station is to protect those involved in serious organised crime investigations or arrests of particularly violent suspects when there is reliable information that those arrested or their associates may threaten or cause harm to those involved. In cases of doubt, an officer of the rank of inspector or above should be consulted.

2.8.8 Code E—2 Interviews and other matters to be audio recorded under this Code

(a) Requirement to use authorised audio-recording device when available

2.1 Subject to *paragraph 2.3*, if an authorised recording device (see *paragraph 1.6(a)*) in working order and an interview room or other location suitable for that device to be used, are available, then that device shall be used to record the following matters:

(a) any interview with a person cautioned in accordance with Code C, *section 10* in respect of any *summary* offence or any *indictable* offence, which includes any offence triable either way, when:

(i) that person (the suspect) is questioned about their involvement or suspected involvement in that offence and they have not been charged or informed they may be prosecuted for that offence; and

(ii) exceptionally, further questions are put to a person about any offence *after* they have been charged with, or told they may be prosecuted for, that offence (see Code C, *paragraph 16.5*).

(b) when a person who has been charged with, or informed they may be prosecuted for, any offence, is told about any written statement or interview with another person and they are handed a true copy of the written statement or the content of the interview record is brought to their attention in accordance with Code C, *paragraph 16.4*.

2.2 The whole of each of the matters described in *paragraph 2.1* shall be audio-recorded, including the taking and reading back of any statement as applicable.

2.3 A written record of the matters described in *paragraph 2.1(a)* and *(b)* shall be made in accordance with Code C, *section 11*, only if,

(a) an authorised recording device (see *paragraph 1.6(a)*) in working order is not available; or

(b) such a device is available but a location suitable for using that device to make the audio recording of the matter in question is not available; and

(c) the 'relevant officer' described in *paragraph 2.4* considers on reasonable grounds, that the proposed interview or (as the case may be) continuation of the interview or other action, should not be delayed until an authorised recording device in working order *and* a suitable interview room or other location become available and decides that a written record shall be made;

(d) if in accordance with *paragraph 3.9*, the suspect or the appropriate adult on their behalf, objects to the interview being audibly recorded and the 'relevant officer' described in *paragraph 2.4*, after having regard to the nature and circumstances of the objections, decides that a written record shall be made;

(e) in the case of a detainee who refuses to go into or remain in a suitable interview room and in accordance with Code C *paragraphs 12.5* and *12.11*, the custody officer directs that interview be conducted in a cell and considers that an authorised recording device cannot be safely used in the cell.

Note: When the suspect appears to have a hearing impediment, this paragraph does not affect the separate requirement in *paragraphs 3.7* and *4.4* for the interviewer to make a written note of the interview at the same time as the audio recording.

(b) Meaning of 'relevant officer'

2.4 In *paragraph 2.3(c)*:

(a) if the person to be interviewed is arrested elsewhere than at a police station for an offence and before they arrive at a police station, an urgent interview in accordance with *Code C paragraph 11.1* is necessary to avert one or more of the risks mentioned in *sub-paragraphs (a)* to *(c)* of that paragraph, the 'relevant officer' means the *interviewer*, who may or may not be the arresting officer, who must have regard to the time, place and urgency of the proposed interview.

(b) if the person in question has been taken to a police station after being arrested elsewhere for an offence or is arrested for an offence whilst at a police station after attending voluntarily and is detained at that police station or elsewhere in the charge of a constable, the 'relevant officer' means the *custody officer at the station where the person's detention* was last authorised. The custody officer must have regard to the nature of the investigation and in accordance with Code C *paragraph 1.1*, ensure that the detainee is dealt with expeditiously, and released as soon as the need for their detention no longer applies.

(c) In the case of a voluntary interview (see *Code C paragraph 3.21* to *3.22*) which takes place:

(i) at a police station and the offence in question is an indictable offence, the 'relevant officer' means *an officer of the rank of sergeant or above*, in consultation with the investigating officer;

(ii) at a police station and the offence in question is a summary offence, the 'relevant officer' means *the interviewer* in consultation with the investigating officer if different,

(iii) elsewhere than at a police station and the offence is one of the four indictable offence types which satisfy the conditions in Part 1 of the Annex to this Code, the 'relevant officer' means *the interviewer* in consultation with the investigating officer, if different.

(iv) elsewhere than at a police station and the offence in question is an indictable offence which is not one of the four indictable offence types which satisfy the conditions in Part 1 of the Annex to this Code, the 'relevant officer' means an *officer of the rank of sergeant or above*, in consultation with the investigating officer.

(v) elsewhere than at a police station and the offence in question is a summary only offence, the 'relevant officer' means *the interviewer* in consultation with the investigating officer, if different.

(c) Duties of the 'relevant officer' and the interviewer

2.5 When, in accordance with *paragraph 2.3*, a written record is made:

(a) the relevant officer must:

(i) record the reasons for not making an audio recording and the date and time the decision in *paragraph 2.3(c)* or (as applicable) *paragraph 2.3(d)* was made; and

(ii) ensure that the suspect is informed that a written record will be made;

(b) the interviewer must ensure that the written record includes:

(i) the date and time the decision in *paragraph 2.3(c)* or (as applicable) *paragraph 2.3(d)* was made, who made it and where the decision is recorded, and

(ii) the fact that the suspect was informed.

(c) the written record shall be made in accordance with Code C, *section 11*.

(d) Remote monitoring of interviews

2.6 If the interview room or other location where the interview takes place is equipped with facilities that enable audio recorded interviews to be remotely monitored as they take place, the interviewer must ensure that suspects, their legal representatives and any appropriate adults are fully aware of what this means and that there is no possibility of privileged conversations being listened to. With this in mind, the following safeguards should be applied:

(a) The remote monitoring system should only be able to operate when the audio recording device has been turned on.

(b) The equipment should incorporate a light, clearly visible to all in the interview room, which is automatically illuminated as soon as remote monitoring is activated.

(c) Interview rooms and other locations fitted with remote monitoring equipment must contain a notice, prominently displayed, referring to the capacity for remote monitoring and to the fact that the warning light will illuminate whenever monitoring is taking place.

(d) At the beginning of the interview, the interviewer must explain the contents of the notice to the suspect and if present, to the solicitor and appropriate adult and that explanation should itself be audio recorded.

(e) The fact that an interview, or part of an interview, was remotely monitored should be recorded in the suspect's custody record or, if the suspect is not in detention, the interviewer's pocket book. That record should include the names of the officers doing the monitoring and the purpose of the monitoring (e.g. for training, to assist with the investigation, etc.)

(e) Use of live link—Interviewer not present at the same station as the detainee

2.7 Code C *paragraphs 12.9A* and *12.9B* set out the conditions which, if satisfied allow a suspect in police detention to be interviewed using a live link by a police officer who is not present at the police station where the detainee is held. These provisions also set out the duties and responsibilities of the custody officer, the officer having physical custody of the suspect and the interviewer and the modifications that apply to ensure that any such interview is conducted and audio recorded in accordance with this Code or (as the case may be) visually recorded in accordance with Code F.

2.8.8.1 **KEYNOTE**

Code C sets out the circumstances in which a suspect may be questioned about an offence after being charged with it. The requirements of Code E do not preclude audio-recording at police discretion at police stations or elsewhere when persons are charged with, or told they may be prosecuted for, an offence or they respond after being so charged or informed. If, during the course of an interview under this Code, it becomes apparent that the interview should be conducted under one of the terrorism Codes for video recording of interviews, the interview should only continue in accordance with the relevant Code.

A decision not to audio-record an interview for any reason may be the subject of comment in court. The 'relevant officer' responsible should be prepared to justify that decision.

Code C sets out the procedures to be followed when a person's attention is drawn after charge, to a statement made by another person. One method of bringing the content of an interview with another person to the notice of a suspect may be to play them a recording of that interview. The person may not be questioned about the statement or interview record unless this is allowed in accordance with para. 16.5 of Code C.

A voluntary interview should be arranged for a time and place when it can be audio recorded and enable the safeguards and requirements set out in Code C, paras 3.21 to 3.22B to be implemented. It would normally be reasonable to delay the interview to enable audio recording unless the delay to do so would be likely to compromise the outcome of the interview or investigation, for example if there are grounds to suspect that the suspect would use the delay to fabricate an innocent explanation, influence witnesses or tamper with other material evidence.

Objections by the suspect or appropriate adult to the interview being audibly recorded are meant to apply to objections based on the suspect's genuine and honestly held beliefs and to allow officers to exercise their discretion to decide that a written interview record is to be made according to the circumstances surrounding the suspect and the investigation. Objections that appear to be frivolous with the intentions of frustrating or delaying the investigation would not be relevant.

2.8.9 Code E—3 Interview recording using *removable recording media* device

(a) Recording and sealing master recordings—general

3.1 When using an authorised *removable recording media* device (see *paragraph 1.6(a)(i)*), one recording, the master recording, will be sealed in the suspect's presence. A second recording will be used as a working copy. The master recording is any of the recordings made by a multi-deck/drive machine or the only recording made by a single deck/drive machine. The working copy is one of the other recordings made by a multi-deck/drive machine or a copy of the master recording made by a single deck/drive machine.

3.2 The purpose of sealing the master recording before it leaves the suspect's presence is to establish their confidence that the integrity of the recording is preserved. If a single deck/drive machine is used the working copy of the master recording must be made in the suspect's presence and without the master recording leaving their sight. The working copy shall be used for making further copies if needed.

(b) Commencement of interviews

3.3 When the suspect is brought into the interview room or arrives at the location where the interview is to take place, the interviewer shall, without delay but in the suspect's sight, unwrap or open the new recording media, load the recording device with new recording media and set it to record.

3.4 The interviewer must point out the sign or indicator which shows that the recording equipment is activated and is recording (see *paragraph 1.6(a)(i)*) and shall then:

(a) tell the suspect that the interview is being audibly recorded using an *authorised removable recording media* device and outline the recording process;

(b) subject to *paragraph 1.13*, give their name and rank and that of any other interviewer present;

(c) ask the suspect and any other party present, e.g. the appropriate adult, a solicitor or interpreter, to identify themselves;

(d) state the date, time of commencement and place of the interview;

(e) tell the suspect that:

- they will be given a copy of the recording of the interview in the event that they are charged or informed that they will be prosecuted but if they are not charged or informed that they will be prosecuted they will only be given a copy as agreed with the police or on the order of a court; and
- they will be given a written notice at the end of the interview setting out their right to a copy of the recording and what will happen to the recording and;

(f) if equipment for remote monitoring of interviews as described in *paragraph 2.6* is installed, explain the contents of the notice to the suspect, solicitor and appropriate adult as required by *paragraph 2.6(d)* and point out the light that illuminates automatically as soon as remote monitoring is activated.

3.5 Any person entering the interview room after the interview has commenced shall be invited by the interviewer to identify themselves for the purpose of the audio recording and state the reason why they have entered the interview room.

3.6 The interviewer shall:

- caution the suspect, see Code C, *section 10*; and
- if they are detained, remind them of their entitlement to free legal advice, see Code C, *paragraph 11.2*; or
- if they are not detained under arrest, explain this and their entitlement to free legal advice (see Code C, *paragraph 3.21*) and ask the suspect to confirm that they agree to the voluntary interview proceeding (see *Code C, paragraph 3.22A*).

3.7 The interviewer shall put to the suspect any significant statement or silence, see Code C, *paragraph 11.4*.

(c) Interviews with suspects who appear to have a hearing impediment

3.8 If the suspect appears to have a hearing impediment, the interviewer shall make a written note of the interview in accordance with Code C, at the same time as audio recording it in accordance with this Code.

(d) Objections and complaints by the suspect

3.9 If the suspect or an appropriate adult on their behalf, objects to the interview being audibly recorded either at the outset, during the interview or during a break, the interviewer shall explain that the interview is being audibly recorded and that this Code requires the objections to be recorded on the audio recording. When any objections have been audibly recorded or the suspect or appropriate adult have refused to have their objections recorded, the relevant officer shall decide in accordance *with paragraph 2.3(d)* (which requires the officer to have regard to the nature and circumstances of the objections) whether a written record of the interview or its continuation, is to be made and that audio recording should be turned off. Following a decision that a written record is to be made, the interviewer shall say they are turning off the recorder and shall then make a written record of the interview as in Code C, *section 11*. If, however, following a decision that a written record is not to be made, the interviewer may proceed to question the suspect with the audio recording still on. This procedure also applies in cases where the suspect has previously objected to the interview being visually recorded, see Code F *paragraph 2.7*, and the investigating officer has decided to audibly record the interview.

3.10 If in the course of an interview a complaint is made by or on behalf of the person being questioned concerning the provisions of this or any other Codes, or it comes to the interviewer's notice that the person may have been treated improperly, the interviewer shall act as in Code C, *paragraph 12.9*.

3.11 If the suspect indicates they want to tell the interviewer about matters not directly connected with the offence of which they are suspected and they are unwilling for these matters to be audio recorded, the suspect should be given the opportunity to tell the interviewer about these matters after the conclusion of the formal interview.

(e) Changing recording media

3.12 When the recorder shows the recording media only has a short time left to run, the interviewer shall so inform the person being interviewed and round off that part of the interview. If the interviewer leaves the room for a second set of recording media, the suspect shall not be left unattended. The interviewer will remove the recording media from the recorder and insert the new recording media which shall be unwrapped or opened in the suspect's presence. The recorder should be set to record on the new media. To avoid confusion between the recording media, the interviewer shall mark the media with an identification number immediately after it is removed from the recorder.

(f) Taking a break during interview

3.13 When a break is taken, the fact that a break is to be taken, the reason for it and the time shall be recorded on the audio recording.

3.14 When the break is taken and the interview room vacated by the suspect, the recording media shall be removed from the recorder and the procedures for the conclusion of an interview followed, see *paragraph 3.19*.

3.15 When a break is a short one and both the suspect and an interviewer remain in the interview room, the recording may be stopped. There is no need to remove the recording media and when the interview recommences the recording should continue on the same recording media. The time the interview recommences shall be recorded on the audio recording.

3.16 After any break in the interview the interviewer must, before resuming the interview, remind the person being questioned of their right to legal advice if they have not exercised it and that they remain under caution or, if there is any doubt, give the caution in full again.

(g) Failure of recording equipment

3.17 If there is an equipment failure which can be rectified quickly, e.g. by inserting new recording media, the interviewer shall follow the appropriate procedures as in *paragraph 3.12*. When the recording is resumed the interviewer shall explain what happened and record the time the interview recommences. However, if it is not possible to continue recording using the same recording device or by using a replacement device, the interview should be audio-recorded using a secure digital recording network device as in *paragraph 4.1*, if the necessary equipment is available. If it is not available, the interview may continue and be recorded in writing in accordance with *paragraph 2.3* as directed by the 'relevant officer'.

(h) Removing recording media from the recorder

3.18 Recording media which is removed from the recorder during the interview shall be retained and the procedures in *paragraph 3.12* followed.

(i) Conclusion of interview

3.19 At the conclusion of the interview, the suspect shall be offered the opportunity to clarify anything they have said and asked if there is anything they want to add.

3.20 At the conclusion of the interview, including the taking and reading back of any written statement, the time shall be recorded and the recording shall be stopped. The interviewer shall seal the master recording with a master recording label and treat it as an exhibit in accordance with force standing orders. The interviewer shall sign the label and ask the suspect and any third party present during the interview to sign it. If the suspect or third party refuse to sign the label an officer of at least the rank of inspector, or if not available the custody officer, or if the suspect has not been arrested, a sergeant, shall be called into the interview room and asked, subject to *paragraph 1.13*, to sign it.

3.21 The suspect shall be handed a notice which explains:

- how the audio recording will be used;
- the arrangements for access to it;
- that if they are charged or informed they will be prosecuted, a copy of the audio recording will be supplied as soon as practicable or as otherwise agreed between the suspect and the police or on the order of a court.

(j) After the interview

3.22 The interviewer shall make a note in their pocket book that the interview has taken place and that it was audibly recorded, the time it commenced, its duration and date and identification number of the master recording.

3.23 If no proceedings follow in respect of the person whose interview was recorded, the recording media must be kept securely as in *paragraph 3.22*.

(k) Master Recording security

(i) General

3.24 The officer in charge of each police station at which interviews with suspects are recorded or as the case may be, where recordings of interviews carried out elsewhere than at a police station are held, shall make arrangements for master recordings to be kept securely and their movements accounted for on the same basis as material which may be used for evidential purposes, in accordance with force standing orders.

(ii) Breaking master recording seal for criminal proceedings

3.25 A police officer has no authority to break the seal on a master recording which is required for criminal trial or appeal proceedings. If it is necessary to gain access to the master recording, the police officer shall arrange for its seal to be broken in the presence of a representative of the Crown Prosecution Service. The defendant or their legal adviser should be informed and given a reasonable opportunity to be present. If the defendant or their legal representative is present they shall be invited to re-seal and sign the master recording. If either refuses or neither is present this should be done by the representative of the Crown Prosecution Service.

(iii) Breaking master recording seal: other cases

3.26 The chief officer of police is responsible for establishing arrangements for breaking the seal of the master copy where no criminal proceedings result, or the criminal proceedings to which the interview relates, have been concluded and it becomes necessary to break the seal. These arrangements should be those which the chief officer considers are reasonably necessary to demonstrate to the person interviewed and any other party who may wish to use or refer to the interview record that the master copy has not been tampered with and that the interview record remains accurate.

3.27 Subject to *paragraph 3.29*, a representative of each party must be given a reasonable opportunity to be present when the seal is broken and the master recording copied and resealed.

3.28 If one or more of the parties is not present when the master copy seal is broken because they cannot be contacted or refuse to attend or *paragraph 3.29* applies, arrangements should be made for an independent person such as a custody visitor, to be present. Alternatively, or as an additional safeguard, arrangements should be made to visually record the procedure.

3.29 *Paragraph 3.28* does not require a person to be given an opportunity to be present when;

(a) it is necessary to break the master copy seal for the proper and effective further investigation of the original offence or the investigation of some other offence; and

(b) the officer in charge of the investigation has reasonable grounds to suspect that allowing an opportunity might prejudice such an investigation or criminal proceedings which may be brought as a result or endanger any person.

(iv) Documentation

3.30 When the master recording seal is broken, a record must be made of the procedure followed, including the date, time, place and persons present.

2.8.9.1 **KEYNOTE**

Preparation before Interview at Police Station

Preparation is essential before any interview (indeed it is the first step in the PEACE interviewing model). This preparation should include the following points:

- Decide where the interview will be conducted. Consider the availability of a room and the timing of the interview.
- The location must have a seat for the person being interviewed (Code C, para. 12.6) and should be adequately lit, heated and ventilated (Code C, para. 12.4). The detained person must also have clothing of a reasonable standard of comfort and cleanliness (Code C, para. 8.5). (It will be a question of fact as to what amounts to adequate clothing and it is suggested that if the clothing is such as to degrade the detained person or make him/her uncomfortable, it may lead to the confession being held to be unreliable.)
- In deciding the timing of the interview, consideration must be given to the detainee's rest period, which should not be interrupted or delayed unless Code C, para. 12.2 applies. Where the interview goes ahead during the rest period under Code C, para. 12.2(a), a fresh rest period must be allowed. Before a detainee is interviewed, the custody officer, in consultation with the officer in charge of the investigation and appropriate health care professionals as necessary, shall assess whether the detainee is fit enough to be interviewed (Code C, para. 12.3 and Annex G).
- If legal advice has been requested you must arrange for the legal representative to be present at the interview unless Code C, para. 6.6 applies.
- If a person has asked for legal advice and an interview is initiated in the absence of a legal adviser (e.g. where the person has agreed to be interviewed without his/her legal adviser being present or because of the urgent need to interview under Code C, para. 11.1), a record must be made in the interview record (Code C, para. 6.17).
- If an appropriate adult should be present, arrange for his/her attendance. (For the definition of appropriate adult, see Code C, para. 1.7.)

- If an interpreter is needed for the interview, arrange for his/her attendance. The provisions of Code C, s. 13 on interpreters for hearing impaired persons or for interviews with suspects who have difficulty understanding English apply to these interviews.
- The reason for the interviewer making a written note of the interview where a person is deaf or has impaired hearing is to give the equivalent rights of access to the full interview record as far as this is possible using audio recording. The interview notes must be in accordance with Code C.
- It is also important to draw up an interview plan and to include any relevant areas that may provide a general or specific defence.
- Look at the evidence available and identify any significant statement or silence by the suspect in order that it can be put to him/her in interview (Code C, para. 11.4).
- In planning for the interview officers should be mindful that a confession can be very damning evidence against a defendant, it is important to provide safeguards that give all suspects the same level of protection. The PACE Codes of Practice recognise certain groups as being in need of additional protection. These groups include juveniles, under 18-year-olds, people who do not speak English, those who are vulnerable and those who are deaf or have a hearing impediment. Such suspects must not be interviewed without the relevant person being present. See Code C, s. 13.

2.8.9.2 **KEYNOTE**

Commencement of interviews

When outlining the recording process, the interviewer should refer to Code E, para. 1.6(a)(ii) and (iii) and briefly describe how the recording device being used is operated and how recordings are made. For the purpose of voice identification, the interviewer should ask the suspect and any other people present to identify themselves.

In considering whether to caution again after a break, the interviewer should bear in mind that they may have to satisfy a court that the person understood that they were still under caution when the interview resumed. The interviewer should also remember that it may be necessary to show to the court that nothing occurred during a break or between interviews which influenced the suspect's recorded evidence. After a break or at the beginning of a subsequent interview, the interviewer should consider summarising on the record the reason for the break and confirming this with the suspect. Failure of recording equipment (para. 3.17).

2.8.9.3 **KEYNOTE**

Objections and Complaints by the Suspect

The relevant officer should be aware that a decision to continue recording against the wishes of the suspect may be the subject of comment in court. If the custody officer, or in the case of a person who has not been arrested, a sergeant, is called to deal with the complaint, the recorder should, if possible, be left on until the officer has entered the room and spoken to the person being interviewed. Continuation or termination of the interview should be at the interviewer's discretion pending action by an inspector under Code C, para. 9.2.

If the complaint is about a matter not connected with this Code or Code C, the decision to continue is at the interviewer's discretion. When the interviewer decides to continue the interview, they shall tell the suspect that at the conclusion of the interview, the complaint will be brought to the attention of the custody officer, or in the case of a person who has not been arrested, a sergeant. When the interview is concluded the interviewer must, as soon as practicable, inform the custody officer or, as the case may be, the sergeant, about the existence and nature of the complaint made.

2.8.9.4

KEYNOTE

Failure of Recording Equipment

Where the interview is being recorded and the media or the recording equipment fails the interviewer should stop the interview immediately. Where part of the interview is unaffected by the error and is still accessible on the media, that part shall be copied and sealed in the suspect's presence as a master copy and the interview recommenced using new equipment/media as required. Where the content of the interview has been lost in its entirety, the media should be sealed in the suspect's presence and the interview begun again. If the recording equipment cannot be fixed and no replacement is immediately available, subject to para. 2.3, the interview should be recorded in accordance with Code C, s. 11. Any written record of an audio recorded interview should be made in accordance with current national guidelines for police officers, police staff and CPS prosecutors concerned with the preparation, processing and submission of prosecution files. Master Recording security (paras 3.24 to 3.30).

2.8.9.5

KEYNOTE

Master Recording

The master recording must be sealed at the conclusion of the interview. Care must be taken of working copy recordings because their loss or destruction may lead unnecessarily to the need to access master recordings. Breaking master recording seal for criminal proceedings (para. 3.25).

The most common reasons for needing access to master copies that are not required for criminal proceedings arise from civil actions and complaints against police and civil actions between individuals arising out of allegations of crime investigated by police.

Examples of outcomes or likely outcomes of the investigation that might help the officer in charge of the investigation to decide whether a representative of each party needs to be present when the seal is broken and the master recording copied and re-sealed might be: (i) the prosecution of one or more of the original suspects; (ii) the prosecution of someone previously not suspected, including someone who was originally a witness, and (iii) any original suspect being treated as a prosecution witness and when premature disclosure of any police action, particularly through contact with any parties involved, could lead to a real risk of compromising the investigation and endangering witnesses.

If the master recording has been delivered to the Crown Court for their keeping after committal for trial the Crown prosecutor will apply to the chief clerk of the Crown Court centre for the release of the recording for unsealing by the Crown prosecutor. Reference to the CPS or to the Crown prosecutor in this part of the Code should be taken to include any other body or person with a statutory responsibility for the proceedings for which the police-recorded interview is required. Breaking master recording seal: other cases (paras 3.26 to 3.29).

2.8.10 Code E—4 Interview recording using secure digital recording network device

(a) General

4.1 An authorised secure digital recording network device (see *paragraph 1.6(a)(iii)*) does not use removable media and this section specifies the provisions which will apply when such a device is used. For ease of reference, it repeats in full some of the provisions of section 3 that apply to both types of recording device.

(b) Commencement of interviews

4.2 When the suspect is brought into the interview room or arrives at the location where the interview is to take place, the interviewer shall without delay and in the sight of the suspect, switch on the recording equipment and in accordance with the manufacturer's instructions start recording.

4.3 The interviewer must point out the sign or indicator which shows that the recording equipment is activated and is recording (see *paragraph 1.6(a)(iii)*) and shall then:

(a) tell the suspect that the interview is being audibly recorded using an authorised *secure digital recording network device* and outline the recording process;

(b) subject to *paragraph 1.13*, give their name and rank and that of any other interviewer present;

(c) ask the suspect and any other party present, e.g. the appropriate adult, a solicitor or interpreter, to identify themselves;

(d) state the date, time of commencement and place of the interview; and

(e) inform the person that:

- they will be given access to the recording of the interview in the event that they are charged or informed that they will be prosecuted but if they are not charged or informed that they will be prosecuted they will only be given access as agreed with the police or on the order of a court; and
- they will be given a written notice at the end of the interview setting out their rights to access the recording and what will happen to the recording.

(f) If equipment for remote monitoring of interviews as described in *paragraph 2.6* is installed, explain the contents of the notice to the suspect, solicitor and appropriate adult as required by *paragraph 2.6(d)* and point out the light that illuminates automatically as soon as remote monitoring is activated.

4.4 *Paragraphs 3.5* to *3.7* apply.

(c) Interviews with suspects who appear to have a hearing impediment

4.5 *Paragraph 3.8* applies.

(d) Objections and complaints by the suspect

4.6 *Paragraphs 3.9, 3.10* and *3.11* apply.

(e) Taking a break during interview

4.7 When a break is taken, the fact that a break is to be taken, the reason for it and the time shall be recorded on the audio recording. The recording shall be stopped and the procedures in *paragraphs 4.11* and *4.12* for the conclusion of interview followed.

4.8 When the interview recommences the procedures in *paragraphs 4.2* to *4.3* for commencing an interview shall be followed to create a new file to record the continuation of the interview. The time the interview recommences shall be recorded on the audio recording.

4.9 After any break in the interview the interviewer must, before resuming the interview, remind the person being questioned of their right to legal advice if they have not exercised it and that they remain under caution or, if there is any doubt, give the caution in full again.

(f) Failure of recording equipment

4.10 If there is an equipment failure which can be rectified quickly, e.g. by commencing a new secure digital network recording using the same device or a replacement device, the interviewer shall follow the appropriate procedures as in *paragraphs 4.7* to *4.9 (Taking a break during interview)*. When the recording is resumed, the interviewer shall explain what happened and record the time the interview recommences. However, if it is not possible to continue recording on the same device or by using a replacement device, the interview should be audio-recorded on removable media as in *paragraph 3.3*, if the necessary equipment is available. If it is not available, the interview may continue and be recorded in writing in accordance with *paragraph 2.3* as directed by the 'relevant officer'.

(g) Conclusion of interview

4.11 At the conclusion of the interview, the suspect shall be offered the opportunity to clarify anything he or she has said and asked if there is anything they want to add.

4.12 At the conclusion of the interview, including the taking and reading back of any written statement:

(a) the time shall be orally recorded.

(b) the suspect shall be handed a notice which explains:

- how the audio recording will be used
- the arrangements for access to it
- that if they are charged or informed that they will be prosecuted, they will be given access to the recording of the interview either electronically or by being given a copy on removable recording media, but if they are not charged or informed that they will prosecuted, they will only be given access as agreed with the police or on the order of a court.

(c) the suspect must be asked to confirm that he or she has received a copy of the notice at *sub-paragraph (b)* above. If the suspect fails to accept or to acknowledge receipt of the notice, the interviewer will state for the recording that a copy of the notice has been provided to the suspect and that he or she has refused to take a copy of the notice or has refused to acknowledge receipt.

(d) the time shall be recorded and the interviewer shall ensure that the interview record is saved to the device in the presence of the suspect and any third party present during the interview and notify them accordingly. The interviewer must then explain that the record will be transferred securely to the remote secure network file server (see *paragraph 4.15*). If the equipment is available to enable the record to be transferred there and then in the suspect's presence, then it should be so transferred. If it is transferred at a later time, the time and place of the transfer must be recorded. The suspect should then be informed that the interview is terminated.

(h) After the interview

4.13 The interviewer shall make a note in their pocket book that the interview has taken place and that it was audibly recorded, time it commenced, its duration and date and the identification number, filename or other reference for the recording.

4.14 If no proceedings follow in respect of the person whose interview was recorded, the recordings must be kept securely as in *paragraphs 4.14* and *4.15*.

(i) Security of secure digital network interview records

4.15 The recordings are first saved locally on the device before being transferred to the remote network file server system (see *paragraph 1.6(a)(iii)*). The recording remains on the local device until the transfer is complete. If for any reason the network connection fails, the recording will be transferred when the network connection is restored (see *paragraph 4.12(d)*). The interview record files are stored in read only form on non-removable storage devices, for example, hard disk drives, to ensure their integrity.

4.16 Access to interview recordings, including copying to removable media, must be strictly controlled and monitored to ensure that access is restricted to those who have been given specific permission to access for specified purposes when this is necessary. For example, police officers and CPS lawyers involved in the preparation of any prosecution case, persons interviewed if they have been charged or informed they may be prosecuted and their legal representatives.

2.8.10.1 **KEYNOTE**

The notice given to the suspect at the conclusion of the interview (see Code E, para. 4.12(b)) should provide a brief explanation of the secure digital network and how access to the recording is strictly limited. The notice should also explain the access rights of the suspect, their legal representative, the police and the prosecutor to the recording of the interview. Space should be provided on the form to insert the date, the identification number, filename or other reference for the interview recording.

2.8.11 Code E—Annex: Paragraph 2.4(C)(iii)—Four Indictable Offence Types for which the interviewer may Decide to make a written record of a Voluntary Interview elsewhere than at a Police Station when an Authorised Audio Recording Device cannot be used

Part 1: Four specified indictable offence types—two conditions

1. The **first** condition is that the *indictable* offence in respect of which the person has been cautioned is *one* of the following:
   (a) Possession of a controlled drug contrary to section 5(2) of the Misuse of Drugs Act 1971 if the drug is cannabis as defined by that Act and in a form commonly known as herbal cannabis or cannabis resin;
   (b) Possession of a controlled drug contrary to section 5(2) of the Misuse of Drugs Act 1971 if the drug is khat as defined by that Act;
   (c) Retail theft (shoplifting) contrary to section 1 of the Theft Act 1968; and
   (d) Criminal damage to property contrary to section 1(1) of the Criminal Damage Act 1971, and in this paragraph, the reference to each of the above offences applies to an attempt to commit that offence as defined by section 1 of the Criminal Attempts Act 1981.
2. The **second** condition is that:
   (a) where the person has been cautioned in respect of an offence described in *paragraph 1(a)* (Possession of herbal cannabis or cannabis resin) or *paragraph 1(b)* (Possession of khat), the requirements of *paragraphs 3* and *4* are satisfied; or
   (b) where the person has been cautioned in respect of an offence described in *paragraph 1(c)* (Retail theft), the requirements of *paragraphs 3* and *5* are satisfied; or
   (c) where the person has been cautioned in respect of an offence described in *paragraph 1(d)* (criminal damage), the requirements of *paragraphs 3* and *6* are satisfied.
3. The requirements of this paragraph that apply to all four offences described in *paragraph 1* are that:
   (i) with regard to the person suspected of committing the offence:
   - they appear to be aged 18 or over;
   - there is no reason to suspect that they are a vulnerable person for whom an appropriate adult is required (see *paragraph 1.5* of this Code);
   - they do *not* appear to be unable to understand what is happening because of the effects of drink, drugs or illness, ailment or condition;
   - they do *not* require an interpreter in accordance with Code C section 13; and
   - in accordance with Code G (Arrest), their arrest is *not* necessary in order to investigate the offence;

   (ii) it appears that the commission of the offence:
   - has *not* resulted in any injury to any person;
   - has *not* involved any realistic threat or risk of injury to any person; and
   - has *not* caused any *substantial* financial or material loss to the private property of any individual; and

   (iii) the person is not being interviewed about any other offence.
4. The requirements of this paragraph that apply to the offences described in *paragraph 1(a)* (possession of herbal cannabis or cannabis resin) and *paragraph 1(b)* (possession of khat)

are that a police officer who is experienced in the recognition of the physical appearance, texture and smell of herbal cannabis, cannabis resin or (as the case may be) khat, is able to say that the substance which has been found in the suspect's possession by that officer or, as the case may be, by any other officer not so experienced and trained:

(i) is a controlled drug being either herbal cannabis, cannabis resin or khat; and

(ii) the quantity of the substance found is consistent with personal use by the suspect and does not provide any grounds to suspect an intention to supply others.

5. The requirements of this paragraph that apply to the offence described in *paragraph 1(c)* (retail theft), are that it appears to the officer:

   (i) that the value of the property stolen does not exceed £100 inclusive of VAT;

   (ii) that the stolen property has been recovered and remains fit for sale unless the items stolen comprised drink or food and have been consumed; and

   (iii) that the person suspected of stealing the property is not employed (whether paid or not) by the person, company or organisation to which the property belongs.

6. The requirements of this paragraph that apply to the offence described in *paragraph 1(d)* (Criminal damage), are that it appears to the officer:

   (i) that the value of the criminal damage does *not exceed* £300; and

   (ii) that the person suspected of damaging the property is not employed (whether paid or not) by the person, company or organisation to which the property belongs.

Part 2: Other provisions applicable to all interviews to which this Annex applies

7. *Paragraphs 3.21* to *3.22B* of Code C set out the responsibilities of the interviewing officer for ensuring compliance with the provisions of Code C that apply to the conduct and recording of voluntary interviews to which this Annex applies.

8. If it appears to the interviewing officer that before the conclusion of an interview, any of the requirements in *paragraphs 3 to 6* of *Part 1* that apply to the offence in question described in *paragraph 1* of Part 1 have ceased to apply; this Annex shall cease to apply. The person being interviewed must be so informed and a break in the interview must be taken. The reason must be recorded in the written interview record and the continuation of the interview shall be audio recorded in accordance with section 2 of this Code. For the purpose of the continuation, the provisions of *paragraphs 3.3* and *4.2* (Commencement of interviews) shall apply.

2.8.11.1 **KEYNOTE**

The purpose of allowing the interviewer to decide that a written record is to be made is to support the policy which gives police in England and Wales options for dealing with low level offences quickly and non-bureaucratically in a proportionate manner. Guidance for police about these options is available at: <https://www.app.college.police.uk/app-content/prosecution-and-case-management/justice-outcomes/>.

A decision in relation to a particular indictable offence that the conditions and requirements in this Annex are satisfied is an operational matter for the interviewing officer according to all the particular circumstances of the case. These circumstances include the outcome of the officer's investigation at that time and any other matters that are relevant to the officer's consideration as to how to deal with the matter. Under the Misuse of Drugs Act 1971 cannabis includes any part of the cannabis plant but not mature stalks and seeds separated from the plant, cannabis resin and cannabis oil, but para. 1(a) applies only to the possession of herbal cannabis and cannabis resin. Khat includes the leaves, stems and shoots of the plant.

The power to issue a Penalty Notice for Disorder (PND) for an offence contrary to s. 1 of the Theft Act 1968 applies when the value of the goods stolen does not exceed £100 inclusive of VAT. The power to issue a PND for an offence contrary to s. 1(1) of the Criminal Damage Act 1971 applies when the value of the damage does not exceed £300.

The provisions of Code C that apply to the conduct and recording of voluntary interviews to which this Annex applies are described in paras 3.21 to 3.22B of Code C. They include the suspect's right to free legal advice, the provision of information about the offence before the interview (see Code C, para. 11.1A) and the right to interpretation and translation (see Code C, s. 13). These and other rights and entitlements are summarised in the notice that must be given to the suspect.

The requirements in para. 3 will cease to apply if, for example during the course of an interview, as a result of what the suspect says or other information which comes to the interviewing officer's notice:

- it appears that the suspect:
  - ~ is aged under 18;
  - ~ does require an appropriate adult;
  - ~ is unable to appreciate the significance of questions and their answers;
  - ~ is unable to understand what is happening because of the effects of drink, drugs or illness, ailment or condition; or
  - ~ requires an interpreter; or
- the police officer decides that the suspect's arrest is now necessary (see Code G).

2.8.12 PACE Code of Practice on Visual Recording with Sound of Interviews with Suspects (Code F)

The contents of this Code should be considered if an interviewer proposes to make a visual recording with sound of an interview with a suspect after 00.00 on 31 July 2018.

There is no statutory requirement under PACE to visually record interviews.

1 General

1.0 The procedures in this Code must be used fairly, responsibly, with respect for the people to whom they apply and without unlawful discrimination. Under the Equality Act 2010, section 149 (Public Sector Equality Duty), police forces must, in carrying out their functions, have due regard to the need to eliminate unlawful discrimination, harassment, victimisation and any other conduct which is prohibited by that Act, to advance equality of opportunity between people who share a relevant protected characteristic and people who do not share it, and to foster good relations between those persons. The Equality Act *also* makes it unlawful for police officers to discriminate against, harass or victimise any person on the grounds of the 'protected characteristics' of age, disability, gender reassignment, race, religion or belief, sex and sexual orientation, marriage and civil partnership, pregnancy and maternity, when using their powers.

1.1 This Code of Practice must be readily available for consultation by police officers and other police staff, detained persons and members of the public.

1.2 The *Notes for Guidance* included are not provisions of this code. They form guidance to police officers and others about its application and interpretation.

1.3 Nothing in this Code shall detract from the requirements of Code C, the Code of Practice for the detention, treatment and questioning of persons by police officers.

1.4 The interviews and matters to which this Code applies and provisions that govern the conduct and recording of those interviews and other matters are described in section 2.

Note: The provisions of this Code and Code E which govern the conduct and recording of interviews *do not apply* to interviews with, or taking statements from, witnesses.

1.5 *Not used.*

1.5A The provisions of Code E which require interviews with suspects to be audio recorded and the provisions of this Code which permit simultaneous visual recording provide safeguards:

- for suspects against inaccurate recording of the words used in questioning them and of their demeanour during the interview; and

- for police interviewers against unfounded allegations made by, or on behalf of, suspects about the conduct of the interview and what took place during the interview which might otherwise appear credible.

The visual recording of interviews must therefore be carried out openly to instil confidence in its reliability as an impartial and accurate record of the interview.

1.6 *Not used.*

1.6A *Not used.*

1.7 *Not used.*

1.8 *Not used.*

2.8.12.1 **KEYNOTE**

Under the Equality Act 2010, s. 149, the 'relevant protected characteristics' are: age, disability, gender reassignment, pregnancy and maternity, race, religion/belief, and sex and sexual orientation. For further detailed guidance and advice on the Equality Act, see: <http://www.gov.uk/guidance/equality-act-2010-guidance>.

2.8.13 Code F—2 When interviews and matters to which Code F applies may be visually recorded with sound and provisions for their conduct and recording

(a) General

2.1 For the purpose of this Code, a visual recording with sound means an audio recording of an interview or other matter made in accordance with the requirement in *paragraph 2.1* of the Code of Practice on audio recording interviews with suspects (Code E) during which a *simultaneous* visual recording is made which shows the suspect, the interviewer and those in whose presence and hearing the audio recording was made.

2.2 There is no statutory requirement to make a visual recording, however, the provisions of this Code shall be followed on any occasion that the 'relevant officer' described in *Code E paragraph 2.4* considers that a visual recording of any matters mentioned in *paragraph 2.1* should be made. Having regard to the safeguards described in *paragraph 1.5A*, examples of occasions when the relevant officer is likely to consider that a visual recording should be made include when:

(a) the suspect (whether or not detained) requires an appropriate adult;

(b) the suspect or their solicitor or appropriate adult requests that the interview be recorded visually;

(c) the suspect or other person whose presence is necessary is deaf or deaf/blind or speech impaired and uses sign language to communicate;

(d) the interviewer anticipates that when asking the suspect about their involvement in the offence concerned, they will invite the suspect to demonstrate their actions or behaviour at the time or to examine a particular item or object which is handed to them;

(e) the officer in charge of the investigation believes that a visual recording with sound will assist in the conduct of the investigation, for example, when briefing other officers about the suspect or matters coming to light during the course of the interview; and

(f) the authorised recording device that would be used in accordance with *paragraph 2.1 of Code E* incorporates a camera and creates a combined audio and visual recording and does not allow the visual recording function to operate independently of the audio recording function.

2.3 For the purpose of making such a visual recording, the provisions of Code E and the relevant *Notes for Guidance* shall apply equally to visual recordings with sound as they do to audio-only recordings, subject to the additional provisions in *paragraphs 2.5* to *2.12* below which apply exclusively to visual recordings.

2.4 This Code does not apply to the conduct and recording in England and Wales, of:

- interviews of persons detained under section 41 of, or Schedule 7 to, the Terrorism Act 2000, and
- post-charge questioning of persons authorised under section 22 of the Counter Terrorism Act 2008.

These must be video recorded with sound in accordance with the provisions of the separate Code of Practice issued under paragraph 3 of Schedule 8 to the Terrorism Act 2000 and under section 25 of the Counter-Terrorism Act 2008. If, during the course of an interview or questioning being visually recorded under this Code, it becomes apparent that the interview or questioning should be conducted under that separate Code, the interview should only continue in accordance with that Code (see *Code E paragraph 1.4*).

(b) Application of Code E—additional provisions that apply to visual recording with sound.

(i) General

2.5 Before visual recording commences, the interviewer must inform the suspect that in accordance with *paragraph 2.2*, a visual recording is being made and explain the visual and audio recording arrangements. If the suspect is a juvenile or a vulnerable person (see Code C, *paragraphs 1.4, 1.5* and *1.13(d)*), the information and explanation must be provided or (as the case may be) provided again, in the presence of the appropriate adult.

2.6 The device used to make the visual recording at the same time as the audio recording (see *paragraph 2.1*) must ensure coverage of as much of the room or location where the interview takes place as it is practically possible to achieve whilst the interview takes place.

2.7 In cases to which *paragraph 1.13* of Code E (disclosure of identity of officers or police staff conducting interviews) applies:

(a) the officers and staff may have their backs to the visual recording device; and

(b) when in accordance with Code E *paragraph 3.21* or *4.12* as they apply to this Code, arrangements are made for the suspect to have access to the visual recording, the investigating officer may arrange for anything in the recording that might allow the officers or police staff to be identified to be concealed.

2.8 Following a decision made by the relevant officer in accordance with *paragraph 2.2* that an interview or other matter mentioned in *paragraph 2.1* above should be *visually recorded*, the relevant officer may decide that the interview is not to be visually recorded if it no longer appears that a visual recording should be made or because of a fault in the recording device. However, a decision not to make a *visual recording* does not detract in any way from the requirement for the interview to be *audio recorded* in accordance with *paragraph 2.1 of Code E.*

2.9 The provisions in *Code E paragraph 2.6* for remote monitoring of interviews shall apply to visually recorded interviews.

(ii) Objections and complaints by the suspect about visual recording

2.10 If the suspect or an appropriate adult on their behalf objects to the interview being *visually* recorded either at the outset or during the interview or during a break in the interview, the interviewer shall explain that the visual recording is being made in accordance with *paragraph 2.2* and that this Code requires the objections to be recorded on the *visual* recording. When any objections have been recorded or the suspect or the appropriate adult have refused to have their objections recorded visually, the relevant officer shall decide in accordance with *paragraph 2.8* and having regard to the nature and circumstances of the objections, whether visual recording should be turned off. Following a decision that visual recording should be turned off, the interviewer shall say that they are turning off the *visual* recording. The audio recording required to be maintained in accordance with Code E shall continue and the interviewer shall ask the person to record their objections to the interview being *visually* recorded on the audio recording. If the relevant officer considers that visual recording should not be turned off, the interviewer may proceed to question the suspect with the visual recording still on. If the suspect also objects to the interview being audio recorded, *paragraph 3.9* of Code E will apply if a removable recording media device (see Code E *paragraph 1.6(a)(ii)*) is being used) and *paragraph 4.6* of Code E will apply if a secure digital recording device (see Code E *paragraph 1.6(a)(iii)*) is being used.

2.11 If the suspect indicates that they wish to tell the interviewer about matters not directly connected with the offence of which they are suspected and that they are unwilling for these matters to be visually recorded, the suspect should be given the opportunity to tell the interviewer about these matters after the conclusion of the formal interview.

(iii) Failure of visual recording device

2.12 If there is a failure of equipment and it is not possible to continue visual recording using the same type of recording device (i.e. a removable recording media device as in Code E *paragraph 1.6(a)(ii)* or a secure digital recording network device as in Code E *paragraph 1.6(a)(iii)*) or by using a replacement device of either type, the relevant officer may decide that the interview is to continue without being visually recorded. In these circumstances, the continuation of the interview must be conducted and recorded in accordance with the provisions of Code E.

2.8.13.1 **KEYNOTE**

Paragraph 2.1 of Code E which is referred to in Code F, para. 2.1 above describes the requirement that authorised audio-recording devices are to be used for recording interviews and other matters.

Interviewers will wish to arrange that, as far as possible, visual recording arrangements are unobtrusive. It must be clear to the suspect, however, that there is no opportunity to interfere with the recording equipment or the recording media. A decision made in accordance with para. 2.8 not to record an interview visually for any reason may be the subject of comment in court. The 'relevant officer' responsible should therefore be prepared to justify that decision.

Objections by the suspect or appropriate adult on their behalf to the interview being visually recorded are meant to apply to objections based on the suspect's genuine and honestly held beliefs and to allow officers to exercise their discretion to decide whether a visual recording is to be made according to the circumstances surrounding the suspect and the investigation. Objections that appear to be frivolous with the intentions of frustrating or delaying the investigation would not be relevant. The relevant officer should be aware that a decision to continue visual recording against the wishes of the suspect may be the subject of comment in court.

Where the interview is being visually recorded and the media or the recording device fails, the interviewer should stop the interview immediately. Where part of the interview is unaffected by the error and is still accessible on the media or on the network device, that part shall be copied and sealed in the suspect's presence as a master copy or saved as a new secure digital network recording as appropriate. The interview should then be recommenced using a functioning recording device and new recording media as appropriate. Where the media content of the interview has been lost in its entirety, the media should be sealed in the suspect's presence and the interview begun again. If the visual recording equipment cannot be fixed and a replacement device is not immediately available, the interview should be audio recorded in accordance with Code E. The visual recording made in accordance with this Code may be used for eye-witness identification procedures to which para. 3.21 and Annex E of Code D apply.

2.8.14 Interviews on Behalf of Scottish Forces and Vice Versa

The CPS, in consultation with the Scottish Crown Office, has produced guidelines in relation to the potential admissibility of interview evidence when officers from England and Wales conduct interviews on behalf of Scottish forces and vice versa. These interviews relate to people subject to cross-border arrest as provided by ss. 136 to 140 of the Criminal Justice and Public Order Act 1994.

2.8.14.1

KEYNOTE

Suspects in England and Wales: Interview Evidence Required for Prosecutions in Scotland or Northern Ireland

Section 137A provides additional cross-border powers of arrest in urgent cases, this section states:

(1) A constable of a police force in England and Wales may arrest a person in England and Wales without a warrant if—
- (a) the constable has reasonable grounds for suspecting that the person has committed a specified offence in Scotland or in Northern Ireland, and
- (b) the constable also has reasonable grounds for believing that it is necessary to arrest the person—
  - (i) to allow the prompt and effective investigation of the offence, or
  - (ii) to prevent any prosecution for the offence from being hindered by the disappearance of the person.

For detention of a person arrested under this power, **see para. 2.6.16.12**. Where the arrest is in England and Wales under this subsection or in Northern Ireland under s. 137(4), the constable has the powers of entry and search conferred by s. 137E.

The specified offences committed in England and Wales to which this power of arrest applies include:

(a) an offence (including an offence under the common law) that is punishable by virtue of any statutory provision with imprisonment or another form of detention for a term of 10 years or with a greater punishment,

(b) any of the following offences:

1 Any of the following offences at common law—
- (a) false imprisonment;
- (b) kidnapping;
- (c) indecent exposure;
- (d) cheating in relation to the public revenue.

2 An offence under any of the following provisions of the Offences against the Person Act 1861—
- (a) section 20 (inflicting bodily injury);
- (b) section 24 (administering poison etc with intent);
- (c) section 27 (exposing child whereby life is endangered etc);
- (d) section 31 (setting spring-guns etc with intent);
- (e) section 37 (assaulting an officer etc on account of his preserving wreck);
- (f) section 47 (assault occasioning actual bodily harm).

3 (1) An offence under any of the following provisions of the Sexual Offences Act 1956—
- (a) section 10 (incest by a man);
- (b) section 11 (incest by a woman);
- (c) section 30 (man living on the earnings of prostitution);
- (d) section 31 (woman exercising control over a prostitute);
- (e) section 33A (keeping a brothel used for prostitution).

(2) An offence under section 12 of that Act (buggery), other than an offence committed by a person where the other person involved in the conduct constituting the offence consented to it and was aged 16 or over.

(3) An offence under section 13 of that Act (indecency between men), where the offence was committed by a man aged 21 or over and the other person involved in the conduct constituting the offence was under the age of 16.

4 An offence under section 4 of the Criminal Law Act 1967 (assisting offenders).

5 An offence under section 5 of the Sexual Offences Act 1967 (living on the earnings of male prostitution).

6 An offence under any of the following provisions of the Firearms Act 1968—
- (a) section 1(1) (possession etc of firearms or ammunition without certificate);
- (b) section 2(1) (possession etc of shot gun without certificate);
- (c) section 3(1) (manufacturing, selling etc firearms or ammunition by way of trade or business without being registered as a firearms dealer).

7 An offence under section 106A of the Taxes Management Act 1970 (fraudulent evasion of income tax).

8 (1) An offence under section 50(2) or (3) of the Customs and Excise Management Act 1979 (improper importation of goods), other than an offence mentioned in subsection (5B) of that section.

(2) An offence under section 68(2) of that Act (exportation of prohibited or restricted goods).

(3) An offence under section 170 of that Act (fraudulent evasion of duty etc), other than an offence mentioned in subsection (4B) of that section.

9 An offence under section 4 of the Aviation Security Act 1982 (offences in relation to certain dangerous articles).

10 An offence under section 127 of the Mental Health Act 1983 (ill-treatment of patients).

11 An offence under either of the following provisions of the Child Abduction Act 1984—

(a) section 1 (abduction of child by parent etc);

(b) section 2 (abduction of child by other persons).

12 An offence under section 1 of the Prohibition of Female Circumcision Act 1985 (prohibition of female circumcision).

13 An offence under either of the following provisions of the Public Order Act 1986—

(a) section 2 (violent disorder);

(b) section 3 (affray).

14 An offence under section 160 of the Criminal Justice Act 1988 (possession of indecent photograph of a child).

15 An offence under section 2 of the Computer Misuse Act 1990 (unauthorised access with intent to commit or facilitate commission of further offences).

16 An offence under section 72(1), (3) or (8) of the Value Added Tax Act 1994 (fraudulent evasion of VAT etc).

17 An offence under either of the following provisions of the Protection from Harassment Act 1997—

(a) section 4 (putting people in fear of violence);

(b) section 4A (stalking involving fear of violence or serious alarm or distress).

18 An offence under section 29(1)(a) or (b) of the Crime and Disorder Act 1998 (certain racially or religiously aggravated assaults).

19 An offence under section 38B of the Terrorism Act 2000 (information about acts of terrorism).

20 An offence under section 3 of the Sexual Offences (Amendment) Act 2000 (sexual activity with a person aged under 18 in abuse of a position of trust).

21 An offence under section 35 of the Tax Credits Act 2002 (tax credit fraud).

22 (1) An offence under any of the following provisions of the Sexual Offences Act 2003—

(a) section 13 (child sex offences committed by children or young persons);

(b) section 16 (abuse of position of trust: sexual activity with a child);

(c) section 17 (abuse of position of trust: causing or inciting a child to engage in sexual activity);

(d) section 18 (abuse of position of trust: sexual activity in the presence of a child);

(e) section 19 (abuse of position of trust: causing a child to watch a sexual act);

(f) section 40 (care workers: sexual activity in the presence of a person with a mental disorder);

(g) section 41 (care workers: causing a person with a mental disorder to watch a sexual act);

(h) section 52 (causing or inciting prostitution for gain);

(i) section 53 (controlling prostitution for gain).

(2) An offence under section 25 or 26 of that Act (family child sex offences) where the offence is committed by a person under the age of 18.

(3) An offence under section 47 of that Act (paying for sexual services of a child), where the offence is committed against a person aged 16 or over.

23 An offence under either of the following provisions of the Terrorism Act 2006—

(a) section 1 (encouragement of terrorism);

(b) section 2 (dissemination of terrorist publications).

24 An offence under section 45 of the Serious Crime Act 2015 (participating in activities of organised crime group).

25 An offence under section 68 of the Policing and Crime Act 2017 (breach of pre-charge bail conditions relating to travel), or

(c) an offence of attempting or conspiring to commit, or of inciting the commission of, an offence mentioned in paragraph (a) or (b), or

(d) an offence under Part 2 of the Serious Crime Act 2007 (encouraging or assisting crime) in relation to an offence mentioned in paragraph (a) or (b).

- Where English officers do not have any statutory or common law powers to detain or arrest a suspect without warrant who is believed to have committed an offence in Scotland and there is insufficient evidence for the issue of a warrant, and the case is not sufficiently serious to justify officers travelling to England or Wales to exercise their cross-border powers under the Act, English or Welsh officers can be requested to invite the suspect to attend an interview on a voluntary basis for interview under caution.
- Where a Scottish officer has attended to interview the suspect, the Scottish form of caution should be given (similarly any variations from Northern Ireland should also be applied).

- English and Welsh constables interviewing suspects in England/Wales when they are aware that the interview is required for a prosecution in Scotland, should comply with the PACE Codes of Practice, save that a Scottish caution should be used in the following terms:

You are not obliged to say anything but anything you do say will be noted and may be used in evidence.

The use of an English/Welsh caution may render the interview inadmissible in Scotland.

Scottish officers should assist the interviewing officers by providing a schedule of points to be covered in an interview and a possible list of appropriate questions.

In all circumstances, officers should ensure that suspects fully understand the significance of a caution or warning.

2.8.14.2 **KEYNOTE**

Suspects in Scotland or Northern Ireland: Interview Evidence Required for Prosecutions in England and Wales

Suspects are not warned that a failure to answer questions may harm their defence. Failure to answer questions cannot harm their defence. Interviews under caution are, however, subject to guidelines which incorporate judicial precedent fairness to the accused.

In investigations of any great seriousness, English/Welsh constables should attend in Scotland, arrest the suspect and bring him/her back to their jurisdiction for interview. If such an arrest is made, the arrested person must be taken either to the nearest designated police station in England or a designated police station in a police area in England and Wales in which the offence is being investigated (s. 137(1) and (7)(a) of the Criminal Justice and Public Order Act 1994).

Under s 137A:

(2) A constable of a police force in Scotland may arrest a person in Scotland without a warrant if—
  (a) the constable has reasonable grounds for suspecting that the person has committed a specified offence in England and Wales or in Northern Ireland, and
  (b) the constable is satisfied that it would not be in the interests of justice to delay the arrest either to enable a warrant for the person's arrest to be obtained and then executed under section 136 or to enable a power of arrest under section 137 to be exercised.

(3) Without prejudice to the generality of subsection (2)(b), it would not be in the interests of justice to delay an arrest for a purpose mentioned in that subsection if the constable reasonably believes that, unless the person is arrested without delay, the person will obstruct the course of justice in any way, including by seeking to avoid arrest or interfering with witnesses or evidence.

There is a similar power for a constable of a police force in Northern Ireland who has reasonable grounds for suspecting that the person has committed a specified offence in England and Wales or in Scotland (s. 137(4)).

Where the arrest is in Scotland under subs. (2), the constable has the same powers of entry and search for the purpose of the arrest as a constable of a police force in Scotland would have if there were reasonable grounds for suspecting that the offence had been committed in Scotland.

The specified offences committed in Scotland to which this power of arrest applies include:

(a) an offence (including an offence under the common law) that is punishable by virtue of any statutory provision with imprisonment or another form of detention for a term of 10 years or with a greater punishment,

(b) any of the following offences:

26 Any of the following offences at common law—
  (a) culpable homicide;
  (b) treason;
  (c) rape;
  (d) assault, where the assault results in serious injury or endangers life;
  (e) assault with intent to rape or ravish;
  (f) indecent assault;
  (g) abduction with intent to rape;
  (h) public indecency;
  (i) clandestine injury to women;

(j) lewd, indecent or libidinous behaviour or practices;
(k) sodomy, other than an offence committed by a person where the other person involved in the conduct constituting the offence consented to it and was aged 16 or over;
(l) abduction;
(m) mobbing;
(n) fire-raising;
(o) robbery;
(p) fraud;
(q) extortion;
(r) embezzlement;
(s) theft;
(t) threats;
(u) attempting to pervert the course of justice.

27 An offence under any of the following provisions of the Firearms Act 1968—
(a) section 1(1) (possession etc of firearms or ammunition without certificate);
(b) section 2(1) (possession etc of shot gun without certificate);
(c) section 3(1) (manufacturing, selling etc firearms or ammunition by way of trade or business without being registered as a firearms dealer).

28 An offence under section 106A of the Taxes Management Act 1970 (fraudulent evasion of income tax).

29 (1) An offence under section 50(2) or (3) of the Customs and Excise Management Act 1979 (improper importation of goods), other than an offence mentioned in subsection (5B) of that section.
(2) An offence under section 68(2) of that Act (exportation of prohibited or restricted goods).
(3) An offence under section 170 of that Act (fraudulent evasion of duty etc), other than an offence mentioned in subsection (4B) of that section.

30 An offence under section 4 of the Aviation Security Act 1982 (offences in relation to certain dangerous articles).

31 An offence under either of the following provisions of the Civic Government (Scotland) Act 1982—
(a) section 51(2) (publication etc of obscene material);
(b) section 52 (taking, distributing etc indecent photographs of children).

32 An offence under section 6 of the Child Abduction Act 1984 (parent etc. taking or sending a child out of the United Kingdom).

33 An offence under section 1 of the Prohibition of Female Circumcision Act 1985 (prohibition of female circumcision).

34 An offence under section 2 of the Computer Misuse Act 1990 (unauthorised access with intent to commit or facilitate commission of further offences).

35 An offence under section 72(1), (3) or (8) of the Value Added Tax Act 1994 (fraudulent evasion of VAT etc).

36 An offence under any of the following provisions of the Criminal Law (Consolidation) (Scotland) Act 1995—
(a) section 7 (procuring prostitution etc);
(b) section 8(3) (unlawful detention of women and girls);
(c) section 10 (parents etc encouraging girls under 16 to engage in prostitution etc);
(d) section 11(1)(b) (males soliciting etc for immoral purposes).

37 An offence under section 38B of the Terrorism Act 2000 (information about acts of terrorism).

38 An offence under section 35 of the Tax Credits Act 2002 (tax credit fraud).

39 An offence under section 313 of the Mental Health (Care and Treatment) (Scotland) Act 2003 (persons providing care services: sexual offences).

40 An offence under either of the following provisions of the Terrorism Act 2006—
(a) section 1 (encouragement of terrorism);
(b) section 2 (dissemination of terrorist publications).

41 Any of the following offences under the Sexual Offences (Scotland) Act 2009—
(a) section 8 (sexual exposure);
(b) section 9 (voyeurism);
(c) section 11 (administering a substance for sexual purposes);
(d) section 32 (causing an older child to be present during a sexual activity);
(e) section 33 (causing an older child to look at a sexual image);
(f) section 34(1) (communicating indecently with an older child);
(g) section 34(2) (causing an older child to see or hear an indecent communication);
(h) section 35 (sexual exposure to an older child);
(i) section 36 (voyeurism towards an older child);
(j) section 42 (sexual abuse of trust);
(k) section 46 (sexual abuse of trust of a mentally disordered person).

42 An offence under either of the following provisions of the Criminal Justice and Licensing (Scotland) Act 2010—
(a) section 38 (threatening or abusive behaviour);
(b) section 39 (stalking).
43 An offence under section 2 of the Abusive Behaviour and Sexual Harm (Scotland) Act 2016 (disclosing etc an intimate photograph or film),

or (c) an offence of attempting or conspiring to commit, or of inciting the commission of, an offence mentioned in paragraph (a) or (b).

The specified offences committed in Northern Ireland to which this power of arrest applies include:

(a) an offence (including an offence under the common law) that is punishable by virtue of any statutory provision with imprisonment or another form of detention for a term of 10 years or with a greater punishment,
(b) any of the following offences:
1 Any of the following offences at common law—
(a) false imprisonment;
(b) kidnapping;
(c) riot;
(d) affray;
(e) indecent exposure;
(f) cheating in relation to the public revenue.
2 An offence under any of the following provisions of the Offences against the Person Act 1861—
(a) section 20 (inflicting bodily injury);
(b) section 24 (administering poison etc with intent);
(c) section 27 (exposing child whereby life is endangered etc);
(d) section 31 (setting spring-guns etc with intent);
(e) section 37 (assaulting an officer etc on account of his preserving wreck);
(f) section 47 (assault occasioning actual bodily harm).
3 An offence under section 11 of the Criminal Law Amendment Act 1885 (indecency between men), where the offence was committed by a man aged 21 or over and the other person involved in the conduct constituting the offence was under the age of 16.
4 An offence under either of the following provisions of the Punishment of Incest Act 1908—
(a) section 1 (incest by a man);
(b) section 2 (incest by a woman).
5 An offence under section 4 of the Criminal Law Act (Northern Ireland) 1967 (assisting offenders).
6 An offence under section 106A of the Taxes Management Act 1970 (fraudulent evasion of income tax).
7 (1) An offence under section 50(2) or (3) of the Customs and Excise Management Act 1979 (improper importation of goods), other than an offence mentioned in subsection (5B) of that section.
(2) An offence under section 68(2) of that Act (exportation of prohibited or restricted goods).
(3) An offence under section 170 of that Act (fraudulent evasion of duty etc), other than an offence mentioned in subsection (4B) of that section.
8 An offence under section 4 of the Aviation Security Act 1982 (offences in relation to certain dangerous articles).
9 An offence under Article 8 of the Homosexual Offences (Northern Ireland) Order 1982 (SI 1982/1536 (N.I. 19)) (living on the earnings of male prostitution).
10 An offence under section 1 of the Prohibition of Female Circumcision Act 1985 (prohibition of female circumcision).
11 An offence under either of the following provisions of the Child Abduction (Northern Ireland) Order 1985 (SI 1985/1638 (N.I. 17))—
(a) Article 3 (abduction of child by parent etc);
(b) Article 4 (abduction of child by other persons).
12 An offence under Article 121 of the Mental Health (Northern Ireland) Order 1986 (SI 1986/595 (N.I. 4)) (ill-treatment of patients).
13 An offence under Article 15 of the Criminal Justice (Evidence, Etc.) (Northern Ireland) Order 1988 (SI 1988/1847 (N.I. 17)) (possession of indecent photograph of a child).
14 An offence under section 2 of the Computer Misuse Act 1990 (unauthorised access with intent to commit or facilitate commission of further offences).
15 An offence under section 72(1), (3) or (8) of the Value Added Tax Act 1994 (fraudulent evasion of VAT etc).
16 An offence under Article 6 of the Protection from Harassment (Northern Ireland) Order 1997 (SI 1997/1180 (N.I. 9)) (putting people in fear of violence).
17 An offence under section 38B of the Terrorism Act 2000 (information about acts of terrorism).

18 An offence under section 3 of the Sexual Offences (Amendment) Act 2000 (sexual activity with a person aged under 18 in abuse of a position of trust).

19 An offence under section 35 of the Tax Credits Act 2002 (tax credit fraud).

20 An offence under section 53 of the Sexual Offences Act 2003 (controlling prostitution for gain).

21 An offence under any of the following provisions of the Firearms (Northern Ireland) Order 2004 (SI 2004/702 (N.I. 3))—

(a) Article 3(1)(b) (possession etc of firearms other than handguns without certificate);

(b) Article 3(2) (possession etc of ammunition without certificate);

(c) Article 24(1) (manufacturing, selling etc firearms or ammunition by way of trade or business without being registered as a firearms dealer).

22 An offence under either of the following provisions of the Terrorism Act 2006—

(a) section 1 (encouragement of terrorism);

(b) section 2 (dissemination of terrorist publications).

23 (1) An offence under any of the following provisions of the Sexual Offences (Northern Ireland) Order 2008 (SI 2008/1769 (N.I. 2))—

(a) Article 20 (child sex offences committed by children or young persons);

(b) Article 23 (abuse of position of trust: sexual activity with a child);

(c) Article 24 (abuse of position of trust: causing or inciting a child to engage in sexual activity);

(d) Article 25 (abuse of position of trust: sexual activity in the presence of a child);

(e) Article 51 (care workers: sexual activity with a person with a mental disorder);

(f) Article 53 (care workers: sexual activity in the presence of a person with a mental disorder);

(g) Article 62 (causing or inciting prostitution for gain);

(h) Article 63 (controlling prostitution for gain);

(i) Article 64 (keeping a brothel used for prostitution).

(2) An offence under Article 32 or 33 of that Order (family child sex offences) where the offence is committed by a person under the age of 18.

(3) An offence under Article 37 of that Order (paying for sexual services of a child), where the offence is committed against a person aged 16 or over.

24 An offence under section 68 of the Policing and Crime Act 2017 (breach of pre-charge bail conditions relating to travel), or

(c) an offence of attempting or conspiring to commit, or of inciting the commission of, an offence mentioned in paragraph (a) or (b), or (d) an offence under Part 2 of the Serious Crime Act 2007 (encouraging or assisting crime) in relation to an offence mentioned in paragraph (a) or (b).

Where Scottish officers do not have any statutory or common law powers to detain or arrest a suspect without warrant who is believed to have committed an offence in England and Wales, if there is insufficient evidence for the issue of a warrant, and the case is not sufficiently serious to justify officers travelling to Scotland, Scottish officers can be requested to invite the suspect to attend a police station on a voluntary basis for interview under caution.

When it has not been practicable for an English/Welsh constable to make an arrest, but a constable has gone to Scotland to interview a suspect following arrest or detention by a Scottish constable for Scottish offences, or a person has voluntarily agreed to be interviewed, the English/Welsh constable should comply, insofar as it is practical, with the PACE Codes of Practice, in particular:

- A suspect not under arrest or detention should be told that he/she is not under arrest or detention and that he/she is free to leave.
- A suspect should be told that he/she may seek legal advice and that arrangements are made for legal representation when required. An appropriate adult should also be present when interviewing a youth or a mentally disordered or mentally handicapped person.
- An English/Welsh law caution should be administered. When appropriate, officers should warn arrested suspects of the consequences of failure or refusal to account for objects, substances or marks (s. 36 of the 1994 Act) and the failure or refusal to account for their presence in a particular place (s. 37).
- The interview should be audio recorded if possible.
- If it is not possible to audio record the interview, a contemporaneous written record of the interview should be made. The suspect must be given the opportu6nity to read the record and to sign it.

Scottish constables interviewing suspects in Scotland when they are aware that the interview is required for a prosecution in England and Wales, should comply with Scottish law. In addition, insofar as it is practical:

- A suspect should be told that he/she may seek legal advice and that arrangements are made for legal representation when required. A solicitor may be present during any subsequent interview if the suspect requires. An appropriate adult should also be present when interviewing a youth or a mentally disordered or mentally vulnerable person.
- When it is certain that the interview evidence will only be used in English/Welsh courts, the appropriate English/Welsh caution should be used.
- The interview should be audio recorded if possible.
- If it is not possible to audio record the interview, a written contemporaneous record of the interview should be made. The suspect must be given the opportunity to read the record and to sign it.

English/Welsh officers should assist interviewing Scottish or Northern Irish officers by providing a schedule of points to be covered in an interview. This could include a list of appropriate questions.

Appendix 2.1

Summary of PACE Code of Practice for the Detention, Treatment and Questioning of Persons under s. 41 of, and sch. 8 to, the Terrorism Act 2000 (Code H)

A thick grey line down the margin denotes text that is an extract of the PACE Code itself (i.e. the actual wording of the legislation). This material is examinable for both Sergeants and Inspectors.

As stated in **chapter 2.6**, Code H has been introduced and applies to people in police detention following their arrest under the Terrorism Act 2000, ss. 41 and 43B; the latest revision applies after midnight on 10 February 2023, notwithstanding that the person has been arrested before that time. In the main, Code H mirrors Code C. The latest revisions to Code H reflect new section 43B in the Terrorism Act 2000. Section 43B provides the power for a constable to arrest without warrant a terrorist or terrorism-connected offender who has been released on licence if the constable has reasonable grounds for suspecting that the offender has breached a condition of their licence and reasonably considers that it is necessary, for purposes connected with protecting members of the public from a risk of terrorism, to detain the offender until a recall decision is made. The updates to the code ensure that there is clarity for the police on the length of time for which the offender on licence can be detained under section 43B and their rights upon first being detained, including to have one named person informed of their whereabouts and their right to consult and communicate privately with a solicitor.

Code H is not reproduced within the Manual but should be available in custody suites and at police stations. Generally, the provisions to Code H are mirrored (with modifications as necessary) in the current version of PACE Code C and vice versa in order to ensure consistency; however, in relation to reviews and extensions of detention there are significant differences from the equivalent provisions in PACE Code C owing to the changes made to maximum detention times by the Terrorism Act 2006.

Code H has been expanded in scope to incorporate provisions relating to the post-charge questioning of terrorist suspects. Part 2 of the Counter-Terrorism Act 2008 provides that a judge may authorise the questioning of a person by a constable after that person has been charged with a terrorism offence or an offence with a terrorist connection. The post-charge questioning provisions of the 2008 Act also introduce a new mandatory Code for the video recording with sound of such questioning.

Section 1—General

This section covers the scope and applicability of the Code (which are, by definition, different from the equivalent provisions of Code C); it also covers the availability of the Code, definitions, applicability to the deaf, blind and speech impaired, and the use of reasonable force, and in these respects follows Code C.

1N The powers under Part IV of PACE to detain and release on bail (before or after charge) a person arrested under section 24 of PACE for any offence (see PACE Code G (Arrest)) do not apply to persons whilst they are detained under the terrorism powers following their arrest/detention under section 41 of, or Schedule 7 to, TACT. If when the grounds for detention under these powers cease the person is arrested under section 24 of PACE for a specific offence, the detention and bail provisions of PACE will apply and must be considered from the time of that arrest.

All persons in custody must be dealt with expeditiously, and released as soon as the need for detention no longer applies. A terrorist offender on licence who is detained under section 43B TACT must (unless recalled to prison or otherwise detained under any other power) be released if (a) a recall decision is made not to revoke the offender's licence, as soon as practicable after that decision is made; or (b) if a recall decision has not been made within six hours beginning with the time of the arrest under section 43B. There is no provision for bail under TACT before or after charge.

Section 2—Custody Records

This section follows Code C. It covers general requirements for making custody records, including the exemption for counter-terrorism officers from disclosing their identities on custody records and provisions as to access to custody records by detainees' solicitors and disclosure of those records to them.

Section 3—Initial Action in Respect of Arrested Individuals

Code H broadly follows Code C in respect of detainees' rights and arrangements for exercising them but differs in a number of respects:

- the record will indicate that the arrest was under s. 41 as opposed to indicating the offence in respect of which the arrest was made—Note 3G indicates that, where an arrest is made on grounds of sensitive information which cannot be disclosed, the recorded grounds 'may be given in terms of the interpretation of "terrorist" set out in ... s. 40(1)(a) or (b)';
- there is a specific provision to the effect that risk assessments do not form part of the custody record and should not be shown to the detainee or his/her legal representative;
- there are provisions relating to the initial steps that may be taken in connection with the identification of suspects;
- the custody officer is allowed to direct custody staff to carry out certain actions in relation to a detainee's rights and entitlements, need for medical treatment and the risk assessment process.
- It should be noted that the power to take fingerprints, intimate samples or non-intimate samples in paragraph 3.12 of this Code does not apply to a person detained under section 43B of TACT.
- Arrests under TACT section 43B can only be made when an officer reasonably suspects that a terrorist offender on licence has breached a condition of their licence and reasonably considers that it is necessary, for purposes connected with protecting members of the public from a risk of terrorism, to detain the offender until a recall decision is made.

Section 4—Detainees' Property

This section of Code H includes a simplification of the circumstances in which a custody officer should search a detainee to ascertain what he/she has in his/her possession but there is no material change in comparison with Code C.

Section 5—Right not to be Held Incommunicado

This section allows a detainee to be visited by those in whose welfare the detainee has an interest. The detainee's right to have someone informed of his/her whereabouts closely follows the equivalent section of Code C but there is much more detailed guidance on visiting rights. A requirement is imposed for custody officers to liaise with the investigation team to ascertain the risks presented by visits. Where visits from relatives etc. present a risk, consideration of more frequent visits from independent visitor schemes is suggested. Visits from official visitors ('official visitors' may include accredited faith representatives and MPs) may be allowed subject to consultation with the officer in charge of the investigation. Note 5B indicates that custody officers should bear in mind the effects of prolonged detention under the Act and consider the health and welfare benefits that visits bring to the health and welfare of detainees who are held for extended periods. However, Note 5G reminds officers that the nature of terrorist investigations means that they need to have 'particular regard to the possibility of suspects attempting to pass information which may be detrimental to public safety, or to an investigation'. For any terrorist offender on licence detained under section 43B of TACT, the right to contact one named person may not be delayed.

Section 6—Right to Legal Advice

The principal difference from Code C is that there is provision for an authorisation to be given whereby a detainee may only consult a solicitor within sight and hearing of a qualified officer (a uniformed officer of at least the rank of inspector who has no connection with the investigation). This section also introduces additional safeguards for detainees who change their mind about wanting advice. For any terrorist offender on licence detained under section 43B of TACT, the right of access to legal advice may not be delayed.

Section 7—Citizens of Independent Commonwealth Countries or Foreign Nationals

Section 7 shows no material change from the equivalent Code C provisions.

Section 8—Conditions of Detention

The main differences from Code C are that there is specific reference to allowing detainees to practise religious observance and to the provision of reading material, including religious texts. Police should consult with representatives of religious communities on provision of facilities for religious observance and handling of religious texts and other articles. The benefits of exercise for detainees, particularly in the cases of prolonged detention, are emphasised. If facilities exist, indoor exercise is to be offered if requested or if outdoor exercise is not practicable. Although the same restrictions on putting a juvenile in a cell apply as under Code C, there is no requirement to include occasions when a juvenile is so confined on the custody record.

Section 9—Care and Treatment of Detained Persons

Section 9 of Code H begins by requiring that, notwithstanding other requirements for medical attention, 'detainees who are held for more than 96 hours must be visited by a healthcare professional at least once every 24 hours'. In all other material respects, the provisions are the same as under Code C.

Section 10—Cautions

Insofar as relevant, the provisions on cautions closely follow those of Code C. There is no requirement to caution a terrorist offender on licence who is arrested under section 43B of TACT. Section 43B is a power to arrest without warrant in circumstances where a breach of licence is suspected, where there is a terrorism risk and it is considered necessary to detain the offender until a recall decision is made by the probation service. It does not depend on the person committing an offence. Following an arrest under section 43B, in the event that a police constable reasonably suspects an offence has been committed, the terrorist offender would need to be rearrested under section 41 TACT or section 24 of PACE and cautioned as appropriate.

Section 11—Interviews (General)

There are no material differences from Code C under this section. The Code H equivalent is, however, much shorter, reflecting the fact that not all instances covered by the Code C equivalent are relevant to detention of terrorist suspects. A terrorist offender on licence arrested under section 43B TACT will not have been arrested on suspicion of committing an offence and so will not be interviewed under caution.

Section 12—Interviews in Police Stations

The only material difference here is set out at para. 12.9:

> 12.9 During extended periods where no interviews take place, because of the need to gather further evidence or analyse existing evidence, detainees and their legal representative shall be informed that the investigation into the relevant offence remains ongoing. If practicable, the detainee and legal representative should also be made aware in general terms of any reasons for long gaps between interviews. Consideration should be given to allowing visits, more frequent exercise, or for reading or writing materials to be offered. See *paragraph 5.4*, *section 8* and *Note 12C*.

Note 12C indicates that consideration should be given to the matters referred to in para. 12.9 after a period of over 24 hours without questioning.

Section 13—Interpreters

Section 13 shows no material change from the equivalent Code C provisions.

Section 14—Reviews and Extensions of Detention

This section contains significant changes from the equivalent provisions in Code C, s. 15, owing to the changes made to maximum detention times by the Terrorism Act 2006. It is set out in full below.

14 Reviews and Extensions of Detention under the Terrorism Act 2000

(a) General

14.0 The requirement in *paragraph 3.4(b)* that documents and materials essential to challenging the lawfulness the detainee's arrest and detention must be made available to the detainee or their solicitor, applies for the purposes of this section.

14.1 The powers and duties of the review officer are in the Terrorism Act 2000, Schedule 8, Part II. See *Notes 14A and 14B*. A review officer should carry out their duties at the police station where the detainee is held and be allowed such access to the detainee as is necessary to exercise those duties.

14.2 For the purposes of reviewing a person's detention, no officer shall put specific questions to the detainee:

- regarding their involvement in any offence; or
- in respect of any comments they may make:
  - when given the opportunity to make representations; or
  - in response to a decision to keep them in detention or extend the maximum period of detention.
- Such an exchange could constitute an interview as in *paragraph 11.1* and would be subject to the associated safeguards in *section 11*.

14.3 If the detention of a person arrested under section 41 TACT is necessary for longer than 48 hours from the time of arrest or, if a person was initially being detained under Schedule 7 to TACT or Schedule 3 to the Counter-Terrorism and Border Security Act 2019, from the time at which the examination under the relevant Schedule began, a police officer of at least superintendent rank, or a Crown Prosecutor may apply for a warrant of further detention or for an extension or further extension of such a warrant under paragraph 29 or (as the case may be) 36 of Part III of Schedule 8 to the Terrorism Act 2000. See Note 14C.

14.4 A terrorist offender on licence who is detained under section 43B of TACT must (unless re-called to prison or otherwise detained under any other power – for example, being arrested for an offence) be released if (a) a recall decision is made not to revoke the offender's li-cence, as soon as practicable after that decision is made; or (b) if a recall decision has not been made within six hours beginning with the time of the arrest under section 43B.

14.5 There are no circumstances in which a person may be detained under section 43B for longer than six hours.

14.6 When an application is made for a warrant as described in paragraph 14.3, the detained person and their representative must be informed of their rights in respect of the applica-tion. These include:

(i) the right to a written notice of the application (see *paragraph 14.7*);
(ii) the right to make oral or written representations to the judicial authority/High Court judge about the application;
(iii) the right to be present and legally represented at the hearing of the application, unless specifically excluded by the judicial authority/High Court judge;
(iv) their right to free legal advice (see *section 6* of this Code).

14.7 TACT *Schedule 8 paragraph 31* requires the notice of the application for a warrant of further detention to be provided before the judicial hearing of the application for that warrant and that the notice must include:

(a) notification that the application for a warrant has been made;
(b) the time at which the application was made;
(c) the time at which the application is to be heard;
(d) the grounds on which further detention is sought.

A notice must also be provided each time an application is made to extend or further extend an existing warrant.

(b) Transfer of persons detained for more than 14 days to prison

14.8 If the Detention of Terrorists Suspects (Temporary Extension) Bill is enacted and in force, a High Court judge may extend or further extend a warrant of further detention to authorise a person to be detained beyond a period of 14 days from the time of their arrest (or if they were initially being detained under TACT Schedule 7 or Schedule 3 to the CT and Border Security Act 2019, from the time at which their examination under the relevant Schedule began). The provisions of Annex J will apply when a warrant of further detention is so extended or further extended. This extension does not apply to the detention of individuals under section 43B of TACT.

14.9 *Not used.*

14.10 *Not used.*

14.11 *Not used.*

14.12 *Not used.*

14.13 *Not used.*

(c) Documentation

14.14 It is the responsibility of the officer who gives any reminders as at *paragraph 14.6*, to ensure that these are noted in the custody record, as well any comments made by the detained person upon being told of those rights.

14.15 The grounds for, and extent of, any delay in conducting a review shall be recorded.

14.16 Any written representations shall be retained.

14.17 A record shall be made as soon as practicable about the outcome of each review and, if applicable, the grounds on which the review officer authorises continued detention. A record shall also be made as soon as practicable about the outcome of an application for a warrant of further detention or its extension.

14.18 *Not used.*

Notes for Guidance

14A TACT Schedule 8 Part II sets out the procedures for review of detention up to 48 hours from the time of arrest under TACT section 41 (or if a person was initially being detained under TACT Schedule 7 or Schedule 3 to the CT and Border Security Act 2019, from the time at which the examination under the relevant Schedule began). These include provisions for the requirement to review detention, postponing a review, grounds for continued detention, designating a review officer, representations, rights of the detained person and keeping a record. The review officer's role ends after a warrant has been issued for extension of detention under Part III of Schedule 8.

14B A review officer may authorise a person's continued detention if satisfied that detention is necessary:

(a) to obtain relevant evidence whether by questioning the person or otherwise;
(b) to preserve relevant evidence;
(c) while awaiting the result of an examination or analysis of relevant evidence;
(d) for the examination or analysis of anything with a view to obtaining relevant evidence;
(e) pending a decision to apply to the Secretary of State for a deportation notice to be served on the detainee, the making of any such application, or the consideration of any such application by the Secretary of State;
(f) pending a decision to charge the detainee with an offence.

14C Applications for warrants to extend detention beyond 48 hours, may be made for periods of 7 days at a time (initially under TACT Schedule 8 paragraph 29, and extensions thereafter under TACT Schedule 8, paragraph 36), up to a maximum period of 14 days (or 28 days if the

Detention of Terrorists Suspects (Temporary Extension) Bill) is enacted and in force) from the time of their arrest (or if they were being detained under TACT Schedule 7 or Schedule 3 to the CT and Border Security Act 2019, from the time at which the examination under the relevant Schedule began). Applications may be made for shorter periods than 7 days, which must be specified. The judicial authority or High Court judge may also substitute a shorter period if they feel a period of 7 days is inappropriate.

14D Unless Note 14F applies, applications for warrants that would take the total period of detention up to 14 days or less should be made to a judicial authority, meaning a District Judge (Magistrates' Court) designated by the Lord Chief Justice to hear such applications.

14E If by virtue of the relevant provisions described in Note 14C being enacted the maximum period of detention is extended to 28 days, any application for a warrant which would take the period of detention beyond 14 days from the time of arrest (or if a person was being detained under TACT Schedule 7 or Schedule 3 to the CT and Border Security Act 2019, from the time at which the examination under the relevant Schedule began), must be made to a High Court Judge.

14F If, when the Detention of Terrorists Suspects (Temporary Extension) Bill is enacted and in force, an application is made to a High Court judge for a warrant which would take detention beyond 14 days and the High Court judge instead issues a warrant for a period of time which would not take detention beyond 14 days, further applications for extension of detention must also be made to a High Court judge, regardless of the period of time to which they refer.

14G Not used.

14H An officer applying for an order under TACT Schedule 8 paragraph 34 to withhold specified information on which they intend to rely when applying for a warrant of further detention or the extension or further extension of such a warrant, may make the application for the order orally or in writing. The most appropriate method of application will depend on the circumstances of the case and the need to ensure fairness to the detainee.

14I After hearing any representations by or on behalf of the detainee and the applicant, the judicial authority or High Court judge may direct that the hearing relating to the extension of detention under Part III of Schedule 8 is to take place using video conferencing facilities. However, if the judicial authority requires the detained person to be physically present at any hearing, this should be complied with as soon as practicable. Paragraph 33(4) to (9) of TACT Schedule 8 govern the hearing of applications via video-link or other means.

14J Not used.

14K Not used.

15 Charging and post-charge questioning in terrorism cases

(a) Charging

15.1 Charging of detained persons is covered by PACE and guidance issued under PACE by the Director of Public Prosecutions. Decisions to charge persons to whom this Code (H) applies, the charging process and related matters are subject to section 16 of PACE Code C.

(b) Post-charge questioning

15.2 Under *section 22 of the Counter-Terrorism Act 2008*, a judge of the Crown Court may authorise the questioning of a person about an offence for which they have been charged, informed that they may be prosecuted or sent for trial, if the offence:

- is a terrorism offence as set out in *section 27 of the Counter-Terrorism Act 2008*; or
- is an offence which appears to the judge to have a terrorist connection. See *Note 15C*.

The decision on whether to apply for such questioning will be based on the needs of the investigation. There is no power to detain a person solely for the purposes of post-charge questioning. A person can only be detained whilst being so questioned (whether at a police station or in prison) if they are already there in lawful custody under some existing power. If at a police station the contents of *sections 8* and *9* of this Code must be considered the minimum standards of treatment for such detainees.

15.3 The Crown Court judge may authorise the questioning if they are satisfied that:

- further questioning is necessary in the interests of justice;
- the investigation for the purposes of which the further questioning is being proposed is being conducted diligently and expeditiously; and
- the questioning would not interfere unduly with the preparation of the person's defence to the charge or any other criminal charge that they may be facing.

See *Note 15E*

15.4 The judge authorising questioning may specify the location of the questioning.

15.5 The judge may only authorise a period up to a maximum of 48 hours before further authorisation must be sought. The 48 hour period would run continuously from the commencement of questioning. This period must include breaks in questioning in accordance with *paragraphs 8.6* and *12.2* of this Code (see *Note 15B*).

15.6 Nothing in this Code shall be taken to prevent a suspect seeking a voluntary interview with the police at any time.

15.7 For the purposes of this section, any reference in *sections 6, 10, 11, 12* and *13* of this Code to:

- 'suspect' means the person in respect of whom an authorisation has been given under *section 22 of the Counter-Terrorism Act 2008* (post-charge questioning of terrorist suspects) to interview them;
- 'interview' means post-charge questioning authorised under section 22 of the Counter-Terrorism Act 2008;
- 'offence' means an offence for which the person has been charged, informed that they may be prosecuted or sent for trial and about which the person is being questioned; and
- 'place of detention' means the location of the questioning specified by the judge (see *paragraph 15.4*),

and the provisions of those sections apply (as appropriate), to such questioning (whether at a police station or in prison) subject to the further modifications in the following paragraphs:

Right to legal advice

15.8 In *section 6* of this Code, for the purposes of post-charge questioning:

- access to a solicitor may not be delayed under Annex B; and
- *paragraph 6.5* (direction that a detainee may not exercise the right to consult a solicitor by consulting the solicitor who attends for the purpose of the consultation, or who would so attend but for the giving of the direction, but may instead be exercised by consulting a different solicitor of the detained person's choosing) does not apply.

Cautions

15.9 In *section 10* of this Code, unless the restriction on drawing adverse inferences from silence applies (see paragraph 15.10), for the purposes of post-charge questioning, the caution must be given in the following terms before any such questions are asked:

'You do not have to say anything. But it may harm your defence if you do not mention when questioned something which you later rely on in Court. Anything you do say may be given in evidence.'

Where the use of the Welsh Language is appropriate, a constable may provide the caution directly in Welsh in the following terms:

'Does dim rhaid i chi ddweud dim byd. Ond gall niweidio eich amddiffyniad os na fyddwch chi'n sôn, wrth gael eich holi, am rywbeth y byddwch chi'n dibynnu arno nes ymlaen yn y Llys. Gall unrhyw beth yr ydych yn ei ddweud gael ei roi fel tystiolaeth.'

15.10 The only restriction on drawing adverse inferences from silence, see *Annex C*, applies in those situations where a person has asked for legal advice and is questioned before receiving such advice in accordance with paragraph 6.7(b).

Interviews

15.11 In *section 11*, for the purposes of post-charge questioning, whenever a person is questioned, they must be informed of the offence for which they have been charged or informed that they may be prosecuted, or that they have been sent for trial and about which they are being questioned.

15.12 *Paragraph 11.2* (place where questioning may take place) does not apply to post-charge questioning.

Recording post-charge questioning

15.13 All interviews must be video recorded with sound in accordance with the separate Code of Practice issued under *section 25 of the Counter-Terrorism Act 2008* for the video recording with sound of post-charge questioning authorised under *section 22 of the Counter-Terrorism Act 2008* (see *paragraph 11.8*).

Notes for Guidance

15A If a person is detained at a police station for the purposes of post-charge questioning, a custody record must be opened in accordance with section 2 of this Code. The custody record must note the power under which the person is being detained, the time at which the person was transferred into police custody, their time of arrival at the police station and their time of being presented to the custody officer.

15B The custody record must note the time at which the interview process commences. This shall be regarded as the relevant time for any period of questioning in accordance with paragraph 15.5 of this Code.

15C Where reference is made to 'terrorist connection' in paragraph 15.2, this is determined in accordance with section 69 of the Sentencing Code. Under section 69 of the Code a court must in certain circumstances determine whether an offence has a terrorist connection. An offence has a terrorist connection if the offence is, or takes place in the course of, an act of terrorism or is committed for the purposes of terrorism. Normally the court will make the determination during the sentencing process, however for the purposes of post-charge questioning, a Crown Court Judge must determine whether it appears that the offence has a terrorist connection.

15D The powers under section 22 of the Counter-Terrorism Act 2008 are separate from and additional to the normal questioning procedures within this code. Their overall purpose is to enable the further questioning of a terrorist suspect after charge. They should not therefore be used to replace or circumvent the normal powers for dealing with routine questioning.

15E Post-charge questioning has been created because it is acknowledged that terrorist investigations can be large and complex and that a great deal of evidence can come to light following the charge of a terrorism suspect. This can occur, for instance, from the translation of material or as the result of additional investigation. When considering an application for post-charge questioning, the police must 'satisfy' the judge on all three points under paragraph 15.3. This means that the judge will either authorise or refuse an application on the balance of whether the conditions in paragraph 15.3 are all met. It is important therefore, that when making the application, to consider the following questions:

- *What further evidence is the questioning expected to provide?*
- *Why was it not possible to obtain this evidence before charge?*
- *How and why was the need to question after charge first recognised?*
- *How is the questioning expected to contribute further to the case?*

- *To what extent could the time and place for further questioning interfere with the preparation of the person's defence (for example if authorisation is sought close to the time of a trial)?*
- *What steps will be taken to minimise any risk that questioning might interfere with the preparation of the person's defence?*

This list is not exhaustive but outlines the type of questions that could be relevant to any asked by a judge in considering an application.

16 Testing persons for the presence of specified Class A drugs

16.1 The provisions for drug testing under *section 63B of PACE* (as amended by *section 5 of the Criminal Justice Act 2003* and *section 7 of the Drugs Act 2005*), do not apply to persons to whom this Code applies. Guidance on these provisions can be found in section 17 of PACE Code C.

Annex A—Intimate and Strip Searches

A Intimate search

1. An intimate search consists of the physical examination of a person's body orifices other than the mouth. The intrusive nature of such searches means the actual and potential risks associated with intimate searches must never be underestimated.

(a) Action

2. Body orifices other than the mouth may be searched if authorised by an officer of inspector rank or above who has reasonable grounds for believing that the person may have concealed on themselves anything which they could and might use to cause physical injury to themselves or others at the station and the officer has reasonable grounds for believing that an intimate search is the only means of removing those items.
3. Before the search begins, a police officer or designated detention officer, must tell the detainee:
   (a) that the authority to carry out the search has been given;
   (b) the grounds for giving the authorisation and for believing that the article cannot be removed without an intimate search.
4. An intimate search may only be carried out by a registered medical practitioner or registered nurse, unless an officer of at least inspector rank considers this is not practicable, in which case a police officer may carry out the search. See *Notes A1* to *A5*.
5. Any proposal for a search under *paragraph 2* to be carried out by someone other than a registered medical practitioner or registered nurse must only be considered as a last resort and when the authorising officer is satisfied the risks associated with allowing the item to remain with the detainee outweigh the risks associated with removing it. See *Notes A1* to *A5*.
6. An intimate search at a police station of a juvenile or a vulnerable person may take place only in the presence of an appropriate adult of the same sex (see *Annex I*), unless the detainee specifically requests a particular adult of the opposite sex who is readily available. In the case of a juvenile the search may take place in the absence of the appropriate adult only if the juvenile signifies in the presence of the appropriate adult they do not want the adult present during the search and the adult agrees. A record shall be made of the juvenile's decision and signed by the appropriate adult.
7. When an intimate search under *paragraph 2* is carried out by a police officer, the officer must be of the same sex as the detainee (see *Annex I*). A minimum of two people, other than the detainee, must be present during the search. Subject to *paragraph 6*, no person

of the opposite sex who is not a medical practitioner or nurse shall be present, nor shall anyone whose presence is unnecessary. The search shall be conducted with proper regard to the dignity, sensitivity and vulnerability of the detainee including in particular, their health, hygiene and welfare needs to which *paragraphs 9.4A* and *9.4B* apply.

(b) Documentation

8. In the case of an intimate search under paragraph 2, the following shall be recorded as soon as practicable, in the detainee's custody record:
    - the authorisation to carry out the search;
    - the grounds for giving the authorisation;
    - the grounds for believing the article could not be removed without an intimate search;
    - which parts of the detainee's body were searched;
    - who carried out the search;
    - who was present;
    - the result.
9. If an intimate search is carried out by a police officer, the reason why it was impracticable for a registered medical practitioner or registered nurse to conduct it must be recorded.

B Strip search

10. A strip search is a search involving the removal of more than outer clothing. In this Code, outer clothing includes shoes and socks.

(a) Action

11. A strip search may take place only if it is considered necessary to remove an article which a detainee would not be allowed to keep, and the officer reasonably considers the detainee might have concealed such an article. Strip searches shall not be routinely carried out if there is no reason to consider that articles are concealed.

The conduct of strip searches

12. When strip searches are conducted:
    (a) a police officer carrying out a strip search must be the same sex as the detainee (see *Annex I*);
    (b) the search shall take place in an area where the detainee cannot be seen by anyone who does not need to be present, nor by a member of the opposite sex (see *Annex I*) except an appropriate adult who has been specifically requested by the detainee;
    (c) except in cases of urgency, where there is risk of serious harm to the detainee or to others, whenever a strip search involves exposure of intimate body parts, there must be at least two people present other than the detainee, and if the search is of a juvenile or a vulnerable person, one of the people must be the appropriate adult. Except in urgent cases as above, a search of a juvenile may take place in the absence of the appropriate adult only if the juvenile signifies in the presence of the appropriate adult that they do not want the adult to be present during the search and the adult agrees. A record shall be made of the juvenile's decision and signed by the appropriate adult. The presence of more than two people, other than an appropriate adult, shall be permitted only in the most exceptional circumstances;
    (d) the search shall be conducted with proper regard to the dignity, sensitivity and vulnerability of the detainee in these circumstances including in particular, their health, hygiene and welfare needs to which *paragraphs 9.4A* and *9.4B* apply. Every reasonable effort shall be made to secure the detainee's co-operation, maintain their dignity and minimise embarrassment. Detainees who are searched shall not normally be required

to remove all their clothes at the same time, e.g. a person should be allowed to remove clothing above the waist and redress before removing further clothing;

(e) if necessary to assist the search, the detainee may be required to hold their arms in the air or to stand with their legs apart and bend forward so a visual examination may be made of the genital and anal areas provided no physical contact is made with any body orifice;

(f) if articles are found, the detainee shall be asked to hand them over. If articles are found within any body orifice other than the mouth, and the detainee refuses to hand them over, their removal would constitute an intimate search, which must be carried out as in *Part A*;

(g) a strip search shall be conducted as quickly as possible, and the detainee allowed to dress as soon as the procedure is complete.

(b) Documentation

13. A record shall be made on the custody record of a strip search including the reason it was considered necessary, those present and any result.

Notes for Guidance

A1 *Before authorising any intimate search, the authorising officer must make every reasonable effort to persuade the detainee to hand the article over without a search. If the detainee agrees, a registered medical practitioner or registered nurse should whenever possible be asked to assess the risks involved and, if necessary, attend to assist the detainee.*

A2 *If the detainee does not agree to hand the article over without a search, the authorising officer must carefully review all the relevant factors before authorising an intimate search. In particular, the officer must consider whether the grounds for believing an article may be concealed are reasonable.*

A3 *If authority is given for a search under paragraph 2, a registered medical practitioner or registered nurse shall be consulted whenever possible. The presumption should be that the search will be conducted by the registered medical practitioner or registered nurse and the authorising officer must make every reasonable effort to persuade the detainee to allow the medical practitioner or nurse to conduct the search.*

A4 *A constable should only be authorised to carry out a search as a last resort and when all other approaches have failed. In these circumstances, the authorising officer must be satisfied the detainee might use the article for one or more of the purposes in paragraph 2 and the physical injury likely to be caused is sufficiently severe to justify authorising a constable to carry out the search.*

A5 *If an officer has any doubts whether to authorise an intimate search by a constable, the officer should seek advice from an officer of superintendent rank or above.*

Annex B—Delay in Notifying Arrest or Allowing Access to Legal Advice for Persons Detained under the Terrorism Act 2000

A DELAYS under TACT Schedule 8

1. The rights as in *sections 5* or *6*, may be delayed if the person is detained under the Terrorism Act 2000, section 41 or Schedule 7, has not yet been charged with an offence and an officer of superintendent rank or above has reasonable grounds for believing the exercise of either right will have one of the following consequences:

(a) interference with or harm to evidence of a serious offence,

(b) interference with or physical injury to any person,

(c) the alerting of persons who are suspected of having committed a serious offence but who have not been arrested for it,

(d) the hindering of the recovery of property obtained as a result of a serious offence or in respect of which a forfeiture order could be made under section 23,
(e) interference with the gathering of information about the commission, preparation or instigation of acts of terrorism,
(f) the alerting of a person and thereby making it more difficult to prevent an act of terrorism, or
(g) the alerting of a person and thereby making it more difficult to secure a person's apprehension, prosecution or conviction in connection with the commission, preparation or instigation of an act of terrorism.

2. These rights may also be delayed if the officer has reasonable grounds for believing that:
   (a) the detained person has benefited from his criminal conduct (to be decided in accordance with Part 2 of the Proceeds of Crime Act 2002), and
   (b) the recovery of the value of the property constituting the benefit will be hindered by—
      (i) informing the named person of the detained person's detention (in the case of an authorisation under paragraph 8(1)(a) of Schedule 8 to TACT), or
      (ii) the exercise of the right under paragraph 7 (in the case of an authorisation under paragraph 8(1)(b) of Schedule 8 to TACT).
3. These rights may not be delayed if the person has been detained under section 43B of the Terrorism Act 2000.
4. Authority to delay a detainee's right to consult privately with a solicitor may be given only if the authorising officer has reasonable grounds to believe the solicitor the detainee wants to consult will, inadvertently or otherwise, pass on a message from the detainee or act in some other way which will have any of the consequences specified under paragraph 8 of Schedule 8 to the Terrorism Act 2000. In these circumstances, the detainee must be allowed to choose another solicitor. See *Note B3*.
5. If the detainee wishes to see a solicitor, access to that solicitor may not be delayed on the grounds they might advise the detainee not to answer questions or the solicitor was initially asked to attend the police station by someone else. In the latter case the detainee must be told the solicitor has come to the police station at another person's request, and must be asked to sign the custody record to signify whether they want to see the solicitor.
6. The fact the grounds for delaying notification of arrest may be satisfied does not automatically mean the grounds for delaying access to legal advice will also be satisfied.
7. These rights may be delayed only for as long as is necessary but not beyond 48 hours from the time of arrest (or if a person was initially being detained under TACT Schedule 7 or Schedule 3 to the CT and Border Security Act 2019, from the time at which the examination under the relevant Schedule began). If the above grounds cease to apply within this time the detainee must as soon as practicable be asked if they wish to exercise either right, the custody record noted accordingly, and action taken in accordance with the relevant section of this Code.
8. A person must be allowed to consult a solicitor for a reasonable time before any court hearing.

B Documentation

9. The grounds for action under this Annex shall be recorded and the detainee informed of them as soon as practicable.
10. Any reply given by a detainee under *paragraph 6* must be recorded and the detainee asked to endorse the record in relation to whether they want to receive legal advice at this point.

C Cautions and special warnings

11. When a suspect detained at a police station is interviewed during any period for which access to legal advice has been delayed under this Annex, the court or jury may not draw adverse inferences from their silence.

Notes for Guidance

B1 *Even if Annex B applies in the case of a juvenile, or a vulnerable person, action to inform the appropriate adult and the person responsible for a juvenile's welfare, if that is a different person, must nevertheless be taken as in paragraph 3.15 and 3.17.*

B2 *In the case of Commonwealth citizens and foreign nationals, see Note 7A.*

B3 *A decision to delay access to a specific solicitor is likely to be a rare occurrence and only when it can be shown the suspect is capable of misleading that particular solicitor and there is more than a substantial risk that the suspect will succeed in causing information to be conveyed which will lead to one or more of the specified consequences.*

Annex J—Transfer of Persons Detained for more than 14 Days to Prison

1. When a warrant of further detention is extended or further extended by a High Court judge to authorise a person's detention under section 41 of TACT beyond a period of 14 days from the time of their arrest (or if they were initially being detained under TACT Schedule 7 or Schedule 3 to the CT and Border Security Act 2019, from the time at which the examination under the relevant Schedule began), the person must be transferred from detention in a police station to detention in a designated prison as soon as is practicable after the warrant is issued, unless:
   (a) the detainee specifically requests to remain in detention at a police station and that request can be accommodated, or
   (b) there are reasonable grounds to believe that transferring the detainee to a prison would:
      (i) significantly hinder a terrorism investigation;
      (ii) delay charging of the detainee or their release from custody, or
      (iii) otherwise prevent the investigation from being conducted diligently and expeditiously.

   Any grounds in (b)(i) to (iii) above which are relied upon for not transferring the detainee to prison must be presented to the senior judge as part of the application for the extension or further extension of the warrant. See *Note J1.*
2. If at any time during which a person remains in detention at a police station under the warrant, the grounds at (b)(i) to (iii) cease to apply, the person must be transferred to a prison as soon as practicable.
3. Police should maintain an agreement with the National Offender Management Service (NOMS) that stipulates named prisons to which individuals may be transferred under this paragraph. This should be made with regard to ensuring detainees are moved to the most suitable prison for the purposes of the investigation and their welfare, and should include provision for the transfer of male, female and juvenile detainees. Police should ensure that the Governor of a prison to which they intend to transfer a detainee is given reasonable notice of this. Where practicable, this should be no later than the point at which a warrant is applied for that would take the period of detention beyond 14 days.
4. Following a detainee's transfer to a designated prison, their detention will be governed by the terms of Schedule 8 to TACT 2000 and the Prison Rules and this Code of Practice will not apply during any period that the person remains in prison detention. The Code will once more apply if the person is transferred back from prison detention to police detention. In order to enable the Governor to arrange for the production of the detainee back into police custody, police should give notice to the Governor of the relevant prison as soon as possible of any decision to transfer a detainee from prison back to a police station. Any transfer between a prison and a police station should be conducted by police and this Code will be applicable during the period of transit. See *Note 2J*. A detainee should only remain in police custody having been transferred back from a prison, for as long as is necessary for the purpose of the investigation.

5. The investigating team and custody officer should provide as much information as necessary to enable the relevant prison authorities to provide appropriate facilities to detain an individual. This should include, but not be limited to:
   (i) medical assessments
   (ii) security and risk assessments
   (iii) details of the detained person's legal representatives
   (iv) details of any individuals from whom the detained person has requested visits, or who have requested to visit the detained person.
6. Where a detainee is to be transferred to prison, the custody officer should inform the detainee's legal adviser beforehand that the transfer is to take place (including the name of the prison). The custody officer should also make all reasonable attempts to inform:
   - family or friends who have been informed previously of the detainee's detention; and
   - the person who was initially informed of the detainee's detention in accordance with *paragraph 5.1*.
7. Any decision not to transfer a detained person to a designated prison under paragraph *1*, must be recorded, along with the reasons for this decision. If a request under paragraph *1(a)* is not accommodated, the reasons for this should also be recorded.

Notes for Guidance

J1 *Transfer to prison is intended to ensure that individuals who are detained for extended periods of time are held in a place designed for longer periods of detention than police stations. Prison will provide detainees with a greater range of facilities more appropriate to longer detention periods.*

J2 *This Code will only apply as is appropriate to the conditions of detention during the period of transit. There is obviously no requirement to provide such things as bed linen or reading materials for the journey between prison and police station.*

Annex K

The documents considered essential for the purposes of this Code and for which (subject to paragraphs 3 to 7 of this annex) written translations must be created are the records made in accordance with this Code of the grounds and reasons for any authorisation of a suspects detention under the provisions of the Terrorism Act 2000 or the Counter Terrorism Act 2008 (post charge questioning) to which this Code applies as they are described and referred to in the suspect's custody record. Translations should be created as soon as practicable after the authorisation has been recorded and provided as soon as practicable thereafter, whilst the person is detained or after they have been released.

There is no power under the Terrorism Act 2000 to detain a person or to delay their release solely to create and provide a written translation of any essential document.

Annex L

The separate Code of Practice that governs the conduct and recording of interviews referred to in this annex is available at: <https://www.gov.uk/government/publications/terrorism-act-2000-video-reco rding-code-of-practice>.

Index

Tables are indicated by *t* following the page number.

E

F

G

H

I

T

U

V

W

X

Y